THE FASHION DIRECTORS:
WHAT THEY DO AND
HOW TO BE ONE

THE FASHION DIRECTORS:

WHAT THEY DO AND HOW TO BE ONE

Second Edition

ELAINE JABENIS
J. L. Brandeis and Sons

MACMILLAN PUBLISHING COMPANY
NEW YORK

COLLIER MACMILLAN PUBLISHERS
LONDON

Cover photo by Terry Lennon

Macmillan Publishing Company
866 Third Avenue, New York, New York 10022
Collier Macmillan Canada, Inc.

Library of Congress Cataloging in Publication Data:

Jabenis, Elaine.
   The fashion director.

   Bibliograph: p.
   Includes index.
   1. Fashion—Vocational guidance.   I. Title.
TT507.J29   1983   391'.0068'8   82-16096
ISBN 0-02-360580-4

Printed in the United States of America

Printing   3 4 5 6   Year   7 8 9 0

ISBN 0-02-360580-4

71847

For MACE
  DIANA
  SARAH MARIE

PREFACE

CHANGE

The most dependable word in the world of fashion is change,—change may be fashion's only constant. Change is what makes the fashion business happen. The newest techniques in fashion merchandising, the look and arrangement of a fashion department, the renovation of a fashion establishment, the style of promoting, the pursuit of a special image, all are in direct response to the restlessness of fashion, a phenomenon that cannot, will not, stand still. (See Chapter 1.)

Change is what pours life into the fashion director's responsibilities. And the change that has taken place in the fashion industry as a whole, especially on the retailing side, has influenced the new job description of the fashion director and guided this revised second edition.

THE NEW FASHION DIRECTOR

A major change. Today's fashion director must be a merchandiser, totally conversant with the "numbers." That is, he or she must be concerned with how the fashion retailer's open-to-buy is spent, what's happening with assortment plans, gross margin, planned increases, growth areas, everything related to making plan. Unlike the fashion director of yesteryear, today's fashion director reads computer printouts right along with the fashion magazines. Even product development will become a major priority for some, another outgrowth of change.

WHAT THIS BOOK OFFERS

This book, like the first edition, written by an active fashion director, not only zeroes in on what a fashion director does and describes how to arrive thoroughly prepared for employment in this area, but also offers valuable guidance to students interested in other fashion merchandising careers.

In this age of specialization and greater competition, those responsible for the merchandising of fashion need strong, professional know-how. A thorough study of requirements, demands, and responsibilities is most essential for the aspiring fashion director, but it is equally essential for the merchandising team who would work with the fashion director to understand the inner workings of this complex merchandising role that can be so supportive of their own efforts. Furthermore, the professional merchandiser can utilize this book to train internal personnel who are prospects for the fashion office.

The book is written from the vantage point of retailing, a field that has been long recognized as an excellent training ground for all careers pertaining to fashion direction or coordination. Later in the text (Chapter 15), when the student is ready to evaluate the information, the book includes all the other areas in which fashion coordination jobs outside retailing are available. These areas are often overlooked by beginners because they are not aware that they exist. In this book the student has a chance, under one cover, to explore all the different possibilities of this field and to decide which path to take.

Those of us who are deeply involved with the fashion industry and who are extremely proud of its contributions are most anxious to attract good people. Practical, realistic tools are necessary to mold such new prospects and this book is designed to serve as one of those tools.

It has been our experience that this book can also serve as a reference book after the student is on the job. It has also proved to be a good guide for the fashion office of any store, plus other departments covered—sales promotion (advertising, publicity/public relations) and display—and is especially valuable to the training director of any fashion institution.

THE ORGANIZATION OF THE TEXT

Chapter 1	Understanding fashion is the first step for anyone serious about pursuing a career in the fashion industry. Thus, Chapter 1 takes that first step.
Chapter 2	So that the student may study the subject with less mystery and to enable the instructor to present an all-encompassing overview at the outset, the second chapter embraces most of the pertinent facts that will be divided and studied in detail in later chapters.
Chapter 3	This chapter provides an important look into American fashion history and a review of how this special fashion career came into being. All this helps the reader achieve the sound foundation and greater sense of adventure that are essential in fashion.

Chapters 4–14	The text has been designed to show exactly how a fashion director works. Each major area of responsibility is dissected within a separate chapter to give the student a realistic blueprint and to provide the instructor with a workable format for assignments. I have tried methodically to give both the teacher and the student what they really need—that is, less of the "should do," and more of the "how to."
Chapter 15	This chapter steps away from retailing and advises the reader where other related careers are available.
Chapter 16	This last chapter is extremely important; it is designed to provide an honest evaluation of this profession, pointing out both the advantages and disadvantages. It makes no effort to glorify or skirt any issue; it makes no bones about what to expect or what to look for.

ROLE PLAYING

The opportunity for innovation in classroom procedure for the instructor and ultimately for the student is enormous. While writing the book I envisioned less lecture and more student involvement. Throughout, I have tried not only to describe the fashion director's responsibilities, but also to give actual examples of how those responsibilities are executed.

The technique of role playing would be highly advantageous in a course of this kind. I would love to see the teacher turn the classroom into a fashion office, directing the students in interpreting the various roles of the fashion office staff. A student could assume one role and the responsibilities connected with that role, then exchange roles with others, until all assignments are covered. Through the playing of roles, the student would not only learn how each area of the fashion office works, but also experience the relationship of interplay with other fashion office members. Before the semester ends, each student would have had a chance to make a fashion presentation; write and produce a fashion show; merchandise a fashion ad; coordinate a TV commercial, a promotion, and a window; create a shop concept, report on a market trip—everything.

Because of the tempo, drama, and creative texture of this profession, the application of dramatic involvement helps the student acquire a more realistic foundation before entering the world of fashion, a place where drama is a way of life.

ELAINE JABENIS

ACKNOWLEDGMENTS

There are so many people whom I am indebted to for their generous cooperation and support. Here are a few, listed in alphabetical order, to whom I wish to extend a special thanks.

Associated Merchandising Corporation

Alan Baer, Chairman of the Board, Brandeis, Omaha, Nebraska

Joseph Bellesi, Director of Special Projects, Bloomingdale's, New York

Bergdorf-Goodman, New York

Bloomingdale's, New York

Bullock's, California

Carson Pirie Scott, Chicago

Kay Corinth

Ebony Magazine

Estee Lauder

Filene's, Boston

Anita Gallo, Vice President, Fashion Merchandising Director, B. Altman Co., New York

Glamour Magazine

Harper's Bazaar Magazine

Macy's, New York

Mademoiselle Magazine

Neiman-Marcus, Dallas

Sidney S. Pearlman, President, Brandeis, Omaha, Nebraska

June Roche, Fashion Director, Milliken

Peter Rogers, Peter Rogers Associates, New York

Saks Fifth Avenue, New York

Sears Roebuck & Company

Seventeen Magazine

Stores Magazine

Vogue Magazine

Women's Wear Daily

Wool Bureau

Lois Ziegler, Fashion Director, J. C. Penney Co.

CONTENTS

THE FASHION DIRECTORS:

WHAT THEY DO AND
HOW TO BE ONE

Pierre Cardin's corrugated looks *(Denis Paget, Courtesy of Women's Wear Daily)*

1

UNDERSTANDING FASHION

WHICH WAY TO THE FASHION OFFICE?

Nearly every day in most large department stores throughout the country, some young person steps off the escalator or elevator and asks:

"Which way to the fashion office?"

It would be difficult to remember how many young people (most of them women) have approached me since I've entered the fashion field, but the moment I see one across my desk, I know who she is and why she is there. I recognize that unmistakable look and, when I see it, I know what is coming. In fact, the speech she is about to make is so typical, I can almost mouth it with her, word for word:

"Could you give me some advice? I have always liked fashion . . . would love to work around clothes . . . I took a modeling course last summer . . . and, well, I kind of thought I'd like to work in this field. So, I wondered if you could tell me . . . how do I get into fashion?"

To begin with, the question itself has always amused me. Over sixty percent of the how-do-I-get-into-fashion inquiries are made in speeches much like the above—a vague statement with a not-so-vague revelation that the inquirer is not too sure about what he or she is asking.

About the only rapport some individuals have with fashion is that they wear clothes. If they turn to this field with no more qualification than that, it is obviously not enough. So, naturally, if an honest answer is to be given, a process of elimination must come first, or at least a setting straight of the record.

The ensuing interview between the fashion aspirant and me usually goes something like this:

"How do you get into fashion? Well, I would need to know what aspect of fashion interests you before I could advise you."

"Oh, I . . . don't know. I'm not exactly sure."

"Well, you said you would like to work around clothes. You could do that by being a salesperson . . ."

"Oh, no. I don't want to sell."

"You mentioned modeling. Would you like to pursue that?" If the answer is yes, we consider her qualifications, advise her about the opportunities and problems on both a local and national level, and the interview is over. If the answer is no, that modeling is fun as a sometimes thing, but she prefers something more challenging or substantial in fashion (not so much a job, but perhaps a career), the interview takes a different direction. If the person indicates a strong interest and aptitude toward fashion illustration, we send her to the advertising department. Display? We send her to the display department. If she has brought with her a presentation of her own fashion designs, we recommend good schools (if she needs further study and instruction) or suggest how she should go about applying for a job in that area.

"What about merchandising?" I usually ask next. "Could you envision yourself as a buyer?"

If interest is indicated, we tell her about our training program for developing young executives, and if she is still interested we direct her to talk with our personnel department or a divisional merchandise manager. If we hear instead, "Oh, no. I had a course in merchandising and I don't feel I am right for it" I know what's coming.

What then?" I ask.

"Well . . . "

"Well . . . what?"

And then it comes. "I'd like to do what you do."

"Be a fashion director?"

We have hit a responsive nerve. "Yes! Oh, yes! I'd be willing to start at anything if I could work with you in the fashion office . . . anything."

It soon becomes apparent that the reason so many young people come to the fashion director about getting into "fashion" is because it seems to be the most glamorous job in the fashion business. And small wonder. Surrounded by intrigue and mystery, the fashion office has had more than its share of puffery to magnify its glamor image.

Of course, the fascination for this area on the part of young aspirants is unquestionably related to the rest of the fashion world, where the environment of fantasy and beauty abounds.

Is it really all that wonderful?

Well, that old cliche "beauty is in the eyes of the beholder" certainly applies here. It all depends on how you look at it.

A Retailer's View

Fashion is, indeed, an exciting business. It has a fast track, a great element of risk, endless change, an aura of drama, constant stimulation. Challenge is a daily ingredient. It encourages creativity, rewards initiative, and it is a haven for self-starters. It is a tester of endurance. But with all these glowing comments, it must be understood that fashion is a very serious business, filling a very real and important need (Americans spend about seventy-five to eighty billion dollars annually for clothes), and anyone who does not attack his or her responsibilities in a serious manner will not happily survive in a high-level fashion career.

There is no way to nullify the glamor image of the fashion world, nor is there any reason to do so. What would be helpful, and perhaps what really is needed, is to dispel some of the mystery.

THE TRUTH ABOUT FASHION

The fashion industry has had good press and bad press. It has been praised and berated—very often simultaneously—so it is no wonder that the fantasy and the reality have become blurred. Because of continuous combinations of boos and bravos, the industry not only lives with a sense of caution, but it is always aware that it will be asked to justify its position. That means, of course, that what the designer creates, what the manufacturer produces, what the retailer stocks to sell, all come under fire when there is consumer resistance.

The retailer, more than any other individual of the fashion community, is held most responsible for unloved fashion newness. After all, it is at the point of sale where the strongest reaction is felt.

Good Fashion Direction

Every member of the fashion business sooner or later experiences the need to defend, explain, and justify a fashion decision. On a retail level, the fashion director is the most frequent target. The secret to a successful retail fashion operation is not to get into the position of having to defend. That is where good fashion direction comes in: being aware of not only what the fashion industry is churning out, but what will be acceptable to the store and its customers.

Nevertheless, there are times, even though objectionable merchandise has not arrived in the store and may never arrive (if a good fashion director is watchful), when cries of protest and disapproval are showered on the retailer all the same.

Examples

A new fashion season is around the corner. Consumers have heard rumblings; a big change in fashion is about to take place. They have read reports of European showings in the daily press and have seen pictures of the proposed new looks in *Vogue, Bazaare, Women's Wear Daily* or *W*. They've heard some distressing interpretations on television. Television comics, recognizing a juicy opportunity, immediately pick up on the new fashion idea and make fun of it. Talk show guests, discovering the latest conversation piece, debate the merits of the forthcoming fashion.

Whenever a radical fashion change is on the horizon, the reaction is usually the same. A target for ridicule and jeering. Shock. Disbelief. Anger. And bewildered consumers, who feel they are the victim (they have not yet heard the true fashion story), become very vocal.

"Where do they get those crazy ideas?"
"Who are they designing for, anyway?"
"How do I keep up with these continuous changes?"
"Am I so out of step I can't understand such bizarre fashion?"
"Where will I wear it? How will I wear it?"

The Traveling Waistline

Whoever said "There is nothing sure but death and taxes" completely overlooked fashion. When it comes to fashion, "change" is as sure as death and taxes. Inevitable. Unavoidable. Regardless to what lengths fashion creators must go to effect change, they must, sooner or later, make it happen. Change in fashion will occur even if every natural line of a woman's body must be ignored.

Consider the traveling waistline. A woman's waistline, for all practical purposes, is located below the rib cage and above the hips, yet fashion can make it move up and down like a yo-yo, depending on the concept of the season. From high empire (below the bustline), to natural waist (there's a novel idea), to a dropped waist (below the natural line), or erradicated altogether with a chemise or "no waistline" look.

So it is with shoulders and sleeves, hips and hems. Fashion changes affect the focus, the size, the placement, the importance. Now you see it, now you don't.

The Terror of Change

Women who see what they feel are outrageous fashion ideas need to know what is going on. When they have to ask "who is going to wear such clothes?" they feel threatened, frustrated, intimidated.

Something that plays such an intimate, consuming role in our lives should not be so devastating. This fear of the unknown can cripple one's ability to interpret, edit, or evaluate fashion, let alone enjoy it.

The Mystery Explained

Women are relieved, even enchanted, when they learn that those "weird" costumes by Claude Montana, Chloé, Kenzo, Cardin, Givenchy, or Yves St. Laurent are presented at the Paris openings in such seemingly outlandish ways for a very good reason—to make the front page.

If leading designers' new collections come down the fashion show runway looking safely like last year's fashion with only quiet little changes, the fashion press would clobber them. They would blatantly chew them up with such accusations as old hat, nothing original, uninspired, totally lacking in inventiveness. That is a review that no prestigious designer can afford, so, to keep their names at the top of the authoritative list of fashion pacesetters, they take a daring, provocative approach to the presentation of a new idea.

Making a Statement

To assure the adoption of their new ideas, leading designers give the fashion press inventiveness. Indeed. They give it to them, figuratively speaking, with fanfare, with rockets bursting and trumpets blaring. After zany servings of fashion flare that often seem to totter on the brink of madness, the press and the fashion industry sit up and take notice. It's exciting. It's news. And, to say the least, it's inventive.

Of course, it is not at all as frivolous as it sounds. Beneath the show business and the theatrics is the onset of a splendid new fashion idea. It is the prelude to change, which is not only inevitable, but demanded.

By exaggerating an idea a statement has been made. For example, if skirts are to be shorter, the designers show skirts extremely high, much shorter than they will be shipped. If necklines are to be high and feminine, they make a bold statement by encircling the neck with ruffles so huge they extend up to the model's nose. If a hat is utilized to emphasize proportion, it might stand a foot high in a startling new shape to eject gasps of surprise from the audience. If large animal motifs are to be a new decor, a designer might present a life-size alligator printed on a dress so huge it seems to envelop the woman's body.

Bizarre? Of course. But, with it all, a statement has been made.

Now, to answer the next inevitable question: why must the "statements" be so exaggerated? To train the eye. To have somewhere to retreat when the more accepted form emerges. Hemlines, whether they go up or down, are a perfect example. Showing the length at the most extreme point indicates that the proportion can work. Those willing to take the plunge can choose the extreme form, and the moderates can ease into the trend with a more conservative approach. But in order to do either, the strong statement must be made first.

"Think the look is great but we could never sell it that short," one buyer might say, "we will need it two inches longer. I think our customers will accept that." And so it goes with every major fashion change. Fashion directors and merchandisers accept or reject or modify every new fashion idea on the basis of their stores and their consumer acceptance.

All change is somewhat threatening and greeted by many with apprehension, even when it is presented in a modified form, but a truly

In a Paris showing of a Claude Montana collection, hats that looked like over-turned canoes reinforced his statement of ethnic tunics and border prints. The bold statement captured the attention of the fashion press (note photographers surrounding the runway). The hats did not become fashion, but the fashion silhouettes did. *(Courtesy of Women's Wear Daily)*

good fashion idea, usually born in just the way described above, eventually can be adopted by the entire fashion world, and, after modification, emerge totally wearable and realistic. Even those women whose first impulse was to condemn or insist "you'll never catch me wearing that" will later applaud the modified version as "beautiful."

From time to time designers do give vent to their deepest fantasies and occasionally indulge in whimiscal expressions, but it should be remembered that if all imaginative designers did nothing but create bad jokes in clothing, they would not maintain leadership, nor would they have any lasting influence.

WHAT CAUSES CHANGE

The causes of change are the direct result of the times in which we live. The economy. Peace or war. Lifestyle. Cultural events.

Listen to the music. If a new trend in music is coming up strong,

Big blouson tops over short, lean skirts, created by America's Bill Blass. Almost two years earlier, a similar, but more bizarre look was created by Pierre Cardin. Compare this picture with Cardin's concept on the title page of this chapter. Fashion trends have their beginnings in bold statements. *(Courtesy of Women's Wear Daily)*

you can be sure clothes will be affected. Through the influence of the beat and what relates to the style of dancing, though the influence of what star performers wear, or just plain inspiration by association. The important thing is, fashion has to be in tune with the tempo.

How could dancers of the twenties have done the Charleston if dresses had not been short? How could swing become so animated in the fifties if skirts had not been full and flared? How could the disco craze of the seventies gained such a sensuous image without the sexy disco dress? And who can separate the popularity of country-western music and country-western dress?

Each decade has its own special fashion flavor, not because the fashion designers so decreed, but because the climate was right. The seventies and the eighties record their own special climate.

According to Morton Salt, the Morton Girl on the box has had six fashion changes because "whenever we start to show our age, we do a little face lifting." Fashion changes are reflected everywhere. *(Courtesy of Morton Salt Division of MortonNorwich)*

The Seventies

During the seventies (the decade writer Tom Wolfe dubbed the "Me Generation"), the cult of the body flourished and fashion followed suit. A devotion to shaping up for health and beauty ran rampant throughout the nation, involving all age groups. For men, women, and children physical exercise, in addition to active sports, demanded active sportswear. Books on running, jogging, and dieting made the bestseller lists. Campaigns against junk food and smoking were launched on a national scale.

The fashion industry didn't create the idea of an active sportswear explosion—it answered the demand.

Also, during this period, the worship of the body beautiful reached an all-time high. The look-at-me syndrome was picked up by men as well as women. *He* unbuttoned his shirt to the waist and filled in the neck area with reams of chains and amulets. A macho image. *She* went braless. Everyone jumped into tight pants.

These trends led to the first major boom in men's jewelry, to the creation of the seamless bra that gave the appearance of being braless, and—the most explosive—the demand for good fitting tight jeans. A direct outgrowth of this body-revealing trend in the success of designer jeans accounted for about ten percent of the five billion dollar jean market. This became a giant classification for men, women, and children. If consumers had not been in top shape or had not wanted to reveal with pride their respective behinds, none of this could have happened. Wearing the designer's label on the back pocket added to the fun and the prestige.

The fashion industry does not get credit for the trend, but it does deserve a great deal of applause for recognizing the potential and successfully providing what consumers wanted. The prestigious designers, who established an element of chic for the jeans story, elevated this product to heights never before achieved. It wasn't long before everyone was getting into the act. Names no one had ever heard of began showing up on those back pockets, each claiming, through extensive advertising campaigns, that theirs provided the best fit. According to *The New York Times*, jeans advertising accounted for the third largest slice of New York area retail television advertising of apparel during this boom period. They showed, claimed, glorified fit. Fit. That was the key. The body-conscious public was on the prowl for the incomparable fit. The demand was there; the climate was right, the fashion industry responded.

This is not to say that the fashion designing world does not create a desire for its product by originating an idea and stirring up acceptance. It certainly does, but, in all truth, it is very likely that the creation came about in the first place because the timing was right, and the timing is right when consumer acceptance is present.

The Eighties

Tom Wolfe also provided us with a handle for this decade. "The Purple Generation" was what we could expect for the eighties. A time of status seeking. Not social status, but career status. And the indication at the outset of the eighties bore this out as a major truth. (Interestingly enough, the top color story for fall, 1980, was one historically associated with status—purple—and it received a royal welcome.)

In keeping with the status climate, classic looks of the most elegant quality became fashion leaders at the outset of the eighties. In all markets, at all price levels, classic was the number one choice. Once regarded as a basic, traditional look, it now took the spotlight as new fashion.

Again, it is a matter of timing. Here was a period when women were expressing a firm desire to be taken seriously in their career efforts. They adopted the sincere tailored suit, the tasteful, understated accessories, the handsome executive attache case—all important props for their climb to the top. The fashion industry again recognized the lifestyle requirement here and filled the bill with beautiful fabrics, impeccable tailoring, and patterns reminiscent of men's success stories in business attire: herringbones, tweeds, subtle stripes, glen plaids, and the mainstay of the Madison Avenue man—the grey flannel suit.

The alert fashion director, who had a finger on the pulse of the buying public, would have alerted management to the need to cater to this huge and growing segment of consumer.

Here is a perfect example of the reason for fashion change. The number of women in the work force has been expanding for some time, not only in numbers but in career-oriented attitudes. All the years of effort to move into more authoritative positions began to reach fruition. This was, of course, the reason for needing appropriate dress to support women's new career roles.

Women Had a Voice

Looking back, we remember how the mini skirt had been in vogue for about nine years when the midi was introduced in 1970. Of course, it is a matter of history that the midi was totally rejected at the time, but, eventually, in a more refined form, the longer length did prevail throughout the seventies. This was not because the industry pushed it onto the fashion consumer (they had already learned this could not be done) but because the time was right. After all, could serious executive women walk into the board room in skimpy little mini skirts? How could they hope to be vice presidents dressed in skirts that made them look like aging cheerleaders?

But, as always, fashion did not stand still. In 1982, when the stores were filled with good, solid classics—exactly as the working women had demanded—the climate suddenly changed. All women, those who worked at home or away from home, grew weary of their basic skirts and blazers. What's more, those in the work force became more secure and were ready for softer, more feminine alternatives for career dressing. Designers turned out new fashion looks that the retailers could sell. After all, that is what the store is there for—to sell.

Energy Conservation. Starting in the late seventies and growing in importance during the eighties, fashion was created to support the turning down of thermostats. Everything from long johns to thermo coats became the order of the day in cold climates. The intimate apparel divisions reacted with warm underdressings. One could get sleepwear with matching snug sacks into which a person could crawl and be warm in a cold room while reading or watching television. The hosiery industry turned a need into fashion by supplying colorful leg warmers, heavier opaque tights, and leggings to be worn with sportswear or with tailored suitings. All these and more fashion ideas appeared on the scene as a buff against cold while the need for energy conservation existed.

IS FASHION IMPORTANT?

Anthropologists' studies have shown that if reasons for dress are listed according to importance, both protection against the elements and covering for modesty would fall below vanity or decor. Certainly this is clearly borne out in the deepest regions of civilization where the temperature is tropical. The almost total absence of clothing among the natives indicates that covering for modesty and the elements are disregarded. Instead, bodies are magnificantly adorned with jewelry, feathers, body painting, and even colorful inlays in the skin—all in the name of beauty. The seeking of beauty seems to create its own place with fashion.

Some time ago when I was interviewed for the Dick Cavett Show, the interviewer asked "Is fashion relevant?" I considered my answer for a moment and said: "Compared to what? International problems? Health problems? No. But man cannot live by problems alone. We need baseball and ice cream and music and, yes, even fashion. Without these things to soften the edges we would all be climbing the walls. But there is more. Fashion's contribution to our economy is enormous. Is fashion relevant? You bet it is. And the more accurately it is used the more relevant it becomes."

The Popular Vote

If there is any truth to the phrase "People get the kind of government they deserve," it is not improbable that fashion is delivered and succeeds in somewhat the same way. If we vote for a trend by supporting it, it will exist. If we veto a trend, it will be voted out and replaced by something more acceptable. It is as simple as that.

Even when a good fashion trend comes into full bloom, peaks, and has a healthy run, it begins to fizzle when the very people who originally cast the affirming popular vote start looking around (often subconsciously) for something new. Then, it starts all over again—the searching for a new idea, the trial and error of initiating the idea, and, finally, selling it. Making sure that the most desirable and acceptable fashion is available to the store's customers exactly when they want it is a large responsibility of the fashion director.

THE PLACE FOR YOU?

There is a great deal more to learn, of course, before the complete truth about fashion comes into focus, but all the foregoing insights represent a strong beginning. As indicated at the outset, young applicants come into the fashion office because it seems glamorous, and ninety percent will admit that they come without really having too much of an idea about what a fashion director does. Therefore, it is time to give you the facts about a fashion director's responsibilities, share an experience, offer workable directions to show you the best way to the fashion office, and find out if a nice person like you belongs in a place like this.

CHAPTER RE-EXAMINATION

Questions

1. How are fashion changes introduced?
2. What are the primary causes of fashion change?
3. Who has the greatest influence on fashion? The designer? The retailer? The customer? How?

Workshop

Assume you are a fashion designer. On the basis of what is happening today and how people are living, what would inspire you? What would you design? Sketch or explain your idea. Explain why you feel it would sell, how it would be used, who your customer would be.

Escalator view of THE GALLERY, shopping mall in Fort Lauderdale, Florida. *(Courtesy of Stores Magazine)*

2

FASHION COORDINATION IN RETAILING

FASHION COORDINATION

The meaning of that phrase—fashion coordination—may conjure up the picture of finding the correct shoe for a dress. You may envision it as meaning pairing up the best jacket for a pant or skirt. It might even telegraph combining the newest colors.

Of course, all of this, indeed, is included in the responsibilities of fashion coordination, but it in no way describes the major contributions made by a fashion director. To get the true picture, perhaps we had better start at square one.

WHAT'S A FASHION DIRECTOR?

Good question. I wish there was a good, simple answer. However, the very fact that the answer is not simple is an immediate clue to the complex nature of the job. Complex, true, but challenging and exciting as well.

Naturally, there is an important basic need a fashion director fills, and therefore, basic responsibilities that must be executed to fulfill that need. But here is the rub—of all the thousands of people working as a "fashion director" hardly two in all the world work exactly alike. In fact, not all have the same assignments.

No need to get stage fright in the face of this bewildering information. This news is an immediate promise of a career that is amazingly elastic, never static, ever changing. Getting in a rut is not likely in the fashion office.

There are many plausible reasons for the variant duties of the fashion specialists, whatever their title, but these three are most conspicuous and seem to show up in almost all cases.

1. The kind of responsibility awarded the fashion office (usually influenced by the firm's personality, management structure, and responsibility breakdown at the rest of their executive level).
2. The amount of true fashion authority and direction taken from the fashion director by his or her firm.
3. The amount of talent, creativity, originality, strength, and vision of the fashion director.

Even as recently as the late sixties and in some cases until the early seventies, the role of the fashion director still was loosely defined in some retail organizations, especially those where the fashion director had not been a long-standing member of the merchandising team.

Very often total involvement on the merchandising side was weakened by the constant flow of other assignments that did not necessarily relate to merchandising decisions affecting the selection and presentation of fashion merchandise, which is, or should be, a primary function of the fashion director. Or fashion merchandise director. Or fashion coordinator. As you can see, there is even an identity problem.

WHAT'S IN A NAME?

Not only do the fashion specialist's assignments and responsibilities differ from store to store, but so does the title. A general merchandise manager, for all practical purposes, is always called a general merchandise manager. So it is with a divisional merchandise manager. And a buyer is always called a buyer. But in all these merchandising careers the responsibilities are usually completely defined and relatively the same. The fashion director's responsibilities are almost never the same. Sometimes the title is clearly indicative of the fashion specialist's position on the store's executive list; sometimes it is deceiving.

There are few careers in retailing that can record the changes and growth as vividly as the role of fashion director can. Perhaps the easiest way to track these transformations is through the title changes.

Stylist

Although the first fashion directors were called "stylists" (see Chapter 3), this name is no longer used in retailing. It has been adopted in other areas, however, such as advertising and photography.

Fashion Coordinator

For many years more people worked under this title in the fashion office than under any other name. It was used for both subordinate members of a fashion office and for the head. It was the updated designation that became popular somewhere in the thirties when the title of "stylist" was eliminated from general use in retail stores. Many stores and related fashion fields have been locked into it ever since.

Fashion Director

About fifteen or twenty years ago, when the role of fashion coordinator began to change even more significantly, so did the title. When it became apparent that this was no longer just a coordinating assignment but much more of a merchandising position where actual direction was paramount, the title of coordinator was ready to be retired along with stylist. Thus the term fashion director came into general use, especially as the title awarded the overall head of a fashion office. This proved more efficient in the office that had other fashion personnel; the subordinates continued to be identified as fashion coordinators.

Fashion Merchandising Director

As further changes came along and retail top management implemented a more sophisticated use of this fashion executive, the role needed a realistic updating once again. Around the mid-seventies, the title of fashion merchandising director was adopted. Although the most important responsibilities are merchandise related, the fashion director may occasionally supply a service that was once the major function of the stylist, may certainly participate coordinating all aspects of the business as did the original fashion coordinator, but today the expanded role—one of much greater importance and value to the company—is that of a merchandiser, working as part of the merchandising team and making merchandising decisions.

Even though this title prevails within the greatest number of leading retail establishments, the position is still referred to, for the sake of brevity, as the fashion director. This fashion specialist will use the full title when signing communications, but in conversation, as throughout this text, the title is abbreviated to fashion director.

Vice President, Director of Fashion Merchandising

As the fashion director's participation on the merchandising side escalated, the title of vice president became a definite possibility for an outstanding fashion director. Regarded as the ultimate title, this one is utilized primarily by large resident buying offices, major retail stores and chains for the top executives of their fashion offices.

In addition to all the responsibility changes and title varieties there is a great deal more that contributes to the somewhat mysterious, elusive image of the fashion director. What is a fashion director? It depends on whom you ask.

The Public View

If you ask those who have no direct association with the fashion director (those on the outside looking in) the director is someone special and awesome. She is the retail glamor girl . . . the head-turning fashion plate who has so much fun working around all those lovely clothes . . . doing all those wonderful fashion shows . . . the one who knows all the inside secrets about what's going on in the fashion world. He is the person quoted by the printed press, radio, and television on his opinions of fashion trends . . . the awe-inspiring fashion authority who makes impressive personal appearances at benefits, civic, social, or cultural events as a representative for the store and is always so handsomely dressed. The director captures the spotlight as a panel member, lecturer, beauty contest judge, commentator, advisor. This lucky person is always dashing off for exciting trips to New York, California, Chicago, or Dallas to view the fashion markets. The fashion director gets to travel to all the fashion capitals of the world abroad—Paris, London, Milan. It is often reported that newly discovered trends take her to India, South America, Copenhagen, Spain, Israel, Canada, Mexico, and the Orient. He or she knows such interesting people—all those glamorous, currently-in-the-news celebrities, fashion designers, fashion magazine editors, stars of stage, screen, and television. What adventure! **Wouldn't you absolutely love to have a job like that!**

Co-workers' Views

If you ask those with whom the director works (those associates whose work-a-day world he or she affects), the fashion director is the fashion know-it-all, a tyrant, an opinionated rock, and a steamroller of fashion information. They find the director sometimes lovable, sometimes fearsome. They might regard the director as a reliable source of valuable fashion guidance and forecasting today . . . an impractical dreamer tomorrow. Associates confess they often lean heavily on the director to do all the advanced leg work, to uncover fashion trends of a coming season; they need the director to *detect*, *direct*, and *project* fashion newness each season. They depend on this person to help ballyhoo, glamorize, and stir up excitement about their merchandise—to stimulate appetites for whatever the store has for sale. They also find themselves admitting that they don't know where she gets her energy. They truly wonder how he covers all the bases he covers. The fashion director's pace is so fast and varied they don't know how the director does it. **Wouldn't have that job for the world!**

The Fashion Director's View

If you put the question directly to a fashion director (by asking what a fashion director is), the answer may have little or no resemblance to the two images just described. Again, it depends on whom you ask.

One fashion director might tell you her duties are far from glamorous. Just reams of directives, magazines, bulletins, and releases to read constantly; a lifetime of revolving doors, overcrowded elevators, and hard chairs (if she's lucky) or standing-room-only in designers' showrooms or at fashion presentations; volumes of note-taking, and a fortune in expendable shoe leather. Another might wear so many hats (handling market research, special events, public relations, youth activities, etc.) he may describe himself as "vice president in charge of headaches."

In the past, many fashion directors have been known to lament the image they had with their companies. "I really don't know who I am . . . and I don't think my management does either." This was heard a great deal during those trial-and-error years when the fashion person was not utilized in as professional a manner as he or she is today. They were regarded with considerable reservation, sometimes even with resentment and not altogether with the clear-cut understanding of their function enjoyed by other executives in the firm. On the other hand, as the recognition of fashion as the lifeblood of retailing came sharply into focus, the fashion director's prestige also grew. In a great many fashion organizations—and certainly among the leading fashion giants—the fashion director is awarded great power and has top-of-the-heap responsibilities for the fashion leadership of the company.

WHY COORDINATION IS NEEDED

As indicated earlier, fashion is the reflection of our lifestyles. It captures and plays back to us with astonishing dependability everything vivid that is happening everywhere, and it does it with mind-expanding speed.

Now, in the eighties, more than at any other time in fashion history because of our immediate and extensive coverage in communications, the buying public is not only better informed about everything, but more quickly informed. What's more, the American consumer, now more sophisticated as a result of communication education, is also quicker to pick up on fashion offerings, with more savvy about what to accept and what to reject.

It is extremely important, therefore, that the selection and presentation of fashion be handled in a most professional manner to better serve a more knowledgeable consumer. Hence, when done with the utmost of speed and accuracy, the coordination of fashion becomes the very lifeblood of fashion in retailing.

Seeing is Believing

Imagine, if you will, stepping inside the door of a major department store.

Look around.

It is only February 1, but if you had any doubts that spring is just around the corner, or had forgotten that Valentine's Day is February 14, the timely displays and fresh, just-arrived spring merchandise effortlessly remind you. In fact, the bank of windows outside had already told you that a vibrant new shade of "loving red" was available in coats, suits, dresses, sportswear, and accessories; you were also exposed to gift ideas that otherwise might not have occurred to you.

A ride up the escalator reveals that the Valentine and spring theme is consistent everywhere. Every mannequin, every display area, and all fashion departments underline the importance of the coming event and the approaching new season.

On one floor is a special "Shop for Lovers," a charming little boutique that wasn't there the last time you were in the store, designed and decorated especially for February 14 fans. It has everything from music boxes to heart jewelry, from romantic record albums to devastating lingerie. Once inside, you hear the latest romantic music, gently emanating from the four walls. You are surrounded with the theme, the mood, the idea.

Not far from the Valentine gift shop is an inspired spring trend shop. A sign reading "A Little Romance" announces with accuracy the kind of fashion apparel accumulated there. Feminine, ruffled blouses. Accents of lace, ribbon, flowers on dresses, all in soft fabrics and gentle colors. All the ready-to-wear pieces, plus the romantic accessories, testified to the beauty and feminity of the romantic trend. Now, in the dead of winter, this early spring forecast, with its light and airy, frothy and sheer fashion, provided early selections with a hint of things to come.

Up on the furniture floor, you might have expected to be completely out of that world of red valentines and the promise of spring, but, here again, the theme is expressed. You wander through a group of model rooms that have new spring fabrics, new spring colors, and (especially created to tie in with the store's total look) a sample "First Home for Young Marrieds" with red carpeting, sleek chrome and white leather furniture and red pillows (some even heart-shaped) tossed generously on everything for that easy-to-live-with look.

If you are especially perceptive, you notice that the continuity does not stop here. In this morning's newspaper a color ad invited you to come see the store with the "loving red" heart. The signing in the windows, in fashion departments, and on applicable counters repeated the same terminology. On television, the store's Valentine's Day commercial, in living color, was aglow with "loving red."

To go one step further, you may become aware that the salespeople who help you know exactly what to advise regarding the newest accessory color or shape to go with your selection of a red costume. They know whether a sheer or opaque leg is best, which jewelry, which handbag is the best choice. A most refreshing experience. It is all clearly spelled out and appetizingly presented. You have learned from the strong message that red is an important color for the season, that romantic looks are in for spring (this reliable store would never present a fashion story so forcefully unless it was important fashion) and, even more helpful for the busy, hurried shopper, you learned how to put it all together.

When customers can enjoy the ease of selecting a wardrobe, with every component part, from intimate apparel to shoes and accessories, available to coordinate with the newest ready-to-wear, they have found a store that literally relates to its customers.

The Link

How did it all come together so well? One would immediately suspect there had to be some kind of well-organized communication system—a definite link that relayed the story, worked out the timing, followed through on the execution.

The link is the fashion director.

The sportswear buyer covers only the sportswear market. A handbag buyer sees only the handbag market. It is very likely that both buyers know little or nothing about what is going on in the other's respective market.

Let's just take a single example related to the handbag buyer. A specific style of handbag comes in a dozen colors. There is no way (and certainly no need) to buy that one style bag in all twelve colors.

How, then, does the buyer decide which colors are best? Also, how will the handbag buyer know what ready-to-wear colors her store will be promoting? How will the buyer know which colors would coordinate best? Should they match? Blend? Contrast? How different will the color story be from what it was last season? A slight change? A drastic change? Of course, the manufacturer might make recommendations, but how valid can those recommendations be without knowing exactly what will be carried in the rest of the store?

There is one person in the store whose responsibility is to know and advise all members of the merchandise team, one person to offer a direction and see that it is followed through—the fashion director.

The Fashion Storyteller

When you see continuity of a fashion promotion, easily recognized and understood because it has been clearly presented in newspaper ads, on radio and television, in windows, interior displays, shops, and signing, you can be sure that a very alert fashion director has done a great deal of leg work and in-store coordination to bring you the up-to-the-minute fashion story, well told. The store's sales personnel, too, credit their fashion knowledge to the fashion director, who instructed them in fashion clinics on the newest trends and how to sell them.

Such a fashion story, with everything moving in the same direction, is a joy to behold. Customers may not be analytical about why they enjoy the store, but they will very likely look forward to the next inspired promotion, and the next, and the next. This, they decide, is an exciting store. They grow to love it and to depend on it. Here is a store that has everything in fashion newness, appetizingly presented, and has it first.

The continuity in all areas didn't just happen, of course. When a promotion is decided on (Valentine's Day is used here because it is a simple, annual example) the system of creative teamwork begins. All who have a responsibility in getting the show on the road—the store's sales promotion director, advertising director, visual presentation director, and fashion director (often referred to as the creative team)—meet to discuss and decide what the direction will be.

Without total continuity, the effectiveness of the "Valentine's Day Loving Red" campaign is watered down or totally lost. For example, if the advertising director decided to call the new color "lipstick red," the display director felt it was more of a "flame," and the copywriter for the television commercial called it "romance rose," the customer might come in looking for three or four different colors, when, in truth, they were all the same. Or, if the junior department decided they had such great looking yellow pieces they would display yellow that week, and the sportswear department hadn't been informed at all about the red promotion and didn't have any red merchandise to tie in, much is lost. It is necessary, therefore, that the coordinator makes sure that everyone knows what is going on. It is even better, if possible, that everyone agrees. A promotion of any kind works much better if everyone involved believes in it and backs it up with that belief.

Communication on what is expected must be set up early enough so that everyone is protected and then must be followed through with all details (scheduling of windows, interiors, ads, television, etc.) to run within a specified time segment. This must be all geared, of course, to the arrival of the merchandise the store is promoting.

More than ever before in the history of merchandising, fashion trends come in and out as fast as a spin through a revolving door. The speeding up of the life cycles of fashion has made it more difficult to coordinate what should be included, what should be omitted, what to play up big, or what deserves only moderate attention. It takes careful analysis. It takes planning. It takes coordination.

Three's a Charm

Three magic words that must constantly be a part of a fashion director's vocabulary, are continuity, timing, and flexibility.

1. Continuity. A promotion or fashion projection must be carried out in all areas suitable for involvement to give the customer the story from all vantage points.

2. Timing. Make plans for a promotion or fashion projection far enough in advance with schedules and releases set so all store personnel involved will be on cue.

3. Flexibility. Keep a fashionable ear to the ground to sound out changes. This important factor requires the careful attention of the fashion director. Occasionally, a fashion trend looks good at the outset, but does not develop as expected. It takes quick thinking and quick decisions to pull out of a fashion plan and then quickly replace it with something else. Also, very often a trend will be a sleeper, but signs begin to indicate that here is the start of something big. A good example of this was back in the mid-sixties when short skirts forced the hosiery manufacturers into the pantyhose business. Many stores who were not watching the fashion trends closely enough were far behind in adding this innovation to their hosiery departments in the strength it deserved. In the seventies the tight-fitting jeans made the use of bikini panties less desirable because of the visible lines. Something else was needed or tight pants would be less salable. Again the hosiery industry answered the need by developing a panty combined with pantyhose; the all-in-one innovation provided a smooth fit, no matter how tight the jeans worn over them. At the outset of the eighties when stretch jeans began to take a big bite out of the sales of rigid jeans, it is very possible that an alert fashion director was the first to bring such newness to the attention of management and the first to have it in stock, thereby contributing to the company's fashion leadership.

RESPONSIBILITIES OF A FASHION DIRECTOR

As indicated earlier, one fashion director seldom works the same as another. Even if their duties are somewhat the same, their system of executing those duties may differ considerably, either by individual choice or that of management. In spite of the variety of assignments and the differences of execution, a fundamental framework exists into which the responsibilities of almost all fashion directors fall.

1. The projection of the fashion position of the firm through the selection and presentation of merchandise. That is, to be responsible for getting the right fashion story to the consumer (presentation of merchandise) and to make sure the store has the right merchandise to back it up (selection of merchandise).
2. The projection of the fashion image of the firm through promotional and public relations activities.
3. The training of store personnel on current and upcoming trends and how they are to be put together.

The first responsibility is totally merchandise oriented. This top priority involves market research, developing fashion trends, and working closely with the merchandising team. The second point, promotional in nature, covers all activities related to display, shops, advertising, and fashion shows. The third responsibility, which is self-explanatory, is by no means third in importance. Obviously, all merchandise objectives must be supported at the point of sale or those objectives may not be fulfilled.

Even within these three areas, a fashion director's responsibilities reach out and involve other areas. Therefore, the ideal breakdown of responsibilities required by the masterminds of most major retail operations follows this outline very closely.

MERCHANDISING RESPONSIBILITIES: BEFORE MARKET

The "market," as the term is used in the retail fashion business, is the place where merchandise is offered for sale at wholesale. The greatest concentration of shopping the market is done during specified market week, when most vendors are ready to show their wares and "open" their showings at the same time for the convenience of the buyers. The market might be New York, California, Dallas, Chicago, Atlanta, or many other smaller regional markets.

Long before the market opens, the fashion director has a great deal of advance work to do.

Research

First comes research. Before fashion directors can make a single recommendation to their companies, they must have substantial facts to back up what they will present as the new season's fashion direction.

They must first visit and consult with fiber companies, fabric houses, and the leather industry on colors, textures, and trends because fashion most often begins at the fabric level; many a clue on what will be uncovered later first shows up here.

Example

When a fashion director sees that every major company is turning out reams of printed fabrics in notably greater proportions than solids, it is a definite clue that a print year is coming up. And, if plaids are more strongly emphasized than any other pattern, then the importance of plaids is undeniable.

In another season there may be such a rush on velour that the suppliers cannot keep up with the demand. Another time it may be a strong demand for velvet or denim that is in excess of the normal expectancy for the season.

Fabric is what designers buy to manipulate their silhouettes into creations that eventually contribute to a season's fashion trends. The fabric, therefore, is the early clue to what trends the season offers. This year it may be crepe, which would indicate soft dressing, next year it may be taffeta, a fabric that would constitute a stiffer, more full-bodied expression of silhouette. Another year it might be the combination of both, which would indicate a season of strong alternatives. It is all there. One need only gather the facts and understand how to interpret them.

Test Your Skill

An interesting and fun way to evaluate how a fabric will influence a fashion trend is to pick a fabric at random and visualize how designers could utilize it in the coming season. Keep in mind the texture, the pattern, and the current use. Will there be taffeta as ruffles? As a fitted coat? As a billowy skirt? Keep track of your fabric interpretations and then watch the first arrivals in the stores and see how close you came.

Next comes working with leading designers and reviewing collections of important resources in New York, California, and abroad. There is major direction here, of course.

Example

After an absence from the fashion scene for many years, knit dressing returned. The clue as to what extent the trend would grow became evident when manufacturer after manufacturer indicated they were "retooling" to accommodate this emerging trend. New yarns and treatments were also developed to turn out better bodies. The indications were clear: the market was equipped and interested in developing this aspect of fashion into a strong trend.

Another great source of early information involves gathering interpretations of projected trends from the leading fashion magazines. Here you can learn what they are carrying editorially in advance issues.

Example

Interest in knit dressing was shown by all the top magazines. Considerable space was allocated to knits or sweater dressing. Some of the magazines offered choice pieces on their covers. Every important fashion voice in the press—magazines and *Women's Wear Daily*—lavished praise on the merits of knit dresses, suits, coats, sweaters that looked like soft blouses, plus a better than usual selection of knit accessories. *Conclusion:* The new yarn in fashion was knits, expressed in new ways.

Reinforcement for everything you have discovered so far can be found by attending seasonal predictive meetings at the store's resident or national buying office.

Example

With actual merchandise or slides and sketches, everything discovered thus far was substantiated. Knit dressing was underscored as being very important.

To obtain a strong overview of the market, I recommend attending New York Fashion Group shows. The Fashion Group, an international organization of women executives in fashion (see Chapter 3), presents at the top of each season a live production of the best of American collections.

Evaluation

In addition to everything the fashion director has learned, he or she evaluates what others have found. An alert fashion director reads the trade publications and leading newspapers daily—especially *The New York Times,* the Fairchild publications, *Women's Wear Daily, Retailing Home Furnishings,* or the *Daily News Record* for men's wear and textiles (depending on the fashion director's area of responsibility), plus *Stores* magazine. The fashion director also scrutinizes the up-to-the-minute forecasts from the store's associated buying office and from fashion consultants.

The fashion director cannot do too much to uncover the facts, verify them, and reverify them. Then, and only then, is the director ready to evaluate. The process of evaluation goes something like this:

1. List all trends in order of importance.
2. Under each trend note the distinguishing characteristics.
   (a) Leading silhouettes
   (b) Leading fabrics
   (c) Best colors and patterns
   (d) New combinations of colors, fabrics, and patterns
   (e) Newest accessory treatments
3. Designate the best timing for promoting each trend.

Next, the fashion director must take a hard, honest look at the entire list and decide which trends are suitable for her particular store and which are not. In some stores all leading trends are promotable and salable. In other stores the same items would die. In some parts of the country, and even within a single company with numerous branches with different clientele, certain trends can be exploded or simply tested. Before completely passing up a trend that seems to have dominant strength, the fashion director must specify the reasons for ignoring it. Too expensive? Too bizarre? Also, budgets must be considered. How many promotions and trends can the store successfully handle? What are the priorities? If necessary, it may be wise to do a few things well, rather than many things not so well. With good fashion decisions one can usually edit a fashion season without sacrificing leadership.

Interpretation

Now that the process of evaluation turned into a process of elimination, the fashion director is ready for the next step. Inseparable from the evaluation and elimination of available trends is interpretation. The fashion director does not simply submit a typed or written list, per se, to management. It is the all-important translation of all the facts, presented orally and visually along with printed material, that makes all the difference (see Chapter 6).

The strength of the fashion director's enthusiasm about what she has found, how she envisions the store's own interpretation of the trend, the extent of business she feels the trend can generate for the company, and the extent of her conviction (awarded only to those things she knows the store must not pass up), all combine to give management confidence as to which way to go.

Obviously, the words "plaid will be important" or "sweater dressing is strong" or "patterns will be mixed" would tell management little. But, if the director dramatizes the availability of extensive, beautifully executed, salable, priced-right, quality merchandise in plaids, or sweater dressing or mixed patterns, and if the director points out exactly what classifications are most important, which resources look best, at what price points or which departments should emphasize this type merchandise, then everyone in the organization will be moved to strongly support the director's recommendation that customers will be "mad about plaids" or will certainly be "knit pickers" next season.

The fashion director might also recommend some appropriate promotional handles, updated terminology related to the trend or special event that would reinforce the trend's effectiveness.

A great deal is riding on her recommendations. No room for a head in the clouds. No place for just hunches. Hunches are fine as long as they are backed up with good, sound research.

MERCHANDISING RESPONSIBILITIES: DURING MARKET

During any market period, the fashion director moves in two directions. He or she shops the market alone to investigate new resources that the store has not formerly carried and appear to have potential, or to discover those that have opened up new divisions, or to contact out-of-the-way designers who have had good reviews, to name a few. Whatever crops up in the market that indicates promise and is not on the buyer's regular resource list should be investigated by the fashion director.

The second direction for the fashion director during market is to shop the resources with buyers and merchandisers:

1. To help guide for good fashion selection and avoid duplications.
2. To help insure against merchandise voids within the fashion trends.
3. To buy for windows, displays, and fashion shows.
4. To introduce buyers and merchandisers to new resources.

With a good basic plan of what the fashion campaign will be in all areas for the coming season, the direction of fashion choices is fairly well spelled out. However, in many cases when shopping resources, good and important things show up that must not be eliminated simply because they do not fit into the master plan. There must be flexibility for additions or subtractions, and decisions very often must be made on the spot while in the market. Therefore, the necessity of teamwork is emphasized again. Everyone should be considered, everyone heard, and then a decision most suitable to the success of store's efforts will result.

MERCHANDISING RESPONSIBILITIES: AFTER MARKET

Based on the orders for merchandise actually placed and the actual development of trends as viewed in the market, the fashion director will now coordinate with management to schedule:

1. Store-wide fashion promotions
2. Departmental fashion promotions
3. Shop or boutique concepts

4. Fashion advertising

    (a) Newspaper
    (b) Radio
    (c) Television
    (d) Catalogs

5. Display changes

    (a) Windows
    (b) Interiors
    (c) Shops

6. Fashion shows and fashion special events

Time and Action Calendar

At this point all decisions have been made as to exactly what the fashion compaigns for the coming season will be, and, with the exception of a new development, the plan is firmed up. Copies of the projection are sent to all department heads and all personnel affected. The fashion director must still organize one more project: the Time and Action Calendar. This is a schedule (see Chapter 9) that provides both display and advertising with timing guidelines regarding the projection of fashion trends throughout the season. It describes what the fashion stories are and the timing for exploiting them.

FASHION TRAINING OF PERSONNEL

A vital part of the action put behind fashion campaigns to make them meaningful in terms of profit for the company and service to the customer is the training of store personnel. It is important that all the store's people, on all levels, have a uniform understanding of what the fashion direction will be and how to use it. Therefore, comprehensive training clinics should be set up and scheduled prior to the arrival of merchandise in the following manner:

1. Merchandising Team

    (a) General merchandise managers (supervisors of merchandising staffs, see Chapter 5)
    (b) Divisional merchandise managers (supervisors of buyers, see Chapter 5)
    (c) Buyers
    (d) Assistants to all the above

2. Store Management

    (a) Director of stores
    (b) Store managers
    (c) Assistants to all the above

3. Advertising Staff

    (a) Sales promotion director
    (b) Advertising director
    (c) Advertising artists
    (d) Advertising copywriters
    (e) Assistants to all the above
    (f) Special events director
    (g) Publicity director

4. Display staff

    (a) Visual presentation director
    (b) Display directors
    (c) Display personnel in charge of windows
    (d) Display personnel in charge of interiors
    (e) Display personnel in charge of shops and special projects

5. Sales personnel

    (a) Sales associates in fashion departments
    (b) Department managers
    (c) Area managers
    (d) Alterations personnel
    (e) Beauty salon managers and operators

And so the story is carried from the top level to the sellers who, after all, make everything happen at the point of sale.

PROMOTIONAL RESPONSIBILITIES

The promotional responsibilities of the fashion director, as opposed to the merchandising responsibilities, are in a somewhat different league. In some stores the promotional area is a major part of the fashion director's contribution; in others it is a small or secondary assignment. In a great many retail operations the fashion director has little or nothing to do with the promotion side of the business. In still others the promotional efforts and the merchandising assignments are so strongly related that there is no effort or intention to separate them. Both areas, many fashion merchants believe, come under the heading of fashion projection, and, therefore, belong together.

FASHION PROJECTION THROUGH VISUAL PRESENTATIONS
1. Coordinate interiors
2. Coordinate windows
3. Help plan and coordinate boutiques and special shops

FASHION PROJECTION THROUGH THE MEDIA
1. Select fashion merchandise and supervise photographic shoots for newspaper ads, catalogs, statement enclosures, and publicity
2. Coordinate merchandise selections for television commercials

FASHION PROJECTIONS THROUGH SHOWS AND EXHIBITS
1. Formal shows—in-store
2. Trunk shows—in-store, departmental
3. Informal modeling—in store restaurant areas, etc.

PUBLIC RELATIONS RESPONSIBILITIES

In some stores this area is the responsibility of the fashion office only when it deals with fashion-related stories. In other cases, the assignment is awarded to a publicity director, advertising agency, and/or public relations director or public relations agency. Whatever the system, the fashion director seldom escapes a certain amount of involvement. The type of public relations efforts that must, of necessity, involve fashion directors and their associates include:

1. Fashion Shows

    (a) Benefits for charitable organizations
    (b) Women's or men's clubs
    (c) Civic organizations or civic efforts

2. Public Appearances

    (a) Speaking engagements—schools, clubs, etc.
    (b) Panel discussions
    (c) Radio and television appearances
    (d) Instructing fashion seminars
    (e) Judging local competition events (beauty contests, etc.)

3. Miscellaneous

    (a) Answer questions and give guidance to customers seeking fashion and etiquette advice
    (b) Help with personal consultation and selection of a wardrobe where a customer requests special assistance
    (c) Maintain a people-to-people relationship with the fashion press and radio and television stations for editorial exposure

FASHION COORDINATION OUTSIDE RETAILING

Retail stores are not the only employers of fashion directing personnel. The field is extensive and varied. The following are only a few of the many possibilities.

The Buying Offices

Another great consumer of fashion coordinating talent is the resident buying offices. These organizations service members of independent retail stores or store groups (chain stores usually have their own buying offices) and have complete departments of fashion coordinators who cover specific markets and report to a fashion merchandising director or vice president of fashion merchandising.

Fashion Consultant Firms

The fashion staffs of consultant firms work in a similar manner to those of resident buying offices. The main function of the consultant firm's coordinators is to research the market. The fashion consultant firms service the retailer or any other subscriber by supplying professional interpretations and evaluations of market research, advice and guidance on coming trends and developments, and direction toward applicable resources for the individual store's needs.

Fiber Producers

The fashion directors of fiber companies not only fulfill an important function for their own employers but become an extremely valuable source of direction for the retailer. The fashion director for Celanese, for example, might provide the retail fashion director with seasonal forecasts on color, pattern, fabric, and silhoutte trends. Celanese also produces seasonal fashion shows in their New York offices when retailers are in the market.

Other fiber producers such as DuPont, Monsanto, Allied Chemical, Hoechst (Trevira) and Eastman might have a fashion director or a fabric/color coordinator or a fabric/color stylist.

Fabric Mills

Such fabric mills as Burlington, Milliken, Ameritex (United Merchants and Manufacturers), and J. P. Stevens enlist the services of fashion directors who project a tremendous influence on the entire fashion industry. Here again the retailer gains extensive support for fashion decisions from the work done by fashion directors of leading fabric mills.

Fashion In Everything

Professionals directing and interpreting fashion trends are called on as consultants or advisors in almost every industry imaginable where products are made more desirable if created with fashion correctness.

The automobile industry is just one example. A car must have fashionable upholstery and appealing fashion colors. Every year, Jane Roche, fashion director for Milliken, goes to Detroit to present her current color stories to help guide the automobile industry in its decisions on fabrics and colors for exteriors and interiors.

The airlines have several reasons for being fashion conscious. Everything from good fashion colors for exteriors, coordinated color and pattern themes for interiors, fashion-right uniforms for flight attendent, plus ground crew personnel all need the expertise of fashion direction. Every time the airlines make a major update of the uniforms of their crews, they carefully choose established name designers to create exclusive fashion looks with which they can be identified. It is not enough for the uniforms to be functional; they must have a special look. So important is the fashion identification that almost every time there is a radical change, the costumes and the designers make the news.

On and on it goes. Everything is fashion. Fashion has invaded every aspect of living—not only what we wear, but what we live with, our cars, furniture, homes, the music we hear, the food we eat. Even the little girl on the box of Morton Salt has experienced a half dozen fashion changes since she first appeared in 1914.

Fashion is big business. Seventy-five to eighty billion dollars are spent annually by Americans for clothing. Fashion is also big news. We have all witnessed its ability to capture headlines, become an international conversation piece, stimulate emotional reactions, and provoke heated debates among officials of schools, churches, and business.

Whether it is applauded for surrounding us with beauty, utilized to reinforce our image, or held responsible for moral behavior, it is, as it has always been, the mirror of our times.

RETAILING—THE GREAT TRAINING GROUND

A fashion career in retailing is rewarding enough in itself, but it has other advantages as well. It is a splendid stepping-stone to other fields that look favorably on applicants with retail background. In fact, retail experience fortifies a person with valuable assets for just about any position that touches fashion. In many cases it is a required prerequisite.

According to Martin Schrader, publisher of *Bazaar,* "When it comes to people with retail background I can't get enough of them. Retail training is the closest thing to the realities of the sales and marketing of most of our advertisers' products. People with retail background know the language."

AFTERVIEW

It is obvious that the fashion director is the store's researcher, advisor, coordinator, instructor, promoter, spokesperson, motivator, and ambassador. One could add other titles, but after finishing this book I am sure you will agree that not one title could be removed.

The fashion director, the store's fashion authority, and its fashion conscience, is also the company's internal link, providing a smooth, uninterrupted connection between buying, displaying, promoting, and selling fashion merchandise.

All these responsibilities are developed in further detail, of course, in the following chapters, but seeing the entire picture pulled together at the outset, as we have attempted to do here, as viewed from the top fashion assignment, helps to clarify the amount of know-how involved, and to determine to what level an aspirant can and should strive.

However, before we move forward, we would like to move backward during the next chapter to examine the roots of the fashion director's role. Although it may be considered a slight digression, it is, in truth, the best of all roads to follow toward the aim of this text. Knowing how the fashion office came to be included as such an important part of the retail store's operation in the first place (not all merchandising careers can track their beginnings as thoroughly) helps establish the entire philosophy of the field, where it began and where it is going.

CHAPTER RE-EVALUATION

Questions

1. Why were the titles of those in fashion coordination changed so often over the years?

2. Why is fashion coordination needed?
3. What happens when a trend, expected to be big, does not develop?
4. Who are the members of a retail creative team?
5. What are three leading areas of responsibility of the fashion director?
6. Why does the fashion director research the market ahead of the buyers and merchandisers?
7. How do fashion directors evaluate which trends are to be recommended to their companies?
8. What does a fashion director look for while shopping the market with buyers?
9. What is a Time and Action Calendar?

Workshop

Review the example of the total-store Valentine's Day and spring presentation. Visualize a fashion trend, holiday, or season and draw up a similar plan as you would like to see it executed.

Goya's portrait of the Marquesa de Pontejos. *(National Gallery of Art, Washington, D. C.)*

3

IN THE
BEGINNING

Back in the days when the "Brave New World" of America was indeed new and brave, no one could have predicted there would some day be such a thing as a fashion director. Not that women were not concerned with fashion in the days of the early settlements. They were. Always. It should also be remembered that many of the women who came over were very young, so before too long they were ready to reach out for what suited their basic nature best, the promise of riches and new status, the things that brought many of them to these shores in the first place.

THE STARTING POINT

The starting point of fashion in America was the fashions the women brought with them. This, of course, depended on their place in the society of their homeland before they came over.

The Women of Virginia

The first women who landed in Virginia (ninety young women came in 1619) undoubtedly brought the dress of the Englishwoman in the last years of the reign of James 1. This was a transitional period for fashion in England, but it is unlikely that these women brought the latest fashions. Some were young widows whose clothes may have been the finely made garments of their trousseaus. But for the most part they were poor maidens looking for husbands and a better life. If one uses the inclination of such women as a guide, they undoubtedly scraped together the finest in whatever fashion their money and means permitted, to help make the best possible impression.

The Women of New England

The first women to settle in New England came to Plymouth in 1620. Most of these women were from modest cr poor backgrounds and without much formal education, similar to their counterparts in Virginia. But, because of a break with the Church of England, some had fled to Holland and lived there for some years before voyaging to America. The combination of the Dutch influence in their dress, and their religious persuasions as Separatists, led them to a simpler and more sober type of dress. They brought "sensible" clothing, devoid of any trimmings, in sturdy fabrics and somber colors.

The Women of New York

The Dutch women of New Amsterdam looked a great deal like the pilgrims of New England. They wore the short waist bodice and full skirt of the early seventeenth-century Dutch, but their colors were brighter. They loved decorated buttons, embroidered collars, and elaborate, pleated ruffs encircling the neck. Chances are, the garments the women brought with them were soon cherished as Sunday best, for church or weddings, and the sturdier clothes needed to meet the greater demands and hardships of those early days were made at home.

Looms and spinning wheels were among the choicest items of home furnishings. The women would spin, weave, and sew all the clothes for the family. The men contributed by processing animal skins for shoes and outerwear. Their fashion guide? They copied what they had—or what their neighbor had. There was little change in American fashion until the middle 1600s.

Earliest Fashion News

As soon as the early years of settling and building were behind them, the women's interest turned to fashion; it was to become a very important part of their society. Early in this new society there was an apparent hunger for some kind of guide, to advise them in the fashionable life they were now able to afford. This was especially true of the women in the towns. They were eager to know what was new and who was wearing it. But news about fashion was mighty hard to come by. Many weeks or months of water separated the settlers from the Old World. Eagerly they waited for news from every ship that docked in their harbors. It is not unlikely that sea captains or newly arrived settlers who brought new fabrics, current fashions from home, and stories of what the ladies were wearing in London, Paris, or Amsterdam, were their earliest fashion authorities.

When new fashions found their way to these shores, the changes in some areas were gradual at first. After all, nothing was thrown away. The handwoven cloth was extremely durable and expected to last a long time. In fact, a beautifully executed costume with handmade lace, precious fur, or some other handsome embellishment, was passed on to the next generation as a cherished gift, used and reused, until only the lace or important trim of the garment was saved as a family heirloom. Also, there was not a change of fashion with a change of season, only a change of fabric, perhaps, from a lighter weight to a heavier one.

**Before the
Revolution**

By the third quarter of the seventeeth century, fashion in home furnishings and dress had flourished into a long-awaited elegance. Rich
fabrics from the looms of Europe and the Orient intoxicated the now
prosperous townspeople of all settlements. Their homes were glorious
with imported porcelains, magnificent woods, Venetian glass, and rich
wall hangings of the finest silks and cottons. All the pent-up desire for
lavish living burst forth with a boundless energy and passion. The last
quarter of the seventeenth century, until the Revolution, was perhaps
the most prosperous and gratifying fashion period in our history.

**The First Fashion
Director**

London was the fashion dictator (until the Revolution, of course) but
direction came strongly from Paris. Fashion dolls, called "babies,"
played the biggest part in transmitting fashion news from country to
country, shore to shore. Dressed by the mantuamakers of Paris in
magnificently detailed replicas of the latest fashions, the dolls were
sent by fast dispatch all over the continent. Those that traveled to
London were next sent to America.

When the "babies" arrived in America, expert dressmakers copied
the creations for reproduction. The copies were adopted for their
wealthy clientele. The creations were usually too intricate for the general populace to copy, so high fashion remained exclusively for the rich
for some time.

**Town and Country
Fashions**

The greatest difference among the women of the New World was not so
much between the settlements, but between the townspeople and the
pioneers in the country. In Virginia, the ladies of seventeenth-century
Charleston stunned the women from the somewhat rustic plantations.

The women of Boston and Salem were less restrained in their fashion
than the women of Plymouth, but the wives of the yeoman farmers of
the New England area might have regarded all the townswomen as
"fancy." Even though the Puritans had dropped many of the rigid
reforms about dress before they came to America, they still maintained
strong feelings about extremes in dress and frivolous nonsense like
bright buttons, braid, or plumes. Laws were passed, stern sermons
expounded, and lists of names of offenders and prohibited dress were
posted, but women still came forth in silks and laces and fur as soon as
the opportunity presented itself.

In New York as well, the gap between the rich town merchant and the tenant farmer was tremendous. Adversity and hardships kept the farmer's wife busy with bare essentials. In town, however, where life was more leisurely, the Dutch maidens were famous for their industrious creations of an abundance of homespun fabrics and fine linen. They accumulated their beautiful linen, enough for generations, for their own use and for the dowries of their daughters.

Sunday Fashions

Fashion was not a day-to-day expression, but, come Sunday the women from the plantations or the farms traveled many miles to attend church, the center of social life, and display their new finery. It was their weekly fashion show. The more prosperous members of the congregation, whose costumes were the latest from London or fashioned after the newest creation dispatched on a fashion doll, strutted in a grand manner for all the parishoners to see.

There was not the slightest concern that such opulent fabrics and magnificent laces and ribbons might not be compatible with the crude and somewhat primitive surroundings. If beautifully hand-carved and finely polished wood was not yet the look of the pews, the wooden plank benches were made all the more endurable with so many beautifully dressed ladies gracing the congregation. One can only guess—but it is a good guess—that church interiors were rushed to glorious revisions to meet the demands of the new lifestyle.

Rivalry in dress was part of this new life style. Clothes were unquestionably a way to announce one's importance and station in the community. Ye Ole Status Symbol, brought over from the mother country, became very big with the colonists.

After the Revolution

The pattern of fashion changes that history has labeled as "trends during war years" and "trends after war years" had its beginning here during the American Revolution. At this time, the greatest fashion changes took place in the larger cities—Charleston, New York, Philadelphia, and Boston. These centers of lively social life were also the fashion centers of America. The British occupation added color and a festive social pattern with lavish formal balls and elegant dinners, and when it was over something of a dull void was left.

Naturally, the elaborate social occasions encouraged extravagance in dress. The ladies bared their shoulders and accented the low décolletage of their gowns with clusters of flowers, real or artificial. They imported the latest hats from the London milliners or sent for those seen in the Paris fashion books. They brought in beautifully handmade fans from Paris and the Orient. It was a grand period, but when the music stopped a sobering time evolved.

Women's fashions became more masculine with fitted jackets and vests. The graceful hoops and panniers began to disappear and were all but gone by the end of the eighteenth century. From then on, throughout the nineteenth century, changes in fashion occurred with greater frequency, a momentum that was destined to increase with every decade thereafter.

The Nineteenth Century

By the middle of the nineteenth century, fashion was taking giant steps in bringing its news and availability to the general population. Isaac Singer patented his new improved sewing machine in 1851, and in 1863, Ebenezer Butterick, a country tailor in Sterling, Massachusetts, cut his first pattern. It started when his wife, Ellen, asked him to draft and grade a pattern for a baby dress for their son, Howard. She suggested that many other mothers would like patterns for their children's clothes, and, thus, a pattern for a Garibaldi suit for little boys became Butterick's first big success.

Women urged Mr. Butterick to create patterns for them, too, and he obliged. Ellen undoubtedly furnished the first measurements. It was the beginning of a big boon to fashion projection for the general public. In 1864 Mr. Butterick opened a New York sales office at 193 Broadway, with patterns for children's clothes. By 1867, he moved his pattern headquarters, which now included patterns for women's clothes, to larger accommodations at 589 Broadway, an area where women shopped for their dress goods and trimmings at the leading dry goods stores.

The Butterick pattern shop became such an important "fashion bazaar," it merited newspaper coverage. *The Buffalo Daily Courier* in 1869 said, "Every day a line of carriages and throngs of ladies on foot crowd the entrance to this establishment. Here has been solved one of the grave social problems which was tending toward a dissolution of the family ties. The making of their own dresses is an occupation that will prove a blessing to restless women who in the bane of their idleness have turned after the false gods of suffrage." *Pomeroy's Democrat* in 1871 said, "The sewing machine has done more than the piano to happyize our homes. And following the sewing machine has come the Butterick pattern." In July, 1871, the *Home Journal* wrote, "They should be ranked with the benefactors of mankind, this firm that has worked out the problem of clothes."

Not only did the availability of the pattern help work out "the problem of clothes," but another "blessing to restless women" was the sewing machine. The sewing machine was no stranger to the many

JUVENILE FASHIONS,
PUBLISHED BY E. BUTTERICK, 192 BROADWAY, N.Y.

BUTTERICK'S celebrated PAPER PATTERNS of all Sizes as shown above. For Sale by

In 1864, during Butterick's first year in New York, Nathaniel Currier litho-graphed the first Butterick advertising posters. The center figure wears a Zou-ave jacket, a colorful braided jacket popular during the War Between the States. *(The Butterick Archives, courtesy of Butterick Fashion Marketing Service)*

women who worked on soldiers' uniforms during the Civil War. The women had sewn regularly in sewing circles on hand-cranked sewing machines furnished by the government.

Expert tailors and dressmakers made the clothes for those who could afford it; others sewed at home. The new patterns, naturally, were a great help to those who did sew, and it was an opportunity for the masses to imitate their idols, the fashionable rich.

Ready-to-wear clothes were in limited supply at first. The clothing manufacturers, at the outset, made garments in only a few sizes, but they were established as an industry by the end of the 1880s. New manufacturing methods soon put the United States ahead of all other nations in clothing production. The American ready-to-wear industry, still unequalled, had an astonishing growth from 1890 to 1920.

Fashion Is News

Many publications in the middle 1800s found fashion newsworthy. As a matter of fact, the day *The New York Times* was born (the first issue hit the streets on the morning of September 18, 1851, for one cent per copy) it included in its first edition of four pages, six columns each, a story of "a furor on Sixth Avenue over a couple of daring ladies' startling new bloomer outfits." This story of fashion innovation undoubtedly caused a great many eyebrows to rise, but as the press and the reader quickly learned, news in fashion has always been something of an eyebrow raiser.

A national magazine that capitalized on this premise by presenting the new in unique ways was *Harper's Bazar*. On Saturday, November 2, 1867, the first issue of a new weekly magazine called *Harper's Bazar*, consisting of sixteen pages, was available for ten cents per copy, or four dollars per year in advance. The Civil War had ended just two years before (April 9, 1865) creating a new kind of woman, one who had assumed duties outside of the home (for the war effort), a position previously unthinkable. It was to this woman, educated, affluent, and fortified with a new initiative, that the new magazine, (introduced by *Bazar* editors as *A Repository of Fashion, Pleasure and Instruction*) was slanted.

Women read in *Harper's Bazar* about women who worked and they poured over large woodcuts of styles, fashion patterns, and serial fiction. They also learned what the prominent families were doing with their holidays and what the ladies were wearing at "The height of the Newport Season."

Vogue magazine began as a weekly also, but a little later (December 17, 1892). This journal was also geared to a fashionable, affluent reader. Women of the upper classes were unquestionably the fashion leaders of the time, and it was the dream of every shop girl to imitate their elegant dress.

The early fashion books, journals, and newspapers were greatly responsible for "getting word around" about new fashion and interpreting its proper use. For many in those days before the turn of the century, the press stood alone as the only available fashion authority.

The Twentieth Century

The speed with which fashion changed and techniques and technology progressed in the first quarter of the twentieth century was breathtaking. But so was the climate of the new America with everything happening at once and fashion, as always, was the mirror to reflect the times.

The lovely Gibson Girl look that graced the early years was replaced around 1910 by a more severe, sophisticated silhouette—straighter, narrower, wrapped in front—sometimes called the hobble skirt because of the way the tight-at-the-ankle skirt caused women to walk. About five years later, tired of hobbling, the skirt did a complete reverse. In fact, it progressed to the first step toward what was to be the most revolutionary period in fashion to date; the skirts became full, and shorter. For the first time, the ankle showed.

World War I

Paris was only half alive early in World War I. People left the city and left homes and shops empty. Despite its problems, Paris continued to create fashions. Many restraints had to be employed because of the war, of course, but new trends evolved. For example, designers turned to velvet, leaving the wool for the soldiers.

At the same time, in the United States, the ready-to-wear industry for women was experiencing great growing pains. Giant stores grew from little dry goods shops as outlets for the new-type fashion business. This was a trial-and-error period for the merchant who was not, for all practical purposes, a fashion expert. Nor were the manufacturers much help. They, too, were struggling for new ideas, and the entire field of fashion was not yet properly coordinated. The manufacturer had excelled in making skirts and shirtwaists, but, with the exception of the wealthy whose dressmakers went to Paris for fashion, there was still a great void in American fashion. The problem was basically the absence of American talent in the field of design. There were no notable "designers," per se, but much was being done to encourage American know-how.

In 1913, Adolph Ochs, publisher of *The New York Times,* ran fashion contests in "The Times," with cash awards for the best designs. At about this time manufacturers, having no store of developed designing talent on which to draw, went to Paris and brought back samples of the latest creations. They began to show a talent that they were encouraged to continue throughout their fashion history—copying and adapting the French creation to American needs.

In 1914, John Wanamaker, a most perceptive merchant who sensed the hunger for new fashion, sent his most outstanding buyer, Mary Walls, to Paris to bring back a collection of Paris originals. Customers swarmed in to see the first collection of its kind in New York.

In addition to John Wanamaker, other giant merchants with an understanding of tailoring and construction and with high-level taste and an eagerness to share it, brought fashion institutions into full bloom in New York. They were men like Edwin Goodwin, Paul Bonwit, and Franklin Simon.

Women's Wear Daily came on the scene about 1910, and in the ensuing years became the great liaison of fashion information and interpretation between the cutter, the merchant, and the consumer. It covered the entire fashion world in detail, the like of which was yet unknown.

Still, the general atmosphere of indecision about how fashion was to be projected, what the customer wanted, and how to advise her to coordinate a costume, was the climate that created the need for someone to pull all of this together. A comprehensive program of fashion coordination or guidance was definitely in order. This was the condition that led to the creation of a new, specialized career in the retail field.

Tobé Coller Davis

Tobé Coller Davis, the first fashion coordinator, went on to become one of the most influential and effective fashion consultants, a business she invented, to service retailers. For one who hated fashion as a child ("I was always being told to tuck in my shirt"), hers is a most remarkable story of an illustrious career in fashion.

Tobé created Tobé & Associates in 1927 with four clients. Her real growth began during the 1930s depression when business was down and retailers were desperate for help. Her incomparable service, a service that did not exist previously, was to research and evaluate fashion trends and translate her findings into workable plans suitable for the individual needs of her clients.

In her business as fashion consultant, Tobé was doing what she had learned as a fashion coordinator at Franklin Simon's. She kept her knowledgeable finger on the pulse of everything happening in the fashion world and the world in general. She was perhaps the first to recognize that "front page news makes front page fashion." This fact, plus the philosophy that "clothes reflect the lives we lead," led Tobé to watch headlines, the economy, cultural and social tastes, and every-

Tobé Coller Davis, the first fashion coordinator (stylist), who went on to become America's most influential fashion consultant for retailers, a business she invented.

thing that would lend a valid clue to what would be new and what would sell. Thus she earned the distinction of being the first person to understand how to predict, present, and merchandise fashion.

Her advice came to her clients in the form of a weekly "Report from Tobé." This confidential report included sketches, swatches of fabric, ad reproductions, prices, resources, and recommendations on how much of a certain item the store should stock. She also went into careful detail on items she felt important, what she expected they would do and why. What Tobé did and what all fashion consulting firms now do on a large scale for a great number of clients, today's fashion director does for her own store on a smaller scale.

Tobé's Background

Tobé's background is a matter of record. She was born in Milwaukee and experienced her first exposure to fashion through her father, Oscar Coller, who owned and operated a large men's clothing store. Tobé had a strong relationship with her father over the years, primarily because her mother had died when she was born. Even though Oscar Coller married again, he discussed all facets of his business with his daughter; his new wife disliked business talk. Thus began Tobé's professional training in retailing.

Tobé graduated from Milwaukee-Downer College in 1914, after which her father sold the store and moved the family to New York. Mr. Coller invested all his money in a men's suit manufacturing firm, an ill-advised investment since the firm soon failed. However, if there is merit in the old adage, "in every apparent failure there is seed of opportunity," this turn of events in Tobeś life bears it out. Tobé was now faced with the need to earn her own living. She considered the possibilities. Since she was not in love at that time, marriage was out. In college she had studied with a possible consideraton of teaching home economics, but that prospect seemed to lack excitement. She chose New York and a job.

If it was excitement she wanted, the first job did not provide it (writing form letters in a mail-order house), but it did provide a lead into her next job. Close to the mail-order house was the office of a man who dominated the ostrich-feather business. Although feathers were on their way out, Tobé was insistent about getting a job there. She urged the feather dealer to give her a job as a secretary, even though she could not type or take shorthand. Soon she was helping her boss replace the dying feather business with a soap-and-towel service and a hat-advertising campaign and was assisting with the decoration of a new store in Chicago. She was paid $12 a week in her mail-order job and now was making $18 a week.

Her days with the feather king ended when she took a job for $25 a week selling hats at Altman's and at Macy's. She was dismissed, however, for not flattering the customers. She moved on to a secretarial job for the owner of a specialty shop, and then to a job as secretary and assistant to Richard Hickson, a leading designer of women's suits.

It was approximately at this time, 1918, that Tobé realized that fashion was for her. At this point, she began doing something that was to be the pattern of her fashion life—watching and learning. She watched what women wore everywhere. She learned everything she could about styling, detail, line, and color. She studied the way clothes were made, and learned all she could about prices, costs, and values.

Tobé left Richard Hickson after a year or so to open a small dressmaking business of her own. She was joined by another Hickson employee and was backed by her future husband, Herbert Davis, a real-estate broker. Tobé confessed that she did not know how to manage a retail business and went broke within a year.

Fortunately, before she closed her doors she met Franklin Simon, who was one of her customers. He was so impressed with her energy and enthusiasm that he offered her an opportunity to create a job for herself in his store. She scouted the store, visiting the various departments, trying to decide where and in which way she could be useful. The decision was made for her—by accident.

One day Franklin Simon asked his advertising manager (according to a story written about Tobé in *Today's Women*, May, 1949), "What kind of gloves and shoes will be best with Easter suits?" The advertising manager said he did not know. It was decided that Tobé be sent over to the Ritz, then the town's most fashionable restaurant, to see what the women were wearing. At the Ritz, Tobé found that smart women were not wearing the high shoes and laced-up gloves, as expected, but were showing up in pumps and pull-on gloves. Franklin Simon, one of the master merchants of that day, made his Easter purchases on the basis of Tobé's findings and recommendations.

Tobe's future career was launched, but not until she had served nine years with Franklin Simon. Her job was to see what fashionable people were wearing and then make sure her store had it. Soon Mr. Simon sent her to Paris to spot exclusive features for the store. Her big scoop was discovering a creation by Madeleine Vionnet, a slipover dress cut on the bias and made without buttons or hooks. On her return from her first trip abroad, *Women's Wear Daily* met her at the dock and in their story named her the first stylist. Her work captured the eye of other retailers, who offered her similar jobs.

She was indeed the first fashion stylist. The job and the title caught on. Soon jobs were created for stylists or fashion coordinators and incorporated in the operation of major retailers all over the country. A new career was born.

What Encouraged the New Career

Tobé's example started a whole new trend, but it also brought to light a question that had existed for some time—how to sell fashion.

After World War I, a big step in the growth of American fashion began. Things were changing. The ratification of the Nineteenth Amendment to the Constitution, providing for woman's suffrage, brought attention to women as those whose opinions counted. This was not only true at the polls, but also in the department stores.

The advent of the cinema, America's newest form of entertainment, was one of fashion's biggest boosters; its influence was tremendous. The movie queens dazzled and stimulated daydreams in the romantic heads of women everywhere. What the star wore, women from New York to Kansas City wanted to wear, hair styles and makeup included.

Meanwhile, back at the local department store, women came to purchase their share of the new glamor. Their demands came faster than many merchants were equipped to meet. The merchants' biggest problem, it seemed, was their inability to understand the "new woman." The more the store provided, the more she demanded. It occurred to the perceptive men who headed the progressive department stores that men alone could not meet the needs of the customers, most of whom, after all, were women. What is it she wants? How do we get what she wants? How, when we do get it, do we pull it all together? Who should do all this?

The First Stylists

Following Franklin Simon's example with Tobé, department stores created a job that started out with the title of "stylist." However, since there wasn't such a thing, as far as professional or business training was concerned, they hired fashionable women of their community, usually with good social background and presumably good taste. Their job was to advise the buyers and merchandisers. Perhaps this desperate beginning of a career that evolved into a profession for fashion coordinators, directors, consultants, or administrators is responsible for a stigma placed on women in these posts, some of which has not yet completely disappeared.

While the lovely ladies serving as stylists had some good taste, it was usually limited to their own social level. They were almost always completely lacking in business knowledge, and, therefore, the advice they gave sometimes translated into a disaster for the store. What the store needed, and often was not getting, was that special style sense translated into merchandising.

**The Professional
Stylist**

Even with what may seem a somewhat false start, the venture did turn up some outstandingly capable women, women whose names have gone on to be noted in fashion's who's who, and thereby proved that the field for fashion stylists had great possibilities. Guiding the buyers and merchandisers to fashion merchandise with customer acceptance obviously, should be a valuable part of a store's operation.

However, retailers discovered that professional stylists were in short supply. This was the big problem hampering the growth of the profession—a staggering lack of properly trained women. Where would the new stylists come from? There was little or no formal schooling available in this field. What's more, many retailers were not too eager for on-the-job training, until they, themselves, had become more familiar with how a stylist should function.

No one was quicker to recognize the need for specially trained personnel to fill the growing demands in fashion careers than the first retail stylist, Tobé herself. She was unable to find enough qualified people for her staff in her fashion consultant business, and the retailers she serviced came to her with the same problem. Where do we find a stylist? Therefore in 1937, Tobé helped create the Tobé-Coburn School for Fashion Careers. Julia Coburn, then fashion editor for the *Ladies' Home Journal,* looking for trained fashion personnel for the magazine and unable to find it, joined forces with Tobé and was responsible for the operation of the school.

**THE FASHION
GROUP**

Recognizing the opportunities available in fashion retailing but still unable to create the techniques and necessary solutions to the huge task in a fast-growing fashion industry, a small group of early stylists banded together to share their problems and, they hoped, come up with some answers.

Such a group of pioneers (to whom every fashion coordinator working today can be grateful) met one stormy night in 1928 at Mary Elizabeth's Tea Room, between Fifth Avenue and Madison Avenue on 37th Street, New York. (It is still there.) It was decided that a "club" or organization of some kind was definitely in order for women working in fashion. The club would serve as something of a "clearing house" for information about what was going on. This would be a way, they felt, to share problems, explore ideas, and air everything pertinent to their jobs.

The "group" did not take off immediately, but in 1930, forty-five women met at the Women's City Club in New York to hear Marcia Connor (then associate editor of *Vogue*) talk about the importance of a "fashion guild." The move was on. In her book, *Always in Vogue*, Edna Woolman Chase, then editor of *Vogue*, gave credit to Miss Connor for seeing the idea of the Fashion Group through.

In 1931, seventy-five women attended a luncheon at the Hotel Pennsylvania and the Fashion Group was born. Its original purpose, to promote good taste and serve as a clearing house for current problems and new ideas, still exists. However, the extensive research and comprehensive programs conducted and expanded by the Fashion Group over the years (beyond any of the founders' wildest dreams) have been responsible in a large part for the fashion world as we know it today.

The Fashion Group's Influence

At the time the Fashion Group was founded, fashion meant mostly ready-to-wear and fashion accessories. But already there were signs that fashion was also interior design and home furnishings. In a story about the Fashion Group in *Charm Magazine*, on the occasion of its twenty-fifth anniversary in 1956, Eleanor Pollock wrote "it would have taken more than a swami to foretell the day when fashion was to mean the upholstery of your new car, the color of your typewriter, the shape of your vacuum cleaner, the design of your kitchen stove, the packaging of your breakfast food, as well as the length of your skirt and the shape of your eyeglasses."

The Fashion Group was highly responsible for bringing together all aspects of the fashion business. They made it possible for fabric people to see what new designers were creating; they encouraged the cosmetic industry to have an awareness of which fashion colors and trends were important; they introduced the hosiery field to the shoe industry. All this interchange of fashion information helped to benefit the entire fashion industry. For example, in the old days the hosiery stylists chose their colors without checking with fabric manufacturers; coordination of fashion, therefore, was difficult.

In addition to the regular luncheon meetings with featured speakers dealing with some phase of fashion, the Fashion Group has become famous for their fashion "spectaculars." Annual fashion shows for members and their guests present collections of the best American designers and foreign designers, as well as shows for home furnishings, accessories, and textiles.

A comprehensive educational program was created by the group around 1954 to help educate girls interested in finding fashion jobs or in improving the ones they had. Proceeds of the Fashion Training Course went to augment the library of the Fashion Institute of Technology.

Fashion Group Chapters

Now, with a membership of over 6000 (over 2,000 in the New York chapter) the Fashion Group has spread its influence and availability to twenty-six major American cities and 16 foreign countries. The Fashion Group regional chapters, in which membership is available only to women who have worked as executives in the fashion field for at least three years, include:

Atlanta	Los Angeles	*Foreign Chapters*
Boston	Miami	Australia
Charlotte	New Orleans	Sydney
Chicago	New York	Canada
Cincinnati	Oklahoma City	Montreal
Cleveland	Philadelphia	Toronto
Columbus	Pittsburgh	France
Dallas	Portland	Paris
Denver	St. Louis	Japan
Detroit	Minneapolis/St. Paul	Tokyo
Honolulu	San Francisco	Mexico
Houston	Seattle	Mexico City
Kansas City	Washington, D. C.	England
		London
		Korea
		Seoul

In addition to the above, there are nonresident members in Switzerland, Venezuela, Brazil, Holland, Austria, Italy, Bermuda, Virgin Islands, and Taiwan, plus many additional U.S. cities.

AFTERVIEW

The study of fashion history is extremely valuable, but not entirely for the reasons many students of fashion have been led to believe. For example, there are some conflicting opinions as to what fashion history actually teaches.

Cycles

Some say that history testifies that fashion cycles are inevitable and take place with predictable regularity. Other proclaim that this is only a half-truth, but repeated so often it has been accepted by many as gospel.

A more reliable truth is that *change* is inevitable (in fashion as in all things), but the *cycles*, try as they may to stubbornly emerge in regular patterns, are often interrupted, jarred, speeded up, or retarded by the economy, wars, science, social, and cultural conditions. These are more realistically the dictators of fashion change, not the calendar. Life cannot be predicted, programmed, or regulated, and neither can fashion.

History Repeats Itself?

Another school of thought proclaims that one can learn where fashion is going by reviewing where fashion has been. In other words, that history repeats itself. To accept this cliché as a truth (when it comes to fashion) is giving history too much credit, or more accurately, the wrong kind of credit.

In fashion, the so-called repeating of history takes the form of revivals. "Revival" is not entirely correct as regards the comeback of a former fashion trend. An impression or an influence, yes, but this is an entirely different thing. The influence might come from any age, country, or culture and still enjoy great acceptability. A draping reminiscent of a Greek toga, an oriental kabuki sleeve, a high-rise Empress Josephine empire bodice, an ancient Aztec or Inca motif, and hundreds of other influences from a time lost in history, return today and tomorrow, again and again.

An influence for fashion is often borrowed from a period similar in temperament to that into which it is resurrected. Timing figures very strongly in the success of a fashion recall. For example, fashion cannot repeat itself too soon after its current reign of acceptance. If a trend is too recent, it would be in the range of passé, rather than from the past. Timing is everything—not just time for a change for its own sake, but time for something frivolous, conservative, seductive, modest, elegant or amusing. Whatever the borrowed trend, it returns not so much as a revival in yesterday's form. Instead, it returns in a form related to the present but smacking of nostalgia.

The Mirror

Fashion is always the reflection of times and places, lifestyles, and people. If one examines the mode of dress during any period of history, remarkable clues found in the fabric, texture, style, or line reveal something of the cultural, economical, emotional, and moral attitude of the people of that time. They were lively, extravagant, and reckless; they were restrained, rigid, and modest; they were preoccupied with fashion or anti-fashion. Fashion mirrors the current needs to glorify, dramatize, disguise, improve, or change the anatomy—its look, its line, its size.

Point of Focus

One of the strong revelations emerging from the study of fashion history is the traveling point of focus on a woman's body. Throughout periods of overdressing and underdressing, exaggerating or minimizing, concealing or exposing, usually one part of the body becomes the focal point of fashion. One time the waistline, another time the hipline, the bosom, shoulders, or legs. One area or another dominates and directs the manipulation of fashion, or the decision to revive a past trend.

What Fashion History Teaches

We need not look to history to predict fashion cycles, but to expect them. We should not look to history to repeat itself, but simply to record. Fashion history is indispensable when it becomes a source from which to borrow influences, usually never in their original form, but a suggestion thereof. Actually, it is not just a matter of borrowing from the past, but learning from it. It is the infallible reference to discover the truth about people and their times as mirrored by what they wore. It may be difficult to always speak the truth about fashion—an area so filled with disception and evasiveness—but when viewed in retrospect, fashion speaks the truth for itself.

CHAPTER RE-EXAMINATION

Questions

1. What was one of the earliest ways women in the New World received fashion direction?
2. Who created the field of fashion coordination? Why?
3. What was the first title used for this fashion expert?
4. Why was the Fashion Group created?

Workshop

Observe the fashion trends visible today, or those recently popular. Indicate which trend (or trends) is a revival or has taken some influence from the past. Note from which time period, culture, and country it came from. Compare the revival with its past interpretation.

The fashion director's desk, a whirl of directives and fabric samples. In a trousered suit by Jones of New York. (*Courtesy of The Wool Bureau, Inc.*)

4

THE FASHION OFFICE

Paradox. This word most accurately describes the structure of the retail fashion office. After all, since the fashion director's title and responsibilities differ so from store to store it certainly is undertandable that the fashion office itself follows no familiar blueprint. The fashion office or fashion department, like no other area in a retail operation, is custom designed by the company it serves.

The size of the fashion director's office (we are talking about size of staff not square feet) is in no way indicative of the director's power or influence in the store. Not at all. The head of a very large fashion office may have less of a voice in the decisions of the store than the head of a small fashion office, where the fashion director wears many hats, covers many bases, and answers to many bosses. This is not because of lack of ability, but often because of the firm's reponsibility structure.

Money Doesn't Count

The size of a store's volume is not always a key to the size of the fashion office. It is not unusual to find a store with an annual volume of $100,000,000 maintaining a fashion office with a staff the same size as a store with an annual volume of $300,000,000. Or an operation topping $400,000,000 employing a fashion office with a smaller staff than another store doing $250,000,000. Everything here depends on the store's projection, whether it is fashion oriented or promotional, and the nature of the power structure.

There are some universal features, however, that are consistent in all fashion offices, if they are at all worthy of the name or are to justify their existence. They are either very small and bursting with activity, or very large and bursting with activity. Large or small, it matters not, the paradoxical fashion office is almost always the scene of remarkable action.

The Important Three

Within the confines of the three largest and most important types of retail fashion operations—department, chain, and specialty stores—the fashion director helps tell the world who and what they stand for as regards fashion. Almost all of the one hundred top-volume department stores (ranging in volume from $55,000,000 to over $700,000,000) maintain a fashion office, headed by a fashion director, who is, in all cases, the eyes and ears as well as the right arm of the merchandising team.

The giant chain stores usually lean heavily on national fashion offices to help guide them in applying fashion that can develop into volume selling.

Specialty stores, who deal mostly in soft goods, are often more image-conscious and depend on their fashion directors to project their special image along with their fashion message.

The major department stores, on the other hand, have a more complicated need. Their fashion image emerges through their fashion leadership at the same time they are seeking and developing fashion merchandise that will translate into volume selling.

THE ONE-PERSON TEAM

The one-person fashion office is not the loneliest job in town. Far from it. It bears little or no resemblance to any other one-person business office, where one might execute a heavy work load in a quiet, uninterrupted atmosphere. The one-person fashion office is a kind of organized madness.

Even though the telephone rings constantly and people wander in and out for one hundred different reasons, the fashion director spends a great deal of time out of the office. The director is so hard to find that associates sometime believe he or she is only a myth. Tracking her down might be tricky, even though she always lets her superior know where she is. She might be in any one of the fashion departments looking over the new arrivals, assisting with the merchandising on the racks, touring the branches to review adjacencies of departments or select a location for a new trend shop, advising on the dressing of a mannequin with a display director, taking clothes to the advertising department for illustration, selecting items for a fashion show, gathering accessories, running off a fashion report on a duplicating machine, conducting a training clinic on the latest trends for the store personnel, being out of the store making a speech or fashion presentation, meeting with buyers or merchandising executives, or preparing to fly off to New York or California or Paris for a market trip.

It's all teamwork, with one facet of the director's personality cooperating with all the other facets. And, in turn, all those elements (that combine and blend into a very diversified "team" that makes up the single fashion director) must also combine and blend with all the personalities of the store.

It is not unusual for a major retail outlet to employ the services of a solitary fashion director. In fact, the fashion director who is on his or her own and does it all is understandably very valuable to a company and certainly can become better equipped to head a large fashion office.

The Fashion Office of Yesterday

From the outset of this fashion career, stores thought of the role in terms of one person and that one person was a woman, as indicated in Chapter 3. (Today some of the leading fashion directors are men.) But even office space for one person (as recently as fifteen or twenty years ago) was mighty hard to come by.

When space in many stores was at such a premium, the fashion "office" might have been a cubbyhole under a staircase, an ex-fitting room, a former storage area behind a wrapping desk, a partitioned-off two-by-four area in the far, far end of a stockroom, or a loft high up, somewhere between the second and third floors, reached miraculously by a ladder-type stairway. Not all fashion office space was like this, of course, but many a veteran retail fashion director (then called coordinator or stylist) will recognize the description.

Not only were the fashion offices remote but they usually were tiny as well. However, many resourceful directors managed to arrange a desk, telephone, file cabinet, clothes rack for merchandise, card table (laden with fashion accessories, trade publications, color charts, press releases, to name a few), and a chair in which no one could sit because it was the catch-all for everything that the table could not hold. And the bulletin board. There was always a bulletin board covered with fabric swatches, new sketches from designers, photographs torn from leading fashion magazines and *Women's Wear Daily*, plus tear sheets of favorite or current fashion ads.

If the above description sounds as though the fashion office was a very unorganized place, let me hasten to assure you that the lack of organization was strictly in physical appearance and not in the performance; in fact, it took—and still takes—a highly organized individual to successfully operate a productive fashion office.

The Housing Shortage

Any resemblance between the fashion director's importance and the quality of the office was strictly unintentional. In order to appreciate the reason for the lack of office space in some retail stores, one must understand that every precious spare foot of space is first regarded as selling space. When one considers that each square foot must be responsible for contributing to the store's total volume, it is understandable why every inch is carefully allocated to the most productive use. For example, a high traffic area that is capable of producing $500 per square foot annually would not be provided for merchandise that would render only $100 per square foot.

When many of the flagship department stores (usually downtown stores) needed to shrink their huge selling floors, more generous office space became available. However, branch stores, experiencing the opposite (a need for more selling space) continued to feel the squeeze for any office.

**Expect the
Unexpected**

While emergencies are apt to appear in any size fashion office, the pressures of such times are obviously more prevalent in the fashion office maintained by one person. Because fashion office responsibilities are often swarming with deadlines, *a sense of urgency* is a top requirement for the fashion director. Words like change, alter, revise, replace, delete, and cancel are not just mere words to the retail fashion director—they are a way of life. If she has a clear-cut idea of what to expect, she will realistically expect the unexpected.

For example, just when the well-organized fashion director has the day's priorities all scheduled he or she can be sure something will come along to rearrange that schedule. Even though a normal day has a dependable amount of deadlines, there are a few more that will inevitably show up. It would not be unusual to get an emergency call from the store president, who has just received an emergency call from an important customer advising that the guest speaker for a city-wide benefit has arrived, but, alas, her luggage is snowed in in Chicago. The speaker has nothing to wear. The fashion director is advised that the distraught guest and the program chairman will be right over, and "would you please fit the lady in something splendid for the event which is less than an hour away."

Or, perhaps, a designer's collection, due in today for a special-invitation showing tomorrow, will not be coming at all because of a transportation strike. The invitations are out, of course, and the show must go on. An entire show must be selected out of stock, fitted, and coordinated to replace the missing collection. Many a fashion director has been called to quickly pull merchandise (selected and signed for before it can leave the department) for a fashion ad that must be put together immediately to replace an ad that is being pulled because the merchandise to back it up will not be in on time.

The emergency-tuned-in fashion director drops everything and rises to the occasion. The director is always rising to an occasion; that's part of the job. Perhaps that is why the one-person fashion office is such a remarkable training ground—the director must do everything and, therefore, not only learns a great deal, but stretches his or her own individual expectations.

The number of stores that maintain a one-person office is considerable. In fact, during an economy crunch, larger departments have pared down to smaller staffs. Excellent opportunities are available for an energetic, enthusiastic person who is ready to set a new track record and is not a clock-watcher. These are important requrements, by the way, for all fashion merchandising careers.

One more comment should be added about the one-person fashion office. Wherever possible, it should be avoided. True, it is a great training ground for a highly energetic person, but there are other drawbacks. For example, it is often a waste of important executive time to handle all the meager details of the fashion office along with the major responsibilities. Also, there is always the danger of diluting efficiency. There must be time for creative thinking. For example, if a fashion director has a great idea for a new shop concept, but hesitates to suggest it because there is no time for follow-through, the talents of this person are ill-placed. Even the assistance of a secretary and/or part-time clerical would be helpful.

Part Time Assistants

In retail stores where only one person is the fashion office and assignments are geared primarily to support the merchandising team, there is time for little else. While researching the market, planning time and action calendars for promoting new fashion trends, working with buyers and divisional merchandise managers on shop concepts, being totally conversant with the budgets, developing growth areas, training personnel on fashion newness and being a part of the store's fashion message through advertising and visual presentation, how would the fashion director rectify conflicts of schedules?

Conflicts on the calendar are inevitable. This is especially true in stores where the fashion director is a strong right arm for the merchandising side and, at the same time, is highly promotional with fashion shows and events. For example, if a market trip and a fashion show appear simultaneously, the fashion director would be hard pressed to be in both places. Under such circumstances, it would be necessary to pull someone else in to assist. Very often, someone from within the store, such as a special events person, steps in to help or take over the event. This person might do everything from coordinating the show to providing the commentary. On the other hand, if such a person is not available within the company, and the fashion director (although very good on the merchandising side) has little aptitude for show business, a free-lance or part-time assistant from the outside might be called in.

It is very possible that the store's fashion director is the only one who can best coordinate the show—especially an important one—because he or she knows the merchandise best and knows what fashion stories the store needs to tell. In such a case, the director might work right along with a temporary assistant, leaving the narrating of the show to a free-lance personality who is brought in specifically for the role of announcer. Sometimes a director writes her own commentary, coming in ahead of the show to view the clothes. Sometimes it is written for her. In other cases, a commentator may be closely associated with the store and with the merchandise (for example, a fashion buyer), and, therefore, capable of making simple notes, and then ad-lib the commentary. We mention all this here because many part-time or free-lance coordinators have found their way into the fashion office as permanent staff members just this way.

Fashion models, too, have very often started on a fashion coordination career through assisting in the fashion office in a similar manner. The store's fashion director asks the model to help coordinate a show, and soon she is learning how it is all put together. If she is a woman with good taste, she is usually very comfortable with the assignment. Next, because she already has displayed good stage presence, she may be asked to assist with the commentary. Soon she may decide this has a better future than modeling, give up the job of mannequin altogether, and accept a full-time job in the fashion office where she can learn more and expand her horizons.

TWO FOR THE SEESAW

When the solo fashion director's office is enlarged to a duet, immediately the vibration is much greater than might be expected, not just twice as strong as before but many times stronger. If one is looking for a challenge, stop here. We are getting into a very lively operation indeed. The two people, usually a fashion director and assistant, become involved in every project under the jurisdiction of the fashion office.

Usually, only the fashion merchandising director goes into the wholesale market for research and making contacts in all areas affecting her job, while the assistant is home watching the store. The watching, however, is a huge job. Follow-through for fashion office procedure never stops. While one season is in progress, another season is being planned. Therefore, the assistant to the fashion merchandising director may be busy with these aspects of the current season:

1. Working with advertising and display on current presentations to assure accuracy.
2. Training sales personnel on in-stock merchandise.
3. Arranging and staging fashion shows.

At the same time, the fashion director, away at the New York market, is working on the coming season:

1. Surveying the market prior to the buyers to determine trends and coordinate fashion direction.
2. Uncovering new resources.
3. Working with fiber and fabric manufacturers on promotions for the coming seasons.

4. Working with fashion magazines for direction on the coming season, plus tie-in promotions and editorial credits.
5. Shopping the New York leadership stores.

THE LARGE FASHION OFFICE

The ideal fashion office of a major store would include a complete staff of specialists, each responsible for covering a specific fashion area and each reporting to the fashion office head, the fashion merchandising director. That, of course, is the ideal setup. In many large stores, where the goals and aims are focused strongly toward obtaining or maintaining an effective fashion image along with fashion leadership, a highly specialized team is more likely to exist.

Listed below is a breakdown of such a team of specialists. It is presented here to show the different types of fashion coordination careers available in retail stores. However, not all titles indicated will exist in all stores, but the responsibilities of all are assigned in some form or other to whatever personnel is included in a specific fashion office.

Who Works in a Fashion Office

Such a staff, as follows, would be the ideal support for the fashion merchandising director of a major store. Area coordinators or fashion directors, reporting to the corporate fashion merchandising director:

Fashion director for ready-to-wear (Misses and Juniors)
Fashion coordinator for accessories, cosmetics, intimate apparel
Fashion director for men's (Ready-to-wear and accessories)
Fashion coordinator for children's and pre-teens
Secretary

There's more. In some cases, the following coordinators (where they exist) report to the corporate fashion merchandising director; in other cases they report as indicated below:

Fashion show coordinator
Branch store coordinator (may report to store manager)
Display fashion coordinators (may report to visual presentation director)
Youth coordinator (may report to special events director)

There are also jobs for assistants to all the above. Even secretaries or administrative assistants in a fashion office get involved with fashion office responsibilities and, therefore, are often promoted in the fashion office or in the store as openings appear.

In addition to all the above, there is a fashion director for the home division, who sometimes reports to the corporate fashion merchandising director, but very often reports to the general merchandising manager or divisional merchandising manager of the home division. Where there is more than one general merchandise manager, it is possible that each may have his or her own divisional fashion director or coordinator. Under this structure, the retailer operates each division as a separate store—men's store, feminine apparel, home store. The budget or basement store is always separate and sometimes has a separate coordinator as well.

WHY RESPONSIBILITY IS DIVIDED

As indicated earlier, it cannot be emphasized too strongly that fashion is in everything and should be expressed and projected throughout the store. Therefore, it would be impossible for all areas to be thoroughly covered in a major store if separate assignments were not allocated to specific fashion people, with clear-cut definitions and directions as to what must be done.

Separate "Stores"

The retail system of dividing merchandise according to customer types into separate "stores" dictates in large measure how fashion office people must work. As mentioned earlier, departments that service men are designated as "the men's store," and, therefore, the fashion director or coordinator assigned to this area will concentrate exclusively on the specific treatment needed here. It may differ from what the fashion director for women's or juniors will be projecting, even though the procedure of research will be pretty much the same. The coordinator for accessories, on the other hand, will be alert for those items or trends that require special attention in that area, but will always keep in mind that whatever accessories the store carries must tie in with or support the ready-to-wear departments.

The timing and theming for the home store may be so different from the fashion divisions that they would work completely independent of all ready-to-wear areas. There are exceptions, of course. For example, when the store is involved in a total store promotion that embraces all areas, then all fashion directors, along with their specific divisions, work in concert to bring about fashion harmony.

A marvelous example of this kind of coordination might be an Oriental promotion. When goods from China became of special interest to the American consumer, several major retailers inaugurated storewide merchandising promotions featuring Chinese products, artisans, personalities, and entertainment relating to The People's Republic of China. For such an event, the singular theme would invade all areas of the store. A customer could find Chinese art pieces in the home store, a Chinese garment in the men's or women's fashion departments, even Chinese menus in the store's restaurant areas. All the plans that made the theme come alive were the direct result of the store's fashion directors' team effort to pull it all together.

Separate Markets

To further illustrate the efficiency of divided responsibility in the large fashion office, the markets where merchandise is to be viewed, reviewed, and selected are divided in exactly the same way.

The junior market is separate from the women's market. The accessory market is separate from the intimate apparel market. The children's market is as different a world as the men's or home furnishings markets. All are comprehensively divided. The separateness in the market, the divisions in the store, the buying staff, and, therefore, the fashion office put every effort into neat little slots that properly belong together.

What surfaces here is that while areas of merchandise and markets are separated, the independent fashion director or coordinator brings together the special information so that the combined effort develops into a beautifully synchronized revelation. This comprehensive system enables the store to present with conviction a strong substantiated fashion story or statement for their customers' shopping pleasure.

To further illustrate the divided responsibilities in the fashion office, listed below are the fashion office structures of two leading department stores: one from New York, one from the Midwest.

Carson Pirie Scott
Chicago, Illinois   Approximate annual volume: (1981) Over 311
million

Fashion Director (Vice President—Director of Fashion Merchandising)
Reports to: Executive Vice President
Reporting to the Corporate Fashion Director:
   Fashion Merchandising Director: Accessories
   (with staff of two coordinators)   Cosmetics
                               Intimate Apparel
   Fashion Merchandising Director: Feminine Apparel

(with staff of 6—3 coordinators, secretary, alterations, stock)	(Misses and Juniors)
Fashion Merchandising Director:	Men's
(with staff of one coordinator)	Children's

B. Altman & Co.
New York City   Approximate annual volume: (1981) over 200
million

Reporting to the Vice President—Fashion Merchandising Director:

Fashion Director:	All women's RTW
(one assistant)	(Misses and Juniors)
Fashion Coordinator:	Women's Accessories
	Men's Wear
	Shoes
Fashion Coordinator:	Suburban Stores
(one assistant)	
Fashion Director:	Home Division
(one coordinator for furniture)	
(one coordinator for soft lines)	
Administrative Assistant:	(for the Corporate Vice President— Fashion Merchandising Director)

If one were delegated to set up a fashion office structure and procedure, the following fundamental framework would be a good guideline, including those elements that suit a specific store's needs and
omitting those that do not. Including or omitting any part of a fashion
office structure, of course, could be helped by taking an intimate glance
at the people behind the titles in the fashion office.

WHAT THE FASHION SPECIALISTS DO

The Corporate Fashion Director

As the driving force behind research, editing, translating, advising,
and educating the merchandising staff regarding fashion, the fashion
director also must be a transmitter of enthusiasm for action.

Perhaps more than in any other area in retailing, colorful personality
types emerge in the fashion office. There is hardly a person in the

country holding this position, if they know their business and execute it well, who is not a totally remarkable individual. It is impossible not to be aware of such people—they send out vibrations that are electric and are almost always vital, alive, interesting, and interested. The fashion director is an inveterate optimist. When she likes something, she likes it with a passion. "I love it! I simply love it," she exclaims, and then proceeds to share her love for it with every member of her staff and eventually management until they are convinced the customer will love it also.

That is the name of the game. Enthusiasm. If, with all the facts available to her, she is convinced a trend is good or big, and if a strong move is in order, she is the first one to generate enthusiasm for what steps are to be taken to make things happen.

This is also a people game. The director must serve, work with, relate to, encourage, inspire, and forgive a world of people, all of whom are so different there are not enough pigeonholes in the universe to classify them. She does this best when she is sure of her ground. An insecure fashion director is not a fashion director. Because her function is primarily that of advisor and because so much is riding on that advice, the foundation of all her fashion evaluations must be solid.

It is all well and good to be somewhat intuitive, or even to cultivate a green thumb for making the right choices, but there can be no substitute for careful, well-planned research. There is no place for guessing or gambling when so much depends on the director's recommendations. Even with hard facts carefully scrutinized, mistakes can be made because of a number of unforseen developments, not the least of these being the unpredictable acceptance of the consumer. Therefore, guessing is out. With facts, there is less chance of missing; at least one's batting average will be far better.

Once the predictions of the fashion direction for the coming season have been made (and approved by management), the fashion director makes sure that every member of the fashion office is well informed of the entire plan. Each coordinator receives directions for expediting the plan and reports back on progress and problems.

The Area Coordinators

We have already established that the fashion departments of a store are systematically divided into areas (also called divisions) or "stores" and, therefore, fashion office coordinators are assigned to those specific areas.

While the overall pre-season research and evaluation are done by the corporate fashion merchandising director, there is a great deal of territory in the market that the assisting coordinator must cover in his or her own area, concentrating only on that area and reporting back on the highlights or on specifics under question. Sometimes market trips are made independently, but sometimes they are made with the corporate fashion director or buyer of that area.

A great deal of his or her contribution, however, is focused on in-store coordination and follow-up. The coordinator will

1. Carefully watch to see that departments have the merchandise arriving to back up projected fashion plans.
2. Supervise the selection of fashion merchandise to tie in with interior displays planned.
3. Make sure each department under his or her supervision has the desired atmosphere or look of the current fashion story.
4. Select merchandise for the fashion story being carried into the tie-in windows.
5. Coordinate and accessorize merchandise for the planned fashion ads.
6. Pull those fashion pieces best suitable for scheduled fashion shows and special events.
7. Act as liaison on any or all publicity necessary for a celebrity, special guest designer, etc., appearing in his or her area.

The area fashion director or coordinator will be more successful by sharing plans with the buyer when possible and looking for input or an okay from the corporate fashion merchandising director.

Example

Miss Area selects three exciting peasant dresses, with assistance from the buyer of Young Designer Dresses. The dresses are to be sketched or photographed for an ad on ethnic style of dressing. Miss Area brings them to the fashion office for the fashion director's approval.

"I think they are great!" the fashion director declares. "The choice of the three different textures is excellent, and the variety of patterns is very good. The only reservation I might have is that the body (silhouette) of the red one might come off looking too much like the yellow one. Perhaps it might be a good idea to replace one piece with something that gives us three more completely different expressions of this ethnic trend."

On reflection, the area coordinator agrees. She hadn't noticed. Three entirely different interpretations of the look would, indeed, make a better fashion story. It would give the customer a better idea of the variety of choice and a clearer picture of what the peasant dress is all about. It is agreed. The change is made and carried out in just that manner—in the ad, in the window, in the department display.

Another area coordinator, for the junior ready-to-wear department, is busy seeing that her departments are turned into pleasant "peasant villages." The junior area, for example, becomes more gypsy, complete with gypsy tent, and fortune teller, and all the colorful gypsy and peasant costumes are dramatically displayed to tell the fashion story from a younger point of view.

The accessory coordinator, whose responsibilities are the same as the other area coordinators, has pulled every facet of the accessory departments together with a marked ethnic look. Bags, belts, neckwear, jewelry—bizarre and unique with a handcrafted flavor—show the influence of countries all over the world. The woman who selects a peasant gown can find the perfect ethnic shawl to complete the look. A junior customer, who found her favorite "gypsy dress," is enchanted with the gypsy earrings that enhance the mood of her costume. It all works. It all goes together. It is fashion coordinated.

The coordinator for the men's and boys' departments is following the "peasant" directive to the letter. Colorful peasant shirts, vests, scarves, and ties all add emphasis to the importance of the trend.

The store is alive with the ethnic looks of yesterday, as interpreted for the eighties. And so it goes with each and every new fashion story. If it is clearly understood by the store and its fashion personnel, it will be clearly understood by the customer. People buy what is understandable.

**Fashion Show
Coordinator**

The fashion show coordinator in the fashion office of a major retail store has a full-time responsibility, zeroing in on this area exclusively. The fashion show coordinator in a small fashion office, however, has other responsibilities as well.

Everything pertaining to fashion shows comes across his or her desk. The coordinator handles all the details pertaining to shows (see Chapter 13) from the booking (scheduling of the date) to the execution of the production. If one needs to know if a particular date is open for a show, they must check with the fashion show coordinator, who keeps the calendar of all fashion office events. In most cases, precedent is given to in-store fashion events. What the store has requested, in connection with the fashion plan, must always come first. After this, if dates are free, and budget permits, shows for benefits, clubs, and the like may be booked. The fashion show coordinator must, like all the other members of the team, get approval from the fashion merchandising director (who is responsible for the budget) on which shows may be scheduled and which refused. Most fashion offices get more requests for shows than the calendar has dates and the energies of personnel will permit.

The scheduling of shows is most effective when tied with the fashion stories planned for a given season. For example, it is at this point that the fashion director might recommend to the show coordinator that during the time the store is projecting the peasant or ethnic looks in all fashion departments, a special "show of folklore" be scheduled in the junior area. She might also recommend that informal modeling be offered during lunch time in the store's restaurant areas during the week of the special promotion.

During peak seasons, when shows and exhibits are given greater priority, and are more desirable, everyone available in the fashion office pitches in. This is also the case when other efforts have pressure periods. The fashion office team bands together for an all-out effort.

Branch Store Coordinator

If the downtown store is treated as headquarters for a retail operation, then the corporate fashion office, along with other executive offices, usually will be found there. However, many retailers no longer regard the downtown store as the flagship and have relegated it to a branch status. In some cases, executive offices are situated in an office building or area relative to the store's distribution center. At any rate, the expansion of retail efforts to branches or suburban stores all over the city, in state and out of state, demands that an on-the-spot person oversees and follows up on everything coming out of the corporate fashion office.

This does not necessarily mean that the branches will have the same atmosphere or the same merchandise. Branches differ because the clientele differs. So it is very likely that one suburban store will cater to the more affluent customer, another in the same organization will cater to a younger, more contemporary customer, while others will offer merchandise for the budget-minded, lower-income customer. The location of the branch and the requirements of the customers patronizing that branch dictate the fashion direction.

If one branch is considerably different from the downtown store or other branches in the group, then plans will vary somewhat from promotion to promotion. The branch coordinator, therefore, feeds back information to the main fashion office as to what the needs are, and a special plan is made for that particular branch.

Unlike the area coordinator, the branch coordinator does not usually travel to cover the wholesale market.

The A-B-C's

In all major retail department store chains or groups there is an assortment of store sizes. They might range in size from a multiple-floor unit that carries everything in soft and hard lines, to a specialty shop concept that features only fashion or one even as small as a twig, which is a mini version of the specialty shop branch. These different size stores are identified as "A" stores (the largest), "B" stores (next size), and "C" stores (the smallest). It is not likely that a branch coordinator would be assigned to a "C" store. Instead, its special needs would be taken care of by the store manager or assistant in the store. In some organizations most "B" and "C" stores would come under the supervision of a coordinator for suburban stores.

If a name designer was being brought in for a special showing of his or her collection, you can be sure the designer would make a personal appearance only at the "A" stores. In all probability, the designer's collection would only be carried in the "A" stores, and, sometimes, not in all. Again, it depends on the clientele of the branch.

In still other situations, where there is no downtown or flagship store in the traditional sense of many department stores (perhaps closed or never existed), the responsibility of more promotional areas would be handled by the branch coordinator. This might include special events, fashion coordination, and even teen coordination and the branch coordinator would possibly report directly to the individual store manager. Merchandising and advertising are usually centralized for the overall responsibility of buying and promotion, leaving the responsibility for fashion presentation (displays and departmental merchandising) and fashion events to the individual stores. They would, however, receive educational material, training guides, and fashion direction from the fashion office, but would be left on their own for execution.

Display Fashion Directors

The branch store coordinator and display coordinator or director in many stores are one and the same. In firms where they report to the corporate display director or visual presentation director but take their direction on fashion correctness from the corporate fashion director, their function is in the area of display only. Under this system the display director for windows is usually separate from the display director for interiors. Then, to unite their efforts, the corporate display director gets guidance from the fashion director, or invites the corporate display staff to check all fashion selections to be used in display with the fashion office. However, for the sake of budget structure and responsibility assignment, the management of many stores prefers that everything relating to fashion projection be assigned squarely on the shoulders of the fashion authority: the fashion director.

In the rare cases where the display fashion people belong solely to the fashion office, they are involved in all aspects of visual presentation of fashion—interiors, windows, shops, shows, and special events. Where the store is extremely large, or these same coordinators or directors are responsible for the branches as well, each of the three visual presentation areas are handled separately:

1. Interiors and cases
2. Windows
3. Special shops, boutiques, etc.

This is the system in a retail giant like Bloomingdale's of New York where the display efforts are so major that a completely separate structure for all areas is maintained. Windows are handled exclusively by the corporate display director and staff, while shops, boutiques, and so on, are designed and created by the director of special projects. The heads of both of these areas work with the store's fashion office for fashion direction.

In small stores any or all display personnel may be called on to handle all details related to special fashion events, as well as the traditional display assignments, such as runways, staging, sets, production, and so on, for fashion shows. These people are indispensable to the fashion office for getting the show put together with lights, sound, technical supervision backstage, and whatever else is required.

The Menswear Coordinator

Not always but very often the role of menswear coordinator or fashion director is filled by a man. As mentioned later (see Chapter 16), there are several men who are corporate fashion directors, even vice presidents, and more are becoming interested in this area of the fashion business. For the most part, however, when men have served as fashion directors or coordinators they have showed up in the men's areas or home divisions.

The history of men in this field was not unlike that of the women. Their earlier roles were simply to coordinate. They had little or no voice in what merchandise was bought; they just tried to pull it all together and make some kind of fashion statement in the departments, in displays, and in ads.

Similar to the women's area, when the men's coordinator was made a fashion director (in practice, not just title) he became an important member of the merchandising staff. All responsibilities of market research, working with buyers, making fashion presentations to management, as done in the women's area, were also executed by the men for their divisions in the same way.

The greatest problem fashion directors or coordinators for the men's division have had is to convince menswear buyers that they are interested in more than just designer merchandise. This problem had also been true in the women's areas, but perhaps more so in the men's because the earlier people, it was believed, never dirtied their hands, so to speak, on anything less than designer collections. Since the men's fashion director is more recent on the retail responsibility charts, there has not been enough time to erase the original image.

The Home Division Coordinator

Here is one area where there have been traditionally more men serving as fashion coordinators or fashion directors than women. From such major retailers as Montgomery Ward's to Bloomingdale's, male coordinators have made impressive marks in their field.

Bloomingdale's.   Perhaps more unique than typical is the fashion staff for home furnishings at Bloomingdale's. Headed by the vice president of home furnishings fashion, the staff of nine, including two senior fashion coordinators for hard and soft lines, are responsible for all home furnishings except furniture, housewares, stationery, and food. The responsibilities of this staff include:

- Editing the market for the buyers.
- Making a fashion statement on the floors (working in conjunction with display).
- Scrutinizing markets all over the world for exclusive products and product ideas for the store's private label programs.
- Developing new products.
- Designing new products.

Because people look to Bloomingdale's for things they cannot find elsewhere, the home furnishings staff is dedicated to extensive efforts to provide such exclusivity for their customers. For example, for Bloomingdale's China promotion, the home furnishings vice president made six trips to China. In the area of product development, the Bloomingdale's staff will come up with ideas and then find a manufacturer to produce them. Believing in the function of design, the Bloomingdale's team tries to reflect this in all efforts and instill this thinking in all staff members. By bringing together new ideas, functionally designed quality merchandise, and inspiring presentations (displays), the fashion coordinators of home furnishings make their roles indispensable to their store.

Montgomery Ward.   Serving as the national fashion coordinator for Montgomery Ward, this chain's lone coordinator services 400 stores. Working differently from a department store coordinator, the Ward's man spends about 35 percent of his time evaluating consumer studies plus working in the field with consumers. Participating in roundtable discussions and also meeting the consumer personally, he learns how the buying public feels about his store and its products. With Ward's change in strategy—that is, offering name brands after a long history of private-label merchandise—it is important for the store to have the fashion coordinator's feedback on fashion statements, consumer preferences, and private design projects.

The Ward's home furnishings fashion coordinator, although he has no open-to-buy in his own budget, works with the buyers, making recommendations on which they have the final decision.

Other Home Coordinators

In the average major retail operation, where home furnishings make a major contribution to annual volume, the fashion coordinator for the home division may report to the corporate fashion merchandising director, to the GMM, or to the DMM. He or she would be responsible for visual presentation in the stores, training personnel, covering the market, as well as working with buyers.

The Youth Coordinator

The youth coordinator, if the store has one, sometimes reports to the special events director and sometimes to the fashion director. This special area has had its ups and downs. Some stores have minimized their youth programs, some have eliminated them entirely. Others, however, interested in capturing the attention of the young customer, have continued and updated such youth-oriented activities. It is only this second group who would maintain a youth coordinator. Even so, in the interest of economy and, again, the extent of merchandising directed to the young customer, the responsibilities of the youth coordinator might differ in proportion.

1. The coordinator might be the same person serving as area coordinator for the junior division.
2. He or she might be the junior buyer serving as a part-time youth coordinator.
3. The person might be a full-time youth coordinator who creates and executes all yout
activities, but also is available for other fashion events when needed by the fashion office or special events director.

In case number 1, the youth coordinator covers the junior market, is in contact with all the young magazines, and provides all departments in her area with events of special interest to the specific age group.

The part-time youth coordinator who is a full-time buyer (number 2) might work on a seasonal basis only (such as back-to-school) with a teen board or school representatives to stimulate interest in this department.

The full-time youth coordinator, if he or she is to make a valuable contribution, is totally saturated in youth-oriented projects, which include everything from merchandising for the young customer to fashion shows and special events, to public service and civic involvement.

THE FASHION OFFICE AS A UNIT

The fashion director of a major store usually travels a great deal, and therefore must have well-informed, well-trained personnel in the office to follow through in the director's absence on all aspects of fashion office responsibilities. Although each member of the staff may have specific assignments for which they have major responsibility, there are some general tasks for which all fashion office people must be prepared to handle. The job may fall to anyone who answers the fashion office telephone.

Telephone Charm

Fashion office phones ring constantly and when there is a customer at the other end, that customer's impression of the store and its fashion image sometimes can be elevated or lowered by fashion office personnel.

Charm. That is a top priority requirement for the fashion office. Tact. Another indispensable talent when answering that fashion office phone.

"I think it's disgraceful the low-cut dresses you showed yesterday in your fashion show. Don't you people have a sense of responsibility?"

"Can I wear velvet in April?"

"I just walked through your store and saw a man undressing a mannequin. I think it's indecent."

"What do I wear on my trip to China?"

"What does the woman wear if the invitation says 'black tie optional?' "

"How do I get my daughter into modeling?"

On and on it goes. Some customers indignant, some seeking help, some just lonely and latching onto any excuse to talk. Whatever their need or purpose, their feelings must be dealt with carefully and with patience.

How would you answer a customer who asks a question that every fashion office must face, sooner or later:

"Why are your models always so skinny? Don't you have any consideration for us fat people?"

The questions are many and varied. Some are amusing, some tough, but all deserve some kind of answer. Everyone in the office should graciously answer the question if possible, or kindly suggest that the caller leave a number and someone will call back.

Etiquette Questions

Hardly a week goes by without several calls coming to the fashion office requesting guidance on etiquette problems. When a store telephone operator gets a customer on the line with a question about etiquette (or anything else the operator cannot classify) the caller will very often be advised "I'll connect you with the fashion office. They know everything there." Of course it isn't true, but what a beautiful compliment! It is nice for a fashion office to have that kind of reputation.

It is certainly to the retailer's advantage that so many consumers look to the local leading department store for answers to a multitude of things. Coming up with the right answers may become a heavy burden at times, but customers do regard the fashion office as *the* authority on everything about proper dress, behavior, manners, entertaining, weddings, and so forth. It is important, therefore, for the entire fashion office staff to be aware of the responsibility to provide answers.

"What are the rules for seating at a dinner party?"

"What do I wear to a garden wedding?"

"What do I wear if this is my second marriage?"

"Isn't it still proper for a boy to go to the door to call for a girl on a date, or is it all right for him to honk?"

If the answer is not known, a good reference library, maintained in the fashion office, would solve most problems. A good beginning for such a library would include:

The Amy Vanderbilt Complete Book of Etiquette
By Letitia Baldrige (Doubleday)

Emily Post's Etiquette—The Blue Book of Social Usage
(Funk & Wagnalls)

The Wonderful World of Weddings by Elizabeth L. Post
(Funk & Wagnalls)

The Bride's Book of Etiquette by Editors of Bride's Magazine
(Grosset & Dunlap)

Even with demarcations of responsibility, every member of a fashion office is strongly intertwined with every other member. Their effectiveness and their very existence depend on each other. If a fashion prediction turns out big, everyone is excited. If a big fashion event is a hit, everyone in the fashion office feels the success personally. If one sees a highly successful fashion office, one sees a great team.

THE CHAIN STORE FASHION OFFICE

The big three catalog-retail mass merchandising chains—Sears, Roebuck & Co., J. C. Penney, and Montgomery Ward—all maintain fashion experts who have huge responsibilities for the fashion direction of their companies. All disseminate their direction from the national offices (Sears from Chicago, Penney's and Ward's from New York). By guiding their fashion buyers and influencing their manufacturers, it is not at all improbable that the combined influence of these retail giants is felt in the industry at large.

All three chains have repositioned their approach by putting stronger emphasis on fashion merchandising for growth in the eighties. Sears, the nation's largest general merchandise retail chain, made its position clear as to the fashion image they were reaching for when they contracted Cheryl Tiegs, a leading fashion model. J. C. Penney, estimated as the largest retailer of feminine apparel, has benefited from upgrading fashion merchandise and Ward's, with their "Discover Ward's" campaign had indicated that they want to be taken seriously as a fashion store to be discovered, for example, by working women who might not in the past looked to Ward's for their wardrobes.

Sears, Roebuck and Co.

Because Sears deals with such a varied source structure, including sources in which they have equity, contract sources, open market, domestic, and import, they take a fashion position with a central theme and color story for each of the five seasons—spring, summer, fall, winter, and holiday. Their fashion consultant team travels all markets and predicts trends that relate to their core customer.

When the central theme of a season is selected, responsibility for its interpretation is awarded to the line buyers. Sears feels that fashion staffs in the marketplace daily should be positioned at sources so that innovations, intricate styling, fabric differences, and color matching can be determined at sewing level for viability of cost and look.

According to Wayne T. Holsinger, vice president of Sears Women's Apparel Group, "We feel that Sears should not set fashion, we should sell fashion." Positioned to raise Sears' consumer level, the Cheryl Tiegs program (a total apparel wardrobe of signature sportswear) was a major success. It also alerted the occasional Sears customer that there was a new "Women's Store" at Sears.

Cheryl Tiegs Signature Sportswear at Sears. Pages of an in-house brochure advising personnel of the fashion merchandise to be featured, and the timing it will be in-store. *(Courtesy of Sears Roebuck and Co.)*

J. C. Penney

The national fashion director for Penney's works under the title of Manager of Fashion Coordination. Assisted by a staff of five people, she reports to the Divisional Merchandise Manager in charge of women's ready-to-wear. The fashion office staff, which comprises three coordinators—one for catalog, one for ready-to-wear (sportswear) and one for accessories, intimate apparel, and dresses—plus two assistants—one for the catalog and one general (covering fabrics and the Fashion Information Center)—handle all the fashion direction for the entire company. This well-organized group working as a service department advises the merchandising team on colors, fabrics, and trends far in advance of the season when buying plans must be committed. For the catalog, they work even earlier.

The fashion director goes to Europe twice a year to attend the pret-a-porter. While the director is gone, the coordinator in charge of the Fashion Information Center strips the walls, which are solid with pictures, fabric, and color samples of the current season. Now illustrations for the forthcoming season begin to go up. This unique room, set up like a conference room, is surrounded on all walls with illustrations of

Penney's issues a color chart for each fashion season.

what fashion stories are to be shared with the merchandising team. To fuller educate their fashion position, a slide presentation is developed by the company's audio/video department, with the fashion director on the set during the shooting to focus on fashion correctness. When translated to cassette with recorded commentary, the presentation is shared with buyers who come in groups to view and discuss. The Fashion Director also develops a colorcard, covering both fashion and volume merchandise and shares this with buyers and key suppliers.

In addition to the slide presentation, a printed report with illustrations on all the recommended trends for the coming season is written by Penney's fashion director. For those who cannot come to New York, the fashion director travels to the company's other buying offices, such as Dallas, Miami, and Los Angeles, to make presentations of the fashion stories. Besides the specific direction given for each season, with a well-trained eye and good taste level, the director helps to make the merchandise look exciting, romancing it with interpretation so that the stores, in turn, will be equally excited about the goods they will have in stock.

Montgomery Ward's

Ward's fashion director is called the national fashion coordinator, assistant vice-president. With a staff of nine assistants, her comprehensive program of fashion direction has helped to show how a fashion office can make an indispensable contribution to the company. Ward's fashion office has done this by being totally conversant with the needs and changes of the company it serves.

In addition to their own meticulous research, which begins with the textile industry, the Ward's fashion office is aided by the company's marketing research department, which interviews customers in Ward's stores. All facts are checked out carefully before moving strongly in any new direction.

AFTERVIEW

Within the walls of all the responsibility assignments indicated previously and those to be diagramed is one remarkable and enchanting fact about the entire field of fashion coordination: each fashion director or coordinator, in addition to routine duties, can almost create his or her own job by adding a new dimension through originality and creativity. Fashion is that kind of world. Therein lies the magnificent beauty of the fashion business. It has rules, yes, but all are vulnerable to being broken, provided they are broken gracefully, tastefully, and innovatively. New rules are always in order when trends and times indicate change.

CHAPTER RE-EXAMINATION

Questions

1. What are the three major types of retail fashion operations?
2. Why is square footage in a store so precious?
3. What personality traits are important for members of the fashion office?
4. What are the advantages and disadvantages of the one-person fashion office?
5. How does the system of separate "stores" and separate markets relate to how the fashion office is structured?
6. How does the area or divisional coordinator differ from the branch store coordinator?

Workshop

Select the specific job you would like to have in a fashion office. Write a short job description of that role.

Mall approach to Saks Fifth Avenue in Fort Lauderdale Galleria. Example of a specialty shop far from the parent store (New York) but still exemplifying its national image. *(Courtesy of Gary Bitner)*

5

HOW TO WORK WITH MANAGEMENT

For management the fashion director is its fashion conscience. The director is the learned arm that embraces all fashion aspects of the business and pulls it all together. If management was called on to spell out succinctly what they feel is the single most important thing for the fashion director to keep firmly in mind, they might easily do it with two words: "be realistic!"

The purposes and objectives of management are the reality that must influence and guide every action and decision of the fashion director. What he or she reports and advises might change the objectives or direction of a store's management, but the decisions and advice the director chooses to offer are always tempered by the needs and goals of the company.

The Kind of Store

The starting point for the fashion director is to determine the purposes and objectives of the store.

> What kind of operation is the director serving?
>   Department store
>   Chain store
>   Specialty store
> Is the store dominant in the area?
> Does the store share in a highly competitive market?
> What is the store's primary direction?
>   Completely fashion oriented
>   Highly promotional (catering to the mass market)
>   All things to all people

Is It Her Kind of Store?

If the store is highly promotional and the fashion expert is not geared for action, nor does she thrive on competition nor relate to promotional-type merchandise, then this store is not for her. If the store is primarily high fashion or at least anxious to obtain such an image, the fashion director must relate to this kind of world, or she will be ineffective.

Perhaps more than any other retail executive, the personality of the store and the fashion director must be synonymous. It is a trait that is almost impossible to fake. It takes a great deal of respect to fulfill requests of retail management and a great deal of sincere appreciation, if not love, to be totally in sync with the store's goals. This kind of rapport not only begets trust, but gets the job done. It guarantees the result that everyone involved is out to achieve; is pulling in the same direction toward a common goal.

What's more, it makes a demanding job more fun. A fashion director works hard, very hard, so loving what he or she does and having fun with it is the secret ingredient that helps make the whole thing work.

The Store's Philosophy

When working with management, the fashion director should never lose sight of the store's philosophy. If the store's philosophy is based on long-standing tradition, naturally, that tradition must be upheld. If the company is trying to pull away from tradition, there are always problems in the process. If the store's policies are designed by a progressive, well-tuned-in management, change will be resisted less—in fact, it will be even welcomed by store personnel and customers alike. The fashion director is most valuable when not only relating to change but anticipating it.

The Checklist

The system of the checklist can be invaluable to a busy fashion director. As regards the store's purposes and goals, such a checklist should be drawn up as soon as the store's direction is known and might include the following goals:

1. To direct all efforts to establish the store as a leading fashion authority.
2. To guarantee the customer the best value at the best price.
3. To provide the consumer with everything of fashion importance that is new and to provide it first.

Then, a secondary list strongly supports the first one. This might include:

1. To be aware of the fashion customer types that come to the store and be sure that those customer types are served with the right merchandise.
2. To be aware of the lifestyles of the women of the community so that merchandise is provided to support those lifestyles.
3. To strive for personal identification with customers, through well-trained fashion personnel.
4. To provide the ultimate in services with courtesy and dependability.
5. To be as involved as possible in community and civic affairs and to make a contribution to the cultural efforts of the community.

If these points constitute a realistic checklist for your company, then mark them indelibly into your thoughts so that your every effort is influenced by these guidelines. *These very well may be the most helpful points in this book.* Such a checklist is also a valuable creed for every executive in the company. In fact, *a great deal of the material offered in this volume especially for the fashion director is also applicable and valuable to every decision-making person in fashion merchandising.*

The Customer Comes First

Notice that almost all the points listed on the preceding checklists consider the customer. This is not a Pollyanna approach, but good sound business. The president's job as well as the fashion director's depends on the satisfied customer. Success can only be measured by the customer's satisfaction. Whenever adding or subtracting from such a checklist, ask how it serves the customer.

How to Make a Checklist

Naturally, the points offered here as a suggested checklist for a professional understanding of management's wishes must be tailor-made for every store. For example, if point number 1—establishing the store as a leading fashion authority—is not your company's wish, then number 2 would possibly come to the top. The important procedure is to pull out of the list those things that are top priority and then support them with every fashion decision. Most leading fashion directors would testify that none of the above goals should be eliminated, for they represent the major service a good fashion operation has to offer. However, it would be wise to draw up a list, then check it out with a dependable source in the company or immediate superior.

As for the last point—involvement in community affairs—this may be the one optional item on the list for some stores. However, since fashion is often regarded as something of an art form, it is repeatedly called on to support benefits (often through fashion shows), so the store's cooperation and sympathy with the customer's interests eventually turns out to be a fair exchange. True, there are times when demands on the store are excessive (see Chapter 13), but a careful budgeting of community involvement can be most rewarding. This last point is included because if this is the wish of management, the fashion director and the fashion office are almost always heavily involved.

WHO IS IN CHARGE OF THE FASHION DIRECTOR?

Here we go again. Just as responsibilities differ, as well as the type of office and staff, so diversity exists in determining who is the director's boss. For all practical purposes, there is a choice of three or four top-level management offices to whom the director might report or with whom her activities are greatly involved.

The President

If the fashion director reports to the president of a large store it is very likely a situation where the president does not want the fashion director's efforts restricted, as it might be if the person to whom she would otherwise report is influencing her paycheck. On the other hand, it may be a method through which the president can best be kept informed about the fashion side of the business.

In cases where the president is also the general merchandise manager, the fashion director would report to the president. This is usually true in smaller operations or when the president is also the owner.

General Merchandise Manager (GMM)

This office is the one to which the largest number of fashion directors or coordinators report. Most retailers agree that this is the most efficient way to utilize the services of a fashion director as an arm of the merchandising team through the GMM. In most large stores there is more than one general merchandise manager (usually one for every "store" division), and sometimes each GMM has a fashion director assigned to that specific division, but most likely reporting to a corporate fashion director, who, in this case, would then report to a senior vice president.

The general merchandise manager has the gigantic responsibility, from a merchandising point of view, of watching the store. All money delegated to each division for buying all goods in the store is under the GMM's control. Not only is the GMM in control of who spends what, but he or she is the trusted guardian of the store's philosphy, the noble overseer who is surrounded with talented people whom the GMM can delegate teach, and inspire. The real leader in this area knows it is a people business. He or she knows how to recognize and encourage talent, bring out the best in associates, and help them to make the store great.

A fashion director, reporting to an inspired general merchandise manager, will take on this manager's flavor. But if the manager is in need of inspiration, the fashion director, recognizing what is needed, can supply it. A truly fashion-oriented GMM, working with an enthusiastic, feet-on-the-ground fashion director, can make a store sing. The manager needs the director's authoritative guidance, the director needs the manager's power and authority.

Divisional Merchandise Manager

In the case of the giant chains (where they are in several businesses), the fashion director may report to the divisional merchandise manager. For example, the national fashion director for J. C. Penney reports to the divisional merchandise manager in charge of women's apparel. In the conventional department store this system is less frequently used. When it does exist, it is usually a fashion coordinator responsible only for the ready-to-wear fashion area, only the accessory area, only the men's area, and so on. This procedure is more likely to be used in the home division than in fashion apparel.

The divisional merchandise manager (DMM) has a responsibility similar to that of the GMM, only this manager concentrates on his or her own division. The money and direction given by the GMM is now delegated to buyers. As in any good system of delegated responsibility, the DMM must translate what has come from the GMM and the fashion director into a workable plan for buyers and their associates.

Sales Promotion Director

Back in the days when the fashion director was not as involved on the merchandising side as today, the director was, as we related earlier, a "coordinator," who was more interested in pretty windows than in merchandise content. And since the rest of the director's time might have been heavily saturated with fashion shows and special events, it was certainly understandable that she report to the sales promotion director. In the stores where she still does, it is more likely that the sales promotion director is involved in merchandising (via visual presentation, shops, etc.) and uses the fashion director in this area. If the store is strongly promotional, the fashion director is not a "director," per se, of fashion, but of promotional endeavors.

When the store's merchandising team (the general merchandise manager, fashion director, divisional merchandise managers, buyers) fill the departments with the fashion they believe is in, it is the business of the sales-promotion director to help sell it. He or she gets the story of fashion to the consumer through newspaper and magazine ads, radio and television commercials, catalogs, statement enclosures, special events, shows and exhibits, and visual presentations through interior displays and windows.

How that fashion story is told, however, and how fashion correctness is illustrated, or updated language, theming, and visual presentation are more accurately accomplished is through the advice and guidance of the fashion director. It is one thing to get the right merchandise into the store, but it is another to get the right fashion story to the customer. Because each is so completely dependent on the other, it is understandable why fashion directors used to be assigned to sales promotion, or why some still are. Even though the fashion director reports to the president or the GMM, the director would work with and assist the sales promotion director just as devotedly as he or she does with the buyers. Most retailers have discovered, however, that a fashion director can be of greater assistance to the sales promotion side if the director reports to the GMM and is totally immersed in merchandising.

THE STORE'S SPECIFIC OBJECTIVES

Once the type of store and its philosophy are defined, the fashion director can proceed to underscore the specific objectives of the operation and contribute to the accomplishment of the related goals. Management sets the objectives; the fashion director helps fulfill them.

MERCHANDISING OBJECTIVES

Several possibilities may be on the list of merchandising objectives of a store.

1. UPGRADING

   (a) Price levels
   (b) Quality levels
   (c) Service

2. ATTRACTING NEW CUSTOMER BLOCKS

   (a) Affluent, moderate, or budget
   (b) Younger
   (c) Advanced, trendy
   (d) Large sizes

     (e) Petite sizes
     (f) Working women

  3. DEVELOPING MERCHANDISE GROWTH AREAS

     (a) Enlarging assortments
     (b) Splitting off departments

Everyone on an executive level is concerned with the store's merchandising objectives, but to discover exactly how these objectives affect a fashion director is our purpose now.

UPGRADING

Very high on the list of an alert, progressive store may be the decision to upgrade. This means that the price and quality level of the store's merchandise is to be moved up to accommodate a growing customer demand.

A particular store may decide to replace low-to-moderate priced goods with moderate-to-better in a specific department. It would mean a decrease in lower-end merchandise and an increase in bigger ticket goods. The plan may be departmental or store-wide. In any case, the fashion director would have a big job ahead.

Changing Price Lines

If the low end of the price line of one women's dress department is too low compared with its high, the plan might be to drop the low-end, move it to a lower-priced department, and use the money allotted in that area for an improved selection of better-priced merchandise. Thus the process of upgrading begins. The department will eventually become a higher-styled, higher-priced area, completely divorced from the lower-priced look that once existed.

Changing a Department's Look

Sometimes the business of upgrading a department has less to do with the price lines than it does with its look. Perhaps it has been decided that department X needs to have younger, trend-setting merchandise. In such a situation all fashion merchandise selected for this area would relate to that specific customer type who preferred what was new, unique, young. It would be hoped that the customer looking for this type of fashion would eventually come to depend on this department for that special look not found in other areas of the store.

New Resources

The purpose of reconstructing departments, of course, is to better serve the customer, a fact we cannot repeat too often. If certain price lines are pulled from a department or a new look is the aim, as just stated, then new resources (manufacturers or designers previously not used) might be needed.

Uncovering new resources is an assignment that very often is delegated to the fashion director. This might require special market trips, or would be accomplished in conjunction with other assignments while in the market. A new resource choice might be a line not carried by the store at the time, one that is coming up important and ripe for picking or one that up to now had no place in the store.

Guidelines for Resource Shopping

Recommending a new resource to management requires a careful basis for selection. Always keep in mind that recommendations for any investment are a way of asking the company to put its money on the line. How strongly do you believe in it? And on what do you base your belief?

1. Who is recommending this resource? Your buying office? Other retailers? The press?
2. What is its track record? How has it performed for retailers who carry it?
3. How are their deliveries?
4. In which department does it belong?
5. Are there already existing lines in that department that are similar?
6. Is it compatible with existing lines?
7. Does it fit the kind of customer who shops that department?
8. Is the quality level and price level in keeping with the department's objectives?
9. Does it fill the void of that department?
10. Is it a line with good growth potential?

Your management might ask any of these questions. Affirmative answers to all questions would be a good basis for a strong recommendation.

If there are several departments for which new resources are being sought in the plan to upgrade, then it cannot be done overnight. In some cases, upgrading would begin as a sampling or testing of a line to judge its acceptability—the store cannot throw out the inventory now in stock or just coming in. It must be done with advance planning and the changeover made systematically.

Underdeveloped Departments

In situations where departments are not getting their share of market, resulting from underdeveloped stock assortments, the expanded use of strong, existing resources that are performing well, plus new resources to fill voids, will change such departments from plodders to producers.

Growth may not always mean enlarging existing departments in a particular branch but it may involve opening a similar department in a branch where it does not exist. In such cases it would usually require the expanded use of existing resources, or—at best—the modest testing of new ones.

Testing

Whether it is a new trend or a new resource, testing or sampling is an excellent way to get a reading on which way to go, or how far to go with a new concept or line. If one is trying to get a reaction to a new look, for example, sampling a new group from an already existing resource would be a possibility. But if one is interested in testing the performance of a completely new resource, then even a capsule collection from that resource would be the way to go.

Tests are best made in "A" stores, or in a store where the specific customer type shops. Usually, one or two stores are sufficient to get some kind of reaction. Money spent on merchandise for testing must come out of the limited open-to-buy dollars of a particular buyer, unless the fashion director has been allocated separate dollars for testing.

Updating Classifications

In addition to upgrading, a store may need a routine updating in merchandise classifications as well as decor. Is junior lingerie still buried within the women's intimate apparel department? Does the sophisticated junior customer (who is probably a young working woman) still have to wade through fashions for the teeny bopper? Are sportswear separates mixed in with coordinates? Every season will present different challenges for updating how the merchandise is housed, creating a need to question the adjacencies, examining a shrinking or expanding of a department's space. Nothing in fashion merchandising is static. The fashion director, as the eyes and ears as well as the arm of management, should be one of the first to alert superiors to the needs for change.

Request Changes with Caution

Changing departments and reshuffling classifications is not easy. Under the best conditions, there is limited space, and a great deal of advanced planning is needed. The plan should include making sure that the move is important to the overall fashion image and leadership of the store and that it better serves the customer. Also, some new fashion concepts indicating drastic changes come and go faster than one can write them down, so one needs to take a hard look at the situation—will it be an ongoing concept or a flash in the pan? While being cautious, a store must also be careful of moving too slowly; can the change be made quickly enough to be effective? A certain amount of courage is involved in being a leader instead of a follower.

The Ongoing Classification

A good example of the ongoing classification—versus the one that might be only seasonal or is good one day and gone the next—involves fashions for petite-sized women. Only a few years ago (approximately 1976), petite-size women lived a very frustrated life when it came to finding dresses and sportswear in their sizes. Few manufacturers cut pieces small enough. These customers were forced to buy clothes and have them cut down to size. It was an unsatisfactory situation at best.

This customer segment began to protest. Small in size but large in numbers, they were vocal enough for the retailer to take them very seriously. The retailer shared this feedback with the manufacturer, who, after careful research, recognized a golden market opportunity that was untapped.

When manufacturers began cutting for this petite customer, they learned that it was not enough to take existing style numbers from their regular line and simply produce them shorter; it was necessary to change the whole proportion of a garment to make it a true petite. The manufacturers, therefore, opened separate divisions to service this customer. When merchandise selection became available in sufficient quantity (that is, enough substantial petite resources), the retailer brought in the petite-size fashions with conviction, opening up separate departments, even assigning the departments to separate buyers.

Petites filled a realistic need. It became big business and the stores that were first to accommodate that customer reinforced their leadership positions.

In many stores it was the fashion director who first became aware of the need, discovered the reaction in the market, and urged management to get into the petite business. The director researched the market, discovered the best performing resources, and made comprehensive presentations to management on the potential of the petite fashion business.

LIFESTYLE MERCHANDISING

The fashion director, who makes it her business to scrutinize the lifestyles of her community, and, therefore, her company's customer, can sense a need for merchandising to lifestyle quicker than anyone in the organization.

A major example, of course, was the working woman. It was no secret that she existed, but in the late seventies the retailer was examining new surveys that revealed conclusively that this customer segment was growing, not only in numbers but in reaching up toward better merchandise.

A few stores opened shops to service this special customer. Most notable was Filene's of Boston. Under the supervision of Filene's fashion merchandising director, a 1,200-square-foot shop was opened in their flagship store, housing updated sportswear and dresses for the working woman and named "Corporate Image." Recognizing that the working woman needed guidance and service, Filene's included tasteful, conservative merchandise that would appeal to all segments of working women, who preferred to look at themselves as having a career rather than just a job. They further paid her the compliment of running ads in *Time* Magazine in addition to local newspaper and television advertising, indicating that business women had as much awareness as business men.

Sanger-Harris in Dallas not only opened a shop but offered a shopping service, as did Filene's. Special personnel gathered merchandise for customers who called in their needs. When they came in they could more quickly make their selections. The store helped these busy women by keeping a record of the customer's sizes, preferences, existing wardrobes, and apparel needs. Brandeis in Omaha had for years offered the working women in their area a "Career Night" at the beginning of each season, demonstrating the various choices available for her wardrobe, how to blend the new with what she already had and how to put it all together with accessories to get more mileage out of her fashion dollar. The program was later expanded to a "Career Week", with workshops on wardrobe planning, hair and makeup techniques, financial guidance, and so on. As fashion director, I inaugurated the program, and was responsible for the entire effort.

Wherever such special shop treatments were opened in major stores, the fashion director was actively involved. When it was established in 1981 that working women accounted for $128 billion in earnings and that these working women spent close to $12 billion just for working

In an effort to service a specific customer block, the working woman, Filene's of Boston, created the Corporate Image shop. Invitation and fashion show held in the shop area. The entire project of merchandise selection and coordination, plus shop management was placed under the supervision of the fashion director. *(Courtesy of Filene's)*

apparel, there was little doubt that lifestyle merchandising was in order.

Active Sportswear

Another area as practical as merchandising to the working woman is merchandising for that other side of the working person's life (men and women)—leisure. As mentioned briefly in Chapter 1, a great segment of the American lifestyle requires active sportswear. The fashion director would not only be sure that his or her company had a special department to service this large customer segment, but had it all year around, not just as a summer project. The director might also keep the buyers aware of the fact that not just joggers and runners purchase such clothes. The comfort-loving American, who had no interest in running or jogging, was buying warmup suits to wear to the grocery store, relax on the patio in, or wear while shopping in suburban malls.

Invitation to "Career Night," a special fashion event for working women. *(Courtesy of Brandeis)*

The Total Picture

To avoid duplication and assure variety, the fashion director must keep in mind the total picture. New resources should supply a missing denominator, not duplication of an existing one. This does not mean, for example, that shirtdresses need be confined to one department. A variety of shirtdresses may exist in any number of departments ranging in price, daytime or nightime looks, misses or juniors. However, too many departments burdened with so many shirtdresses that are too similar, creating a great lack of other important looks, defeats the secret of balance.

LONG-RANGE OBJECTIVES

To assist a fashion director in effectively executing duties on a day-to-day basis, knowledge of the store's long-range plans is a definite plus. To keep abreast of changing times, all outstanding fashion merchants keep their place in the leadership position by constructive, carefully researched information about what to expect tomorrow. Tomorrow not only means next week or next month, but next season, next year, five years from now, ten years from now. No one reads more, keeps a more vigilant watch, or holds an ear closer to fashion sources than the retailer. Experience has taught the retailer that all things are relative and whatever is happening on the changing scene today will have an effect, one way or another, on what happens in a store tomorrow.

Several possibilities may be on the list of long-range plans.

1. REMODELING
    Renovating or updating existing plants.
    Adding or changing shops or boutiques.
2. EXPANSION
    More branches of the existing type store.
    Addition of free-standing specialty stores.
    Additions of twigs or capsules.
    Addition of a discount operation.

Everyone on an executive level is concerned with the long-range plans of a store, but to discover exactly how these plans affect a fashion director is the purpose here. We need to indicate to what extent the director is involved, and in which way he or she makes a contribution.

STORE PLANNING— REMODELING

When a store is upgrading merchandise, it is very likely to take a hard look at its physical plant as well and decide to give it a good face lift. It is difficult to house new fashion in a yesteryear atmosphere.

If the remodeling is to be major it most likely will be put on a long-range program, possibly over a year or two. If the plan includes the fashion departments, management is wise to consult with its fashion director along with all the other people involved. Having lived with some of the inadequate facilities and antiquated floor plans, the director (along with the buyers and merchandising managers) should have some strong feelings about what must be done.

Let us assume that the young fashion customer is not being accurately handled in the existing department. The buyer, area manager or department manager, and the fashion sellers are in agreement. The department, they say, is too obscure, badly lighted, lacking in good dressing room facilities, and unattractive and inappropriate in decor with inefficent fixtures for hanging merchandise. The fashion director, while completely aware of all these ills, enlarges on the whole problem from a fashion vantage point.

As soon as a young customer comes up on the escalator, the view should clearly reveal the tempo of merchandise sold here. If it is the

Two features create greater shopping pleasure for the customer in Bullock's of Northern California.
(1) Open floor space and racks merchandised to make ready-to-wear visible and accessible.
(2) Merchandise benefits from natural lighting on sunny days (augumented by artifical lighting system) under a tent-like fabric roof.
(Courtesy of Stores Magazine)

young customer who is to be lured, the decor should be alive with a contemporary feeling of what is happening in the young world at the time.

The fashion director is aware of a color story that would serve as a good backdrop for the merchandise housed there; she is aware of a new art form that is currently exciting young people. She can suggest these approaches and more. Spotlights on mannequins and other departmental displays, plus proper lighting of the merchandise throughout the department, would provide an immediate improvement. But what is of greater concern to the fashion director is the lack of fashion statements, not due so much to the merchandise itself, but the way it is merchandised on the racks. Addressing that, too, could bring about an immediate improvement. But to do it all most effectively would mean a change of fixtures, a better utilization of wall space, a redirection of aisles, a remodeled treatment that would be colorful and dramatic so that it would pull the customer's eye all the way into the department, creating a desire to come in and look and touch.

The Store/The Theatre

Very often, the extent of remodeling that is necessary to feature merchandise that otherwise would go unnoticed can be very minimal. The important thing is that someone notices that it needs to be done, and the fashion director, always on the watch that fashion merchandise is provided with the atmosphere it deserves, can alert management that sales would improve if the stage had a better setting. The store has always been regarded as "theatre." That is why so many people regard shopping trips as entertainment. A new season in fashion always means a new act, a new set, a new merchandise performance. The fashion director, with a sense of drama, can direct and choreograph the show.

STORE PLANNING—THE EXPANSION PROGRAM

Retail store expansion plans are demonstrated in several ways.

- Expansion and remodeling of existing units for the purpose of updating.
- Revitalization of downtown areas, either within existing plants or replacing them with more modern facilities.
- Regional expansion into new markets with either full-line stores or specialty store units.
- National expansion to take advantage of a national reputation (e.g., Lord & Taylor, Saks Fifth Avenue, Neiman-Marcus).
- Diversification of a major department store operation to include specialty stores or discount store divisions.

Whatever different form companies' expansion plans take, they are likely to all share the same purpose:

- To provide the best growth opportunity.
- To protect their share of the market.

Since store planning is not only concerned with remodeling but also with building, here will be the opportunity to create shop concepts or include departments that were not possible in the old store.

Now the fashion director may be consulted again. Management may wish to know the director's view on the best way to handle certain fashion areas, based on the newest fashion direction. What may have seemed a good idea a couple of season ago has not developed as expected and can be eliminated. On the other hand, what may have seemed unimportant a couple of years ago when the original plans were drawn up, is now showing up as very important.

Example

When such an emphasis was placed on conservative, tailored dressing for the office, the advent of soft dressing for social occasions became highly desirable. There was an obvious desire for a change of pace, for day and for night. Softer, relaxed lines and gentle fabrics better suited the working woman's mood after five o'clock. What's more, she had come to understand the idea of separates dressing—separate jackets, skirts, pants, blouses, shirts, sweaters—that could be mixed with pieces throughout her work or daytime wardrobe. When the opportunity for separates dressing became available for evening wear—evening separates—she understood it and was ready for it. A dressy separates department, therefore, set apart from the regular dress department seemed definitely in order.

When a fashion director brought such an idea before her management, she not only substantiated the merit of the segmentation, but suggested some new resources, which, up to now, did not have the proper area in which to hang.

The point is that the fashion director makes recommendations on well-substantiated evidence of a need. A director never recommends big changes because they seem like a fun idea. Large or small, all changes in store planning stem from the same direction, or at least should: customer need, customer interest.

When to Live Dangerously

This phrase does not mean that a fashion person need be a mouse. Far from it. She can be a tiger. She can wander in up to her neck if she dares but only if she knows there is no quicksand. Sure ground, as far as one can determine, no matter what the apparent dangers of sinking, will usually deliver her and her idea safe and sound. The director must, at times, live dangerously and take a risk, but only if it is a calculated risk. Otherwise, she would be thwarted in recommending things she believed in. Even if she is the only one who can see it, and she had checked all her information and all answers come up "go," then it is her responsibilty to fight for innovation, whatever it is—a new resource, a new classification, a new shop concept. New ideas are almost always met with reservations, but without them fashion merchandising could not exist.

REACTION TO THE GIANT STORE

Little dry goods shops into massive, giant department stores grew . . . and grew . . . and grew. The department store grew so large, in fact, that a bewildered and exhausted public found itself dashing off to small stores for special attention and less confusion in making decisions. In the big stores' attempt to give great selections and more of everything, they forced customers to throw up their hands in despair.

Of course, the great selections of merchandise is one of the things shoppers love about department stores. They can find a tremendous range of sizes, colors, prices. But, with this, they have lost the intimate feeling of the old family store. After all, the department store tradition began when life was vastly simpler. The basic concept of the department store was to bring the customer everything under one roof. However, with the staggering growth of our society and even more staggering growth of our technology, marketing methods, expanded merchandise classifications, and constant, more rapid change, putting everything under one roof has become a tough order.

The Shop Concept

The successful development of the branch stores and shopping centers indicated beyond a shadow of a doubt that "specialty shops" (after all, that is what shopping centers are made of) had a great deal of appeal.

Retailers traveling in Europe found that the women there loved to shop in "boutiques." Paris, for example, was a delight with boutiques everywhere, beautifully done, with strong fashion appeal on a small, intimate scale. This fashion treatment was not new to Paris. The first fine fashion shops for accessories opened in Paris in the seventeenth century.

According to the dictionary, a boutique is a "stall" or small "specialty shop." With guidance of the "word," and the living example as illustrated in Europe, department stores began to put little stalls in the store, and soon the specialty shop was brought inside the department store—a store within a store. The old standbys (the maternity shop, the swim shop, ski shop, bath shop) have been undeniably successful and a great testimonial to the merit of the shop concept. However, even with all its great advantages, it is literally impossible and certainly not advisable to "shop" everything.

In planning new shops and boutiques, the fashion director's participation should be major. It is important for a director to know, however, exactly what makes a good shop, what it takes to make it work, how it is merchandised, and what its primary purpose is, before one can advise and guide in this connection.

**What Makes a
Boutique Work?**

Undoubtedly, there are several reasons why some boutiques take off like the wind and others never get off the ground. But basically there are less chances for failure if a checklist, similar to the following, is reviewed carefully by all involved before action is taken.

1. Does it fill a strong customer need?
2. Is it in keeping with the objectives of the fashion department to which it will be added?
3. Will the profit margin justify the space, cost of operation, cost of promotion?

These answers must come first, and the answers must be yes to all three, no matter how fascinated the fashion director may be with the new shop idea. Remember the precious selling space and costly square footage. It must pay off.

Even after the above points have been justified, there are still more factors to be considered. It is one thing to have a great idea, but it is another thing to have a good plan. Without it the chances of success are slim.

To throw a shop together, helter-skelter, just because a competitor has one or one has heard of one someone else has in New York or London is to court disaster. After all, if the new shop is not better than the competitor's not much is gained, and what may have worked in New York or London may not be feasible at all in Mobile or Denver.

But after all things are considered, the shop idea does rate the effort, then it should be included in the fashion plan, with certain provisions. A shop concept works if, and only if, it offers:

1. A clear-cut fashion message.
2. The right merchandise to back up the message.
3. The right accessories (in merchandise and decor) to punctuate the message.
4. The location, atmosphere, and decor blending in to make the message ring true.

In some stores such a shop might include merchandise that is ski-inspired, that is, with a ski look for people who like the concept but who have never been on a slope and never intend to. Such a shop might also be the home for rugged wear—fashion inspiration taken from the hiker, camper, hunter, and so on. The possibilities are created by what fashion is prevalant at the time, but whatever it is, when drawn into an inspired shop presentation, the customer can identify what he or she sees there with how to use it.

Shop for a Classification

It is not unusual for an entire classification to become receptive to a shop treatment. If there are many alternatives to pant dressing (a wide variety of silhouettes, body designs), a shop might be in order. Even a shop for a single fabric story is a possibility—silks or knits or denim.

Let's explore the possibilities with denim. Long, long ago, denim left the fields of farming in the country and became incorporated into city life, with new interpretations of design, weight, color and purpose; denim continued year after year to be an indestructible fabric, in more ways than one. In every area of the store—for men, women, juniors, and children—denim persisted. So, how could a retailer make a particular selection of denim fashion more desirable than a competitors'?

Segmenting this major business into a special department and then fortifying it with a shop look can intensify the fashion side of the classification. Let us assume that the junior shop will be called "The Denim Depot." An atmosphere of an old-time train station with railroad lanterns, mock ticket window, and a depot bench can telegraph a casual, fun, nostalgic reminder of the early use of denim. A mock-up of the rear of a train's caboose can be a delightful way to display mannequins in the new denim looks. Music piped in (new versions of old favorites such as "Orange Blossom Special" and "Chattanooga Choo Choo") would enhance and enliven the whole idea. If a "Denim Depot" is utilized in the children's department, a small table with an electric train would add motion to the theme.

Within the merchandise mix of basic and fashion denim (both are needed), including novelty skirts, pants, jackets and vests, there should be coordinating tops and accessories.

A more sophisticated treatment would be in order for the misses denim sportswear area. A "Singing the Blues" shop might be supported with titles and platters of new blues recordings on a back wall, with a denim-clad manequin or two at the front of the department holding a microphone.

Shop for a Name Designer

An ideal way to merchandise for the fashion customer is the special shop that houses a single designer's creations. A Saint Laurent Rive Gauche Shop for the fashionable woman, or a Giorgio Armani Shop for the designer-conscious man are examples. Such fine merchandise might be segmented into a separate "room" on the fashion floor, walled off enough to announce that this area is special.

The Trend Shop

A place where forthcoming trends can be tested ahead of the season's peak periods for that kind of merchandise is a technique used very successfully by most leading merchants. The trend merchandise is brought in in limited numbers and spotlighted in a small shop concept to establish a reaction (especially if it is a faddish or innovative idea) before a large investment is made. It is far better to take a markdown on a few hundred pieces than on thousands.

Trendy merchandise, featured in a shop where customers know they can find the last word on what is coming up new, can be an exciting way to track consumer reaction. While the merchandise would change, say, every month, the shop itself would continue year around.

In most retail stores the fashion director is highly if not totally responsible for such a project. The director would provide management with:

1. Trends to be shown.
2. Timing for each trend's showing.
3. Resources to be included, complete with style numbers of specific merchandise.
4. Investment dollars required.
5. Necessary theme, title, and decor needed to reinforce the trend.
6. Location (which store or stores, space within the store).

In many cases the director would be completely responsible for merchandising the shop and the director might even be awarded an individual budget so that the shop's content would not come out of the buyers' open-to-buy.

Everything that appears in a trend shop would very likely be sixty days ahead of peak periods in the parent department. That gives the merchandise division time to see if a trend is hot, lukewarm or to be in and out in a hurry or eliminated altogether. The economy in recent years has taught the retailer to research everything carefully and relate to customer preferences. Testing in a trend shop is a valuable tool toward this end, and the fashion director is strongly responsible for its execution.

The Twigs

The "twig" shop or "capsule" unit is a shop offering edited versions of the store's full stock of some accessory and/or fashion departments. They appear in shopping centers or in concentrated commercial areas away from the parent store, perhaps even in communities located elsewhere in the country.

Such shops are geared in a strong fashion direction to exemplify the fashion image or leadership of the parent operation. If a fashion director is involved with the buyer in helping decide on the selection and presentation of such fashion merchandise, the director will, of course, be guided by the purpose of the shop, the existing image of the store, and the clientele it will service.

The Free-Standing Specialty Shop

In the free-standing specialty shop, be it a furniture store or a women's ready-to-wear store, the fashion office might be called on to help "pull" suitable specialty items. Specialty shops excel in fashion treatment, so this would be place where the fashion specialist could advise and direct a fashion idea and execute responsibilities in exactly the same way as in the parent store. A fashion coordinator, from the fashion office, may be assigned this special responsibility along with other duties. If the specialty store is devoted to furniture and home furnishings, the home furnishings fashion coordinator would have the entire assignment.

SEASONAL OBJECTIVES

Many of the projected plans under "long-range" could be included under "seasonal," because it is by taking a step or two forward each season that some of the long-range plans are finally accomplished. Seasonal planning, therefore, should contribute to the long-range plan.

Work Ahead—Far, Far Ahead

One of the greatest contributions the fashion director can make to management is to plan far in advance of the coming season. Six months ahead, she will have started her research on what's coming, and five months ahead of the season, she will make her initial presentation to management with recommendations of her findings (see Chapter 6).

It is from these early evaluations that management is able to anticipate what steps of action are to be taken. If, for example, the coming fashion trend justifies a new shop concept, buyers' budgets can be set up for it, the display director or store architect can be enlisted to design for it, carpenters can be scheduled to build it, and new arrangements can be made for the merchandise coming out of that area to make room for the shop. It all works together, and all because the fashion director assures management that this is the way to go.

IMMEDIATE OBJECTIVES

Everything that deals with in-season or current season fashion projection comes under this heading. The merchandise is in, the windows and interiors are decorated as planned, the ads are scheduled, the radio and television time is bought, and the sales personnel has been trained to interpret the fashion trends to the customer. All is in readiness. Everything that was planned for months ago has arrived. It is now the fashion director's job to see that all those well-laid plans do not run amuck. The director and staff coordinate all aspects of the fashion projection to the customer with continuity and dramatization.

AFTERVIEW

Perhaps the most desirable working relationship between fashion director and management is not only the fashion director's thorough understanding of the company's needs, but management's knowledge of how to utilize the services of a fashion director. When management knows how to lean on that fashion arm of the merchandising team, truly relates to the director as its fashion conscience, the rewards are extensive. There is so much management needs to have pulled together and the fashion director is the ready asset to do the job.

In understanding how to work with management, in relating to the philosophy and objectives of the store, the fashion director finds the clue to what makes his or her presence on the team important.

The fashion director is not concerned with pleasing just one boss, because in theory the director supports the entire merchandising team. A director serves every level, every area, and if she does it well she is never like the waitress in a restaurant who says, "Sorry, but this is not my station." All executives in merchandising, all fashion departments, all divisions, are indeed the fashion director's station.

So, whether the director reports to the president of the store, the GMM, the sales promotion director, or any other, his or her effectiveness will be felt by all who serve on the merchandising side. The director may not always be sure who is boss, but management will never have any question about who is the fashion director.

CHAPTER RE-EXAMINATION

Questions

1. Why is it important for a fashion director to be aware of customer types?

2. What is the value of a checklist of management objectives?
3. What are the general responsibilities of the general merchandise manager?
4. To whom do fashion buyers report?
5. What is the advantage of having the fashion director report to the GMM instead of to the sales promotion director?
6. What is the purpose of looking for new resources?
7. How does a store test a new fashion idea?
8. What is the difference between updating and upgrading?
9. What is meant by lifestyle merchandising?
10. How has the fashion retailer helped customers shop with greater ease in a giant store?

Workshop

Design a trend shop. Select a current fashion trend or utilize an imaginary one. Describe how you would house this trend in a shop, describe the merchandise, the look of the shop, give it a name, and identify the type of customer who would shop there.

The fashion office reviews color, fabric, and trend information with fashion merchandisers prior to trips into the market. *(Ken Karp)*

6

INFLUENCE OF THE FASHION OFFICE

Fashion directors are messengers. They bring back to their stores the fashion message gleaned from their research. The director and staff refine, document, and interpret the message for the store. Once approved (and purchased), this team translates and dramatizes the message to be carried to the customer. Thus, the influence of the fashion office is a buying and a selling one.

BUYING INFLUENCE

When merchandisers and buyers go into the wholesale market to make their selections for the coming season, they are greatly aided in making an astronomical task less so, and certainly more efficient, if they are fortified with advance information.

When one considers the tremendous numbers of resources available for every departmental classification and the multiple choices at each resource from which to select a bushel-full of fashion trends, it staggers the imagination to know how it can all be covered, how decisions can be made on what to buy and what to pass up. As if this were not enough, the buyer has limited time in which to make selections, and limited money to cover those selections. A strong buyer, capable of evaluating recommendations made on fashion trends, will be delighted and eager to take the fashion director's predictive information right along as an authoritative guide on which way to go.

Every buyer in a specific division, may accept the fashion plan with enthusiasm—every buyer, perhaps, except one who defies the whole thing and proclaims that it is not for her department, not for her customer. She may be right, or, perhaps, only partially right. In any case, the final decision on which way to go rests with the buyer, unless he or she is so far out of line that intervention by the merchandise manager is in order.

When the merchandising staff, including the merchandiser, the buyer, and sometimes the assistant buyer, has a definite direction of what the store believes in as far as (1) trend-setting fashion and (2) dominant-sell fashion, they are in a better position to come home with the right kind of merchandise to back up the fashion plan.

What to Buy?

The fashion plan or what to buy depends on the philosophy and goals of the store. Let us assume we are dealing with a store that regards itself as a fashion leader and, at the same time, is dedicated to the principle of doing volume business. Contradiction? Not necessarily. Can the two be mixed? Certainly.

Fashion Leadership

The purpose of fashion leadership is to give the consumer a consistent flow of fashion merchandise that represents the newest, most important fashion trends appearing on the fashion scene—and to have them first. Such fashion merchandise with consumer acceptance (and it can only be fashion if it does have consumer acceptance) merchandised with clear statements, accessible presentations, housed in a fashion-right ambiance, presented early enough to testify to the store's ability to be a leader instead of a follower, establishes that merchant's fashion authority. Such fashion authority begets confidence and confidence begets sales. Sales, in large numbers, equals volume.

The Magic of Newness

If customers say too often, "They never have anything new in that store . . . just the same old things . . ." even the "same old things" won't sell as well. Customers will, strange as it may seem, prefer to buy the same old things from the store with fashion leadership if the prices are reasonable rather than patronize a store with no leadership at all. It may be because they feel safer with a fashion authority. In fact, customers even prefer, it seems, to buy markdowns and follow the sales at leadership stores. The bargains are sweeter.

Leadership/Image

Every store has an image, of course, whether it is favorable or unfavorable. The customer who is impressed with a store's prestigious image might wish to be identified with that store. Another customer, aware of a store's ability to always have the best selections on the latest and most desirable fashion merchandise, and to be first in the community to provide that fashion, has found a store with fashion leadership. It may not necessarily be high fashion (preferred by a small segment of fashion consumer), but current fashion priced within the reach of the larger segment of customer.

In the early days of merchandising fashion, image evolved accidentally or deliberately by perceptive merchants, especially during the thirties, forties, and fifties, when catering to the customer who regarded clothes as social security. Images were born through snob appeal, status ratings, or just plain sensationalism.

A store's prestigious image is very often recognized or saluted during gift-giving occasions such as Christmas. One is often impressed by the name of the store on the package when giving or receiving a gift. "A gift from Tiffany's! How grand!" A compliment both to the giver and receiver. Christmas catalogues with impressive gift suggestions have made some stores famous, bringing them into the news year after year. For the person who has everything—what about a solid-gold bathtub? Or perhaps his-and-hers airplanes? Neiman-Marcus of Dallas was repeatedly in the news for just such fabulous gift ideas.

The high-fashion image of a store, however, may project so strongly that many customers are afraid to walk in for fear they may be slapped with a cover charge. In the times when status-seeking customers make their selections on the basis of store and label, the combination is perfect. The arrival of the seventies, however, brought a strong indication toward "anti-status" and many an astute merchant recognized the fact that customers buy merchandise, not image. That is, many customers will not buy from a store because of its image alone, but because the merchandise is right.

Therefore, if the store's image shouts "expensive" or "exclusive," its fashion direction naturally follows that line. If a store is regarded as a young store, a conservative store, or whatever, they are invariably obligated to back up that image if it is to be maintained. However, many leading merchants on today's scene have recognized "you can go broke trying to live off of an image."

It is all a matter of timing. When times change, the fashion story (always the mirror) changes with the times. For example, there was a time when mink was very high on the list of status symbols. At first mink was only for the rich. However, imitating the rich has long been a practice of the general populace, and the bigger and stronger our middle-class population became, mink began wrapping multitudes of women. A working girl might walk up four flights to a little two-by-four apartment to save money to pay for her mink, her status symbol. However, when the mink stole became a uniform, showing up on everyone, everywhere, and when the maid was wearing mink on her day off, it was time for the lady of the house to turn to something else.

At the outset of the seventies, flaunting status symbols, such as haute couture designer labels, not only were resisted but were considered downright vulgar. There were too many issues of grave importance on the scene. At the end of the seventies, seriousness about dress had reached a new high. "Investment" was the new buzz word. Investment dressing was the new trend. Dressing for success had become a full-scale preoccupation for both men and women, but most assuredly for women who were now determined to climb the executive ladder and look the part. They had learned that in order to be taken seriously they needed to have their image compatible with their goals.

There was another aspect to the image story regarding dressing for success. In the past, when women worked, it was usually out of necessity and seldom an element of self-expression. "Have to" work as against "want to" carried no status. However, when the world had seen the Gloria Vanderbilts, Charlotte Fords, Diane Von Furstenburgs and Jackie Onassis' go to work, a career became far more chic for women than it had ever been in our nation's history. Furthermore, we saw women in broadcasting move with distinction from modest roles as weather girls to major roles as anchorpersons. With horizons seemingly unlimited, accomplishment became the answer to fulfillment for legions of women.

The eighties, therefore, quickly became identified as a time for status seeking. As mentioned in Chapter 1, it was not however a time for the seeking of social status but instead career status. High achievers surfaced in all fields of endeavor and the race for accomplishment was on. In addition to reaching for more and better educations these individuals studied the importance of proper dress and the vital task of personal packaging escalated.

Fashion. Proper choices. Quality. Wardrobe planning. All these gave the business of wearing apparel new clout. It also gave the industry new responsibility. Thus, the consumer's concern with personal image reverted back to the retailer. Clothes were important again. Customers were looking to the knowledgeable retailer for support in this effort—with good selections, professional direction and advice, with quality and workmanship that would be a compliment to their lofty endeavors. Winners, or potential winners, wanted to do business with winners. Therefore, retailers with fashion leadership were in a winning position to service this new gigantic block of customer.

Whatever is socially acceptable during a given time affects the peaks and valleys of so-called image stores. For example, in a period when young-looking fashion is preferred, a store with a very conservative, stodgy image would fall from favor. But stores with fashion leadership (always keeping current), and not necessarily strictly image notable, usually are in a position to better serve a changing society. For the eighties, even the major fashion stores with grandiose images strongly incorporate fashion leadership merchandise along with high-fashion collections. One area fortifies the other. That is, the statusseekers enjoy buying fashion merchandise from a store known for high fashion, even though they are not high-fashion customers.

Thus, the fashion director must thoroughly understand the fashion aims of the store. If leadership is its goal, leadership must be uppermost in fashion plans. And, in cases where it applies, if the store has leadership potential and customers are urging for it, the fashion director should inspire management to accept the role of leader. Every market area is different, of course, but how well the customer is served ultimately becomes the store's image.

In today's highly competitive arena, a retailer cannot exist without image. The retailer who achieves a desirable image, whether as a top-rated discounter or a celebrated fashion authority, ultimately can also take the leadership position.

Know the Customer

As mentioned at the outset of this chapter, the choices in the fashion market are legion. Knowing what to buy comes from two decisions that influence the fashion director when laying out a fashion plan for the buyers.

1. Available fashion trends
2. The customer to be serviced

There may be a dozen available trends in a given season. The fashion director might edit them down to six, those that are suitable for the company's customer. One cannot, or should not, buy everything, but a strong store's stocks should reflect the top trends with choices within those trends that provide consumer acceptance. What is good in one part of the country may not be good in another. Climate, lifestyle, and economy affect all fashion decisions. A good example of this was the western trend that swept the country at the outset of the eighties. Eastern cities were fascinated with dressing up like cowboys and Indians. The traditional west, who lived with the western look on a day to day, year after year basis, was not impressed. It was not until the industry began interpreting the western look with new fashion expressions that the westerner reacted. The difference now enabled customers to buy a new variety of western looks in the traditional department store instead of just in western specialty stores. Until the trend took on that new dimension, most western-located stores passed up the western trend for something else.

Types of Merchandise

There is a certain rate of speed with which all customer types can accept new fashion ideas. Some resist change totally, some ease into it cautiously, and still others (the smallest group) hunger for it. These three customer types (and they exist in most communities but in different proportions) must be identified by each company. This is another aspect of knowing the customer. For example, the fashion director can quickly eliminate a certain trend from her recommendations if she feels strongly that "no one in our town would buy that."

To facilitate the proper covering of the market, resources and their merchandise are divided into three distinct groups.

1. Advanced
2. Updated
3. Traditional

Some stores may cater solely to one group or the other, but most traditional department stores would encompass a portion of all three.

Advanced Fashion

Some specialty shops might base their image largely on catering to the advanced customer with very forward-looking fashion merchandise. Their clientele would be that group who longs for change and dares to be different. These customers are very often the trendsetters. The advanced customer, while a very welcome one because she leads the way with new fashion ideas, is more difficult to service in the traditional department store because of her limited number and varied fashion tastes.

Nevertheless, the traditional department store, trying to be all things to all people, will attempt to accommodate this small group, but will do so in proportion. That is, they might use advanced merchandise (which may someday be regarded as updated when it has greater acceptability) to test a trend, but during that early testing period or while it is still very forward-looking, their stocks would reflect only about five percent.

Updated Fashion

In stores that stock everything from advanced fashion looks to conservative ones, updated fashion might be considered the middle of the road. In others, where the very forward-looking examples of a trend are not stocked, the updated looks would be the height of available fashion.

This customer type, for many stores, is the largest consumer group around. She may prefer fashion with an updated flavor, but she may occasionally opt for something that is advanced, and, then again, she may be the same customer who selects certain fashion looks that are traditional or conservative.

Updated merchandise is usually the treatment given that fashion that has the greatest acceptability of a proven trend. For example, a tailored jacket in a basic color and fabric, with a conservative notched collar and plain buttons, would be considered traditional. The same jacket with a less conservative fabric and color, perhaps with a more unique collar and button treatment, would be updated. The jacket that would be even more unique in fabric and color and with very bold, exaggerated lines in shoulder, collar, and trim would fall into the category of advanced.

Like the advanced merchandise that may someday be regarded as updated, the updated look may someday be regarded as traditional. Nothing remains static in fashion.

Traditional Fashion

Most retailers could not exist without a large portion of their fashion stocks dedicated to the traditional customer. Some stores obtain their image as a traditional store by catering in large part to the conservative customer. Such stores, however, as many will testify, can be boring if not mixed with a strong selection of updated fashion.

To eliminate confusion for the customer, many stores separate their traditional departments from all other fashion, providing that customer with her own special area. This occurs also with updated and advanced departments. A great deal depends on the individual store's approach to servicing the customer, or which customer block they are most interested in attracting. Unlike the updated customer, the traditional one will not shop in the advanced departments.

Traditional or conservative may not be as lacking in fashion as these identifying words may sound. There are periods, and the most recent was during the late seventies and early eighties, when traditional suits, sportswear separates, and shirtdresses were important fashion, even though they were what the traditional customer had always worn, because of the tremendous return to classic dressing. The advent of investment dressing, mentioned earlier, was responsible for this great acceptance and demand for traditional fashion looks.

So, once again, contradiction in fashion, always waiting around the corner with a new season, requires that all statements about fashion be accompanied with timing.

Basic Fashion

There is still another area that will be found in most department stores. This group, which has undoubtedly been around a lot longer and will be forever, is merchandise that is not always regarded as good taste—the "dumb coat," the "nothing dress," the sweater or blouse repeated in exactly the same way season after season, year after year because there is a customer out there who demands it. And, sometimes, it is good taste merchandise, but not necessarily fashion.

Veteran retailers have often referred to this type merchandise as "bread-and-butter" goods—a term borrowed long ago from the food business. In a food market, such staples as bread, butter, milk, and sugar are always available to the customer, no matter how many other food products—ready mixes, frozen items, gourmet selections—are added to the shelves. So it is with fashion merchandising. Regardless of how many fashion innovations appear, the good old basics that sell day after day, must be stocked. True, there is the usual amount of updating from time to time—a newer fabric, an updated color, a slight revision of line—but the look appeals only to the basic customer.

Even in this area there can appear some contradiction. For example, when jumpers are not fashion they are basic; when jumpers are in, they are fashion. Of course, the designers interpretation may be different (updated), but the principle is undisputable.

Balancing Fashion Merchandise

The balancing act in fashion merchandise is what makes some retailers great. It is easier for the store that takes a single direction—that is, decides to be known as a conservative store, a young store, an advanced store. These operations cater to a single customer type. But for the complex department store or chain, interested in attracting all customer types, the juggling of balls in the air takes skill.

In any sizeable operation, catering to a wide variety of customer types, with price lines running the gamut from high to low, all phases of merchandise must be represented. The fashion director's responsibility in helping accomplish the balance is often astronomical. The director knows that trend-setting merchandise must be present for fashion leadership. The director also knows that the competition will have the same type of merchandise eventually, but the store that has it first has the greater ingredient for leadership. Everyone follows the leader—the customer certainly and the competition inevitably. In both cases, it is the endorsement of success and the ultimate compliment.

Volume or Dominant-Sell Merchandise

Along with the fashion customer who wants to be first in her circle to show up in something new and different, there is the customer who wants fashion that is established and accepted generally. Such merchandise comes under the heading of volume or dominant-sell. Since this is the strength of most major retail outlets, it is the fashion director's responsibility to be constantly on the outlook for trends or items within trends that have the potential of developing into volume selling.

An example of this evolution was the status jean that appeared in the late seventies as a major fashion trend with one or two top designer resources. It grew to such proportions, with a constant flow of new resources and a widening of customer demand from women very young and slim to older women not so slim, that many stores gave this single item its own department. Until the trend softened it was a volume item. Those merchants that were into it early and right enjoyed volume business from this exploding classification. When it began to subside (as all trends do) something else had to be found to replace it. Consequently, the fashion director's search for volume items never ends.

Influencing the Buy

Since it is a major responsibility of the fashion director to be guardian of the store's fashion image and encourage its fashion leadership, it follows that the director must be sure that the store has the proper balance of fashion merchandise servicing the advanced, updated, and traditional customer. That is the fashion director's guideline when influencing what the fashion buyers bring into the stores.

Buying for Special Events

In some stores the fashion director does no buying at all. The director may only suggest and guide. In other operations, the fashion director may be given some "open to buy" money, to be used for "sampling" pieces for testing, for consideration of a new line, a new look, a new item.

In other situations, the fashion director buys, or requests the buyer to include in orders, special pieces necessary for fashion shows or special events. An entire show or a scene in a show, may depend on a specific fashion illustration. It would be necessary, therefore, to buy especially for that show. Fashion show pieces sometimes must be purchased for a specific model—size or type. This is more likely to occur when a guest model (important customer, club woman) is representing the store in a show instead of a professional model. It is imperative in such a situation to buy what the nonprofessional can carry off, what her particular figure problems, personality, or age will permit.

Sometimes, "show pieces," not as readily salable and therefore not usually carried in stock, are necessary to add excitement and emphasis to a fashion production. Also, for an important show or promotion, part of the impact is to present pieces previously unseen in the department.

Windows also come under the heading of special purchases by the fashion director. When a theme or promotion is big and important, it is often more efficient to have the fashion director actually pick and pass judgment on those things necessary to carry out a fashion idea for the store's windows.

When the unique or bizarre are part of the fashion impact, these special fashion pieces are excellent as illustrations or attention-getters. The buyers, however, cannot always sacrifice precious dollars from their "open to buy" allotment to contribute to show pieces. Thus, the fashion director's show budget is established, so he or she may do the buying.

THE PREDICTIVE PRESENTATION

After the fashion director's research has been accumulated, refined, and evaluated, it is time to share findings with top management and all executives of the merchandising staff. As the company's chief communicator of fashion information, the fashion director exerts initial influence on buying through the predictive presentation, submitted before the merchandising staff goes to market to shop and place orders.

The purpose of the predictive fashion presentation is just what its title implies—predict what the buyers will find when they shop for goods. Of course, it is not a crystal ball kind of predicting; only facts, as solid as the fashion director's research provided, are presented in a well-organized outline form. It is through this presentation that all findings for the coming season, from all areas of the market, are brought together and offered as guidance before the market opens for business.

It's All Confidential

No one will lock the doors, but those attending a predictive fashion presentation are usually requested to keep all information shared with them strictly confidential. It is at this meeting that the trends the company believes in will be revealed and, at this point, one does not share the store's plans with any personnel other than those immediately affected and responsible. Thus, this meeting is devoted to those in decision-making positions only.

Who Calls the Meeting

The fashion director sets the date for this presentation, checking with the store calendar and travel plans of those expected to attend. The director stategically selects a time just before most market trips are planned to start buying the very merchandise she will be discussing. Since the meeting is seldom repeated, it is important that everyone involved be present. Those invited (this should be done in writing with an r.s.v.p. requested) must be advised far enough in advance to firm up the date and to insure the best possible attendance.

Advance Preparation

In addition to the research done by the fashion director, there is much preparation before the future fashion story is ready to be revealed. First, the fashion director tabulates all findings and censors and evaluates all available fashion possibilities (see Chapter 2) before she is ready to interpret and translate all the facts into a workable plan.

Because there is so much territory to cover, and limited time in which to relate the entire story, the utmost of discipline should be exerted to reduce the whole thing down to a succinct, comprehensive presentation. An economy of words and an extravagance of illustration is a desirable balance. It should be understood that there are places where there is no substitute for oral explanation, but where visual illustration can assist oral explanation, it should be included.

Provide a Passout

When so much important material is being disseminated and so much must be absorbed, a brochure or booklet, written by the fashion director, and, if possible, illustrated by a member of the fashion office or an artist from the advertising department, or even with pictures clipped from fashion periodicals, serves as a most valuable aid in many ways.

1. As a text to follow, and perhaps, as an outline for taking notes during the presentation.
2. As a way to review highlights of the presentation before going to market.
3. As a reminder or reference book to take along into the market.

How to Make a Predictive Presentation

It is preferable that the booklet or brochure be organized in the same way the presentation is made. That is, each page can relate to the facts and points presented if it is compiled in the order of presentation.

At the very outset of the presentation, the fashion director should give a brief and revealing summary of what the coming season has to offer. Setting the tone and mood of what can be expected is most helpful to those following the details presented later. This tone-setting summary should be a blanket comment, all embracing and certainly inspiring. The inspiration should be educational as well as stimulating. It could sound something like this:

"The coming spring/summer season could very well be promoted under the overall banner of "Free and Easy." There will be a freedom of movement with separate pieces that can be put together in unexpected ways. Fabrics and colors and patterns will transcend boundaries that previously were unexplored. There will be a freedom of expression with soft, easy clothes. Relaxed silhouettes with clean lines will make this a welcome season for free spirits.

"It will be a season of stabilization after a season of experimentation. Those fashion ideas that tried their wings last season, flew too high for a while, then quickly fell, exhausted, overexposed and overdone, will not be around. The new spring fashion skies will be filled instead with floating lines that move gently and easily.

"There will be a great deal of stress on packable fabrics for people on the go. There will be great respect for fashion items that can live a double life. Double-duty clothes are important for busy people. Less clutter. Easy to transport. Easy to live with.

"Easy. That's the key. Free and easy. The kind of spring we have been waiting for. The kind of spring that should have great sales acceptance."

The mood is set. Everything that follows will enlarge on and illustrate that opening statement.

Although trends change from season to season and year to year, there are certain basics that must be covered in all predictive presentations, all of which help mold the format. The format should include:

1. PRESENTATION OF PREDICTED LEADING FABRICS

   How to Illustrate:
   (a) Use a series of colored slides showing closeups of fabrics, divided into groups according to separate fashion stories.
   (b) Use fabric swatches, mounted on a board, or on several fabric posters. Each board or poster can tell a different fabric story.

   Point out:
   (a) Which fabrics are new, which are in greater demand, which are important in which markets (couture, better, budget; women's, juniors).
   (b) Which fabrics will be directional (advanced).
   (c) Which fabrics will be for leadership (trends).
   (d) Which fabrics will be dominant-sell.
   (e) What the new fabric combinations will be.
   (f) Which fabrics will be best for fashion and which best for promotion.

2. PRESENTATION OF IMPORTANT NEW COLORS

   How to Illustrate:
   (a) Use color slides, alone or together with sketches or photographs of how they will be used in garment types.
   (b) Use color charts or color fabric swatches. Separate charts for each color family are best to show the degrees of color changes.

   Point out:
   (a) Which colors are directional (advanced).
   (b) Which colors are for leadership (trends).
   (c) Which colors are dominant-sell or volume.

   (d)   What new color combinations are in the offing.
   (e)   What color or color family is number one.
   (f)   Suggest a color or color family that would best suit the store's needs as a seasonal backdrop in display.

3.   PRESENTATION OF NEW TEXTURES AND PATTERNS

How to Illustrate:

   (a)   Slides.
   (b)   Samples of fabrics and leathers.

Point Out:

   (a)   The important features of the new textures (surface interest, nubby, smooth, etc.).
   (b)   The leading patterns (prints, dots, stripes, plaids).
   (c)   Edit the pattern story down by selecting one or two that might be major (if it should be floral prints, advise if they should be petite or large, delicate or bold, realistic or abstract, etc.).
   (d)   Which texture can be combined together, which patterns can be worn in combination.

If possible, color chips, fabric samples, or yarn clips should be attached to the booklet passed out to all attending the presentation. Such color, fabric, and pattern samples are especially important to buyers going out of the country to buy imports. This kind of direction is needed at least six months in advance of when the goods will be delivered.

Visual Aids

After the fabrics, colors, textures and patterns have been revealed and evaluated, it is time for a brief forecast of the trends that will continue strong, those falling away, and those that will be coming up new.

Sketches, color slides, or film of the new looks should be presented now to illustrate what will be seen in the showrooms when they go into the market. It is one thing to see the fabric and the color, now they need to see how it will be manipulated. Many fashion directors have found video tape a great help in presenting their forecast story. Once the slides have been accumulated for the presentation, they can be transformed to video tape, duplicated, and shown repeatedly at various branches if necessary.

Presentation of Trends

Every season the same categories of wearing apparel are available—coats, dresses, sportswear, and so on—but the manner in which they are expressed differently is influenced by a new trend idea. These changing interpretations of how a dress is to be cut in the body and what details are to be featured are the result of a trend that has infiltrated the fashion picture. Therefore, when new merchandise decisions have to be made for a coming season, it is important to know what the trends are, how many are available, and which trends an individual store believes in and can support.

In preparation for this presentation, the fashion director will have edited the available trends, presenting most or all to the company for education purposes, but recommending that they support what the director considers the most important five or six.

HOW TO ILLUSTRATE:
(a) Use sketches, slides, film or video tape.
(b) Show examples of all categories of wearing apparel under each trend.
(c) Present the trends in order of importance.
(d) Offer suggestions for timing; allocate a period on the seasonal calendar for promoting each trend.

POINT OUT:
(a) The features or details that identify the trend.
(b) Which colors and fabrics reinforce the trend.
(c) The trend's potential. (Is it something to get in and out of quickly? Does it have the promise of staying power—lasting for more than a season or two? Can it be developed into a volume seller?)
(d) New resources that support the trends.
(e) Resources already being carried whose new collections look good.
(f) The accessories needed to support the trends.

The recommendation of trends is the most important part of the presentation. All fashion plans and buying commitments will be made on the basis of this information. It cannot be repeated too often—fashion directors must do their homework. This involves careful research, intelligent interpretation and translation, with recommendations made on the basis of the individual company's needs.

Live Illustrations

There is nothing like a live illustration of a new fashion look—a costume worn by a live model. Everyone can then see how it falls, clings, floats, moves, whatever. They can also see the costume accessorized to get the total picture from head to toe. This is how their customer will look in the forthcoming season.

Whenever it is possible to get samples (at this early stage it is not always possible), it is obviously a great advantage. If a retailer is located near a fashion capital, such as New York or Los Angeles, then borrowing samples for a special showing is more likely. However, most stores far away from such sources would have a much more difficult time. Obtaining samples before merchandise is in stock is often arranged through a personal contact of the fashion director or other member of the merchandising staff, who might arrange with a manufacturer's sales representative to loan them to the store for one day.

If the actual merchandise is not available from a manufacturer, then filmed models, moving in the new fashion expressions, are equally helpful. These films may sometimes be begged or borrowed from fabric mills who have developed them for their own fashion presentations. Color slides are often available early from the fashion office of the store's resident buying office.

Recommending New Ideas

Along with the incoming trends, the fashion director should pass along any and all ideas that are significant to updating lines or departments.

If a new cosmetic line is appearing on the horizon and the director has obtained some significant facts and figures to prove its effectiveness, the cosmetic buyer might appreciate this information so that it can be investigated further when the buyer is in the market.

If a new jewelry designer, just beginning to get reaction to new creations, looks good, it behooves the fashion director to pass along the word to the jewelry buyer.

If the director has learned that a leading fashion designer is planning a new subdivision, with a completely new and different line to supplement his higher-priced couture fashions, perhaps with a younger and more moderately priced look, the buyer affected should be advised.

If a new shop idea fills a gap the fashion departments have been needing, the director should accumulate all the information (theme, resources, price lines, space needed) and present the idea for consideration in the plan of major additions for the new season.

Everything of importance, or seeming importance, available for the coming season, should be passed along to management and the merchandising staff for consideration.

Well, Almost Everything

A certain amount of censorship, of course, must take place. After all, there is just so much time, so much money, and so much space in the store. The fashion director must be aware of what could not possibly be utilized. These things, out of good judgment, should be eliminated from the presentation. However, there are exceptions in this connection. There might be something that could contribute to management's being well-informed about what is happening or help influence other decisions, even though it is not suitable for the store itself.

Promotional Recommendations

After relating the complete fashion story for the coming season and listing all facts as they relate to the whole picture, the director is ready to present recommendations for promotable trend-setting fashion stories. She has recommended proper timing for each of the trends (perhaps a time and action calendar will accompany her printed pass-out); now it is time to cover these additional points:

1. Which trends deserve the most support (dollars).
2. Which trends should be promoted store-wide (involving all fashion departments).
3. Which trends are promotable for a specific department (i.e., some are suitable only for juniors).
4. Which "items" are promotable. (Each season specific items show up that are promotable on their own. For example, there may be a trend of T-shirt dressing, but within that trend, one T-shirt may emerge that is so sought after it deserves to be promoted individually.)

The Fashion Plan

All the previous information presented by the fashion director in her predictive presentation is the fuel for the store's fashion plan for the coming season. In addition to the trends and how they will be promoted, new shop concepts, even new classifications may evolve. Management, evaluating all they have seen and heard, will decide the final direction. They will meet later with the fashion director and finalize the new season fashion plan.

The Total Picture

This predictive presentation may be the only time the entire merchandising staff and management will see and hear the entire fashion picture of the coming season.

Remember, the junior buyer goes only into the junior market. A jewelry buyer sees only the jewelry market. It is most revealing and most advantageous for all fashion buyers and merchandisers to get the prediction of all markets in order to see how one relates to the other and what the possibilities are for the total store. After all, the jewelry buyer will certainly have more confidence selecting jewelry for the neck if she knows about the new necklines. The shoe buyer will not be led down the garden path if he knows in what areas he must be covered in order to relate to the new skirt lengths and new lines.

Thus, the buying influence of the fashion director is one of guidance and fact finding. It is one of stimulating in management reaction and action for those important fashion facts. However, as they say in the trade, "we buy to sell," so the director's work has just begun.

THE FASHION DIRECTOR'S SELLING INFLUENCE

It is thrilling to find great fashion trends, believe in them, and buy them. It is even more thrilling to see all those efforts succeed; they succeed when they sell.

No fashion directors worth their salt will drop the ball at this point, not here, where it really counts. They will very likely sit close at the elbow of the general merchandise manager and sales-promotion director during planning meetings for the coming season. They will hope that they made their points clear enough and strong enough to encourage these individuals to include exciting advertising programs, display plans, and good exposure in the radio and television media for the fashion trends recommended. Directors will hope also that all trend-setting action will be scheduled early, in order to be first in the community with the important fashion news.

Telling the Fashion Story to the Customer

The fashion director's first step is to help guide the store in getting the right fashion merchandise into the departments. The next step is getting the fashion story to the customer.

Fashion-impact newspaper ads and fashion magazine ads will help; radio and television commercials, carrying waves of excitement, will contribute; inspired windows and interior decor, displays, and vignettes will help. Fashion shows and special events bringing the story to life can help tremendously in repeating the fashion story to the consumer. But the most important help of all comes at the point of sale. If the selling staff does not have the fashion story down pat, the whole network of effort could be wasted.

FASHION PRESENTATION FOR SELLERS

As carefully as the predictive presentation was researched, planned, and presented, so must the fashion presentation for sellers be coordinated.

Every fashion seller from every department and every branch should be scheduled to attend seasonal fashion training sessions. At the top of the season (when the new season's merchandise is arriving), the meetings should be scheduled to educate the selling staff on everything that is new, how to sell it and how to put it together.

How to Make a Seller's Presentation

The sellers have not been to the fashion market. They have seen none of the samples, heard none of the predictions. Perhaps a few rumors have filtered down to them, or perhaps they have picked up bits and pieces of fashion news, but it is very possible that the bits and pieces have not been properly interpreted. Also, there is no way for the seller to know, at this point, what the merchandise in the department will look like throughout the season or what the store's fashion point of view will be. It is up to the fashion director's presentation, therefore, to provide all the answers.

First, a short summary of the general "flavor" of the coming season, much like the one given in the predictive meeting to the executive, is in order. The director might explain:

"You have had bulky springs and bright springs, daring springs, but this year will be different. Spring will be a little 'soft' this year."

He or she should paint a picture, stir the imagination, light a fire, incite their interest. The director might continue to explain that the fabrics, colors, and lines will all go "soft." Whatever words the director chooses, whatever techniques she applies to describe the season they are about to sell, she must be sure she projects enthusiasm and belief in the fashion direction the store has taken.

Since this is not a decision-making body and the plan has already been formulated, many of the details offered at the predictive meeting should be omitted. In the interest of time, and to eliminate the risk of confusing the group, it is usually best to present only the top or leading features in each category. For example, the director would present:

1. Leading fabrics
2. Leading colors
3. New fabric combinations
4. New color combinations
5. New fashion trends
6. New accessory treatments

Illustrate Everything

Illustrations, many of the same kind used at the predictive presentation, are most important. At this date, however, when merchandise is already arriving, plenty of samples should be available from stock to model and coordinate.

When selecting merchandise for a sellers presentation, it is most wise to use samples from as many departments as possible. There is no finer way than to have many departments represented, so the sellers can see how their own particular fashion pieces look on a completely accessorized model.

Assume Nothing

Advise them about all promotions that will help influence their thinking. The promotions also encourage them toward inspired selling and help them know to what degree their efforts are backed up. Fill them in on any new shops affecting their area. Nothing is more demoralizing to personnel than to walk into their department one day and find it dismantled, with no warning about what is going on. Include them in your philosophy of what fashion should be today, how the things you show are to be worn, and where if it is not obvious.

Assume nothing. The story is not new to the fashion director; he or she has been living with it for weeks. But it is all new, surprising, confusing, and perhaps resisted at first by this audience seeing the season put together for the first time.

A selling job is part of the fashion director's efforts here. Before the fashion seller can *sell* the customer with conviction and understanding, the fashion department must do a bang-up selling job itself. Sometimes selling the sellers on a new idea is a gigantic challenge.

Something to Remember

Whenever possible, supply all the sellers with a brief résumé or booklet on the highlights of the presentation. It should be simply done, easy to understand, (all new trends clearly identified) and illustrated for easy reference.

Videotape

Many major retailers have developed video studios within their plants to serve as an educational and training tool. Not only are they capable of producing very professional fashion films, but now can make extensive use of films supplied by vendors on videotape. An extensive film library, therefore, can be maintained, all for the education of store personnel and the customer.

A major advantage of videotape is the opportunity to duplicate any effort and send copies to all branches where it can be viewed at the convenience of personnel, regardless of the staggered hours in most suburban stores. It can also be viewed over and over again if review is necessary. Since it is not always possible to get all fashion sellers together, and it is not always possible for the fashion director and her staff to personally reach all branches, videotape is a very efficient communications system.

Another great advantage is the instant replay. When a video film is in production, the fashion director, supervising on the set, can view a shot instantly to be sure the necessary fashion statement has been made.

Producing Video Films

If a special training film is to be made in the store's video studio, the fashion director is usually totally involved. A film illustrating the fashion trends the store believes in may become the responsibility of the fashion director—to write, coordinate, produce, and even direct it.

The first step, of course, would be to organize the trends to be illustrated. A written outline, noting the order each trend is to be filmed, should be shared in advance of shooting time with the photographer and studio manager. Settings have to be arranged, shooting time scheduled, and a reasonable amount of camera angles planned in advance. Then there are the fashions themselves to be assembled (some samples flown in for the shooting and quickly returned to the manufacturer), models booked, and the script put into work and on film.

Even with the use of film, many companies prefer the personal presence of a member of the fashion office to reinforce what the viewers are seeing.

Question-and-Answer Period

There are bound to be questions, even after the most comprehensive presentation. In fact, asking questions is a good sign. It indicates that the fashion director has stimulated the audience's interest to contribute, debate, challenge, or seek further information. Great ideas come out of such sessions, and involvement is a vital part of a good presentation.

Since the audience may not volunteer questions, it might be wise for the fashion director to mention at the outset that a question-and-answer period will follow. It is an ideal time to clear the air; the fashion director learns what points did not reach the audience clearly, those attending are able to express their feelings about the season and how they think their customers will react, and all present can hear what the other person is thinking.

PRESENTATION FOR ADVERTISING, DISPLAY, AND PUBLICITY DEPARTMENTS

These three specialized fashion people, the teams responsible for delivering the fashion message to the consumer, should be included in all presentations—the predictive, the sellers, and for emphasis on specifics that do not necessarily affect other associates (which calls for a special presentation). For example, a special session in the fashion director's office, exclusively for members of the display department, is often scheduled at the start of a season and repeated at regular intervals as needed, when new merchandise comes in or new promotions are ready for execution.

In a session for display people, examples of how the new looks should be draped, worn, and accessorized is most vital. The tone or theme of a promotion will influence the kind of mannequins used, props, decor, style of presentation. If any fashion directive needs clarification in this connection, this is the way to do it. The fashion director can review any fashion points regarding the windows, interiors, or shops. The exchange of ideas here may turn up something that had not been considered previously.

The Language Barrier

In addition to learning the season's new fashion story, the creative staff needs to be filled in on the new language. Along with every big fashion change and with every important fashion story, the terminology changes.

Some fashion words are standardized. That is, they exist permanently in the fashion vocabulary to describe a particular fashion concept or treatment. For example, a peplum is a flared, extended portion of a bodice that comes below the waistline. A blouson, although a French word for blouse, is a bloused treatment at or below the waist. Even so, a new season and a new interpretation of the peplum or blouson bring new meaning to the words, which, in another season may completely disappear from the fashion language, buried but not forgotten until another inspired designer revives them again.

Standardized fashion terms are universal and are used in one form or another throughout the industry and can be found in any good fashion dictionary or glossary. But one would be hard pressed to find new and constantly upcoming words, created specifically for an innovative fashion idea. For example, what's a baggy? It was a loosely fitted style of pant that had a very successful run a few seasons ago. When the trend disappeared, as trends do, the word, so important while it had its place in the sun, has gone the way of the trend. Into the archives. However, while the trend exists the right word is absolutely essential. When the trend disappears, it is replaced with not only a new look but a new word.

What's Wrong with this Picture?

There was a time in fashion ads and fashion magazine editorial pages when the models stood in a stilted manner with a hand on one hip. This was fine in the day when she had a parasol in one hand. The hand on the hip seemed to belong with the hourglass figure. It was the attitude of the time. However, figure lines and body movements change. Whether they change to accommodate a mode of dress, or dress changes to accommodate new attitudes toward the body, the fact is the look of the posed model, as against a natural or candid treatment, had to disappear as surely as the bustle.

Sketches or photographed illustrations must have the look, pose, and motion of the current trend. The fashion director, watching the fashion story from all angles, must be sure everyone knows what that newest trend is. For example, a new trend might require that the model pictured have a hair style that reinforces the intent of the garment. Or, if the model is shown with the length of skirt out of proportion to the new concept, an entire fashion statement might be misinterpreted. The fashion director can be of great service to help the advertising staff produce fashion correctness in their illustration and/or fashion photography.

**BEING A SELLING
INFLUENCE BY
EXAMPLE**

It is only natural that customers and business associates alike should look to the fashion director and members of the fashion office to serve as a fashion authority by what they do as well as by what they say. Usually when a new trend is evolving in fashion, the "fashion people"—coordinators, buyers, and models—are among the first to lead. If they do it well, their example is readily followed. They add emphasis, inspiration, and endorsement for those less courageous.

Taste, Above All

Often, fashion pioneering takes courage, but for a fashion person to wear what is new just for the sake of doing so, whether or not it is suitable to her own personality, figure, or lifestyle, is a number one sin. She should be a good example in the censorship of dress as well its endorsement. Everything is not for everybody. What is right for her adds favorable support to the trend; what is wrong for her creates a distaste for it. Many fashion people, overwhelmed by a sense of responsibility to join, defeat their purpose. In any given season, there are many great fashion stories to choose from, enough from which to pick only those one can tastefully support.

If the fashion director has a great high-fashion look, if she is dramatic enough, tall enough, and lean enough to get away with most difficult-to-wear trends, she is wise to capitalize on this fact. Adding impact to fashion in this manner, particularly through personal appearances for the store, can be very rewarding.

On the other hand, regardless of her size, it is important for the director not to be too slow to adopt a new length, a new color story, new pattern treatment, new look. She cannot afford to be asked "If this is such a great idea, why aren't you wearing it?" That old adage "Do as I say not as I do" is not very workable in the fashion director's life.

All fashion stores prefer their employees to show up in the latest trends as soon as possible. To encourage updating of work wardrobes, most retailers provide generous discounts on fashion merchandise. It is much easier to indicate to customers that this is a fashion look they must have if the people selling it are at least current fashion, even in a modest way. Overdressing, however, is a danger. One should not outshine the customer any more than a hostess should outshine her guests.

**INFLUENCE ON
THE YOUNG
CUSTOMER**

Along with the fashion office's buying and selling influence comes its influence on the young customer. The influence on the adult or mature customer is covered in every aspect of this chapter and throughout the entire text (whether it is through advertising, displays, shows, or special events), but a special area must be set aside for the young customer. This potential customer of today, and it is hoped in the years to come, is a completely different consumer, whose interests require special attention. Many stores depend entirely on the effectiveness of its fashion office to attract and influence the young consumer.

The Teen Customer

Perhaps the first awareness a young lady has of herself is in regard to her appearance. "I look fat. I look skinny. I look tall. I look pretty." She is concerned about what to do with her hair. She looks at makeup with mixed feelings, wondering how to use it, if to use it and what kind to get. She pours over *Seventeen,* identifying with the lovely young models throughout the issue, wondering how she would look in something like that. The next thing she knows, she is wandering through the junior department of a store, spots something she saw in the magazine and tries it on. Her fashion rapport has begun.

She is a little unsure of herself at first. However, there is usually one thing about which she is not in the least unsure—she would like to be a model. She has heard her friends at school talk about modeling schools and modeling classes. She has heard them talk about the fashion boards at the store. Everybody, it seems, "comes to the store" for almost everything.

This may be one of her earliest experiences as a young adult in associating with "the store." And it seems to follow, that if there is something that she wants, in the way of information, a course, a service, advice, news, or instruction, she will call the store. They will undoubtedly have it, know the answer, or know where to guide her to get the answer. The store may grow a little weary (foolish if it does) of being expected to be all things to all people, but it is this image that is indispensable, especially in gaining the homemaker or career woman of tomorrow, as well as the buying power of the youth of today.

Give the Young Customer What She Wants

Since the young consumer is enchanted with the idea of fashion modeling, and the retailer is enchanted with the idea of getting her into the fashions that are for sale, the offering of a modeling course serves a dual purpose. The young potential customer gets acquainted with the store's service and she is now coming into the store where she can discover at first hand what is the fashion department for her and what is being shown.

"How can I sign up for your modeling course?" she will ask.

"Right here," the secretary-receptionist of the fashion office sings. "Just have a seat and I'll call the youth coordinator" (see Chapter 4).

Most applications come by telephone or mail in answer to an ad about a new course.

The Educational Program for Youth

The youth coordinator (who may also be a fashion coordinator), responsible for all events pertaining to the youth market, is also an educator. In the case of special classes, she will usually follow a procedure something like this. She decides what kind of classes seem most in demand and draw the best attendance:

1. Modeling classes
2. Good grooming and beauty classes (makeup and hair)
3. Wardrobe planning
4. Exercise shape-up classes

Much depends on the trend of interest at the time. What was good last year could be losing ground this year and completely out of the picture for next year. There is very little loyalty, either in interest of activities or to the store, where most young people are concerned. It is imperative, therefore, that they be captured again and again.

It may be decided that a four or six-week course, including all of the above considerations, be offered in one or several branch locations, depending on the availability of space and the desirability of the location.

Scheduling of Classes

Timing, of course, is of the utmost importance in scheduling the classes under the youth program. There is greater interest in exercise classes, for example, before the bathing suit season, or at the beginning of a new fashion season where the new looks are more revealing. However, even modeling classes and instruction on wardrobe planning are more effective at the top of a season when interests are new. Therefore, classes should be scheduled at the onset of a season instead of in the middle of one.

In addition to scheduling the right classes at the right time, the rest of the fashion calendar must be consulted. Too many events must not be scheduled at the same time, both from a standpoint of personnel need and space availability. For example, a store may use the same people from the fashion office to do a number of things. One could not lecture a class and conduct a fashion show at the same time. As to space, a store may have only one auditorium or classroom, therefore, space must be reserved far enough in advance to avoid conflicts. Other departments in the store also have activities, meetings, classes, and so on, which require space.

When the schedule of classes is firmed up, copies of the intended program should be sent to everyone in the store who might be affected. Communication with the buyers of the young fashion departments is especially important; buyers and their salespeople are asked most often what is being offered. A calendar of events, posted in all the young departments, announcing "what's going on and what's coming up" of special interest to the young customer, will be most helpful.

Instructor for the Classes

The Youth Coordinator usually finds herself the teacher. Because of limited budgets, if the store is to provide such services, all aspects of the project must be executed by the person in charge.

The youth coordinator would get support, however, from other specialists in the store. For example, in the week when a class is devoted to makeup, a makeup expert from the cosmetic department or someone provided by a cosmetic vendor (another term for manufacturer or resource) would take over the instruction of that class. This also works with instruction on hair care and styling—someone from the store beauty salon would be ideal as an instructor for that portion of the course. Even though these specialists would take over a class without charge, they would be developing new customers for their own departments. Even the junior buyer might get into the act; discussing the fashion she has in her department would certainly help create interest in what she has to sell.

Very often, experts in a field come in from outside the store to instruct on a public relations basis. A physical fitness expert from a local gym or beauty spa might come in to direct a class on exercising or aerobic dancing for health and beauty.

Fees for Classes

While the store encourages activities such as a youth educational program for the purpose of public relations, most courses (especially those that run several weeks) carry a charge or at least a registration fee. The charge is usually nominal—much lower than would be charged at a modeling school, for example—perhaps just enough to offset the overhead.

The student, too, is benefited. Attendance is always much better and more faithful when an investment has been made, no matter how small. Also, there are supplies that often are included in the course, and the tuition usually covers all the required work tools. A charge also guarantees the limited number permitted in a class, making room for those who are really interested rather than those who might just drop in out of curiosity.

Fashion Boards

For many years, fashion boards on high school and college levels were very high on the list of importance in youth activities offered by retail stores. Applicants from all local schools were screened and an outstanding young woman was selected to represent her school on the store's fashion board. This fashion board system was used extensively by almost every large or small department store, specialty store, and chain operation in the country; they were at their height in the midfifties and sixties. *Seventeen* and other magazines geared to the youth market gave great emphasis to youth programs and helped refine and expand their purposes and activities.

To be selected for membership on the teen board of a store was an honor. After all, to represent one's school as the leading "fashion example" of a sharp, well-dressed young woman, was a mighty nice feather to wear in one's cap. Stores hoped that what one learned as a member of the fashion boards one would take back to one's classmates at school.

Even though the fashion boards were beginning to disappear in the seventies and it appeared there was little hope for them in the eighties, those stores that maintained such programs felt bound to them, either as a tradition or because they still found them valuable.

The College Board

With many retailers, the college board began as a fashion advisory body. A membership on the college board very often meant a summer job, working where all the new back-to-campus clothes were shown. Besides selling, the job included the role of advisor or guide for incoming freshman on their way to campuses everywhere about what to take, how much, and what was to be worn for what (campus, class, dorm, social, etc.). This worked in the fifties and early sixties before jeans became a campus uniform. When dress codes changed, the board advisor lost her job.

The Back-to-School Show

One of the activities of the school fashion boards that existed the longest (and, perhaps, is one of the strong reasons some still exist) is the back-to-school fashion show, usually held in early August.

For many girls it was their first modeling experience. Sometimes they were given special modeling instruction by the fashion office, which, in itself was a helpful experience. Some shows were small (on a runway in the junior department) catering to walk-in trade, some shows were major, highly advertised and extensively staged in the store's auditorium, an outside ballroom, or theater. Sometimes the board members were enlisted for informal modeling in the store's restaurant areas, photographed for the store's newspaper ads, and appeared on television. Besides being fun, it was a time of learning about fashion and the retail business as a possible career.

With high costs, the economy, reduced in-store staffs, and a greater need to focus on realistic merchandising problems, the back-to-school show, along with board activities, fell from the company's priority list. However, this trend, like fashion trends, has a tendency to fade or disappear, only to be revived again, sometimes bigger than ever.

The Pre-Teen Boards

Although not as many stores were involved in this area, many did give a try, for a time, to fashion boards for pre-teen girls. The girls learned about fashion appropriate for them, had field trips, slumber parties, contributed to civic needs (sang Christmas carols during the holiday season, delivered pumpkins to orphanages during Halloween, and gave food baskets to the poor at Thanksgiving). Their fashion shows were usually held in the pre-teen departments, usually before Easter and back-to-school fashion periods, and they were a joy to behold, especially for their parents and grandparents.

Some of the Pre-teen Board members eventually graduated to the store's high school fashion board, and the high school members sometimes continued their association long enough to join the College Board. The entire picture was a very worthy, wholesome kind of undertaking. Everybody wanted to be a part of it. Everybody seemed to have a good time. Everybody benefited.

The Changing Scene

No one will deny that the entire life-span of the teen fashion boards, from the middle forties through the sixties, had a remarkable record of excellence in public relations for the store, and were good training grounds for young people who excelled in interest and involvement. The record clearly shows that many a Teen Board member, getting her first taste of the retail business, decided this was the field for her. Some of the finest youth coordinators and fashion coordinators had their start in retailing in just this way—as a member of the store's fashion board.

In the late sixties, however, the scene was beginning to change and the seventies brought a new kind of young student into the picture. She was far more sophisticated. She literally preferred to go to summer school or tour Europe. There were more distractions, more demands on her time. There was evidence everywhere that she was more concerned with the real issues of the world and her environment. Her social conscience was showing. She not only knew what was going on in the world, but wanted to do something constructive about it.

The college student was becoming a deep concern to retailers—"antifashion." She thought less about what clothes to take to school with her than she did about what political group she would join and what social cause she would support. There was less shopping at home for the customary back-to-campus wardrobe. After all, rules about campus dress had long since fallen away. Pants-dressing for girls, once forbidden, met approval everywhere. Jeans and "grubbies," once deplored, were now applauded by both men and women students and accepted in the classroom. If she needed any clothes, she picked up things in shops where she was going to school. She felt she knew it all when it came to fashion, and what she didn't know, she made up. It was easy to do; fashion had become an original, individual thing.

Boards of the Seventies

An awareness of what changes have taken place directs what changes should be made internally in the store's program. This is a very big part of the youth coordinator's function, because it is she who is in a good position to keep a constant finger on the pulse of the young market. In the early seventies, the boards were made up of student body delegates or representatives who were no longer enchanted with doing a little fashion show, throwing a party, or holding a dance. This new group was happy to show up at board meetings at the store, if, and only if, they felt they were doing something important.

The New Programs

The early seventies brought ecology programs all over the country. The fashion boards were excited and delighted to meet and plan what to do about pollution. They went door-to-door, distributing educational literature on the pollution problem, collecting protest signatures, even appearing on the floor of their state legislature to speak out on behalf of the youth of the community about what the problem meant to future generations. Many of the letters written to soldiers in Vietnam and prisoners of war came from fashion boards of department stores. Many made a valiant effort to see that mail reached soldiers on a regular basis. They even raised money to send delegates to the Paris Peace Talks and carry their mail to the proper liaison officers abroad protesting the treatment of the prisoners of war. Many similar social programs (raising money for medical research, for the handicapped, for the underprivileged) became the work of fashion boards. They met to discuss sex, overpopulation, religion, poverty, and racism, none of which were treated with anything but the greatest concern.

Boards of the Eighties

In the late seventies and at the beginning of the eighties some department stores that had dropped such youth programs reinstated them. The campuses were cleaning up their fashion act. Students were dressing again. Personal image (maybe influenced by the status-seeking attitude existing around them in the more adult world) became relevant once more. Fashion stores kept their programs simple, relating everything to the business at hand—fashion.

Even if fashion *boards*, per se, are outmoded, fashion *programs* never will be, as long as the program fits the time and the need. Fitting the time and the need is what retailing is all about. Therefore, whatever it takes to keep abreast, to be in touch, to be of service must be done more immediately in this area—the youth area—than in any other. Here is where the temperature rises and falls most quickly in reaction to what is happening.

AFTERVIEW

Since presentations to management and store personnel are such a constant part of the fashion director's contribution, for which the director must write (succinctly and in terms that will not be misunderstood) directives, booklets, brochures, reports, or releases, it is advantageous to have an aptitude for writing. Perhaps some kind of writing course would be helpful.

Also, because the director must speak before astute and knowledgeable bodies, including management, associates, the consumer, plus the listening and viewing audience of the electronic media, and because the director is often called on to address special interest groups, clubs, and organizations of all kinds interested in her views and reviews on fashion, it is most desirable that her speaking voice be pleasant. If one has an inborn talent, wonderful, but for the person who needs training, some education in speaking techniques or voice cultivation is worth considering.

The qualities of speaking well and writing admirably are secondary, of course, to the qualities of taste, judgment, vision, and enthusiasm. With these, a director's influences on buying what is right for the fashion departments and helping to sell with effectiveness to the consumer are undeniably vital, and, when executed with skill, justifies the director's position as a power on the merchandising team.

CHAPTER RE-EXAMINATION

Questions

1. What is meant by fashion leadership?
2. What does "image" mean to a store?
3. What are three types of fashion merchandise and what does each mean?
4. How does a fashion director influence what buyers select?
5. What is a predictive fashion presentation?
6. How does the fashion director influence the store's fashion sellers?
7. Why is it important for the fashion director to provide the store with current fashion terminology?
8. How can a fashion director contribute to the store's fashion ads?
9. What is the purpose of youth programs in a store?
10. When are back-to-school shows held and what purpose do they serve?

Workshop

Draw up a predictive fashion presentation. Use past, current, or imaginary fashion trends. (The different aspects of the presentation might be divided among two or three people, i.e., one presents the trends, another colors and fabrics, etc., but the fashion story must relate throughout.)

Some of the leading American apparel marts (clockwise)—Los Angeles, San Francisco, New York, Dallas and Chicago.

7

COVERING THE MARKET

Every fashion decision the fashion director makes for the company is related to, affected by, and the result of how the director covers the market and what he or she finds there.

DEFINITION OF "THE MARKET"

In retailing, "the market" is anywhere manufacturers and designers (also referred to as resources, vendors, or cutters) offer their wares for sale at wholesale, to merchants to sell in their stores at retail.

For buyers the initial time to "shop the market" for a coming season is during the so-called "market week" or whenever the market opens. It is then that the designers and manufacturers show their proposed collections or lines from which buyers make their selections and place orders. It should be noted, however, that while the "market week" occurs during the opening of a season, there is basically no such thing as a restricted "market week" for most buyers who come to New York almost every month, even twice a month, because of constant new developments.

While the giant retailers may cover all the domestic markets from New York (the largest and most important) to California (Los Angeles and San Francisco), other merchants may cover only the regional markets and bypass the two coasts. For example, some retailers may shop the Dallas market or the Chicago market, or those in Miami or Atlanta because they are closer to their region. Even so, these regional markets provide their customers with showings of major resources from both coasts, who, in addition to their showrooms in New York and California, also show at some of the other markets. However, since New York is primarily the center of American fashion, this chapter will deal with covering the New York market, a procedure that is applicable, for the most part, to all other markets.

The Fashion Capital

7th Avenue in New York is Fashion Avenue.

Throughout the world of fashion—at home and abroad—New York is regarded as the fashion capital of America. Gigantic as it may sound, the New York market, for women's ready-to-wear, is for the most part concentrated on two famous streets: Seventh Avenue and Broadway.

Seventh Avenue has become more than the name of a street. It is the phrase that is synonomous with American fashion. "Seventh Avenue says . . . ," or "Seventh Avenue predicts . . . ," or, as *Women's Wear Daily* reports, "SA believes . . ." Even though many outstanding designers are to be found elsewhere in America, Seventh Avenue has the image as the American authority for New York's couture, designer, and better ready-to-wear. In fact, the street sign in the garment area reads "Fashion Avenue." Broadway, on the other hand, famous for great American sportswear for women and juniors, is where more of the mass or volume cutters have their showrooms.

The California Market

Going to New York is often synonymous with going to "The Big Apple." In a like manner, the California fashion world feels "The Big Orange" epitomizes their image. There is no comparison when it comes to the strength of their nicknames (The Big Apple seems better known), but when it comes to comparing the two fashion markets, it's like comparing apples with oranges.

New York has the greatest concentration of leading American designers and the fashion direction emulating from them is undisputed. California, on the other hand, younger in the fashion picture, has grown to major proportions in fashion leadership when it comes to sportswear, swimwear, activewear and young, spirited innovations. Their courage with color, for example, has awakened many a fashion trend previously too shy to emerge.

Retailers, once they discovered the special excellence available in the California market, realized their need for both coasts' expertise, each unique and important in its own way. Shopping the market in California has proved more effortless and less time consuming than in New York because most of the major resources are located in or near The California Mart. So important is this system that New York, at this writing, is accepting bids for the consideration of a mart and the redevelopment of the 42nd Street and Times Square areas.

The MAGIC Show

In addition to a strong market for women and children, the men's market is regarded by most major retailers as a must when it comes to the MAGIC Show. MAGIC (Men's Apparel Guild in California) created in 1934 as a showcase for West Coast manufacturers, has long since expanded to international proportions and includes manufacturers from throughout the world. Held during the first week of October and March each year in the Los Angeles Convention Center, with an estimated 1500 exhibitors with presentations in 3000 booths, MAGIC is touted as the largest men's wear show in the country.

The California Mart in the "Big Orange"—Los Angeles—provides retailers with news of events to be offered during market dates.

HOW A BUYER COVERS THE MARKET

It is important for everyone in the fashion coordination field to understand how a buyer buys—what problems he or she must face—before the fashion director or coordinator can establish a good rapport with the buyer and provide a good service. If communication between the fashion director and buyer breaks down or does not exist, the goals and objectives of both can be seriously impaired. It is nice for a fashion director to have a buyer's respect, but it is also important to have his or her cooperation.

The buyer comes into the market with a plan. How much to spend and how much to select in each classification for each department or departments for which the person buys is specifically spelled out before leaving on a buying trip.

How a Buyer Draws Up a Market Plan

"Forget the past," may be a nice philosophy for anyone wishing to get off to a fresh start or a better future, but the past, as far as a department's sales performance is concerned, is what every buyer has to live with.

Before the buyer makes the first scratch on the proposed buying plan, he or she must check the open-to-buy, stock condition, and sales performance of the comparable period last year. Guided by this past of units and dollars, plus a plan for growth in any specific area, the buying plan is formulated. Naturally, the system or procedure the buyer follows to fulfill the buying plan differs with the type of operation (chain, specialty, or department store), but the purpose is the same.

The Dress Buyer

In the very large retail operation, there would very likely be a separate dress buyer for every dress classification and price level. However, for our purpose here, the example of a store where the better dress buyer is responsible for all classifications is more typical of the greatest number of operations throughout the country.

Let us assume that last year the better dress buyer had her departments broken down into street dresses, ensembles, and social occasion dresses. For the upcoming season there seems to be strong development of two-piece dressing for day and separates dressing for evening. Because these two classifications will be considered explosive (very good sellers), special funding will be necessary for either or both new developments. If these new categories are to be taken out of existing open-to-buy, then purchases of other merchandise would have to be pared down or eliminated. Every season presents new considerations. Some classifications are strengthened, some shortened, some added, and some completely eliminated. The decision of what the new classifications will be depends on the new trends researched and recommended ahead of market time by the fashion director.

Each classification is identified by a special number, and each number is awarded a certain dollar amount. The total of all the better dress buyer's classifications make up the amount the buyer will spend to fill the stock requirements of the buyer's department or departments for a given period.

Before the buyer gets the money, so to speak, the plan must be submitted to the divisional merchandise manager for review. It is very likely that the DMM will take the plan of the better dress buyer and all other buyers' plans for the division to the general merchandise manager for approval. When the better dress buyer's plan is approved, the DMM gives the go-ahead and the buyer is off to the market.

Let us assume that the buyer is going into the market in November. At this time, open-to-buy money for February and March may be spent. The buyer would not, however, spend every cent of each month's open-to-buy. The wise buyer would hold back enough for expected reorders and new developments. It would be sad, indeed, for any fashion department, if something hot or new showed up and there was no money left to cover it.

A Day in the Market

If the fashion buyer is with a department store that is associated with a resident buying office in New York, the buyer undoubtedly would meet with the merchandise representative (MR) of the buyer's area before shopping any of the resources. The resident MR is a specialist. He or she knows the buyer's area thoroughly; the MR also knows the buyer's store and its needs. Therefore, he or she is in a position to say to the buyer:

> "I feel you should drop resource X this season. It is not looking good and they are overpriced. I feel, on the other hand, you should take a look at resource W which is new and catching on very well. Several of our other associate stores are doing very well with them and some are stores very much like yours."

Both the buyer and the fashion director can take advice like this, check it out, and decide if it applies to their store and their customer.

Next, the buyer probably sits down at the telephone in the store's New York office and starts calling to make appointments for showings of those manufacturers or resources on her list with whom she has not already booked before coming to New York. She calls the Oscar de la Renta showroom. She identifies herself by name and store. She calls every designer on her list until her appointment calendar is filled.

Showings are booked at least an hour or an hour and a half apart (most shows last about forty-five minutes, but seldom start on time), leaving only enough time for lunch (sometimes) or more phone calls. She is on Seventh Avenue from early morning until the market closes, about five or six o'clock.

During each show, while carefully scrutinizing each model, she makes good notes so that when she goes back later—if she is interested enough to return—she will remember the pieces she would like to consider.

Many major fashion lines do not have formal shows, per se, but simply "open" their lines at a given time (not all lines open at the same time) and buyers call for appointments or are called by the vendors themselves to make an appointment to view the collections.

In cases of important resources, the fashion director will usually accompany the buyer to the showings. The director may or may not return for writing of the order; it depends on where the fashion director is needed most at the time.

Writing Orders

Viewing the collections in formal shows and reviewing lines in showrooms is only the beginning for the fashion buyer. Now the real work starts. If she has not set up a follow-up appointment with a resource, another round of phone calls must be made. The buyer calls back the resource whose show she has seen and liked well enough to consider buying some pieces. "I would like to make an appointment to write," she says this time. "Eleven o'clock tomorrow morning? Fine. Thank you." When she arrives the next morning at the showroom, she is careful to be on time. She is seated behind a desk, well supplied with order pads, pencils, and is offered a cup of coffee or juice. (Buyers are always thirsty or hungry so to alleviate the pressures of making hundreds of decisions, little gestures of hospitality in the form of coffee, juice, or food are offered in some form or other in most showrooms. Sometimes, if a buyer is writing during the lunch hour, a sandwich might be provided as well.)

The representative or salesperson with whom she works, after making sure the buyer is comfortable, brings over the racks of clothes to be reviewed and considered. The buyer may wish to look at the entire line once more before making any final decision if she is planning on buying in depth or may wish to look at only those numbers noted on her program during the show. When shopping the better houses, it is not likely that there will be much "in depth" buying. At the urging of the fashion director, or a decision of the DMM, the buyer is more likely to select only the choice pieces of many manufacturers, thus giving her department a more "item" look. The customer can then enjoy greater selection with less duplication.

Leaving Paper

There are two phrases that are music to the ears of every fashion house. The first is "take numbers" and the second is "leave paper." When a buyer takes numbers (style numbers), she is indicating interest in buying that item. If she carefully fills in on her order pad not only the style numbers but the preferred colors, sizes, and number of pieces to be ordered, it is a good sign. But the best sign of all is when the buyer signs the order form, tears it off (keeping a duplicate copy for herself), and hands it to the salesman, thus fulfilling what all manufacturers love and prefer—the business of "leaving paper."

Leaving paper means to leave the order on the spot. Many buyers, however, may take the order away with them, either to reconsider their selections as compared with other selections available in other houses, or to submit the order, along with all others she plans to place, to the divisional merchandise manager to approve and sign.

Passing Orders

Even though a specified open-to-buy has been awarded to each fashion buyer, a certain disipline as to how that open-to-buy is spent is administered by requiring that orders be reviewed with the DMM and the GMM. When the orders have been signed by superiors, the buyer then can consider his or her order "passed."

Whether the order is left on the spot or mailed in later, the amount of "paper" the manufacturer receives on a certain number determines whether or not it will be "cut." In other words, if a particular creation does not stimulate enough interest from all the buyers who have seen it, it will be eliminated from the line completely and not be put into production. That is why sometimes after a buyer has gone home, after submitting a bona fide order to the fashion house, she will be advised that a number or two she has ordered will not be available. The success or failure of a style number in a line, or of an entire line for that matter, depends on the buyers who "leave paper."

The paperwork a buyer must do in order to expedite responsibilities is considerable. Many evenings, after covering the market all day, are spent in a hotel room writing orders, reviewing notes, trying to make the best possible decisions on how to spend that open-to-buy. All of this is part of making sure the buyer's department or departments are covered to back the trends the fashion director had recommended.

HOW THE FASHION DIRECTOR COVERS THE MARKET

To a buyer, covering the market means *her* market or *his* market. For example, to the shoe buyer it is the shoe market; to the hosiery buyer, the hosiery market; to the junior buyer, the junior market; to the coat buyer, the coat market. Each covers his or her own market, and that market only.

When a fashion director covers the market, it is a different story. The director is not only interested in each buyer's market individually, but in all of them collectively. It is only by seeing the entire fashion picture, piece by piece, department by department, and then put together, that one is able to interpret the strength and direction of coming fashion trends. Differing from the buyer, the fashion director does not come into the market with a buying plan; he or she comes in with a routine.

The Routine of Appointments

Like buyers, fashion directors line up appointments, by mail or telephone, identifying themselves by name, title, and store. Wherever possible, not knowing in advance how much time will be necessary to cover each source, they leave enough time between appointments to avoid overlapping or arriving late. It is also helpful if appointments in one building or area are made consecutively; much time is lost in travel between addresses.

Time is a valuable commodity, not only for the visiting fashion director, but for all those people who are making space on their calendar to see the director. A respect for the time of those granting the interview is a must; it is best to be a little early and wait. If an unavoidable conflict arises, the original appointment must be notified as soon as possible and a new time set up. To make an appointment and not appear, regardless of how justifiable, is unforgivable. Next time, that door may not be opened as readily. Since a fashion director can use all the help he or she can get, diplomacy, good manners, and expressed gratitude for all aid extended (even if it is their job to do so) are not only good business but will make her next trip to the same source more pleasant and more valuable.

Without Pencil

In the market the manufacturer regards the buyer as "the person with the pencil." That is, the person who literally writes the orders is the most important person visiting the manufacturer's showroom. When people "without pencil," such as fashion directors, although capable of influencing buyers, request special showings of merchandise or special meetings, it is a courtesy that must be acknowledged with thanks. Most manufacturers are aware of the influence of fashion directors, but their schedules are as heavy and complicated as the fashion directors'.

Establishing Market Relationships

Respecting people's time and keeping appointments are two kind elements that get a fashion director off to a good start with relationships in the market. The fashion director, who is consistent in visits to a particular source—that is, visits them as often as possible when in the market—can establish that she is interested in their efforts, has a respect for their guidance and is, therefore, making them a partner, in effect, with what she is trying to accomplish. If she has been instrumental in bringing the resource and the buyer together, all the better. By being visible, asking advice, and expressing gratitude for their expertise, the fashion director gets on a first-name basis with many sources. Good market relationships are invaluable to the fashion director who needs all the friends she can get to help her successfully cover all the bases that need thorough covering.

Before the Market

Before the buyers come, before the market opens, before the director is able to make recommendations to her management and the store's merchandising staff, the fashion director begins with research (see Chapter 2) on the stuff of which fashion is made: fabrics. The director not only discovers in the fabric market what important fabrics are available but learns what the designers are selecting.

Designers go into the fabric market to see what is being produced—colors, textures, fibers, treatments, and weights. They want to know about performance of a new fabric, perhaps get a pattern confined (exclusively theirs) and, therefore, get an inspiration from the goods they will work with. How it can be manipulated, combined, and disciplined very often influences a designing trend.

The fashion director is very much like a reporter out to uncover a story. She follows the line of action. She traces the story line back to its source. Thus her routine is formulated.

The First Stop

Before the fabrics come the fibers that go into the fabrics. Therefore, to track down clue number one, the fashion director calls on giants like DuPont, Celanese, and Monsanto as well as other fiber people whose research experts have done an amazing job of anticipating what will be in demand or what will be accepted. They have combed the fabric markets of the world, such as Interstoff, for direction. To show the fashion director what is new, the fiber authority may take him or her into a fabric room stocked with swatches, panels, and books of new direction. The fashion director will also learn what is getting the action, what the mills are producing, and what the cutters are buying. From this area the director will get a clue or indication of several things:

A new fiber type appearing on the market
A new color direction
A new texture
A new weight

The fiber people might tip the director off as to where they discovered a certain color or texture. Perhaps it came from a brick color of a castle in Spain or a Picasso art exposition or a favorite color of an international celebrity.

Things worth noting are beginning to show up. New trends, a strong comeback of an old trend, a repetition, with a new twist, of a currently established trend. Conclusion: if so much interest is being expressed in these trends, there must be something going on in the fashion designer's studio and in the manufacturer's cutting room relative to all this. At this point, however, no decision is made by the fashion director, nor does the director jump to any conclusions. The director has hardly seen or heard enough to evaluate the whole picture, but now has a strong indication of what to watch for.

The Second Stop

The director's next stop will be to an assortment of fabric people. What the mills are making is all important. If major mills are producing a certain fabric in huge volume, it is very likely they have good reason to believe in it and/or the cutters are buying it. Heavy purchases of an item by manufacturers is a most dependable clue.

If a fashion director learns that a mill is finding it difficult to supply the demand on a certain fabric, it is certain that garments in that fabric

While in the market, fashion directors and other retail executives can take advantage of exhibits created by the industry. Pictured is a view of the "Laboratory of Knits" display, sponsored by the Knitted Textile Association at Parsons School of Design. About 250 innovative knitted fabrics for men's, women's and children's wear were included. (*Courtesy of Knitted Textile Association*)

will be flooding the fashion scene. One year I learned that there might be a shortage of velour. Sure enough, the trend toward velour tops, dresses, sportswear and more was tremendous. Every season brings its favorites, some predictable, such as denim was several years ago, some totally unexpected, like panne velvet one year; when it was gone, it was gone. Manufacturers were hard pressed to come up with additional panne velvet to fill reorders.

The fasion director does not ignore the lesser trends, those that look good, even if they are not giants. It takes more than one fabric, one color, and one trend to make a season or fill a store.

The Chains

In addition to working with stores or store groups, the fabric producers (the mills) work very closely with the chains. Very early, the fabric people make presentations to the fashion departments and merchandising executives of the chains. An exchange of ideas takes place. The chains learn what the mills can and will do, what they believe in and why. On the other hand, the fashion departments of the mills learn what the chains feel strongly about, what direction they might take, and what specifics they might like developed. What such giant retailers regard as important is always worth noting.

Leather Sources

Leather producers also work far in advance of seasons, carefully evaluating colors, textures, and marketing possibilities. Will total garments, in addition to coats and shoes, be expressed in leather? What about accessories? What new combinations will be acceptable? Here again, it is imperative to check and see if the designers are including new uses or new expressions of leather. In which way? To what degree? You can be sure the shoe industry and handbag market are checking into what is happening in each other's camp.

Designers Come Next

Good contacts among strong designers can be invaluable. Even though they may not be in a position to reveal everything about a collection, they might agree to give you a glimpse or a feeling about what trends look promising. "Almost all of my collection will be soft. All fabrics will be manipulated into soft lines; the fabrics themselves will be soft in texture—very touchable—and soft in color," one designer might confide to a visiting fashion director. The designer may express thoughts about which silhouettes he or she has faith in and which ones the designer feels are not for his or her market. The fashion director, as part of her routine, makes good notes of all she sees and hears. She is getting the picture.

How the Designers Work

Having some idea about how leading designers go about creating their collections not only helps to dispel some of the mystery about the birth

Good contacts with leading designers can be very helpful to a fashion director. The author with Oscar de la Renta in New York and Pierre Cardin in Paris.

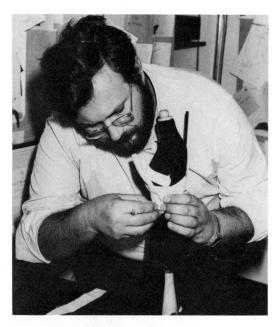

Designer Gianfranco Ferre of Milan works out details of a garment on a miniature dummy. *(Photo by Tim Jenkins, courtesy of Women's Wear Daily)*

of fashion, but fosters an enormous respect for the hard work that goes into it.

Most designers begin work on a new collection almost immediately after the showing of the one just finished. In fact, the completion and reaction to one collection often triggers a "feeling" or inspiration for the next. Fashion themes and color stories may be the outgrowth of a past season or a complete departure, but one thing is usually fundamental—most collections stem from fabric. Most designers agree that the fabric is the strongest inspiration. How the fabric is manipulated, of course, differs with every designer.

More unique than typical is how Gianfranco Ferre of Milan, Italy, works. Ferre will sketch details such as necklines, hips, belts, even faces with makeup, independent of the total look. Ferre edits his collection from about 300 sketches, full-figure and partial. According to *Women's Wear Daily*, he uses the unique approach of doing his fittings in the fabric in which his creation will be made. Many designers use toile (muslin pattern) for fittings. Another unique technique utilized by Ferre is using a miniature dummy on which he works out details of a garment (see illustration).

It is not unusual for designers to work almost up to the last minutes of when a collection will be presented, to refine, correct, or adjust, any detail he or she feels can be improved.

Consultations with the Buying Office

If a store belongs to a buying office that provides its members with good advanced information, the fashion director is greatly aided. The staff fashion director of a resident buying office in New York (usually titled the vice president of fashion merchandising) has had the market thoroughly researched and is in a position to advise fashion people from member stores about the findings. This advice can be shared in personal conference with the individual fashion director or in group meetings. Comprehensive group meetings are scheduled on a regular basis especially for fashion directors of member stores to carry back to their management. Such meetings would be offered at the top of each season—spring/summer, fall/winter, and holiday. The resident buying office fashion department provides the member fashion directors with direction in advance of market openings, so they in turn can make edited versions of the presentations to their store executives (see Chapter 6) prior to their coming into market to place orders.

Perhaps the most complete fashion office of any buying group at this time is the Associated Merchandising Corporation (AMC). The fashion office of AMC, for women's and children's apparel, fashion accessories, and intimate apparel, includes six fashion coordinators, each responsible for a separate fashion area and reporting to the fashion merchandising director (vice president of fashion merchandising). Also reporting to this vice president of fashion merchandising is a fashion merchandising director for men's and boys' wear, and the European fashion consultants located in the AMC Paris office.

In the seasonal predictive fashion directors' meetings, each AMC coordinator presents the findings and evaluations of his or her specific market area. The stores' fashion directors attending the meetings, who see at least eight or nine market areas (sportswear, dresses, coats and suits, juniors, children's, intimate apparel, shoes, and fashion accessories) together with new direction for fabrics and colors, have an opportunity to see how the coming season's trends are expressed throughout all markets.

These presentations are made with the assistance of sketched illustrations of actual merchandise, incorporated into a very inspiring multi-media colored slide presentation, including photography of trend examples from leading designers as well as fabric and color samples. Also, live models wearing samples from influential designers, guest speakers from the industry, and individual evaluations of each classification by the AMC fashion coordinators offer the member fashion directors excellent, dependable guidance to reinforce their own research.

The Composite

At this point, the fashion director, in an effort to get solid advanced information about the coming season, has interviewed leather sources, fiber companies, fabric mills, and designers, and has attended group meetings and private conferences with fashion people in a resident buying office. Each area and each interview has provided another piece of information, another point of view (more than one opinion is very important) relating to coming fashion trends. Still the director's work is not finished.

Look and Listen

Along with a good, sturdy pair of legs, (and comfortable shoes) for the endless work of calling on, tracking down, and chasing after anyone who has new and reliable fashion information, the fashion director also needs a good pair of eyes.

Reading reams of printed information, predicting, forecasting, and revealing what's to come, helps supplement other information or add impetus to those clues that have surfaced thus far. A fashion director is wise to have such subscriptions of material as *Women's Wear Daily* sent directly to her home. She is likely to find there is more time for leisure reading away from office interruptions and busy phones, with a better chance to concentrate and reflect on the steady flow of material.

Talking with other fashion directors, magazine editors, merchandisers, buyers, and anyone related to the fashion business gives a fashion person on a hunt an undeniable feel for what is in the air.

Also, it is important to talk with the big cutters. If the big companies are investing big money on a trend by "putting the knife to it" (that is, actually cutting the style numbers) the director will get closer to what is actually happening.

Shopping helps to enlighten and educate the visiting fashion director. New York, or wherever market trips are made, provides examples of good merchandising in the local leading stores. Boutiques, too—elegant, unique, trendy—provide excellent indications of trends and taste. Shopping uptown, downtown, on the Avenue (Fifth Avenue), in the Village, in Soho, and in many out-of-the-way places provides new clues and new inspirations. It is the composite of all this activity that adds to the validity of a fashion director's recommendations.

HOW TO WORK WITH THE BUYER IN THE MARKET

Everything the fashion director learned through her research she has shared with her management and merchandising team before they all go off to market. All of this she documented and presented in her predictive presentation, followed by an establishment of a time and action calendar for the coming season. Now, with the sanction of management, everyone is off to buy according to plan.

Out-of-town retailers visit leading New York retailers while in the city on market trips. Stops at Macy's, Bloomingdales, Saks Fifth Avenue, Lord & Taylor, Bonwit Teller, Bergdorf Goodman, B Altman's, Henri Bendels, to name a few, are a must. *(Courtesy of Women's Wear Daily)*

Fashion Presentations for Retailers

By day, the fashion director and buyers usually cover the market in showrooms, either for formal showings of collections or viewing fashion lines, piece by piece. Often, in hotel ballrooms, for breakfast, lunch, or at night, after the showrooms have closed, some of the major fashion houses or organizations in the fashion industry offer fashion presentations for retailers in the form of Broadway-like productions.

From such events, the retail community can get an overview of what is available in the market and arrive at individual vendor appointments with a better idea about what to buy.

Covering the Showrooms

When the fashion director accompanies the buyer to couture and designer openings of collections the buyer calls ahead of time as mentioned earlier (usually from the office before coming to New York) to make reservations for seats. "I would like to reserve two seats at the showing of your new collection," she will say when calling the designer showroom, "one for our fashion director and one for myself." This is usually in response to an invitation; most such collections are by invitation only—those who buy the line or those expressing an interest to do so.

The Show Begins

Usually seats are reserved. The major stores and the press are seated in the front rows, the smaller customers are toward the back. Very often, the printed program placed on the viewers' seats is a statement by the designer revealing the designer's philosophy of the coming season and his or her own fashion statement.

At each show, the buyer and fashion director take notes on impressive features and jot down style numbers if they are available. The packed showroom, filled with buyers, fashion directors, merchandisers, store presidents, representatives from resident buying offices, and the press, view a swift parade of models moving down a narrow ramp or along the floor, sometimes tracing through two or three rooms and even a hallway, if the crowd is overflowing. Standing room only crowds usually appear for most important showings. There is very little description available, except on the printed program, and that is very seldom. Sometimes a designer will appear to greet the audience, make an opening comment or two, and then disappear. Sometimes the designer's collection will be received with enthusiastic applause and the designer will be called to take a bow at the end of the showing.

Since the collections shown are unedited versions of what later will actually be cut and sold, the presentation is fairly long. While the famous Seventh Avenue models move in and out to appropriate music, the professional people watching soon get the message of what the designer is trying to say. Because most buyers buy by items, that is, select choice pieces, rather than entire collections, especially in the better markets, the notes they take are to identify, for later reference, those pieces they feel will fit into their fashion departments. By choosing only items, the buyer gets the choice pieces from every collection and those best suited to her customer; the buyer also builds a stock that has greater versatility and better selection. If the buyer's notes include a great number of style numbers, it is a good sign he or she has a strong interest in the collection. If only a couple are noted, the buyer may consider it unsalable or unsuited to the store's needs.

If the buyer and fashion director are sitting next to each other during the show, they may compare notes, exchange opinions, and express ideas. Perhaps they are sitting at opposite ends of the room (lucky to have squeezed into the overcrowded showroom). It is also possible that, due to conflicting schedules, the buyer and fashion director do

At a showing of his collection for retailers, a Bill Tice creation on the fashion show runway. *(Courtesy of Intimate Fashion News)*

not attend the same performance of a showing. If they don't, they might compare notes at a later time during the day, but almost always before they return home.

Showroom Presentations

It may be necessary for the formal showing to be bypassed altogether. It is very possible that the buyer and/or the fashion director will not be in New York the week of the show and would, therefore, review the line in the showroom with a sales representative. Even though the purpose of the show is to give the fashion community an overview of what the designer's fashion position is, all buyers must ultimately make showroom appointments to write the line, if they should decide to do so.

Not all lines provide formal shows. Because of the high costs even those designers who traditionally held such showings have eliminated them. Most ready-to-wear lines are viewed from racks in the manufacturer's showroom one piece at a time, presented for consideration by a showroom representative or salesperson. Occasionally, a piece from the group will be shown informally on a live model. The buyer may feel unable to judge the line of a certain garment on the hanger and may request that it be shown on a live model.

When accompanying a buyer at a show or showroom, the fashion director takes her own notes and is wise to sit quietly while the buyer does her work. THe director does not interrupt or contradict an opinion or conversation the buyer and showroom representative may be having.

To assist the retailer in note-taking while reviewing a line in their showroom, the manufacturer often provides a descriptive list, complete with style numbers, fabric content, available colors, prices, and estimated delivery dates. Illustrations may also be included, especially when the line is extensive and remembering all details would be impossible. Such printed descriptive material is extremely helpful when the buyer sits down to write orders.

Why the Fashion Director Is There

When accompanying a buyer, the fashion director keeps a watchful eye on what she is seeing and hearing, always remembering why she is there. It must be reiterated that the buyer is seeing the market from her vantage point only, but the fashion director is seeing it total store. Because of the fashion director's premarket presentation, the store has decided on certain trends in which they believe, and the fashion director is here to see that merchandise is being selected to back them up. She is also on hand to select certain provocative pieces from the lines she sees that are great examples of a trend and that will lend drama or excitement for shops, windows, displays, and fashion shows she has planned to help sell the trend.

"I'd love to have that for a fashion show," she might say to the buyer during a showing.

"Then you should buy this group of three pieces," the showroom representative might suggest. "It would make a great window."

The buyer and the fashion director might or might not agree. They sometimes do buy a group for display or window illustration, but they also might select separate pieces from separate lines to do a better job of telling their fashion story.

The fashion director is also on hand as advisor. A buyer may be undecided about certain pieces or about an entire collection. She may, after viewing a line, turn to the fashion director and ask, "Does this group have the look you were talking about?"

"Frankly, I don't feel that they are doing the new look as well as some other houses. Also, I think they are overpriced."

"I'm inclined to agree. What's the alternative?"

"I ran across a new resource that might just fill the bill. Would you like to look at it?" the fashion director might suggest.

The discovery of a new resource might come from any number of directions; from the resident buying office, or from other fashion directors who have seen the line, and report, "If you haven't seen this line you should. We might even open a special shop featuring this collection—it's that good." A new resource might be one that the buyer formerly was familiar with, one that went out of business and re-opened under a new label. She knows his workmanship. She knows his reputation.

"Let's take a look." They call for an appointment. It may prove to be the greatest line yet, it may be completely unsuitable for their needs. However, if the fashion director has done her homework well, she will not recommend that any buyer sacrifice valuable time to look at a line that would not be suitable for their store. First on her list of evaluation would be, "Is it right for us?" The fashion director is a merchant. He or she is interested in seeing buyers and departments involved with merchandise that is right and salable. The director is careful to keep out of it, to regulate personal tastes and prejudices. A director's personal likes and dislikes don't count. When working with buyers in the market, the fashion director keeps an eye on fashion objectives.

The Fashion Director's Objectives in the Market

The following objectives are uppermost in a director's mind while covering the market.

1. To be sure the correct fashion items are being selected to cover the new fashion stories.
2. To watch for good coverage from new and ongoing resources to back up new shop concepts.
3. To see that the right kind of merchandise is selected for windows, displays, and fashion shows.

In addition to the above, if a new trend, a sleeper, or a hot item seems to be showing up, the fashion director must check it out (as with other trends) and immediately advise merchandisers and buyers of its importance. The director must, if the conviction is strong, urge the merchandising team to include the new item. This should include communication with the GMM, in case additional money or change of plan is involved.

The Styleout

Instead of waiting until all the merchandise selected in the market arrives at the store, many stores use a system called the styleout to see what a department will look like. In essence, it is a procedure through which every division and every department within that division can view in advance what merchandise will be stocked.

For example, if a blouse department hangs up all the selected pieces (one sample of each) side by side, the DMM, GMM, and fashion director can see at a glance:

1. If the selection is representative of the important current trends.
2. If there are enough alternatives to styling, fabric, and color.
3. If there are any duplications (one does not need six similar plaid shirts from six different resources).
4. If there are any voids.

The styleout serves a very real purpose in giving a department good balance. It also alleviates the risk of investing too many open-to-buy dollars in one category while another equally important goes begging.

Also, this is a good time for the fashion director, who has discovered some new resources in the market that the buyers have not seen, to bring in samples for consideration. If what the director brings is a duplication of what a buyer already has, the item can be eliminated. But if, on the other hand, the item supplies a void in a particular department, the merchandising team may decide it is worthy of being incorporated. The buyer then would be asked to go see the resource with the fashion director and select what she or he feels is needed; a new resource is thus introduced into the store.

The styleout also provides the store with guidance on what might be purchased from the import market, those things that are not available in the domestic market or provided at a better price or better technique abroad.

The samples brought in for the styleout (perhaps in a meeting room in a resident office in New York) are loaned by the resource from whom the purchase is to be made and returned immediately following the styleout.

Covering the Import Markets

Just as New York was used in this book as an example of covering the domestic markets, the European market will be the example for the import fashion market. The procedure is applicable to most other foreign markets.

Unlike New York, the couture market in Europe opens after the ready-to-wear market. In Europe, couture collections are usually introduced in January (spring) and July (fall) the pret-a-porter (ready-to-wear) in late March or April (fall) and October (spring). Some years the timing varies, but these approximate time slots are fairly traditional. The pret-a-porter opens early for fall to enable buyers to commit for fall and before the U.S. fall market opens. The couture, originally intended for private clients, had no need to open so early.

A typical European schedule might look like this:

OCTOBER

3–9	Fashion Showings	Milan, Italy
9–12	Fashion Showings	Florence, Italy
12–14	Designer Collections	London, England
17–21	Pret-a-Porter	Paris, France
20–23	Fashion Week	London, England

Most major retail executives might make all these dates, but not all buyers will cover them all—buyers are interested only in those relating to their specific areas.

European Couture in the Seventies

At the outset of the seventies, the haute couture of Europe (primarily Paris) failed to give the fashion direction for which it has always been famous, for which it has always held leadership. Throughout our modern experience with fashion, leadership and direction has always migrated from the top, the haute couture. But the sixties started a new influence, from the bottom—the Village in New York, communes in San Francisco, Kings Road in London, the Left Bank in Paris, and boutiques in Copenhagen. Influence came, in fact, from everywhere, anywhere, on almost any street, except where fashion had always been born and bred: Paris and the other fashion capitals of the world.

The European fashion leaders, instead of being creative, began to get their inspiration from the same places—the streets, the discoteques, and the scattered communities of rebellious youth. Thus, the looks that started out as put-ons or antiestablishment were picked up by the so-called fashion establishment, endorsed, sanctioned, and glorified.

It was in such a climate, together with the grave issues of the day (the Vietnamese War, racial issues, pollution, overpopulation, inflation), that created an antistatus atmosphere. It was a climate that turned people away from any extravagant display of "show." Even with those who could afford it, what was extremely expensive in fashion seemed unnecessary. Fashion dictation from the European haute couture, therefore, seemed to have another strike against it. And, since little direction was offered, little direction was taken. In addition to this, the lifestyle of the people had changed, and there was no longer the same need for couture leadership.

The pret-a-porter showings, on the other hand, held more interest. They were ready to compete with Seventh Avenue, and Seventh Avenue (strongly dependent on inspiration from European couture) was challenged to come up with originality of its own. Thus was the flavor of fashion direction at the beginning of the seventies.

European Couture for the Eighties

The eighties brought an entirely different attitude within the couture and toward it. It was well known that the couture did not make money in itself. But—no matter—the spinoffs on the prestigious names were enormous. Endorsements, fragrances, accessories, and merchandise of every conceivable kind bearing the famous couture designer's name were sufficient for guaranteed sales.

At the outset of the eighties, in a period of economic upheaval, Paris wanted to see women beautifully dressed up. As the bard of Paris, Yves Saint Laurent indicated very clearly in his collections that in a time of recession and tight money women wanted to move in the opposition direction. No one wanted to appear sad and poor. There was a great deal to be said for the look of prosperity; the appearance of success might attract the reality. Certainly the working woman had been utilizing this principle for some time. Now success dressing took on an opulent flavor. Designers went all out with lush, rich fabrics manipulated in extravagant new cuts. Embellishments with accessories were dramatic, sophisticated, ornate. Even colors of precious metals and stones added to the ambiance—black onyx, copper, pewter, pearl, silver, gold (especially gold), ruby, and sapphire.

The Influence

Yves Saint Laurent took the lead by reaching back to Shakespearean times, to Elizabethan elegance. It was a Renaissance of the Renaissance. The designer also made elaborate tributes with fashion interpretations to Matisse, Ingres, and Van Dyke. It was, indeed, a return to elegance.

It was a time to appeal to all sides of a woman, or to offer women an abundance of alternatives. The Paris designers came forth with a sense of humor as well and fashion reflected this with amusing, costumey creations. For still more alternatives they offered a return to prettiness. Femininity was saluted with ruffles and flounces and bows, billowy taffettas, moire, velvets, silks, and lace.

The fashion observers of the world learned what fashion historians have always known—fashion it not unlike the weather; if you wait a while it will change. That is why constant vigilance is necessary in the fashion business. One can never be entirely sure from which authority or area of life fashion influence will come. One period from the streets, another from haute couture. Fashion being what it is, the entire power structure could turn around tomorrow. Couture on top again. New designers on top. Those who have dropped down, pulling up again. New reasons, new life styles, new needs. Fashion reflects them all.

Georgio Armani, putting finishing touches on a collection, at his ancient palace in Milan, Palazzo Durini, where he houses his entire organization. Armani, who designs for both men and women has wardrobed major celebrities from Diane Keaton to Mick Jagger. *(Courtesy of Women's Wear Daily)*

European Travel Schedule

Since more retailers attend the pret-a-porter openings than the haute couture, we will deal here with the "pret," the word used by the fashion industry when referring to the pret-a-porter (ready-to-wear) showings in Europe.

Usually, Paris takes the lead, setting its date first, then the others plan accordingly, so buyers can go from one fashion capital to the other. Usually, the schedule would include a few days each in Milan, London, and Paris.

Milan

The first stop is Milan. For many years the Pret showings were held in Florence (knit shows are still held in Florence) but in the mid-seventies the major markets switched to Milan, which is Italy's industrial center. The seasonal ready-to-wear mart there, the Milano-Vende-Moda, may provide as many as two hundred firms specializing in medium-to-high priced apparel for men, women, and children.

At Milan's Sample Fair Hall 4, the showplace for the Modit show mart and designer runway presentations, buyers and the press might see two collective runway shows, each with 150 items selected from 15 leading firms. In addition, more than forty designers show their lines at the Hall on different dates. The Modit collective show and lines are geared to export rather than the domestic market, and the designer shows complement Modit.

In addition to viewing the runway shows, buyers and fashion directors will visit the booths or showrooms of various designers to view the pieces of the collections on an individual basis, just as they did in New York.

Price and Shipment

When shopping an import market, a great deal of careful consideration must be given to shipping dates (merchandise not in the stores on time defeats the purpose), and price, which differs for every part of the world. There is, first of all, FC or First Cost (the wholesale price of the garment). Then there is LC or Landed Cost (what the garment will cost shipped to our shores). The total cost of bringing a garment into the store must be considered. Next comes the store's markup. If what the garment must be sold for at retail is comparable to the same quality available in the domestic market, or provides a look that is far superior or unavailable among American designers, then the purchase is justified. To avoid delivery disasters or price changes, it is wise to place import orders as early as possible.

Observe the Community

In addition to viewing the collections and reviewing the lines, the fashion director gathers additional information and inspiration from the community. She visits the boutiques, searching for special boutique items that can be exclusive and unique. She carefully notes how the women in Milan dress. In fact, every city she visits will be excellent ground for research on what women of the world are wearing for what occasion and how they are putting it together. Once again, the fashion director becomes an observer, a reporter. What she sees she reports to the buyer and to management back home.

The Next Stop, Paris

During the Pret (as this fashion week in Paris is called), Paris on the Seine becomes Paris on the Scene. And the fashion scene in Paris—regarded as the world's biggest fashion show—is always alive with almost unbearable excitement. When you consider all the strong, vibrant, complicated personalities that make up the fashion community, that's a monumental amount of executive power poured into a concentrated area. Combine this with a tremendously aggressive press, which often runs up to 1,000 during a Pret showing, then add the drama, glamor, intrigue, and star-studded countenances of the French designers, models, and fashion creations, and you have an electric situation.

If it wasn't enough that Paris is Paris—with its great hotels and magnificent restaurants, its inspiring boutiques, and historical beauty—along comes show time for its leading industry, fashion, and it is staged and reviewed like a Broadway production.

A great deal of the drama is created by the way the collections are shown. From those of Saint Laurent, Cardin, Ungaro, or Givenchy shown with a flare unique to each in their private salons, to the tents in Forum des Halles where thousands of eager attendants fight and scratch and kick and scream, waving their invitations above their heads, trying desparately to get in to see the choice shows, the Pret is more circus than theater at times. Regardless of the undignified struggle to get into a show, the mad scramble for seats, the pushing and shoving, there is less pain in the fight to get in than in missing an important one. Whether one sees Emanuel Ungaro at the Theatre des Champs Elysees or Claude Montana in a tent in Les Halles, the result is the same—an unforgettable fashion experience, which could very well include the witnessing of a moment in fashion history being created. The following day, not only are the outstanding pieces pictured in the press around the world, but so are some of the celebrities in the audience, who dress with equal attention-getting skill.

In addition to the formal shows, there is the Porte de Versailles, Salon du Prêt â Porter Feminin. The thousands of spectators who do the Salon (that is the expression) can spend days viewing hundreds and hundreds of booths, without hassle, without hurry. Here one can discover new talents, carefully review lines, make important fashion decisions. Do we have the customer for this look? Will the customer pay this price? Is it in keeping with our fashion image?

Again, shopping the boutiques in Paris (the fashion world's greatest) and the modern Parisian shopping center (the 40,000-square-meter Forum Des Halles where the show tents were erected) and observing what the people wear, where they wear it, and how they put it together is extremely instructive for the fashion director. As many clues about what's new are found on the streets of Paris as in the shows. There consumer acceptance is indicated, a direction not to be denied. The role of observer can enable the fashion director to come home with not only new fashion looks but great ideas for displays, windows, shops, advertising, and fashion shows.

To document the inspiring windows or shops or displays the fashion director might take colored slides and offer a special presentation to the sales promotion division when he or she returns home.

Sometimes the designer agrees to make an appearance at the end of the showing of his collection (at its initial introduction or at a benefit). Here is Claude Montana after a showing of his Paris collection, being applauded by some of the 35 models that participated. *(Courtesy of Women's Wear Daily).*

The London Market

Dates for the London market coincide but do not conflict with the French and Italian dates. In each of these three leading European markets, retailers will find desirable choices unique to each country's special talents.

For example, buyers would select knitwear in Italy of a type they would not find in Paris. In London they would seek out wonderful hand knits, woolens and tweeds better done here than anywhere else. The procedure of reviewing the foreign markets, seeing the shows, observing the people and shopping the stores is the same here as in New York.

Keep in Touch

The touching of fabrics is a good practice whenever shopping a resource, at home or abroad. A garment on a runway, under very complimentary lighting can appear very different from when you see it up close. Also, a fashion piece on a rack or shown several feet away in front of potential buyers can also be deceiving. It is always wise to ask to have a garment brought forward and touch it with your palm or the back of your hand or even hold it against your face (itchy fabrics will anger your customers). Turn the garment over to inspect construction. It is not necessary to do this with every piece, only those in which you have a serious interest. This is especially important when shopping in foreign markets.

Product Development

Newest in the job description of the very experienced fashion director is the assignment of product development. With this major undertaking the director can be of great assistance to the manufacturer as well as the retailers served.

As a start, perhaps the director finds some select fashion pieces while in Europe (very often from retail outlets). It might be something hidden away in a remote boutique or it might be something that is showing up repeatedly in the shops, being worn by people on the streets. The garment has a strong appeal because the director feels it is the beginning of a trend that the customers of the store would understand, and, therefore, be likely to buy. At this time there is nothing like it being manufactured in the States. So what does the director do? She buys a sample or two, takes it home. First she discusses her find with management. Then, if they are in accord, she takes the sample to a manufacturer with whom she and the store have a good relationship and asks what their interest might be in incorporating a similar look in their line.

It is possible that the manufacturer has also been to Europe and, yes, saw the look, but not this particular sample, which he likes. Together they discuss how it should be adopted for the American market (along with the manufacturer's designer), and it is agreed that with certain changes—either because it would have greater appeal to the American woman or because of production costs—the garment would be put into production. For a giant retailer or chain the garment might be made exclusively for them, but for a smaller retailer the final product could be shared with everyone.

The Copiers

It is also possible that the fashion director would find pieces in the domestic market that she would like to see altered, revised, reinterpreted—either by the manufacturer who owns it, or by another manufacturer who could develop a similar piece for less money. Even without any suggestions from the retailer a tremendous number of manufacturers "knock off" fashion designs created by other designers. The piece could be copied from a foreign or a domestic one. The practice is universal and openly accepted. Most manufacturers are proud of their copies, announcing with pride that "this is that new Bill Blass dress," "this is the Oscar de la Renta blouse." Of course, it is the ultimate compliment and reinforces the power of the leading designers, at home and abroad, but the copies are never the same nor are they intended to be. They are only "knock offs" of the originals. Some manufacturers are so strongly involved with this kind of production they are known solely as "knock off houses." Almost any day in New York you can see an artist standing outside a window of a leading fashion store sketching what is displayed on a window mannequin. Or, the manufacturer does as the fashion director does—buy the garment at retail, take it back to the workroom, take it apart to learn its secrets of construction.

While a designer's new line is kept secret before it is exposed to the public and the press, once it hits the runway of the show, and the cameras flash to capture what's new for the reader, it's open season. One can copyright a name or a single creation but not an idea. That is why a trend sweeps through the industry like wildfire. If it catches on, everybody will be doing some version of it.

Developing Imports

Many merchandisers, buyers, and fashion directors are involved in some form of product development every season when it comes to certain imports (e.g., when working on imports from the Orient). If the fashion director goes over before the buyers, she might work on fabrics, colors, and patterns. She would be interested in incorporating the best fashion choices of these elements even before the kind of "bodies" (silhouette, line of the body of the garment) are discussed. After this initial trip that might have been scheduled in November, she might return with the buyers in January to further develop import products. This time those fabrics, colors, and patterns would be assigned to specific bodies, with specifications on everything, from what would be the best collar to the most desirable button. This could be done in concert with the buyer, who, in turn, would place orders for the store.

Because so many retailers feel that if they had such-and-such a dress or sweater or jacket put together in such-and-such a way (knowing their customer) they feel they could sell it in volume. And since volume business is the aim of most major retailers (even those with fashion images) product development is of great importance. The giant chains have used this practice for years, developing products to their "specs" (specifications) to better serve their customer.

Since product development is a very real goal for many retailers, it is not unlikely that a major part of the fashion director's time would be spent in some form for this effort. Buyers, too, would be part of the system.

The Fashion Team

Teamwork, exemplified through relating to the efforts of each, is essential to the effectiveness of the buyer–fashion director relationship. In some organizations a buyer is rated on his or her ability to use the fashion director. The buyer is way ahead who understands that the fashion director's goals and the buyer's goals are one and the same: to select merchandise the customer wants, to keep the cash register ringing, and to make a profit for the company.

The fashion director, on the other hand, needs to understand the road the buyer must travel to arrive at where they are both going. The buyer is faced with space problems, open-to-buy limitations, goals for growth, pressures to make figures, markdowns, concerns over deliveries, personnel problems, and customer acceptance, to name a few. The fashion director can read vibrations and anticipate trouble spots by asking questions relating to those trouble spots, and working closely with the buyer on specific plans and promotions. When a fashion director is aware of what the buyer must face, the director is not likely to make recommendations that do not support that buyer's efforts.

For example, a new pant silhouette was seen extensively in Europe by the fashion director on her recent trip. It was worn primarily by young women. In her eagerness to see a junior buyer have a good season and to be sure that the store was covered on what appeared to be a strongly emerging trend, she suggested, "Your department represents a real fashion authority for your young customer. What do you think of flying in a few pieces of this new pant?" Or, "I know of a domestic resource who is already turning these out." The junior buyer likes the idea and knows that the fashion director will follow through by urging management to support the effort with an ad, or a request for additional open-to-buy, if it is needed. The result of this teamwork enabled the store to scoop the city to be the first to stock the new pant look. The item turned out to be explosive and buyer exceeded her plan for the quarter's sales.

Good fashion directors can be worth their weight in gold to receptive, fashion-minded buyers, and the buyer who knows how to use a fashion director has a huge plus in his or her corner.

AFTERVIEW

More than at any other time in the history of retailing, buyers are extremely busy people. They have many more tracks to cover than ever before. Buying has become a more exact science and more exact performances are required. Besides the initial duties of buying merchandise and supervising their departments, they have many branches to visit, cover, and protect. The more branches, outposts, specialty shops, the more paper work, and, of course, responsibility. These busy people need help.

With fashion trends firing in and out, up and down, it is vital to the lifeblood of the buyer's area to call on the fashion director for advice and guidance to help select the most effective merchandise, and to help get the fashion message over to the customer, and the department's managers, and fashion sellers. Also, the fashion director, keeping on top of all trends, knowing when they have peaked, supplies a much-needed service to the buyer.

The fashion director, if he or she can look and really see, listen, and hear, will be unafraid to take a position on what is needed. If the director must push hard to convince the skeptical or the unseeing, then push it is. If it concerns an important fashion issue, the director is duty bound to see that management or the buyer in question understands its importance. If the fashion director sees the goal as attainable and profitable, and if customer interest is indicated, the director may have to fight the buyer for the sake of the consumer. The customer comes first. To take a position with conviction takes courage, but it helps make the store authoritative.

On the other hand, if the fashion director is a beginner, or new with the store, he or she is wise to permit a good buyer to be a teacher in many things—how to cover the market, what to look for, and so on. Many fashion directors making their first trips abroad have had some generous, knowledgeable buyer or merchandiser to thank for showing them the ropes. The best way a director can repay the buyer is to learn the lesson well and some day give the buyer the assistance needed to make a good fashion department even better.

CHAPTER RE-EXAMINATION

Questions

1. How do the New York and California markets differ?
2. What is the MAGIC Show?
3. What guidelines does a buyer follow in drawing up a market plan?
4. What is meant by "leaving paper"?
5. How does the way a fashion director covers the market differ from the buyer's way?
6. How does a resident buying office help the fashion director?
7. What is the pret-a-porter?
8. What is meant by landed cost?
9. What is a knock-off house?
10. How does the fashion director help buyers with developing imports?

Workshop

Assume you have been to Europe and discover a new fashion idea. Describe what you have found and how you would go about introducing it into the U.S. market.

(Elyse Rieder)

8

SOURCES OF ADVANCED FASHION INFORMATION

A fashion director has a world of unseen friends. They are scattered everywhere. Some are known personally, some are never met. Nevertheless, the director receives constant communications from these friends, who are dedicated to helping the director keep on top of every aspect of current or coming fashion trends.

These remarkable fountains of valuable information flow from such sources as national fashion magazines, trade publications, fiber companies, industry associations, leather industry, shoe industry, and cosmetic companies, most of which are unsolicited but generously dependable.

Also, indispensable information flows from resident buying offices with which a store is associated, from fashion consultants whose services the store employs, and from organizations of the industry to which one may enlist membership, such as the Fashion Group, National Retail Merchants Association (NRMA), and so on. With a little help from friends such as these, in addition to the director's own organized scratching, there is very little that should escape the perceptive fashion director.

RESIDENT OFFICES

The resident office, known since its inception as the "resident buying office," was created for the purpose of up-to-the-minute direction for a business that is fast-paced and ever-changing.

Back in the days when a trip to New York meant crossing the country on a slow train, when computers did not exist, and long distance telephoning was not so common, buying offices in residence, acting in behalf of the absentee retailer, were a must. The buying office did exactly what its title indicated—buy merchandise for the member unable to make enough trips to the hub of American fashion: New York. Later, when Los Angeles and the Orient developed, the buying office represented the retailer in these markets as well.

With the advent of air travel, retailers found New York closer, no matter how far they had to fly. Trips became more frequent until now, most buyers, merchandisers, and fashion directors are in New York almost every month, sometimes twice a month. They also make their own trips to Los Angeles and the Orient or any other part of the world that fashion dictates.

Why, then, do most notable retailers still maintain resident offices? There are several reasons.

Why Stores Belong

Even though the role of the resident office has changed in recent years, it is still a very necessary arm for the retail business. In a business that is highly diversified and plagued with constant change as retailing is, membership in an effective resident office, staffed with top professionals in their field, is a must for the progressive merchant.

While the services and purposes of a resident office are many, the most universal advantages include:

1. Thorough fashion direction from people who are close to the scene every day.
2. An opportunity for all member stores to exchange information, ideas, experiences, and plans.
3. An opportunity to share figures.
4. A chance to learn what items or trends are doing well in other member stores.
5. A way to save buyers endless leg work. The resident office staff, through advanced market research, edits the available resources. (e.g., A resident staffer might tell a sportswear buyer, "Out of these hundreds of sportswear resources, this group is not worth your time, this group is good but not for your store, but these you must visit.")
6. A system of keeping pace with departmental structures that are subject to revisions as a result of the changing fashion trends.
7. An opportunity for combined buying power.
8. The advantage of having buying office branches in foreign markets.

The sharing of ideas, plans, and figures is not a problem with stores regarding competition with a resident office membership, because each group usually represents only one store in any major market area.

Types of Resident Offices

Some offices are store owned (AMC—Associated Merchandising Corporation); some are corporations that own their stores (ADG—Associated Dry Goods); some are privately owned (Felix Lilienthal, Inc.); some family owned (IRS—Independent Retailers Syndicate), and some are extensions of giant operations (chains such as Macy's Corporate Buying Division, Sears Roebuck & Co., J. C. Penney & Co., and Montgomery Ward & Co.)

In their updated roles they regard themselves as merchandising and research organizations or retail consulting firms. Whatever they regard themselves, the actual services rendered depend on the kind of operation served. However, the stores are provided with indispensable support systems through the resident office's research departments that issue a steady flow of directives on the newest of everything pertinent to the store member's business.

Resident offices specializing in service to department stores are separate from those servicing specialty stores. There is even a resident office available for retailers in the large-size fashion business for women. Each kind of business has its own set of problems and goals and each requires specialized, professional service.

Some buying offices maintain facilities on both coasts—New York and California—to service their members in both markets. Regarding imports, the existence of foreign offices are in a better position to research the world market for new developments and opportunities.

The Resident Fashion Office

A top source of fashion information should be constantly available from the fashion department of a resident office. A unique and excellent example of a most comprehensive setup for such service to the fashion directors of member stores is the Associated Merchandising Corporation.

AMC's fashion office, completed with a fashion director and divisional fashion coordinators working in concert with the merchandising staff of AMC, provides all of its stores' fashion directors with up-to-the-minute fashion information. AMC's philosophy is that disclosure of all fashion information to the store's merchandising and executive staff "should go, initially, through the store's fashion director so that

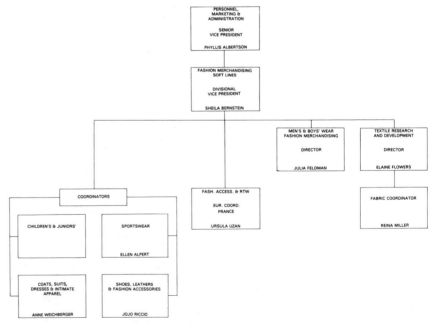

The fashion office structure of Associated Merchandising Corporation. Fashion directors of member stores may receive advice and guidance from this fashion office staff, individually or collectively.

she may decide, along with her merchandisers, what part of the fashion message will be emphasized to the customer. Any predictive ideas that may initiate with the merchandisers, need to get screened through the fashion office, where the decision will be made, in general agreement with the merchandising staff, as to the AMC position on news in fashion and the timing of its release."

Realizing that such responsibility must be fortified with accurate fashion information, a network of authoritative guidelines it provided. It is on the basis of this system that the AMC fashion office provides, immediately and in explicit detail, those vital guidelines for fashion leadership. Such guidelines come in the following forms:

Fabric Report—Issued semiannually. Forecast for spring/summer and fall/ winter. Includes swatches of complete fabric market in terms of important color families, patterns, prints, and classified textures.

Advanced Colors—Issued semiannually. Forecast for spring/summer and fall/winter. Colors presented in categories by color family and new color combinations.

Advanced Leathers—Issued semiannually. Same as colors.

Holiday Color Report—Issued annually. Color and fabric news is researched and translated by AMC's director of textile research and development. By attending the major textile fairs in Paris (Premier Vision), Como, Italy (Ideacomo) and Frankfurt, Germany (Interstoff), the forthcoming themes and trends are uncovered.

Advanced Trend Information

In addition to these, other published material comes semiannually in the form of a Paris Report, a Europe Report, and a report on American fashions (as a seasonal forecast), all supplemented and kept up to date with regular development reports on all fashion trends in all areas.

In the New York facility, where the AMC fashion office headquarters are located, the AMC fashion merchandising director or any of the divisional fashion coordinators are available by appointment for consultations. Since store members have individual offices in the same building, there is the provision of meeting rooms, board rooms, eating facilities, and, therefore, the ease of a closely knit working situation.

Whatever the structure of the buying office, the purpose is the same—to provide stores with professional advanced guidance for their activity in the market. Since the fashion office of a store is responsible for the evaluation and interpretation of the facts provided, it is the director who catalogs all the guidance from all the sources and what surfaces with great conviction becomes a go ahead for direction for a particular store. In other words, a buying office can report on the

AMC fashion staff keeps member stores informed of new developments by a constant coverage of domestic and foreign fashion markets.

market in general, but the store's own fashion director knows his or her store best—what is right for them and what is not.

FASHION CONSULTANTS

Not all stores subscribe to the services of fashion consultant firms. They feel capable of doing their own research of trends, or depend on the combination of their own fashion office and that of a resident buying office. However, those who do subscribe might use such reports as religious authority or as supplementary information.

Reports from fashion consultants, if they are used as supplementary material by the fashion director, can provide another viewpoint. A fashion director is wise to keep an open mind. The viewpoint that is different just may be the one that uncovers a sleeper.

The fashion consultant firm usually has a staff of fashion coordinators who give their full attention to a specific area in the same way that fashion coordinators in a buying office work or the divisional fashion coordinator of a store operates. Each covers a specific market, and feeds back the information necessary to contribute to the report. The fashion consultant is especially effective in dealing with specifics concerning a particular store. "This item is a natural for you." "This is not for your type of customer."

Confidential, Please

The material provided in reports from any service (including resident buying offices), is regarded as highly confidential. Subscribers, after all, are paying for an information service to help them obtain fashion leadership. If it is shared with anyone not directly responsible for its utilization, its purpose is not served. One is not in the business of educating or training one's competition.

The fashion director carefully reads the reports from the fashion consultant. The director might consult with management on certain points to obtain their reactions and compare them with her own. "This bears careful watching," they might all decide. In such a case, as in all instances of fact finding, the director will keep a sharp lookout for other references in this connection and check out everything on that specific area. The best lesson a fashion director as researcher and fact finder can learn is *never assume anything*. A director would never assume what one source says—no matter how reliable—is the only way to go. That, in essence, is the beauty of all the pieces of advice that come across the director's desk. The composite is more dependable than any single opinion. All together they help the fashion director decide: "Is the idea just a fluke? Or is this where the smart money will be going?"

FIBER COMPANIES—FABRIC COMPANIES

Very early on the scene, usually six or eight months ahead of a forthcoming season, the fiber companies announce their predictions. The fiber people release their findings sometimes a year in advance, but most fashion directors find the six-month forecast of more immediate use. The chain stores, however, along with buying offices, consultant firms, designers, mills, and converters must have predictive information much earlier. However, if a particular specialty or department store is planning on confining a special pattern or print as "our very own," it is imperative to work much further ahead. In such a case, the fashion director, along with the buyer, will be greatly involved in the research and selection of what that confined fabric look will be.

Color Cards

If advance color information is a vital issue for a long-range projected promotion or special event, the fiber and fabric people are good early sources. It may be necessary to know a year in advance if yellow will be good, and, if so, what shade of yellow will be the best choice. A review of the fiber and fabric color cards, leather chips, and predictive information from sources such as Cotton Inc. or the Wool Bureau Inc. would turn up some pretty reliable suggestions.

Whether a year in advance or six months in advance, all the color cards and releases come up with a rainbow of new and impressive names, even for standard colors. A brick color becomes Spanish Tile, Red Fox, or Hot Ginger. A blue becomes Ink, Blue Persian, or Blue Night. When the brick or the blue has a new hue that is a bit different from a season or two ago, it must also have a new name. It is all part of its "image." Some very good suggestions of what to call a new color come from releases of the leading fiber and fabric producers.

Mademoiselle once editorially identified a new color that combined tones of brown and green as "Breen." Manufacturers and retailers who had been at a loss as what to call the new color that was neither green nor brown, picked up *Mademoiselle*'s inspired idea and used "Breen" in their promotions.

The Fabric Books

Swatches of every conceivable fabric anticipated in the fashion market come in fabric booklets or charts from the fiber and fabric sources. Again, these are usually unsolicited and provided at no charge. The fabrics are identified as to trend, texture, and use. For example, a page on sheers, with swatches showing examples of chiffons, voiles, batistes, and silks, might be classified as the new "soft trend." A page might be classified as the "new nubbies," with swatches illustrating these new textures. And, as examples of uses of the fabrics, pages or groupings might point up "the new skirtings," "the new shirtings," "the new coatings," and so on. All the presentations are very comprehensively prepared for effortless reading and easy reference.

Additional Fashion Information

It would seem service enough if the fiber and fabric people saw fit to supply retailers with color and fabric forecasts alone. Surprisingly, the service does not stop there. Their printed presentations also include their version of the fashion trends in ready-to-wear silhouettes and accessories. Naturally, the total picture gives more authority to their fabric and color predictions, but it also helps to relate these predictions with the overall fashion picture.

Color slides, too, are often available for the fashion office's use, showing the predicted fabrics, colors, and fashions from resources using their ingredients. These are usually available on request for use at training meetings or fashion shows.

THE INTIMATE APPAREL INDUSTRY

The manufacturers of intimate apparel have designers who are as concerned about what is happening in fashion as any other branch of the industry. After all, if soft, sheer, or revealing fabrics are to be prevalent in a given season, the intimate apparel designers must create the correct undergarments. Whatever the fashion trends in wearing apparel must be supported with coordinating accessories, and that would also include intimate apparel.

Designers of intimate apparel are as concerned with new color stories as they are with trends; colors, too, must be fashion-right and capable of fitting into the entire new-season picture.

Fashion designers are very helpful to the intimate apparel people because without their direction, how would they be able to support a full skirt with a full petticoat, or a sheer blouse with a lace camisole?

To assist the retailer, intimate apparel vendors supply beautifully illustrated releases, showing what to wear under what. This offers not only excellent guidance for the fashion director, but for buyers and fashion sellers as well. Very often, slide presentations are available for employee or customer training. During intimate apparel market weeks, many resources invite the retailer to major fashion shows to introduce their new lines as well as to educate their customers about the look, use, and care of their products.

THE COSMETIC INDUSTRY

Helpful information comes from almost every imaginable area of the fashion world. In cosmetics beautiful and imaginative releases pour forth to keep the fashion office of a store "au courant" with the important beauty innovations. Some of the most enchanting adjectives and inspired product or color titles emerge in romantic glory from releases and forecasts of cosmetic companies and fragrance houses. New and "never-before-so-effective," "never-before-so-glamourous," "for-the-first-time-natural-beauty secrets" are announced dramatically and poetically in kits addressed to the fashion director.

It is a most worthy service. The fashion director notes that the fabric and color charts show a strong interest in new shades of warm neutrals for a coming season, and then along comes the cosmetic forecast that tells of "peaches-and-cream face for the new, warm, neutral fashions." People have done their homework. It is generally known that the leading cosmetic houses go to Paris for fashion direction, sometimes even before the couture market opens. All major cosmetics authorities seek fashion guidance from the experts to assist them in making decisions about what the new fashion face should be.

All of this is an excellent illustration of how the entire fashion industry—every part of it—coordinates its fashion direction. Such coordination makes fashion what it is. If the trend is futuristic, makeup would need to be more imaginative, perhaps stark or angular. If the soft look is in, pastels in makeup are likely to appear. If colors and textures are bright and heavy, the soft look in cosmetics would not be suitable that season. It is necessary to emphasize "that season" because what might not work one season might be just the ticket in another. At any rate, one needs to know what is being planned.

In the cosmetic forecast, along with the glowing names and inventive descriptions of new products, comes the cosmetic industry's version of the coming fashion trends, as they relate to the new "faces." If exotic fashions are expected to be important, the exotic eye might be designed. If a truly romantic, feminine fashion treatment is predicted, the exotic eye would hardly be suitable. Naturally, all cosmetic companies will not be doing the same thing, but in one way or another, the leaders will all manage to be fashionably accurate and well informed about the future fashions.

To be sure that the customer is well served, the fashion director will be as anxious to get fashion stories to the cosmetic buyer as to the dress buyer. It would be quite disturbing for the fashionable woman to buy a costume in the new rustic-red tones and be unable to find a lipstick that would match or blend. The perceptive fashion director, while scrutinizing the fashion forecasts he or she trusts, from all areas of the industry, will discover that, sure enough, if rustic-red is going to be good in ready-to-wear, there will be rustic-red tones in makeup. This revelation points out another fact for the fashion director. If the color is being picked up in many areas, there must be a great deal of confidence in it. Exposure and availability of a color throughout the fashion market makes it a good possibility for a promotional color.

In addition to color, texture plays an important part in the cosmetic fashion story. For example, the look and hand (fashion industry term for feel) of fabrics or their special use in our lifestyles influence the matte face, the shiny face, the dewy face, or the transparent face.

When sheer, transparent fashions were making the scene, see-through makeup was created to tie in. When Yves Saint Laurent presented a return to elegance, with opulent fabrics, the "velvet look" was designed. The fashion director and staff would do well to check cosmetic releases for just such fashion tie-ins.

Lifestyle also influences the cosmetic industry. When at-home fashions became very desirable, because home entertaining became more prevalent, and when just plain leisure time was being spent at home, "fragrances for the home" became big business. Everything from room and closet sprays to cold water wash for lingerie, blankets, towels, and bed linens was offered. Special fragrances were suggested to tie in with each room's decor—Early American or country (sporty or casual), Oriental (exotic), romantic (feminine).

In addition to color, textures, silhouettes, and lifestyles, the cosmetic industry supports seasonal efforts. At cruise time there are skin bronzers for tan without sun; at ski time skin moisturizers and protectors; for joggers, tender treatment for the feet.

The season, the look, the trend, and the mood are all translated by each fashion area of the industry to relate to the other.

THE CONSUMER MAGAZINES

In the process of accumulating factual material for their editorial pages, the consumer magazines have developed fashion editors and fashion departments whose reputations are synonomous with fashion authority. Even though all retailers will not agree with all magazines nor recognize the extent of their influence, there are few who will deny that as documents of record, interpreters of total fashion, and innovators of fashion presentation as an art, they are incomparable. In the area of fashion presentation as an art, they are incomparable. In the area of fashion presentation, the magazines, especially the high fashion ones, have been accused of soaring too far over the average woman's head. They have not been accused, however, of talking down to women.

It would follow, therefore, that a medium that regards fashion as something of an art form and is so articulate in glorifying its creations, would certainly be worthy of a fashion director's attention, especially when it is help they are offering.

From Whence Cometh Your Help

In their eagerness to be valuable, perhaps even indispensable, to the retailer, the consumer magazines reach out a helping hand in many forms. Choice information on advanced issues is one of them. These advanced information kits come thoroughly documented, usually with illustrations or tear sheets, along with a complete explanation of what fashion direction the issue is taking, what will be shown, who makes it, how much it is (cost and retail), what the promotional opportunities are, and suggestions for windows, displays, ads, and fashion shows.

Whether or not the fashion director is in a position to accept an offered promotion from a magazine, he or she is benefited greatly by the information passed along in the process. It is hoped, therefore, that even when the official promotion is not consummated, the fashion director can advise the customer in other ways concerning the authority or advice of a magazine. Perhaps in the commentary of a show or in a television interview the director might relate, "*Bazaar* feels so strongly about this new look they are devoting a large part of their April issue to it." Or, "*Seventeen* says this is going to be the new girl on campus. You will find this merchandise tagged 'Seen in *Seventeen*' in our junior department."

Magazine Foreign Reports

Twice each year, following the couture or pret-a-porter collections in Europe, traveling magazine editors who have been on the scene to cover the foreign import markets will share their findings and feelings about trends with retailers. Fashion directors find reports from such fashion editors a welcome plus. A Paris Report from *Bazaar* or *Mademoiselle* for example, might not only include the highlights of trends in fabrics, silhouettes, accessories, makeup, and hair fashions, but even such revealing information as preoccupations and conversation in Paris at the time regarding art, food, and health. All of this additional information provides direction of lifestyles, moods, and appetites, all of which affect fashion.

The stacks of advanced fashion information supplied by national magazines helps the fashion office of any store keep an effortless finger on the pulse of their thinking, endorsements, and interpretations. These, incorporated into other stacks of information, either underline what the director already believes or emphasize something she might have felt more or less lukewarm about before reading another point of view.

Magazine Fabric Reports

Unlike the other materials and information provided free of charge, the magazines do require a subscription fee for their color and fabric reports that are prepared twice a year for spring/summer and fall/winter.

Major fashion magazines, such as Bazaar, and Glamour provide the retail fashion director with valuable reports on fabrics and colors from the world's best sources.

In addition to retailers, buying offices and fashion consultants buy the magazine fabric books, undoubtedly to keep a close check on what all fashion people are thinking and doing.

Seasonal Seminars

Before market, most of the leading national fashion magazines that headquarter in New York send out invitations to store executives and buyers to be their guests at a seminar or predictive presentation of a forthcoming season. One magazine may make their presentation at a coffee hour in a morning session or cocktail hour in an afternoon session. Others may be held in strictly formal meetings. Usually, reservations need to be made as to which session is most convenient.

At these sessions, which usually never last more than forty-five minutes, one or two editors preside, showing color slides, films, sketches, or actual merchandise to be featured in a forthcoming issue. In addition to the visual presentation and the editor's comments, each guest is usually provided with printed resource lists advising exactly what will be incorporated in the issue, piece by piece. Each piece is identified by manufacturer, style number, and wholesale cost. In this way the magazine acts as liaison between manufacturer and retailer. The manufacturer gains additional exposure and prestigious attention while the retailer gets an opportunity to know in advance what merchandise will be featured editorially and, therefore, consider including it in their orders while in the market.

The magazine seminars also have good educational value from a "how-to" point of view. How to accessorize a new look, how to merchandise a new idea, how to combine new proportions. Thus, an important part of covering the market for the fashion director includes covering the magazines. From the magazine resource lists the director can indicate to the buyers that here is a house worth checking out, here is a style number or two they might like to consider. "It looks very good and is priced right. Let me know if you buy it, and we'll get you magazine credit."

Also, before or after the seminars, it is possible to have a consultation with a magazine editor, to discuss any questions or problems regarding their service or their promotion plans. It is not necessarily the business of the magazine to decide what will be big or important in fashion; it is their function to point up those things in which they believe and those things they regard as fashion, according to the magazine's philosophy and readership. They will tell you, however, when asked how enthusiastic they are about any given area of fashion.

Magazine Slide Presentations

Another service from the magazines is edited copies of the slide presentations they show retailers in their offices. These, too, must be purchased. For stores that do not have access to other visual fashion presentations the magazine's slides can be helpful for in-store education. Magazines sometimes produce films relating to a specific customer segment (e.g., the working woman), which also may be used as a training vehicle or at a consumer level. These films also are available for a fee.

The *Seventeen* Show

Another source of education and inspiration provided by the magazines for the industry is the major fashion production, presented at a time when large numbers of retailers are expected in New York. Because of rising costs and the adoption of other programs, most magazines have eliminated their June show, with the exception of *Seventeen*. Geared to their August issue, specifically a back-to-school edition, and the September issue of fall fashions, the show provides the audience with an insight into a season's leading fashion ideas for the young customer.

Everyone attending is provided with a detailed program that includes, in the order of appearance, a breakdown of scenes or categories and the manufacturers and style numbers represented.

If a store is interested in bringing such a show to their own store, a package is usually available for a substantial fee, for a road show version, plus a traveling fashion merchandising coordinator for a personal

Each year, Seventeen holds a June show, to acquaint retailers with new looks and trends in young fashions from their August and September issues. Pictured, a finale scene of suggested back-to-school fashions. (*Courtesy of Seventeen Magazine*)

appearance as commentator. If this is not possible, the show stimulates ideas that a store might utilize on its own.

Other Magazine Programs

Other magazines, such as *Mademoiselle* and *Glamour* have comprehensive programs, also available for a fee, for which the store will receive the services of fashion and beauty coordinators who will appear at the store to conduct fashion and makeup seminars and demonstrations. These have proved to be good traffic builders for those stores who have subscribed to such formats as *Mademoiselle*'s "On Location" or *Glamour*'s "Glamourworks."

Fashion Group Shows

Members of the Fashion Group (see Chapter 3) enjoy a wealth of professional analysis of fashion trends. One of the outstanding ways the Fashion Group of New York analyzes and interprets fashion is through an annual schedule of remarkable fashion productions: twice a year, European collections; twice a year, American collections; special shows for all other fashion divisions—fabrics, children's, sportswear, cosmetics, home furnishings. In addition to these, each year's Fashion Group calendar brings newly spotlighted fashion happenings, such as imports, art exhibits, special costume collections, and so on. If it's important, the Fashion Group will bring it to its membership's attention.

The advantage of viewing a Fashion Group show (such as the American collections show) is that you are able to see the best of the American fashion market all in one production. The image of a season, the strength of a color, the vitality of a new silhouette surfaces with emphasis when shown in several versions from top designers.

The Fashion Group's shows are usually presented at the New York Hilton's grand ballroom—one performance at breakfast and one with lunch (sometimes a third performance is added). Over 100 waiters serve an audience of 1,750 spectators at each show, dramatically presented with 30 New York models. It is an electric experience, an unmistakable strong statement for the importance of fashion as a international industry.

The Awards Show

The Coty American Fashion Critics' Award "Winnie" statuette.

The motion picture industry has its Oscars, the television industry its Emmys, the recording industry its Grammys, and fashion has its Winnies. The awards to the fashion industry are many, but one of the most coveted is the Coty American Fashion Critics' Award, founded by Coty, Inc., in late 1942. Presented each year to American designers whose work during the previous year has had a significant effect on the American way of dressing and whose creations have won the applause of the fashion press (who vote on the winners) it is regarded as highly important recognition.

From the first Coty award winner, Norman Norell in 1943, every influential name in American fashion (couture designers, leather designers, furriers, designers of lingerie, children's fashions, men's, fashion accessories, and cosmetics) have been included at one time or another in this prestigious awards night. Sometimes the awards were made at a gala black tie evening, with a highly paced fashion show, but in 1981, Coty abstained from their usual show format and made the Coty awards at a private luncheon.

An alert fashion director, whether or not attending such award shows, will consider such news-making fashion events worthy of attention. Award winners get there through great efforts and are recognized by panels of astute judges. Therefore, the special interest created for their designs from the store's and the customer's viewpoint has merit. The promotional value is obvious.

AFTERVIEW

After taking a look at the avalanche of advanced information that pours down on the fashion office, one might get the idea that making decisions about what should be incorporated into a coming season would be a snap.

Not so. Judgment is still the most important factor. A barrage of predictions could cause a bad case of confusion if the fashion director has a problem with judgment, direction, or the ability to evaluate the given facts. But a fashion person well indoctrinated with his or her own research and taste and with an awareness of consumer needs and desires can intelligently edit everything that comes into the office.

What is good for one store, one market area, is bad news in another. Although the differences are not as great today—because of the onslaught of immediate communications—lifestyles and people still differ from one community to another. Even when the differences are slight, they are enough to make one fashion look sell well, another not so well.

In a store where a fashion coordinator is new in a job (when one is new one may not yet be called a fashion director), sources of fashion information, such as those noted in this chapter, come as a blessing.

A fashion director from one of the most highly regarded fashion stores in the country interviewed for this book, exclaimed: "I would have given anything if someone had spelled out for me where to go for information or guidance, what to look for, and how to use what I found. Having it all set down, even if you are knowledgeable, is like having someone hold your hand. The touch of a dependable hand is not a bad idea. Especially in this business. Who doesn't need it?"

CHAPTER
RE-EXAMINATION

Questions

1. Why was the resident buying office system created?
2. How does the current resident office differ from the original?
3. What is the advantage of having so many diversified sources of advanced fashion information?
4. How do fashion magazines service the retailer?
5. What does the fashion director gain from Fashion Group shows? From *Seventeen* shows?
6. Why would fashion awards be of interest to the fashion director?

Workshop

Assume you are a fashion director who has heard conflicting rumblings about color stories for the coming season. One rumor indicates that bright colors will be the leading story, another that soft neutrals are number one. Show how you would check out which way to go, what your final decision would be, and how you would justify your findings to management.

A storewide country and western fashion promotion can be reinforced with a shop concept such as the one shown here. *(Ken Karp)*

9

PLANNING FASHION PROMOTIONS

The fashion director, highly responsible for the fashion content of the store, is also responsible for helping to promote it. Of course, every major store has a highly skilled creative team whose specific job it is to promote what the store has for sale, but they do it with valuable input from the fashion director, who, very often is included as an indispensable member of that team.

THE CREATIVE TEAM

Headed by the sales-promotion director, the creative team includes the advertising director, visual presentation director, special events director, and publicity director. The orchestration of these creative specialists makes it possible for the customer to relate to newspaper ads, catalogs, radio and television commercials, store windows, interior displays, shops, and special events that all work in concert to bring forth a clear, exciting, comprehensively told fashion story. It is the well-blended harmony of all areas of the advertising media (sometimes called "beating the drums") plus visual presentations in the stores that make fashion happen.

From the birth of a fashion promotion idea to its planning and execution, the fashion director has a great deal to offer. Although the fashion office is not involved in sale promotions (clearance sales, special purchases sales, and so on), fashion promotions that enhance the store's good fashion and quality image have a better chance for continued acceptance of merchandise on a day-to-day basis and even after it has been marked down. In other words, the spin-off of effective fashion promotions is considerable.

What the Fashion Promotion Does

Fashion promotions help build acceptance. Since most retailers of a comparable type in a community will, sooner or later, have merchandise of a similar nature, what would be the reason for a customer to shop at one store over another? Realistically, there are several contributing factors—location, ambience, service—but the first and foremost influence (assuming that prices are comparable) would be the magnetic fashion promotions that create a strong, irresistible appetite for whatever is being touted.

A fashion promotion cannot mean simply that just because some new merchandise has arrived it is time to run an ad. Running an ad is running an ad. But running a fashion promotion is backing up that ad with exciting displays, sales training, and perhaps even a special shop concept. True, not every fashion statement deserves that kind of attention, but the ones that do should be utilized to the fullest extent.

The Campaign

To promote fashion with impact, the technique of pulling the season's stories or even a major fashion story under a single theme or "umbrella," with all aspects of the promotion corresponding to that theme—ads, radio, television, displays, shops, and special events—that is a promotion. That is a campaign. And that is what we are concerned with here first—the fashion promotion that really "beats the drums" to build traffic.

How Fashion Promotions Are Selected

Selecting and developing an effective fashion promotion is one of the special thrills of the retail fashion director. Here creativity can blossom. All the director's groundwork—the research, the recommendations, presentations, and time and action calendar plans—is on the threshold of coming to life. When the racks and counters and cases are filled with those things the fashion director said were good fashion, and when the advertising campaign announces to the customer "It's here!," the great reward is to see those things "barreling out of the door" because customers are responding with "I'll take that."

Fashion promotions come from at least three different directions. Some are automatic, some are offered, and the major efforts are created. For example:

CREATED

New trends
New colors
New fabrics
New products
New departments
New shops

OFFERED

Vendor co-op promotions (resource that splits or contributes to the ad cost)
Fiber companies, fabric mills, ingredient institutes (wool, cotton, etc.), co-op promotions

AUTOMATIC

Holidays—Valentine's Day (see Chapter 2), Mother's Day, Father's Day, etc.

Seasons—Back-to-school, spring, summer, fall, holiday, etc.

The automatic promotions literally write themselves into the promotion calendar and very often serve as an additional slot to promote those listed under *created* promotions.

The *offered* promotions are of special interest to the fashion director. If what the vendor or fabric or fiber company offers is in line with those promotional ideas that the store will be "creating" during a given season, then the offer would be encouraged by the fashion office. If it is completely contrary to the fashion plan, then the offer might better be passed up. It is very tempting for a store to accept a promotion that offers co-op money (i.e., money offered by a supplier to help pay a part of the advertising campaign expense to encourage the promotion of their product). However, even very large stores can handle only a certain number of promotions per season, and being selective is part of presenting the best fashion image and at the same time producing the best sales results. The day is gone, at least at this writing, when dear dollars, whether they be the store's, the vendor's, or the fiber or fabric company's, can be delegated for anything that is not directly related to selling.

The promotions that are *created* or tailor-made for the store's needs and season's specific fashion trends are the biggest responsibility of the fashion director. It is this type of promotion that depends on the fashion director's recommendations.

The fashion director reported that the return of pant dressing was strong; the great alternatives available in the market testified that this was true. The director claimed that the romantic look was highly promotable and the market supported this belief with great selections. The director urged a new approach to classic dressing and the buyers, equally enthusiastic, brought it in with conviction.

The new season is coming. The new merchandise is coming. Promotion-planning time, scheduled far enough in advance, now translates into promotion-action time.

The Retail Calendar

The retail year is divided into four selling periods, each called a quarter. The breakdown is based, of course, on seasonal selling and merchandise is stocked accordingly. The four quarters are:

First Quarter:	February—March—April	(Spring)
Second Quarter:	May—June—July	(Summer)
Third Quarter:	August—September—October	(Fall)
Fourth Quarter:	November—December—January	(Holiday/ Early Spring)

All fashion plans are tied into the four quarters, but the appearance of certain merchandise crosses over the boundaries all the same. For example, testing of summer merchandise might appear in the store in March; testing of spring merchandise might show up in December. It depends on the trend and availability of merchandise. Early testing is very important, as indicated earlier, but the periods of peak selling for a season always appear within the quarter.

THE TIME AND ACTION FASHION CALENDAR

If the calendar in question is for the spring season, the fashion director would provide the merchandising team with a proposed Time and Action Calendar as early as the preceding September or October. The calendar would designate the exact fashion trends available for promotion, the timing for promoting each, what it is to be called, how it is to be signed, what color, fabrics and accessories are to be featured.

For example:

SPRING/SUMMER FASHION PLAN
TIME/ACTION CALENDAR

Timing:	April 13–May 3
Theme:	THE ROMANTICS
Defined:	Feminine, soft, romantic—a delicate, demure, almost Victorian expression. Lingerie touches.
Key items:	Feminine blouses (ruffles, lace, pin tucks).
	Graceful yokes, dimpled or puff sleeves.
	Flounced, tiered, soft skirts.
	Lacey sweaters.
	Soft dresses (blouson, tiered)
	Romantic separates (pants, camisoles, soft jackets).
Colors:	White.
	Sun-washed pales—coral, blue, pink, aqua, sand.
Patterns:	Romantic prints (roses, petite florals)
	Embroidery.
Fabrics:	Voile, organza, georgette, lace, batiste, linen.
Accessories:	Lalique feelings in jewelry. Pearls, cameos, bows, flowers.
	Shoes—ballerina flats, strippy sandals.
	Hosiery—pale colored, sheer.
Signing:	A LITTLE ROMANCE
Special events this period:	A flower show

Notice that the timing allows a three-week period for promotion of "The Romantics" trend. With everything clearly spelled out, the display department will know what kind of merchandise to put on all the appropriate store mannequins, what kind of windows to create to reinforce the romantic theme. (See Chapter 10.) The signing in the stores and the terminology in the supporting advertising are verly likely to be similar if not exactly the same. So that the customer clearly gets the message and is fully aware of the fashion statement being made, when she reads or sees that there is "A Little Romance" awaiting her in the store's fashion departments, the theme's title should be repeated in all media.

Following this three-week period, all displays, mannequins, windows, signing, ads, television spots, and so on, would be changed to follow the direction of the next trend to be promoted, as indicated on the Time/Action Calendar for the season's fashion plan. Thus the entire season is put together, with one trend getting the spotlight after another, featured, of course, during the time segment most appropriate for that type of merchandise to be in the stores.

HOW TO WORK WITH THE SALES-PROMOTION DIRECTOR

The sales-promotion director is responsible for selling the store and the merchandise in it. Working with the merchandising staff and the fashion director, it is the sales-promotion director's responsibility to pull all the facets of a promotion together and supervise its execution.

At meetings with the GMM, DMMs, and the fashion director, decisions are made as to which promotions take precedent over others, which will get the big treatment, and which the small. Some will go storewide, some divisional, some departmental.

At an initial planning meeting, called by the sales-promotion director to get the promotion plan into the hopper, everyone involved makes a contribution. The GMM endorses what the fashion director has offered, the DMMs offer their acceptance or rejection of what is proposed, and the go-ahead is given.

Next, the sales-promotion director calls in his or her own team—the advertising director, visual presentation director, publicity and/or special events director—and together with the fashion director the action starts.

For example, the fashion promotion in question is a country-western look. Everyone present has a copy of the fashion director's seasonal directive—the Time/Action Calendar. It tells them almost everything they need to know, but further discussion with the fashion director might be in order.

"In which departments will this trend be stocked?" the sales-promotion director might ask.

"All divisions' sportswear areas," the fashion director answers. "We will be carrying the look in some form or other in women's, men's, children's, and junior departments." This indicates that the promotion will be storewide. They decide on giving it the big treatment.

To the advertising director this means that a series of ads will be necessary to cover the story, undoubtedly separate ads for each division, but presented under a single theme. To the visual presentation director it means that decor throughout the apparel divisions must tie together with the promotion theme. Wheels start turning in the heads of the publicity director and special events director. What kind of excitement can they drum up to stimulate traffic and what kind of editorial coverage can be obtained?

But first a word from the fashion director, at the request of the sales-promotion director. "The look is predominantly urban cowboy-cowgirl yet there is a lot of beautiful American Indian influence with Indian motifs and beading and fringe. It is very spirited. In juniors and young men's departments you will find it more costumey. In misses areas (women) it is mostly an influence, a suggestion, in fabric, patterns, and trimmings. In children's it's all fun and comfort and amusing. Little cowhands. Little country girls. It's pure Americana."

From what the fashion director has said, everyone present gets the idea that the promotion must be handled in an easy, lighthearted manner.

"Exactly," the fashion director agrees. "It should be all cooked up country-style."

That's it. The theme's handle or banner phrase has surfaced. "Make Mine Country." "The New Fashion Frontier." "Best of the West." One idea triggers another. Eventually the creative team will make a final decision as to which one looks best in print or can best support their visual display plans.

The whole promotion, it is decided, will be very folksy. The approach must be unpretentious, cozy, and friendly. Everyone is caught up in the excitement now. Enthusiasm projects from all sides of the room.

"Maybe we should have some live country music on the opening day of the promotion. Maybe country rock."

"Maybe a square dance in the parking lot."

"What would you think of bringing in a country music star?"

And so it goes. The fashion director watches in all directions to be sure that everything from the title of the theme to the interpretation is in keeping with the fashion look. It is the director's job to see that the terminology in ads and signs and the decor in display tell the fashion story accurately. The sales-promotion director will note all suggestions and contributions offered in the meeting and later draw up a finalized promotion plan that assigns everyone his or her responsibility. The sales-promotion director will request the fashion director to review all fashion aspects of the promotion to be certain that the fashion theme rings true and does not get lost or misinterpreted along the way. The fashion director will meet with the fashion office staff and delegate their assignments.

The divisional (or area) coordinators will be responsible for all details in their area, and the display coordinators will be given explicit details of the plan. The fashion director will schedule a "fashion show of country folks" to tie in with the appearance of the celebrity to be brought in as well as coordinate informal modeling in the restaurant areas of the store during peak lunchtime hours. The fashion director will also communicate with the buyers to select exactly those fashion pieces that are to be put on the mannequins and in windows during this period. The director will also select merchandise to be modeled in the television commercials.

All this is why the fashion director was in the market with the buyers. The director saw what the buyers selected, knows what will be coming in, and knows what can be counted on for windows, ads, interior displays, television, and shows. The promotion, completely coordinated, is put into production.

The Storewide Promotion

We just sat in on a storewide fashion promotion that included all ready-to-wear divisions. Although this may be considered storewide in most companies, others, who are strong into hard lines as well as soft lines, would consider this a ready-to-wear promotion only. Another store, interested in including all aspects of their business, would make every floor of the store reflect a single promotion. For example, a color story could be embraced for total store exposure. Assume that it was a season presenting a new palette of bright colorations. The sales-promotion director together with the fashion director decide to display the store with "Bright Ideas." All mannequins would show fashions in the new bright colors, but in the home division "Bright Ideas" might represent bright colors and/or innovative decorative suggestions.

The Import Promotion

Another exciting direction the storewide promotion can take involves an import event. If one cannot travel around the world, a good substitute is a trip to the local department store, where collections of wares are brought in from exotic places to bring variety and intrigue to shopping trips.

The annual fortnight event at Neiman-Marcus, Dallas, featuring a different country every year, is indicative of how an inspired thematic approach can cover a store, from art to gifts to food to ready-to-wear. When interest in China and Chinese goods came to the attention of the American retailer, storewide promotions were a natural. Bloomingdale's of New York, the first to successfully offer its customers a chance to buy Chinese goods in a major way, was much in the news with this promotion. Carson Pirie Scott of Chicago had a "China and Other Oriental Expressions" promotion that was a major campaign to create excitement in their stores, tying everything, right down to the shopping bag, into the theme.

How an Import Promotion Is Created. When Bloomingdale's noted that fashion was requiring quality fabrics and customers were showing an appreciation for items such as handknits, they determined that a full-scale five-week, chainwide promotion on Irish merchandise was in order.

After a year-long effort and one hundred trips to Ireland, working with Irish designers, manufacturers, weavers, and craftspeople, plus having things made with Irish fabrics by American and European designers, "Ireland, That Special Place" was ready for Bloomingdale's shoppers.

In specially designed shops, some looking like Irish castles, some

View of Neiman-Marcus furniture area during their storewide import promotion called Fortnight-Orientations. *(Courtesy of Neiman-Marcus)*

with thatched roofs, Irish merchandise (much of it exclusive and developed by Bloomingdale's) included apparel and accessories for men, women, and children, cosmetics, fragrances, home furnishings, and food. Totaling over five million dollars, the Irish import fair was launched at Bloomingdale's New York flagship store with a black-tie gala.

Such a promotion contributes enormously to a store's leadership image.

The Automatic Promotions

National holidays, new seasons, annual civic events, all become routine for major exposure by the retailer. In fact, the general public literally expects the store to embellish a holiday with inspired interpretations in decor, merchandise, and entertainment. They can take their cue from the store as to when it is time to shop for a holiday, get ready for a new season, or plan for an upcoming important special event. The store is the first to tell when it is time to think of Christmas, time for back-to-school, time for the cotillion ball. These are automatic promotional vehicles because they happen every year.

The Co-op Promotions

The promotion that is "offered" to a retailer with a co-op tie-in is very instrumental in getting over a fashion idea that is benefical to the supplying company as well as the retailer.

An example is a promotion offered by companies such as Du Pont, Celanese, Milliken, or Monsanto. The idea usually originates with the company who makes a presentation to the retailer. With a completely organized campaign, including suggestions for ads, broadcast copy, visual aids for display, the company's representatives spell out how the special promotion should work and what the available resources are, establishes the timing, and even offers to provide special training sessions for store personnel involved.

What the Fashion Director Contributes

If the co-op promotion is fashion-related, the fashion director is in charge of those things that fall under the fashion office's jurisdiction. For example, from the list of available resources provided by the fiber company proposing the promotion, the fashion director can check those the store uses, work with the buyers on which numbers will be purchased, and see that the store is covered with merchandise of the right kind to back up the effort.

If the event transcends one division to another, the fashion director gets involved in a coordinating situation. If it is a storewide promotion, the director would call all coordinators together to unite their plans.

Let us assume it is a Celanese promotion. Each coordinator would check the resource list of their division to see which contained Celanese fibers. Celanese would advise each division what resources are available for their products. The home furnishings coordinator, guided by Celanese and his or her DMM, might project that division's fashion story by creating model rooms containing fabrics made from the promoted fibers. The coordinator may also do a fashion window, dramatizing the synthetic fibers with carpets, drapes, and furniture. The coordinator would select pieces to be illustrated in the newspaper ads and those items to be used on television.

The fashion director of the ready-to-wear area would meet with the home furnishings fashion coordinator to learn what the coordinator is doing. The director would then make a list of things that would support what the home furnishings coordinator has planned and thereby enhance the entire promotion. The director might

1. Put a live model or a display mannequin wearing Celanese loungewear in the model bedroom on the home furnishings floor.
2. Place such a display mannequin in the home furnishings window.
3. Arrange a special Celanese fashion show.
4. Select and coordinate Celanese fashions that the buyers and DMMs wish included in newspaper ads, TV, and display.

If the fiber company in question does not provide a sales training seminar, it may be a task assigned to the fashion office. The fashion director would schedule the meeting, inviting the fiber people to participate. After all, they know their product best—especially the specific selling points that need to be shared with the fashion sellers. The fashion director might provide models to show the pieces that will be featured in the promotion, advising the group about the performance of the fabrics and how to care for the garments.

All is in readiness. The right goods are in the departments to back up the promotion. The in-store areas have been decorated, signed, and displayed to tell the customer about what is going on. A bank of windows has been devoted to the event. The ads, illustrating merchandise selected and accessorized by the fashion office, are scheduled. Radio and TV spots are scheduled. The sales-promotion director has arranged for publicity in the local press (if there is a newsworthy story). The fashion sellers have been educated. The storewide co-op promotion selling Celanese fashion is under way.

**The
Fashion-Inspired
Storewide Promotion**

Some of the most exciting storewide promotions originate in the fashion office. This type of fashion exposure is most important to the store, because it is tailor-made, self-styled, and relates immediately to what the store has to sell. If the GMM and sales-promotion director are in sympathy with the idea, very likely it will get the big treatment.

Take, for example, a spring season that reveals a newly expressed interest in ethnic-inspired fashion. About every decade, and sometimes sooner, there is a resurgeance of some kind of ethnic-type fashion incorporated into a fashion season. Sometimes it is costumey, but for the eighties it appeared more as a salute to our countries of origin, refined, reflective, more as an influence than authentic. On the basis of this, more salable selections were available for all ready-to-wear departments.

If it is big enough to warrant it, the fashion director may advise a major treatment. It is agreed. Men's, women's, and children's ready-to-wear divisions, and, of course, the accessory division are scheduled to fill the store with "Pleasant Peasants," or "Nouveau Natives."

The sales-promotion director, enthusiastic about the idea, arranges to bring in some artisans who will make handcrafted jewelry and accessory pieces. They would be located near the related accessory areas and focus on fascinating skills while customers watch. The sales-promotion director might also bring in a collection of folklore art for a limited presentation. Or, some folkloric dancers. An arrangement might be made with the restaurant areas of the store to feature a different ethnic menu each day during the promotion.

The fashion director's responsibility is, again, to advise the buyers on what the new ethnic influence is in their particular markets, to set the timing for the promotion, and to see that merchandise is scheduled to be in stock at that time. The fashion director would coordinate all fashion aspects of the promotion—the shows, ads, displays, windows, and commercials. The director will instruct the fashion office, advertising, display, and fashion sellers on the new way to accessorize the looks. The director sees to it that everyone knows what the fashion message is and what merchandise is involved.

A fashion promotion of this type is a busy time for all members of the fashion office as they make sure that their departments have the correct look and that the racks of merchandise being featured are brought forward, It is during such promotions that subordinates in the fashion office, in need of learning the ropes, can latch on to an assignment, no matter how small, and discover something about their aptitude. Every event produces a new wrinkle. Even if the beginner is only typing up a bulletin or directive of procedure for the promotion, he or she can take notice of the words being typed and observe later as it all unravels—how it started, how it developed, how it all turned out.

Departmental Promotions

The promotion that concentrates on a specific fashion department is the one most dear to the heart of the buyer involved. The enthusiasm the buyer exudes is a joy to behold. If there is ever a time for the fashion director and buyer to be buddy-buddy, this is it.

The idea for the promotion might come from the buyer, the DMM, or the fashion director. The DMM may have requested a fashion promotion in a given department, wanting to see more action, or wishing to promote a new collection, a new designer, or a new shop concept. The buyer may have originated the idea through associations in the market. A designer or fashion celebrity may have offered to come to the store during a tour around the country.

The fashion director, whose job it is to keep a steady fire burning under the store's fashion pot to be sure that something is always cooking to perpetuate or stimulate the store's fashion position, might offer to create a special fanfare for a departmental fashion promotion.

The director would talk with the buyer first. "If we can get everybody's blessing, how would you feel about our doing a fashion promotion with your merchandise exclusively? Your department could give us the kind of leadership we need for the looks we'll be trying to promote." The conversation might have been prompted by the fashions they both saw in the market earlier, or it may have come about at the prospect of a new shop opening or a new trend that is unique to that department. If the buyer is in accord, the fashion director might submit the idea, either verbally at a forthcoming promotion meeting or in writing to obtain the necessary "blessing."

To: General Merchandise Manager
           Divisional Merchandise Manager
           Sales-Promotion Director   cc: Buyer
From: Fashion Director
Subject: Fashion promotion
           Designer shop only

This shop is new. We feel that a lot of beating of the drums will be necessary to attract the right customer. We submit to you the following promotion plan for your consideration:

1. A grand-opening kind of event in early September—such as a continental breakfast and formal fashion show, by invitation only. The event would be in our number one "A" store only.
2. Informal modeling every day for a week in the department, publicized by signs throughout the store and a newspaper ad.
3. Personal appearances of attention-getting young designers with their collections. Extend some type of hospitality (coffee, tea,

etc.) to customers for a sit-down formal show followed by informal modeling the balance of the day the designer is in the department. These might begin late August and continue through September.

I have discussed this with Mrs. Buyer and she is eager for our help. She is willing to contact whomever necessary to get the right designer into the department to help push the pieces and collections she is buying. We anxiously await your prompt opinion regarding the above. Any suggestions or amendments you can offer will be greatly appreciated, but I strongly feel we must get the consumer as excited about this new department and our new fashion direction as we are.

Timing Is Everything

Timing, one of the vital three magic words in a fashion director's life (see Chapter 2), is everything in the business of planning fashion promotions. All promotion ideas must be dreamed up and submitted for consideration far in advance of execution day. If the plan for a storewide promotion is due for execution in August, it should be in the making in May. If a divisional spring plan is under consideration for March, January is not too early to start. Two to three months ahead, for an important divisional promotion, should be the minimum time allotted for preparation, four to six months for storewide promotions.

It cannot be repeated too often, however, that if a strong and unforeseen trend climbs up, all conditions for latching on must be go. Flexibility, another magic word, is indispensable to meet the unexpected and is part of the fashion director's challenge. Rigidity, or jealously guarded, neat little plans cannot coexist with the unpredictable nature of fashion; neither can they coexist in the nature of the fashion director. Flexibility is a must.

As stated, storewide promotion plans are usually projected about four to six months in advance. This long-range plan, of course, would include all types of promotions (special events, fashion promotions, volume promotions, and sales) for all divisions. It is into this major plan, established to be elastic, that special, indispensable, and unanticipated promotions are interwoven.

Approval of the Fashion Promotion

When management examines the merits of a proposed promotion, they need to read concise, uncluttered information that gets right to the point.

1. How much business is the event expected to generate.
2. What will it cost to produce and advertise.

For the answer to the first point, the fashion director can get the figures from the buyer or divisional merchandise manager. For the second answer the director can consult with the special events director, who can provide estimates for all costs. What will surface will be a budget that should balance with the projected results.

When approval of the promotional idea comes through, there would be a need, of course, for further budget meetings to determine how much is to be spent for food, show production, music, flowers, and so on. It would also be necessary to meet with all personnel who would be involved in expediting the event. The results of the meetings would be put into writing, perhaps in the form of a responsibility sheet.

Purpose of the Responsibility Sheet

A good responsibility or work sheet, designed to record the details of a promotion, makes life more pleasant for everyone concerned. Again, brevity is the key, but above all—ASSUME NOTHING. Therein lies the secret of having all bases covered without a hitch. A fashion director, like a good teacher, would do well to place these words, big and bold, in full view of everyone in the office. Assume nothing, then nothing is likely to be overlooked. To assume that the printer knows when to have the invitations printed and delivered (He can see the date of the event on the copy, can't he?) is unfair. To assume that every model knows there will be two performances of the show instead of one (We usually do it that way, don't we?) is a grave mistake. Spell it out in delicious detail. It saves such a lot of grief later.

Drafting the Responsibility Sheet

Every promotion is different. A responsibility sheet, directive, or work sheet (whatever one wishes to call it) is a tailor-made document advising everyone involved about what is needed and what is expected.

Continuing with the departmental promotion for the designer shop as the example, each idea on the approved promotion will have a separate responsibility sheet. The following is for the first event, the grand-opening breakfast and fashion show. Copies of the following, sent out from the fashion office, will go to all executives mentioned, plus the GMM, DMM, sales-promotion director, publicity director, and everyone in the fashion office.

After all concerned have their assignments, one person in the fashion office, usually the fashion director's secretary (a good training spot for a would-be coordinator), draws up a checklist and follows through, right up to show time, to be sure every objective has been accomplished.

FASHION OFFICE RESPONSIBILITY SHEET

Event: Sit-down breakfast and Fashion Show
For: Designer Shop Grand Opening
Date: Wednesday, September 3
Time: 10:00 a.m.
Place: Special Events Auditorium—Crossroads Store

Name	*Responsibility*	*Please Note*
Special Events Director	Please reserve Special Events Auditorium for Sept. 3, plus day before for set-up.	
Special Events Director	Please book a music group as background Something light and easy; remember this is breakfast. The fashion look will be elegant and casual.	Music needed for 10:00 a.m. to 1 p.m. Walk-in and walk-out music, plus the show.
Advertising Director	Copy for invitations on attached requisition. 1,000 needed.	Invitations must be printed and mailed not later than Monday, August 15.
Advertising Director	There will be no ad. This one is invitation only.	
Buyer Designer Shop	Please have your special mailing list compiled and ready for addressing August 15.	
Buyer Designer Shop	Please assign someone in your Dept. to accept reservations beginning August 21.	Invitations will be mailed August 19 and 20.
Director of Food Service	Menu attached, per our conversation. Serve at 10:00 a.m.	Reservations expected: Approx. 250–300. A final count will be provided by the designer shop. Contact Buyer or assistant
Supervisor of Porters	Tables and chairs for approx. 250–300 people.	Seat 4 at card tables, 6 at round tables. Final count will come to you from Director of Food Service.
Manager of Flower Shop	Centerpieces for approx. 30 tables of 4, and 30 tables of 6. Color scheme will be autumn orange, gold, and brown.	A final count will be provided by Director of Food Service.

FASHION OFFICE RESPONSIBILITY SHEET (cont.)

Name	Responsibility	Please Note
Display Director	The ramp set up in T-shape as discussed. The set design you suggested will be great, but keep to soft earth tones. We need the colors of the clothes to project without competition.	If more reservations come in than expected, it may be necessary to take out one section of ramp to make room for more tables. Will advise.
Fashion Show Coordinator	Show time is 10:45 a.m. immediately following breakfast, Show approx. 30 to 40 pieces. Select from designer shop only. Use all designers.*	Please discuss with me which models to book, fitting dates, and rehearsal time. *For this show we are not interested in promoting specific collections but the total fashion picture of a new department.

The Item Promotion

To create excitement for the fragrance, Epris, Jacyln Smith made a personal appearance at Macy's New York. (*Courtesy of Macy's New York*)

We have examined illustrations of the storewide, divisional, and departmental promotion. One more vital promotional avenue is still available to help get the fashion story to the customer. The item promotion. The individual item, important enough and hot enough to merit attention on its own, might show up in a single department or embrace an entire division, maybe even more than one division.

The item promotion may focus on a single silhouette, label, concept, or classification. Although it may enjoy an easy-come easy-go appearance on the fashion scene (something that the retailer may get into and out of in short order), nevertheless, when it is showing up big and strongly acceptable, an item promotion is in order.

One example involves the separate jacket. It is a season when all sportswear departments—both misses and junior—are offering the customer who is interested in separates dressing a jacket that can be worn in combination with a multitude of tops and bottoms. Even the dress department is being provided by dress resources with a separate jacket that can be coordinated with a number of dress silhouettes. In other words, the separate jacket need not match the component parts and can slip over all kinds of fashion pieces.

Let us assume that it is a time of economic crunch, a time when the working woman is faced with a lot of competition for her disposable income. She is inclined to purchase those things that offer considerable versatility. All signs indicate that the separate jacket fills a real need for that consumer. Therefore, the fashion director advises management that the fashion market has responded to this consumer need and that great variety of choices are available in all feminine markets and at all price points, from designer to budget. It is agreed that the separate jacket is, indeed, a promotable item.

How to Merchandise an Item Promotion

Management gives the fashion director the go-ahead for the item promotion for the separate jackct. First, she decides the best target date for the promotion. Next, she informs all concerned divisionals and their buyers of the plan and target date. Next, when in the market each buyer involved might be requested to bring to the office a sample of the jackets being considered. When all samples are hung side by side it would be easy to see if there was enough variety in silhouettes, colors, fabrics, and patterns. This system as spelled out earlier in the text (The Styleout, Chapter 7) affords everyone on the merchandising team the opportunity to see if any voids or duplications exist.

Following this, the buyers would provide the fashion director with specifics as to what is actually purchased, how many units, and for which stores. Through this system the director and management will see at a glance to what extent the promotion will be backed up.

Now comes planning the overall theme for signing and advertising, the decision of whether or not to "shop" the promotion (pull the separate jackets into a shop concept), and educating display on how the separate jacket should be presented visually in the stores and in windows.

From what is coming in for the jacket promotion, the fashion director with help from the buyers can have specific examples flown in ahead of the arrival of the first receipts (merchandise in stock) to be sketched or photographed for ads and/or television commercial shootings. The director would undoubtedly pick a variety of styles to give the customer an accurate picture of the scope of the item and would also represent a variety of preferences for different customer types. An item could be promoted very effectively with a double-truck newspaper ad—two full facing pages.

To further unite this effort, the fashion director and coordinators would pull specific pieces for the display directors, to illustrate in the stores what the customer saw advertised.

Continuity. We cannot repeat too much the need for continuity. When the ad breaks, and/or television commercials are viewed, the customer must be able to come into the store and see the fashion statement visually made wherever that separate jacket is housed. It reinforces her confidence to observe exactly how this separate garment works with other pieces. It is entirely possible that on seeing a handsome illustration of what goes with that jacket she will buy all the component pieces she sees on the mannequin.

Going one step further—and a very important step—a T-stand with a jacket statement should be placed wherever possible near every mannequin displaying the jacket story.

Certainly, if any fashion shows are scheduled for this time, the separate jacket can be presented in numerous ways to show the customer the merits of such a purchase.

All put together (in displays, windows, ads, TV commercials, and fashion shows), the customer can see the item expressed effectively and with authority. There can be no doubt in her mind that this fashion item is important. She gets the message. And well-planned promotion did it.

DIVISION-PLUS-DIVISION PROMOTION

Let us assume that the season's leading color is a berry-red. It is dominant in ready-to-wear, at all price ranges, and in accessories. Reacting to the dominant color palette, the cosmetic industry developed supporting berry-red colors in makeup. The tie-in is a natural. Displays, introducing the cosmetics' delicious "berries," reflected mannequins dressed in berry-red fashions in a setting with baskets of berries, plus samples of products (berry lipsticks, cheek color, blushers) nestled in the baskets. The signs reading "It's Berry Picking Time" capture the imagination of the shopper.

It is not likely that the related fashion statement would have been made if the fashion director had not contacted both divisions, advising them of the opportunity. The director might even have suggested the technique of tying the two areas together. In any case, the director would have followed through on the concept, making sure it was all developed into a viable fashion statement.

Divisions lap over beautifully from time to time when important designers lend their name and talent to a field other than their original one. For example, when fashion designers Yves Saint Laurent, Pierre Cardin, Oscar de la Renta, and Geoffrey Beene created designer collections of linens and towels, stores who carried other merchandise by these designers could, if they chose, do a tie-in promotion to show their customers to what extent they are a designer store. With or without an ad, displays could include the designer's fragrances, their scarves, their belts, their luggage. Many stores carry a designer's accessories even though they may not carry the designer's couture or ready-to-wear fashions.

Chanel, by the way, was the first haute couture designer to come up with a personalized fragrance bearing her name. Before this, perfumes were available only from perfume houses. This innovation started a trend with big name designers everywhere. One can buy a fragrance, scarf, towel, belt, jewelry, shoe, luggage, men's, women's, and children's fashions, lounge or sleepwear, even chocolates—all bearing the same famous designer's name or signature. Thus division-plus-division promotional tie-ins are always available. The fashion office, usually aware of a leading sportswear designer coming out with a new line of coordinating accessories, alerts the divisionals of the availability and, if the line is purchased, helps pull the two divisions together for promotion purposes.

Does the Name Matter?

When Liz Claiborne, a leading American sportswear designer, created a line of accessories, the fashion director could advise the accessory buyer or division about the amount of investment the store would be making in Claiborne sportswear. The sizable investment tells the accessory division that the store has a solid Claiborne customer and, yes, it is possible that the accessories would be meaningful if the right silhouettes were available.

PROMOTIONS FOR SPECIAL CUSTOMERS

To intensify the importance of its Liz Claiborne collection, Macy's New York provided its customers with a personal appearance of this American designer. *(Courtesy of Macy's New York)*

Certain customer types are best serviced through promotions that are designed especially for their needs. Just as bridal events are traditionally held to bring together those features that are specifically of interest to the bride-to-be and her family, so it is with other customer blocks, such as working women, petite sizes, or full-figured women, to name a few.

Let us take a look at the promotional value of relating to the full-figured woman. Because she has certain figure problems and cannot be fit with regular-size merchandise, she has been given a department of her own in ready-to-wear.

Understanding that problems of proper fit for this large-size customer does not stop with ready-to-wear, the intimate apparel industry came forward with fashion for what to wear under that ready-to-wear. Formfit Rogers, for example, with their comprehensive Cut Above program, offered these women glamour and fashion for their intimate apparel just as was enjoyed by the smaller-sized women.

To promote this service, leading fashion retailers across the country tied in with Formfit Rogers to bring their customers advice through seminars and shows. For example, Brandeis in Omaha, Nebraska, pulled ready-to-wear, intimate apparel, accessories and cosmetics together in a spring and fall fashion clinic and fashion show, with the added party touch of an ice cream social. The response by a once-neglected customer type was enormous.

Formfit Rogers, in cooperation with retailers, brought in a New York model to the stores to illustrate the glamour available to the full-figured woman. *(Courtesy of Formfit Rogers)*

Flyer-invitation passed out to customers, inviting them to the show. *(Courtesy of Brandeis)*

The Magazine Promotion

All the leading fashion magazines have some sort of tie-in proposal from time to time. The magazines propose promotions based on their editorial pages for the purpose of making their fashion selections available in stores throughout the country where their readers might shop. In the process, the magazines' advertisers are also likely to benefit.

Sometimes the promotion offered by the magazine requires no special investment on the part of the retailer, sometimes it involves the purchase of a number of advertising pages in the magazine, either on a regional or national basis. That is, the purchase of an ad in a regional issue constitutes the exposure of that ad only in the specific part of the country where the particular retailer is located. For example, a store in Nebraska would not very likely benefit from an ad run in New York, unless they were strictly interested in prestige. Several stores do buy national ads in leading fashion magazines just for that purpose. Also, such stores might be in an area enjoying a great deal of tourism; a national ad would bring attention to that store. There is a considerable difference in cost, however, between regional ads and national ads. Therefore, a retailer must decide which approach best serves its needs.

The Early Promotions

Mademoiselle began promotional tie-ins with retailers with their first August college issue in 1935. *Mademoiselle* editors, recognizing that retail stores were faced with a doldrum month in hot, between-season August when business was slow, created a merchandising concept that would give stores an earlier "kick-off" for fall, back-to-college selling. At first, a small group of stores tied in with the magazine, and, as the word got around, more stores became involved. About 250 stores in each major trading area of America latched onto the August college issue tie-in.

Vogue, one of the first to tie with a major retailer outside New York, created a great deal of attention from merchants and consumers everywhere when they tied with Neiman-Marcus for a college promotion in 1937. Its success led to more, the *Vogue* 1937 Christmas issue, and in early 1938, a tie-in with *Vogue's* Americana issue, spotlighting the best of the American designers. In 1924 *Harper's Bazaar* began to furnish stores with information on editorial content and direction of the magazine.

What the Magazine Provides

The national consumer fashion magazines have a great deal to offer the retailer.

Authority   That is perhaps the most important ingredient the fashion magazine has to provide its readers and advertisers and, consequently, the retailer. Through a long and dependable track record, the fashion books (an inside word used by magazine staffs) have supplied the consumer with up-to-the-minute reporting on what's happening in the fashion world at home and abroad. Both pictorially and editorially they have delivered the message the fashion designers send out. They have done this so effectively that such phrases as "seen in *Bazaar*. . ." or "*Vogue* says. . ." are undeniably attention-getters. So powerful is their name as credentials that fashion models will accept modeling assignments at a fraction of the fee (far less than they would command elsewhere) to appear on those fashion pages. To have had a magazine cover is, of course, an even greater credential.

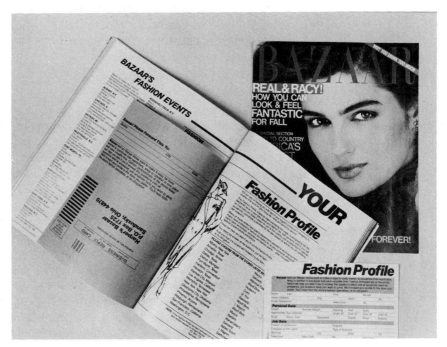

Bazaar offered career and fashion seminars to retail stores to service customers looking for authoritative direction. *(Courtesy of Harper's Bazaar)*

Glamour   The fashion press can take almost full credit for creating and stimulating a continuous aura of glamour for fashion. Their role, in fact, has been intensified because of their ability to "glamourize" almost every aspect of fashion.

Service   By sharing the advantages of their authoritative and glamorous image, the fashion magazines offer a special and unique service to the retailer through tie-in fashion promotions. Sharing their expertise and image provide a service not easily available elsewhere.

Through their constant research of what is happening in the fashion industry, plus what the fashion consumer wants and needs, the fashion magazine creates packaged promotions. For example, *Seventeen* might offer a back-to-school promotion or a bridal promotion, all geared to the young customer. *Mademoiselle* and *Glamour* might focus in on the young woman needing professional advice on her appearance—hair, makeup, and wardrobe—in preparation for entering the work force. *Bazaar* might concentrate on helping the retailer service the business woman who is an executive or aspires in that direction.

Some magazines might go even further to assist the retailer in its efforts to be an indispensable fashion store. They might provide training sessions for store personnel, or produce slides or films (available at a fee) suitable for in-store training or consumer viewing. Whatever direction the magazine promotion takes, when it is accepted by a specific store it is usually exclusively theirs in their city.

The Magazine Promotion Kit

Well tuned in to the retailer's needs and manner of operation, the magazine provides the fashion director with most of the working tools necessary to get the show on the road. Once the promotion has been accepted by the store (usually handled by the fashion office), the magazine in turn sends out a promotion kit. Every magazine has its own technique, but in almost all cases, the kits are works of art.

Nothing is overlooked. Slick, color blow-ups of the cover of the issue involved . . . sketches of promotable fashion looks . . . resource lists of merchandise in the tie-in issue . . . suggested commentary for shows . . . suggested advertising copy or fashion slogans . . . logos, for advertising reproduction . . . sketched ideas for windows or displays. In short, a completely designed promotion idea and how to produce, create, and exploit it. If a store fashion director needs help, the fashion books are prepared to graciously and effectively give it.

The Resource List

The resource list is received from the magazine far in advance of a tie-in, often ahead of the promotion kit. This gives the buyers and the DMM time to check the list and order those pieces that will appear in the magazine issue that are suitable for the store. The idea is to have the merchandise in stock at the time the promotion breaks.

The Guest Editor

Perhaps the most supportive element of a magazine promotion is the personal appearance of a fashion editor. Her presence reinforces the fashion authority of the effort. It is possible to have a guest editor (or a team of magazine people) arrive the day before the event, help pull it all together, and execute the event as well.

The guest editor is available to narrate a fashion show, conduct a training seminar for store personnel, and orchestrate a fashion clinic for customers, which could include a demonstration of makeup and hair. When a guest editor is part of the package, the magazine provides the store with glossy pictures, biographical materials, and so forth, for publicity and in-store signing.

A magazine promotion that proved its ability to build store traffic—Mademoiselle Magazine's On Location in-store promotion. It brought attention to all fashion areas—ready-to-wear, accessories, cosmetics, and even the store's beauty salon. Pictured is a question and answer portion of the On Location program. *(Courtesy of Mademoiselle Magazine)*

The Store's Responsibilities

When tying in with a magazine, the store has certain responsibilities to help make the effort a success. Not all the following are necessarily required in all cases, but most are likely to be under consideration for one type of magazine promotion or another:

1. Patronizing some of the resources featured editorially in the specific tie-in issue of the magazine.
2. Publicizing the promotion with newspaper ads, displays, signing, television and radio.
3. Buying pages of advertising in national or regional issues (as part of the package).
4. Documenting all efforts in connection with the promotion—pictures of the fashion show, windows, interiors, copies of ad tear sheets, newspaper publicity, duplicates of radio and television copy, samples of invitations or programs used for the event.

The Magazine Promotion for Special Customers

For a more sophisticated approach of what they have to offer the retailer, the fashion magazines have turned from simply providing a guest editor to narrate a fashion show to supplying (perhaps in conjunction with a show) specialized services. For example, they may offer a "makeover" program, where volunteers from the audience are shown how a change in the use of makeup or a new hairstyle can improve one's fashion look. This was often done for students as part of a back-to-school program.

Very popular with customers in department stores is the magazine program that related specifically to the working woman. Showing her which clothes were most suitable for her specific job, helping her plan a workable wardrobe, and providing fashion tricks on how to blend the new things she bought with what she already owned proved to be a much-needed and welcomed service. By zeroing in on special customer types, the magazines became more service oriented than they had in the past.

The Shelter Magazine Promotion

Not all magazine promotions are devoted to ready-to-wear. Occasionally, a magazine will offer a beautifully laid out fashion promotion dedicated to the home furnishings division. The idea may include anything from "design your own room" to "fashions for table settings" to "how to entertain" or "how to cook for two." All are geared to acquainting the customer with the home furnishings area of the store, plus stir interest and recognition of products advertised or editorially featured in the magazine.

The home or shelter magazines, such as *Better Homes and Gardens* or *House Beautiful*, would be of special interest to the fashion coordinator for the home division. Most coordinators for the home division also read consumer magazines such as *Bride's Magazine* and *Modern Bride*. Heading the list of trade publications would be *Retailing Home Furnishings*. Other valuable trade periodicals would include:

Curtain, Drapery & Bedspread
Totally Housewares
Housewares
Giftware News
Gifts and Accessories
China, Glass

Toy and Hobby World
Showcase (luggage)
Merchandising Magazine
Chain Store Age
Entre (gourmet, housewares)
Home Fashions Textiles (A Fairchild Publication)

The corporate fashion office might get involved with the fashion coordinator for the home division if the coordinator's promotion required the accent of ready-to-wear. For example, let us assume there was a home magazine promotion that focused on "patio living." It is very possible that the fashion office might be called on to supply a capsule show with live models wearing appropriate patio clothes, staged in the home division where model patios have been erected. Since most retailers consider fashion a total store responsibility, the tie-in is ideal.

Selecting Magazine Promotions

Most magazine promotions would never happen without the sanction or urging of the fashion office. However, it might be wise for the fashion director to evaluate the results or benefits. As a guideline, the following list of questions might be applied:

1. Does this promotion have the potential to be a big traffic builder (i.e., will it lure large crowds) for the store?
2. Does it have the ability to attract the kind of customer the store needs?
3. Is the budget or cost of the promotion realistic? Would the same money be better spent another way?
4. Does the store have the facilities and personnel to carry off such a promotion successfully?
5. Would the promotion result in immediate sales?

Consider all of the preceding questions carefully. If one can answer yes to all these questions the effort is worth pursuing. It is essential to be aware of the company's attitude toward such undertakings.

For example, if one cannot answer yes to the last question—will the effort result in immediate sales?—it is possible that just the building of good will and attracting people to the store would be satisfactory for some stores—hoping, of course, that such an event might eventually pay off in sales. However, some merchants, faced with an economic squeeze, would veto any effort that did not bring immediate results as well as traffic into the store. These facts must all be weighed and judged on their merits as they relate to the individual operation.

AFTERVIEW

The important thing about any promotion is to have a plan. Although magazine people offer good service to tie-in stores, the follow-through by the store's own people is indispensable to the success of such efforts.

Regarding the store's own promotions, the routine used to coordinate an item promotion is applicable to almost any promotion—storewide, divisional, or departmental. The work sheet or responsibility sheet used in the departmental promotion example is certainly flexible enough to be employed for any size promotion. The important thing is to use some vehicle that provides good communication.

It might also be well for the fashion director to realize that not all fashion promotions enjoy the dedicated interest and sympathy of the merchandising staff, selling staff, display, or advertising that the director feels is deserved. However, if fashion leadership is what top management wants, the director must stand unwavering in enthusiasm for what must be done. The fashion director must always remember: if the store does not see a promotion as important, the customer will not. Better to do fewer promotions and do them well.

CHAPTER RE-EXAMINATION

Questions

1. Who makes up the creative team of a store and what do they do?
2. What justifies a storewide promotion?
3. How does an item promotion differ from a storewide promotion?
4. How does an import promotion contribute to a store's image?
5. How do fiber or fabric companies help with store promotions?
6. In which way can a fashion director of ready-to-wear assist a fashion director of the home division in a promotion?
7. What are at least three important guidelines to follow when planning a fashion promotion?
8. Why is a responsibility sheet important to a fashion promotion?
9. What are two advantages a retailer can gain from a magazine promotion?
10. What guidelines should be used in selecting magazine promotions?

Workshop

Draw up a fashion promotion proposal. Indicate

1. Merchandise to be included
2. Department or departments to be serviced.
3. Name or theme of promotion.
4. How it should be promoted.

Include a responsibility sheet for execution.

A single mannequin, a single word on the floor announcing the designer's name—Armani—give a dramatic example of the designer's collection. (*Courtesy of Saks Fifth Avenue, New York*)

10

FASHION PROJECTION THROUGH VISUAL PRESENTATION

A starry-eyed young woman is stopped in her tracks by an enchanting department store display. She is looking at a group of ten beautiful store mannequins, arranged behind a fence-like prop, all dressed in spectator sportswear (holding banners, programs, binoculars, popcorn bags, or hot dogs), as though they were watching a race or a game, cheering for their favorites. She can almost hear the make-believe crowd noises because the effect is so real, so stimulating.

But more important, the young woman can see at a glance the pants, shirt, sweater, jacket, and accessories proposed in a lifestyle situation that she can identify with. She sees them all put together in a color story she would not have considered previously.

The happiest thing about this energetic scene is that the customer has discovered an outfit she really wants to own. She heads for the department. "I want the whole thing," she tells the fashion seller, "just the way it's put together on the mannequin."

This situation is not unusual. Stores with effective displays experience this reaction continually. Displays sell. They also do a great deal more. In this case:

- First, the customer was entertained.
- Next, she was shown what the store had for sale.
- Then she learned the new way to wear the looks and how to accessorize.
- Also, she was able to view the great number of alternatives available in a spectator look.

True, not many displays include ten mannequins (Macy's in New York did it), but even with two or three grouped together all the preceding four points can be transmitted to the customers passing by.

THE POWER OF VISUAL PRESENTATION

When the title of the display director was changed to visual presentation director (very often, vice president), it became obvious that the old title (which carried the stigma of someone who arranged plastic flowers and dressed and undressed dummies) had to be replaced with a title more indicative of this executive's role in modern merchandising.

A survey by *Women's Wear Daily* in 1979 of 4,500 women revealed that store displays generally rated in first place as their most important source of fashion information.

Both working and nonworking women rated store displays first, but working women to a greater extent. Catalogs rated next in importance in the overall tabulations, although among women 50 or older, and among women in the $25,000 to $40,000 household income bracket, daily newspapers rated second (moving catalogs to third place with this group). Since all three of these areas are utilized extensively by retailers, it is plain to see where most American women get their fashion direction: from the stores.

If visual presentation is the leading source of fashion information for the customer, then the fashion director's input is indispensable in this area for communicating fashion statements.

Since all stores of a comparable type and size have approximately the same merchandise, the way the merchandise is presented is in large part what makes the difference. According to Macy's senior vice president, Michael Stemen: "the variable is presentation."

The belief in this fact, and the ultimate demonstration of its truth, is now a matter of retail history in the case of Macy's. After Edward S. Finkelstein, chairman and chief executive officer of Macy's New York, completely revitalized Bamburger's downtown store (the New Jersey division of R. H. Macy & Company), which was aided in consistently exceeding its sales plans by the technique of wonderful displays and inspired visual presentations, he applied that technique (along with unprecedented marketing/merchandising strategies) when he went to Macy's San Francisco. It worked. Mr. Finkelstein changed the San Francisco store into a class store, making it competitive with all others in that area, and putting Macy's into first place.

When he became CEO and chairman of Macy's New York, where his multimillion dollar renovation required redesigning the store floor by floor, the concentration on visual presentation continued. The remodeling of the store's basement into "The Cellar," for example, with its inspired mall of shops, offering housewares, gourmet food, fresh produce, bakeries, a replica of P. J. Clarke's East Side restaurant, plus hundreds of other exciting accommodations, helped bring Macy's New York into that city's leading position. The Cellar shopping bag became the most carried on the streets of New York, plus on every departing plane. It was an effort that made the entire retailing world take notice.

In fact, most of the leading New York stores, where competition is fierce and image is the big draw, are dedicated to constant excellence in visual presentations. At Bloomingdale's, a most impressive model for all of retailing, the visual presentations of fashion merchandise in their windows, shops, and throughout their fashion floors make visiting the store a must when in New York. (Queen Elizabeth did.)

Even with the prospect of home computers and cable television for shopping from home, the excitement of milling around tastefully presented merchandise—seeing, feeling, touching, and actually being a part of the experience, is expected to grow even stronger, provided the creators of visual exhilaration continue to inspire and be inspired.

Fashion window that makes a memorable statement: a lifestyle window—the swimwear emerges with strong color statement on white ground. *(Courtesy of Bloomingdale's, Howard Meadows, Corporate Display Director)*

MAKING A FASHION STATEMENT— VISUALLY

Through visual presentations, perceptive merchandisers can look at any store and know immediately that store's merchandising position. They can see when it is not just handsomely decorated but is also the last word in fashion leadership. They know at once whether it is a promotional store or a fashion store. They can tell if it is a leader or a follower. Customers, too, although not as analytical as professional retailers, know what the store is all about by what they see.

It is estimated that the attention span of the average customer, when looking at a store display, is less than seven seconds. That is, unless the display has captured the customer's imagination. In any case, whether one sees it out of the corner of the eye, or stands and contemplates it, several images emerge. For example:

1. *The personality of the store.* Display and visual merchandising should reveal how the store sees itself—elegant, contemporary,

avant-garde, conservative, entirely one or the other, or perhaps a bit of each assigned to specific areas in an attempt to be all things to all people.

2. *What is new.* If fashion leadership is the goal of the store (a comment repeated often throughout this book because of its importance), visual stimulation is a must. Bringing what is new forward on display testifies to the store's convictions.

3. *Projection of peak trends.* Even the customer who is well informed and knowledgeable about what is going on currently in fashion must still be reassured that the store is equally knowledgeable and right on top of peak trends. By underlining these trends visually, with impact and conviction, the retailer indicates the strength of the store's position on any fashion story.

THE WINDOWS

Outside the store, before the customer takes the spin through the revolving door, she knows something of what is going on inside, but, more important, her appetite has been intensified or she has been given a bright new idea.

The customer has learned a great deal more. (People tend to look at

A dramatic window of black and white Bill Tice lingerie/at-home fashions. *(Courtesy of Bloomingdale's, Howard Meadows, Corporate Display Director)*

windows longer than at interior displays; perhaps this is because there is less distraction once the window has been noticed.) Window shoppers will learn:

1.   An important new color story (a bank of windows all done in blue and white has impact).
2.   A new fashion silhouette (a new fashion proportion—long or short, full or slinky, always brings gasps of surprise or admiration).
3.   What fabric is leading in importance. (Every season brings its innovations with fabric—new textures, new manipulation. The showcase treatment in windows encourages customers to go to a department they might otherwise bypass.)
4.   A new designer collection (plus the personal appearance of a fashion celebrity, with signing of time and place).
5.   A special event of storewide caliber, such as an import fair.
6.   The advanced view of a coming season. (How else in July would a woman know it is time to buy a winter coat? Where else could she see the new silhouettes of bathing suits in February? Even though it is January, a bank of bridal windows for June weddings are traditional with some stores.)

Through the stores' efforts to instruct and sell, retail windows have been dramatized throughout retail history with such inspiration and glamour that they have become famous as entertainment.

Unfortunately, windows are not always available in shopping centers in the same way as they are in downtown or flagship stores. However, where they do exist (especially in cities such as New York, Chicago, or Beverly Hills where the traffic of pedestrians is continuous) their effectiveness can be tremendous.

Out-of-towners take special joy in going window shopping. During a special event or holiday season, people will travel far from surrounding communities to a large city to see the store's Christmas windows, for example. When conventions are in town, 80 percent of those attending will include "shopping the stores" as part of their sightseeing.

Therefore, with the dual responsibility of retail windows (1) to inform and (2) to entertain, the planning should be thorough and inspired.

The Beginning of Image

Image building, from a visual point of view, began with the store's windows. Of course, no retailer would want their impressive windows to be written off as "just so much window dressing." This would only happen if the image created by those windows was not substantiated by what the shopper finds inside—that is, a continuity of excellence in interior displays and comprehensive fashion merchandising on the floors.

INTERIOR DISPLAYS

Although windows are depended on to make good first impressions, enticing passersby to come in, interior displays are first in importance. Many new stores, particularly in shopping malls, have no windows at all, per se, and others are actually "see-through" windows (i.e., through them one sees directly into the store). In any case, interior displays, near or in the fashion departments, are closer to the point of sale.

Unique Sales Personnel

Unusual as it may seem, the limited availability of live salespeople on fashion floors of many stores, especially in branches, because of high selling costs, transforms the lifeless display mannequin into the high-powered seller. In other words, the customer very often sells herself with the "suggestive selling" and "advice" she receives from the handsomely dressed display mannequin. Although this is not as likely to happen in designer or couture departments, where service is part of the ambience, it is certainly true in stores from coast to coast in areas where volume merchandise in all price ranges—budget, moderate, or better—is sold.

Display for the Eighties

There was a time when displays were jazzed up with a lot of goop and gobs of flowers and tinsel and an overwhelming amount of props. So many distractions, crowded into a display area, upstaged everything else in the department, not to mention the mannequin buried among it all. Everything was getting attention except the merchandise.

Today, with expanded classifications and the rush of changing trends and stepped-up seasons, stores have realized that the merchandise itself can come front and center. The merchandise itself is exciting, or at least it should be. Interior displays, therefore, can function somewhat like a headline on an ad—it announces what the fashion story is all about and what is being offered—and then permit the merchandise to emerge as the feature itself.

Lifestyle displays are magnificent theater. When mannequins are shown in a real-life situation, the effort relates more immediately to the way some departments are merchandised—according to lifestyle. *Where* does one wear this look? *How* does one wear it? *When?* Lifestyle illustrations in display provide answers.

In some cases, simplicity is the only way to go. For high fashion merchandise, in the same way it would be advertised in a newspaper or magazine ad—with lots of white space—the display unit would be clean, uncluttered, making a single statement about a very special garment.

Sign Here, Please

The use of signs in many retail outlets would be better described as the abuse of signs. Here is a golden opportunity for enchanting, inspiring, amusing, or just providing plain good fashion communication with the customer, yet an astonishing number of retailers have never learned the real value of sign language.

Just following a few basic rules would increase the effectiveness of in-store signing.

1. All fashion signs should be in one uniform size and color.
2. All type or lettering for fashion signs should look different from type size and style used on sale signs.
3. Wording should be held to a minimum.

Interior display for Father's Day, using unique mannequins. (*Courtesy of Sanger-Harris*)

4. Terminology on fashion signs should speak the language of fashion.
5. Trite language should be avoided at all costs.

Some stores use little or no signing; they are more right than those who use signing incorrectly. The sign is the store's voice. The fashion director, the guardian of the store's image, might use an understanding of effective signing to elevate the fashion message as it relates to fashion displays. Very often, the fashion director is requested to provide names for fashion trends to be used on signing. The director has the perfect opportunity in this regard to reduce the title or phrase to a few stimulating words. A succinct message is one that is read; a wordy, rambling one is often ignored.

Updated Mannequins

Not all stores believe in mannequins. Some very successful operations use few or none, but most find, for all the reasons mentioned previously that life-like illustrations provide valuable answers to fashion questions. The old one-picture-is-worth-a-thousand-words adage has supported many fashion merchants throughout the world.

A great contribution can be made to a store's fashion image by the types of mannequins used. Mannequins are expensive. However, for the customer to empathize with what she sees displayed, the "model woman" should be a complement to the customer's own self image. Quality clothes require updated mannequins with the last word in makeup and hair fashions. Large-size fashions need to be on a figure that is at least in some measure acceptable to that customer. The same for petite clothes. If displayed on a tall mannequin, the proportions would be all wrong. Young figures belong in the junior department, ethnic and minority groups appreciate their own special look reflected in display. In other words, all customer types need special treatment in display.

The fashion director, perhaps more sensitive to the incorrect image being projected, should work closely with the visual presentation director in this regard and perhaps go along into the market when new mannequins are selected.

Because trends in fashion change and people change, mannequins in a store must also change from time to time. For example, one store had invested heavily in mannequins when hemlines were short and when the hemline dropped they were reluctant to dump them all and start all over again. They tried for some time to make do with what they had, but the legs were all too short and, eventually, to do justice to the new looks, a new population of plaster people had to be brought in.

BOUTIQUES AND SHOPS

Perhaps the most beautiful example of how the merchandise itself is the feature is found in special boutiques and shops, created for the express purpose of spotlighting deserving merchandise.

Back in the fifties, when Geraldine Stutz of Henri Bendel, New York, created a "street of shops" in the store, it was an inspiration to other retailers to incorporate this merchandising technique into their own plans. In 1982 she gave Henri Bendel another new look with "Bendel's Arcade" a complex of shops for intimate apparel. As mentioned earlier, the idea of the "shop" was borrowed from the old world, where giant department stores did not exist or were less desirable than the individual boutique, vis-à-vis Paris.

The Purpose of Shops

Buzz words like ambience, segmentation, individuality, impact, and statement come into conversation when talking about shop concepts. The shop, carved out within the department or specialty store, can serve several purposes, but each requires a separate shop treatment.

1. To give special attention to a hot trend.
2. To service a special customer segment.
3. To intensify a lifestyle classification.
4. To distinguish a special designer.

The Trend Shop

The shop has a great deal to offer in regard to the first purpose—featuring a hot trend. Here is an opportunity to pull together into one concentrated area the best representative merchandise of a specific new fashion idea. By intensifying the story with a wide and varied selection on a single theme, the customer will experience the intended impact of the area and is assured by the statement that here is something important. The trend's effectiveness might not take off as quickly without such a shop, nor would the customer be as well served; here she can see how it all is put together. A good trend shop pulls in the related accessories along with the ready-to-wear; multiple sales are possible when the customer sees what goes with what.

Contents of trend shops change as new trends surface. Thus a trend shop becomes a "swing" shop (a shop that swings from one fashion trend to another). The location of the shop remains the same, only the contents and themes change. A famous example of this treatment is the junior swing shop in Bloomingdale's New York. Working with the

Famous for their swing shop for juniors, Bloomingdale's maintains their third floor area with regular changes to bring together fashion merchandise with a specific theme to capture a current trend. When folkloric dressing was in, the shop became a haven for "Folklore" junior fashions. *(Courtesy of Bloomingdale's, Joseph Bellesi, Design Director of Special Projects)*

fashion office, the director of special projects designs the theme and decor to relate to the merchandise. So inspired are some of the translations of merchandise into themes that they are often the subject of much press coverage, plus customer interest. Also, maintaining the swing shop in exactly the same place month after month has created a following; people come to see what is new.

Shop for the Special Customer

Servicing a special customer segment is another strong reason for utilizing the shop concept. Women of a specific type or size might find shopping more convenient (certainly less frustrating) if their choices were segregated into a separate area. The retailer has long understood the need to do this for the half-size customer. Next came the recognition of the petite customer and the large size woman (not the same as the half-size customer), who needed a shop of their own.

Then along came another huge block of customer type: the working woman. True, the existence of the working woman was not new, but her goals and roles in business had changed and, therefore, so did her working wardrobe. If she was not an executive, she still wished to dress like one. Taking up the banner that it was wise to dress for the job she wanted not the one she had, she looked to her favorite department store for advice and fashion guidance.

Most notable of such shops was Filene's "Corporate Image." (See Chapter 5.) In their downtown store in Boston, Filene's fashion director was given the responsibility of merchandising this shop concept for the working woman. The shop's manager reported directly to the fashion director, so they could have a direct line of communication as to what the customer needed and was asking for.

Also, the advanced customer—the one who wants a manner of dress that not everyone would find acceptable—can be serviced with a shop concentrating a collection of bold looks into a special area for special tastes.

The Lifestyle Shop

Shops for lifestyle dressing cropped up all over the country in response to customer needs. Of course, fashions changed as lifestyles changed, but the pattern for shops in this regard became deeply entrenched in merchandise plans. The active sportswear shops were an example. In the spring and summer they offered fashion choices for the jogger, runner, skater, bike rider. In the fall and winter fashion choices included warmup suits, hiking gear, ski looks, and more. Even those who did not jog or ski selected such sports-inspired fashion as leisure or weekend dressing.

The fashion director, who very likely had been the designer of the shop, works with the display department to be sure the fashion image intended is expressed in the shop's look and location.

The Designer Shop

This one is almost automatically written in the shop plan when the merchandising team decides to buy a special designer collection. For example, a Rive Gauche shop is almost essential when carrying Yves Saint Laurent's ready-to-wear line. That is, if the investment is extensive; otherwise it would be included within a general designer shop. Same with a Perry Ellis, Calvin Klein or Anne Klein collection, or any important designer group. The fashion director would base the recommendation for a shop on the basis of dollar investment, plus the advice of the visual presentation director as to location and proper adjacencies. An ill-placed shop is a defeated effort.

Whatever the shop type, there must be good communication between the fashion office and the display department. Customer types, involving taste levels, economic plateaus, and lifestyle convictions must all be considered in designing shops.

Judging from the list of shop alternatives noted here as examples, one can readily see the unlimited possibilities in merchandising fashion in shop concepts alone, in developing separate "businesses" within the business. Recognizing what the growth areas are in fashion is one of the major contributions of the fashion director. Recognition comes first, then choosing the technique through which to explode the potential.

HOW TO WORK WITH THE VISUAL PRESENTATION DIRECTOR

All this direction about display is not included here for the fashion director to tell the visual presentation director how to run his or her department. It is, in fact, for the other side of the coin, to help directors run their own departments.

When working with the visual presentation director, as with every other executive to whom the director must relate, the fashion director must have a basic knowledge of the function of that executive. The director needs to relate to the objectives of the visual presentation director, be aware of that director's problems, expectations, deadlines. In short, the fashion director must know how to speak the visual presentation director's language.

The Display Staff

The size of the display staff, of course, depends on the size operation, but for most major department stores the following people would be included:

Visual Presentation Director
  Display Director (corporate)
    Display Manager (for each individual store)
    Assistant Display Manager (for each individual store)
      Display associates
    Store Planning Draftspeople
    Sign Department Manager
      Sign department associates

In the larger stores there might be a separate display director for windows, one for interiors, one for shops, or a director of special projects. The fashion director would work with the visual presentation director initially, share approved plans with the display director, and help with training on all new fashion for the display managers and their staffs. In other words, the entire display department would depend on the fashion office for fashion direction.

Change—The Magic of Display

Display as an art form. When sleek, architectural lines are expressed in fashion, display props, such as these pictured here, effectively reinforce the clean, uncluttered feeling of the gown. *(Courtesy of B. Altman & Co., Andrew Druschilowsky, Display Director)*

If fashion departments are to enjoy fast turn of their stocks, they need the assistance of effective displays, interiors and exteriors, that also turn fast. Racks and cases might be filled with newly arrived merchandise, but unless the display areas are changed often enough no one would know it. A customer shopping in the store every week could enjoy the surprise of a new look in the departments she frequents almost every time she stops by. In fact, that is primarily why she does stop by. Something new has arrived. Without asking anyone or being told, she can see it. She sees it if it is displayed.

The change may be a simple thing—a new color grouping on a T-stand, a new pattern story, expressed in several ways, displayed together for emphasis. It may be a new designer sampled on a mannequin, just one, but changed so often it seems as though there is an endless stream of new ideas available.

We have established that display, hour after hour, day after day, makes fashion statements more continuously than any other means. The use of merchandise as the central feature of display is bringing fashion into what many believe it really is—an art form. Just as people love to walk the halls of museums, there is a similar feeling as they walk the aisles of a department store.

Guidance for Display Choices

If a display staff member was left alone, to wander through a fashion department and select any garment that strikes his or her fancy for the display mannequin of that department, it is possible that the item may not have sufficient comparable pieces to back it up, or it may not be representative of the fashion trend featured by the store during that period. It also may be out of focus with the color story the store wishes brought forward. It may not be at all representative of the store's fashion image. Store displays are too important to be selected at random; someone has to direct traffic.

The Time and Action Calendar

All direction for the display department in regard to fashion comes from the fashion office. The fashion director, working far in advance of a season's schedule, will provide:

- Trends to be featured in display.
- Timing when the trends are to be featured.
- A trend and timing schedule for windows.
- What departments are included in each scheduled trend.

This information is based on the Time and Action Calendar drawn up by the fashion director. Guiding when to change displays, plus what those changes should be, is the fashion director's explicit and detailed Time and Action Calendar for all areas of the company—buying, advertising, and display.

Special information, intended especially for the display department in order to install and change displayed merchandise, is furnished by the fashion director in the form of a Front and Forward Program used in conjunction with the Time and Action Calendar.

Front and Forward Schedule

The visual presentation director and staff need a great deal of special information to expedite their responsibilities for displaying fashion. The fashion director's display plan, which we will call the Front and Forward Schedule, will list:

- Vendors
- Style numbers
- Department numbers
- Classification (i.e., jacket)
- Brief description (i.e., "wool flannel cardigan")
- Color story
- Total investment
- Name of trend/timing for display
- Recommended signing
- Stores where the merchandise is available

Because the fashion office has checked with all the appropriate buyers about delivery dates of the involved merchandise, and has followed through to make sure it "hits the floor" on time, the system works beautifully.

**How to Check
Delivery Dates**

Usually the buyer will check delivery dates of orders and advise the fashion director, who might have asked about some specific merchandise expected to support a Front and Forward display installation.

Example:

The Time and Action Calendar lists a nautical theme to be featured throughout the store December 15. Ads are scheduled to appear on that date, and when the customer comes in the store, certain major displays (as requested on the Front and Forward schedule) are to illustrate the nautical theme. However, as of December 1, the fashion director discovers the merchandise promised on the Front and Forward schedule has not arrived and the buyer is on vacation.

Since the fashion office is responsible for the follow-through of the plan, the fashion director takes action. The director pulls the orders in question, calls the customer service departments of the resources from which the merchandise is expected, and learns that the merchandise was shipped, as promised. The next step is to check the store's distribution center (central warehouse where all merchandise is sent first before being delivered to the specified branches) and have the merchandise located. The director learns that it will take exactly four days for the merchandise to be processed and delivered to the stores and another day or two before it hits the selling floor. That means that by December 6 or 7 the merchandise will be available for the display people to select and incorporate into their displays. That is a close call (more typical than unusual), but everything will be in readiness, on target, as planned for December 15.

In regard to the preceding incident, it is important for a fashion director to understand the system of delivery dates, so that plans relating to the arrival of new merchandise are realistic. The director should also know how long it takes to get merchandise from the time it arrives at the distribution center, is processed, ticketed, trucked to the designated stores, checked in, and put on racks on the floor. A Front and Forward schedule should not be sent to the display department without assurance from the buyer or resource that the merchandise will arrive on time for display installations.

**How the Display
Staff Works**

Armed with a copy of the fashion director's display schedule, the display manager and staff set out to select the designated pieces for their mannequins. They have no problem tracking down the correct merchandise; they simply follow the road-map of directions. First, they locate the specified vendor (found on a label or tag on the garment), check the classification (i.e., a jacket); they then read the hang tag for the style number. The color story calls for "camel," so as soon as they find the suitable size for the mannequin, they are on their way to the next step.

The fashion director has included some special instructions about what goes with the jacket—skirt or pant, blouse or shirt—plus accessories. The display people pull all the necessary pieces to complete the new fashion look. When all the mannequin changes have been made in all departments, the visual presentation director and fashion director will tour the stores to review the results.

**Fashion Meetings
with the Display
Staff**

An endless stream of fashion ideas and imaginative approaches are necessary to perpetuate the fashion authority of a store through display. No display department, no matter how well informed and creative, can do this continuously without a little help from its friends. And, the fashion director, on the other hand, knows full well that one of the most important friends of fashion is the display department.

Much of fashion's success comes directly from the inspired and their inspirations at the retail level. The sharing of that inspiration through the exchanging of ideas helps dispel the mystery of how current fashion trends are to be handled. Many stores report that their creative areas—fashion, advertising, and display—meet on a regular basis to clear the air.

"Just what do you mean by unconstructed?"
"We are not clear on the do's and don't's when mixing patterns."
"What's a tyrolean jacket?"

These and many other questions come forth when display and fashion departments get together. Not everything can be successfully explained on paper. Visual demonstrations should be part of the communication between these two areas. To answer all the questions, the fashion director and/or members of the fashion office can present actual merchandise. Even the construction of a sample display can be offered to be critiqued.

"We have never put jewelry on this type of garment before," a display person may protest.

"Well, we do now," the fashion director explains. "It has all changed."

After having seen a new idea repeated so often when in the market, the fashion director must remember that display people, many of whom never make a single trip into the fashion market, have a limited frame of reference regarding fashion change. This is one of the reasons the fashion director works so close to the market—to be on top of every emerging development and be in a position to share findings with all areas of the company.

How Fashion Change Affects Display

Change is the one thing most dependable in the world of fashion, as stated so emphatically in Chapter 1. This is a fact that makes it impossible to rely on last season's thinking, sometimes even last month's. For example, the visual presentation director goes into his or her market many months ahead of a season, and must know at that time what items will be necessary to tie in with anticipated fashion trends. The visual presentation director will buy Christmas display needs in June and Spring/Summer in December.

We touched earlier on the appropriate mannequins for specific customers types (petite, large size, junior, etc.), but there are other considerations concerning mannequins when planning a new season. One season a particular department might be well served with modern, impressionistic display treatments because the merchandise justified such a look. However, if a whole new flux of romantic, feminine merchandise is coming into that department, the current mannequin concept would be jarring. A department with headless, faceless, stylized mannequins can hardly present the desired delicate, demure, gentle image of the incoming romantic fashions.

Hair fashions, too, must be carefully planned. The fashion director must advise the display people far in advanced of their market trips that wispy, soft hairdos will be needed for the young romantic looks, or that the new hair proportions (as they relate to the new fashion proportions) will be full, long, short, severe, or casual. The full, flamboyant, tossled hair fashion on a sensuous display in the lingerie department would not be suitable, of course, for a tailored, reserved, executive-looking suit in the corporate image boutique for working women.

There are also contradictions in fashion looks from season to season. What might have been serious fashion one year shows up as frivolous another, or vice versa. The correct interpretation, therefore, must be shared with display. "This fashion idea must not be taken too seriously. We should not play it too straight—a gag treatment or fantasy flavor would work," the fashion director might advise. Display would never dream of taking this kind of liberty without sanction. Naturally, there are many ways to approach any theme, but only a few are correct and one or two are likely to be more powerful. The more accurate the interpretation, the more attractive the sales.

In all fashion situations that affect display, advance planning is a must. There should not be too many surprises tossed into the lap of the display department. As any store will testify, there are many occasions when surprises are unavoidable. The visual presentation director is a genius of improvisation, and has had to prove it over and over again, but it's not a favorite way to live. Therefore, a well-organized rapport with ths fashion office is a tremendous asset for display.

Display for the Male Customer

While women tend to identify with the physical structure of a mannequin (a junior figure used in a mature woman's department might make a customer angry), men do not. A handsome face on a male mannequin doesn't do too much for the male customer. It might for the woman who shops for him, but when he shops for himself, he would more likely identify with the mannequin (depending on the man, of course) if it were standing in a window or a display area in a lifestyle situation. A male surfer with a window full of bathing beauties, or a total masculine environment, such as models in hunting or fishing gear, might catch his eye.

In most cases, men are more easily content with seeing a half mannequin, that is, the body of a suit with no legs and no head. They like to see the cut of the coat, the drape of the line, the fit of the collar, and the new width or knot of the tie. Men would be aware of the color and fabric combinations. The rest be hanged.

Display and the Color Story

Perhaps the earliest information the visual presentation director will need from the fashion director will be color direction for the coming season, sometimes even two seasons out. Even though the display staff attends the predictive presentations of the fashion director, there is a special need, in regard to color, to discuss the choices and alternatives. Color will set the tone of many display decisions. Earth tones will speak one language, electric or neon brights another.

If management and the fashion director decide that one powerful color is the best way to support a season's fashion story, then display is responsible for making the visual statement happen. However, the visual presentation director will need to know *exactly* what that color is to be as to shade, tone, intensity, and so on. Just saying orange, red, yellow, or brown tells nothing. The visual presentation director needs an exact color sample or fabric swatch of the color in question. The new season's blue may be like none other. With the exact and unmistakable color in hand, plus a good idea of how it will be used in ready-to-wear and for what divisions (women's, men's, children's), the overseer of display can buy all the necessary props and trim to add exciting emphasis to the fashion story.

VISUAL MERCHANDISING

Display is only one aspect of the huge responsibilities of the visual merchandising director and staff. As mentioned earlier, display is similar to a headline that announces what the fashion story is all about; the department where the display merchandise comes from is the body of the story itself.

Working with the merchandising executives, the visual merchandising director is responsible for creating a layout for the selling floor, with a consistent format, workable adjacencies, and efficient fixtures that both support the merchandise and serve the customer. Not an easy order.

Basic Fundamentals of Visual Merchandising

How the selling floors of a store are laid out depends on the store's image and philosophy. However, certain basic guidelines are applicable to most stores.

1. Classify merchandise within each department.
   Example: All jeans, within their respective departments, are pulled together.
   All coffee pots, pulled together in small electrics department.
2. Determine proper layout for each department.

All fixturing within an area should be set on a grid system. The fixtures should form straight lines from aisle to back wall and left to right. This allows for open aisles for the customer to walk easily into the department. Whenever possible, the department should run from front to back. (See Figure 1.)

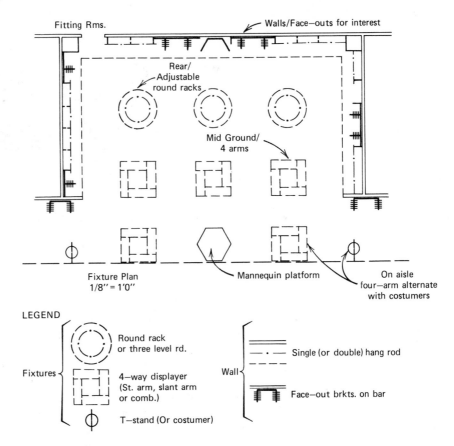

Figure 1.

3. *Colorize Merchandise.*
   Colorizing should be done left to right, and light to dark by color value. (See Figure 2.)

4. *Coordinate fabrications.*
   In order to make clear-cut fashion statement, it is important that fabrications are segregated.
   Example: Do not mix:
   Raincoats and cloth coats on the same fixture
   Knits and wovens on the same fixture
   Cottons and wools on the same fixture

5. *Segregate clearance merchandise.*
   Merchandise that has been marked down and will not go back up in price comes under the heading of "clearance." Clearance merchandise should be placed at the rear of the department. Each ready-to-wear department should have a wall section designated for clearance, or round racks at the rear of the department. Clearance in hard lines departments should also have a wall section

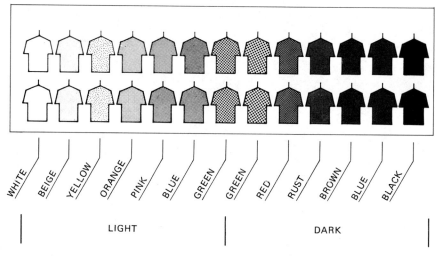

Figure 2.

designated for clearance, or tables at the rear of the department. In all cases, the designated clearance area should be so signed.

6. *Designate sale merchandise.*

Sale merchandise has been marked down for a certain period, but at the end of that time will return to its regular retail price. The fixture holding the sale merchandise should be signed "Sale," and will stay in the same location within its classification.

Example: If a coordinate group is normally shown at the front of a department, the fixture will remain in that spot, with a sale sign added on top of the fixture for the duration of the sale that is removed when it is over.

MERCHANDISING FIXTURES

In some stores the fashion director is involved in or assists in planning how merchandise is presented on the various styles of fixtures. In others, the fashion director, policing the results, can verify or suggest ideas that might better serve the fashion currently needing special or preferential attention. In any case, every retail executive should understand the workings of visual presentation for several reasons:

1. Size of fixtures often influence the number of pieces purchased in a classification.
   Example: A *rounder* can hold 120 to 150 tops. If a full rounder is to be filled, that many pieces will need to be purchased.
2. The way merchandise is hung or displayed affects the buy of small groups.
   Example: Certain fashion items, brought in in minimum quanti-

ties, perhaps to test, may only fill a T-stand or two-way waterfall 12 to 18 units). The fashion director, concerned that such a small group might get lost, might communicate with the display department to make sure the group gets its proper feature spot when it hits the department.

3. The way merchandise is hung affects color selections.
   Example: If merchandise in a single classification is purchased from one designer in two colors, it is important that the two colors, hanging together, are compatible. One would not very likely buy black and navy, but would purchase one or the other plus a complementary color, perhaps camel or red.

4. The way merchandise is hung affects the choices of patterns.
   Example: Whenever merchandise is selected, the fashion director and the buyer must always consider how will it look on the floor. If patterns are in question, and destined to hang on a single display unit, it might be the wish of the buyer (depending on the desired investment) to have one unit for plaids and another for solids. If the investment is limited, it must be remembered that these two will hang together if they are of the same fabric (i.e., both wool).

FIXTURE CAPACITY INDEX

As a guide of how to buy for available fixtures in a department, and how to plan the merchandising of an area, it is wise to bring along or memorize the following when shopping the market.

Small four way	40 units (dresses, 24 units)
Large four way (standard)	80 units
Two way (waterfall)	12 to 18 units
T-Stand	12 to 18 units
Rounder	120 to 150 tops or pants/or 60 coats
Tri-level rounder	75 to 90 units
Rectangular rack	Suits 35 per side/70 total Pants 60 per side/120 total
Wall hanging	4-foot section (single hung)
	60 to 85 tops
	50 pants
	25 coats
Face-out	10 to 12 units

(see illustration in Figures 5 and 6)

The Purpose of Consistency. When a format is created by the visual presentation director, it is usually decreed that nothing or no one deviates from that plan. A firm rule regarding the consistent manner in which a fixture is merchandised is important for two reasons:

1. The customer comes to depend on a certain style of merchandising; she can travel to any store in the company and find the system consistent.
2. Fashion departments, with uniform merchandising formats, look clean, uncluttered, and inviting.

The Finishing Touch. Even when a single item is being presented on a fixture (such as a jacket or sweater or coat), it is effective to layer or accessorize the front piece to illustrate how it can be worn. For example, a jacket might be hung over a shirt and/or sweater.

Illustrations of Fixture Usage

To further identify how a consistent format in merchandising fixtures might work, the following illustrations (Figures 3–13) are offered. Of course, there are other ways to present merchandise. These are ones used by Brandeis, Omaha, Nebraska, plus many stores throughout the country.

T-Stands—for Coordinates (Figure 3)

For all ready-to-wear areas, this fixture is helpful in highlighting a single item. It should always be used at the front of a department for maximum exposure. Ideally, it is used to present *one look* or *item* in a full size range.

Merchandise used on these units should be changed frequently based on stock and need for exposure and coordination with displays.

T-Stands—for Separates (Figure 4)

For all ready-to-wear areas, this fixture helps to highlight a single item. It should always be used at the front of a department for maximum exposure.

Merchandise used on these units should be changed frequently based on stock and need for exposure. Where possible front garments should be layered.

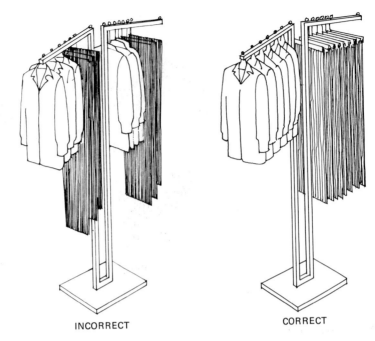

INCORRECT   CORRECT

Figure 3.

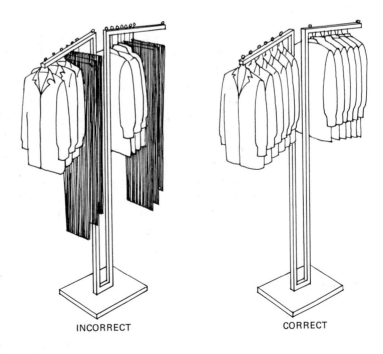

INCORRECT   CORRECT

Figure 4.

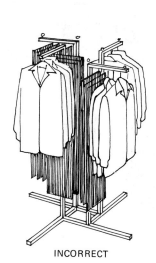 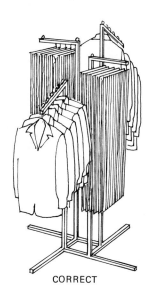

INCORRECT   CORRECT

Figure 5.

Four-Arm Face-Out Rack—for Coordinates (Figure 5)

This is a very useful fixture, making an organized and neat presentation of related separates or items. It is suitable for all ready-to-wear departments.

Merchandising by classification is important when using this rack as is merchandising by coloration. The entire unit may tell a color story, or each arm may make an independent color statement. This fixture always creates a better impression when only tops or only bottoms are shown on an arm. Versions of this rack may be all straight arms or may vary with some waterfall arms. When a waterfall arm is used, that arm should indicate the front of the rack and should always face the aisle. Face-out items should be layered where possible. The height of the arms holding tops will be lower than the arms holding bottoms. Tops should be shown on a slant arm and bottoms on a straight arm.

Four-Arm Face-Out Rack—for Separates (Figure 6)

For an organized and neat presentation of related separates or items, this is a useful fixture in all ready-to-wear departments.

Merchandising by classification is important when using this rack as

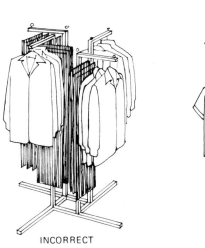

INCORRECT   CORRECT

Figure 6.

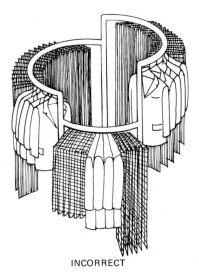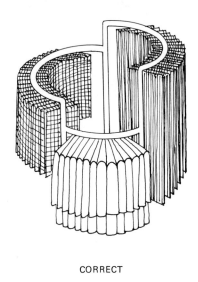

INCORRECT   CORRECT

Figure 7.

is merchandising by coloration. The entire unit may tell a color story, or each arm may make an independent color statement. Versions of this rack may be all straight arms or may vary with some waterfall arms. When a waterfall arm is used, that arm should indicate the front of the rack and should always face the aisle. Face-out items should be layered where possible.

Three-Way Adjustable Round Rack—for Coordinates (Figure 7)

This fixture is vertically adjustable in three equal sections, making it useful for presentation of separates or coordinate groups in any department. Each of the three bars should be at staggered heights, with the lowest bar to the front. Heights should be appropriate to the merchandise with pants and long skirts on the tallest bar.

Three-Way Adjustable Round Rack—for Separates (Figure 8)

Only one classification of separates should be represented per fixture.

The Quad Rack (Large Four-Way) (Figure 9)

Although this rack has some adjustability, it is rather limited in usage.

It is suggested for heavy merchandise, such as jeans, suits, and coats. It is also very good for coordinate groups. This fixture should be placed in the middle of the department, but not on a aisle. One item should be shown on each arm.

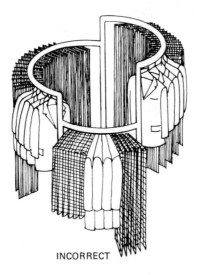
INCORRECT

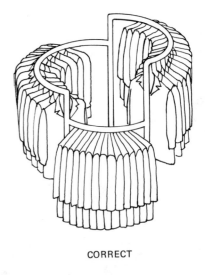
CORRECT

Figure 8.

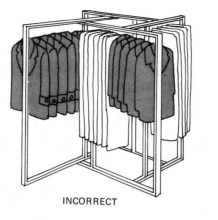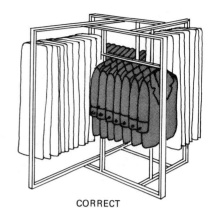

INCORRECT   CORRECT

Figure 9.

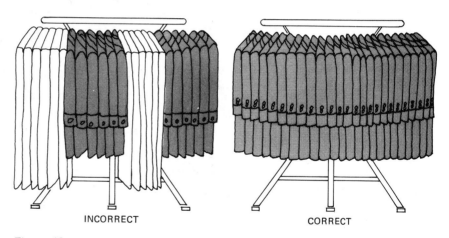

INCORRECT   CORRECT

Figure 10.

The Round Rack (Figure 10)

This rack is volume oriented and should be used to house a large amount of stock. Rounders should be placed toward the rear of the department.

Merchandise on round racks should be colorized and sized within a color range whenever possible. A form or T-stand draper may be used on top of the round rack to display an item of the merchandise housed on the fixture.

Too much merchandise on a rounder gives an untidy appearance and makes it difficult for the customer to make a selection.

Wall Projections

Jet Rail, Keystripping, Hang Bars (Figures 11–13). Never hang jet rail or bars in one continuous row. Break the monotony by staggering for a more appealing visual impact. Many different arrangements can be created to fill space as well as give back wall areas an exciting customer appeal.

Walls should always be merchandised. In the clearance months of July and January, if stocks are low, remove fixtures from the floor, and always keep walls merchandised.

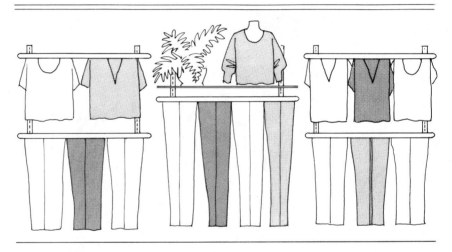

Figure 11.

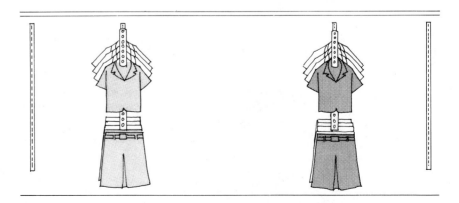

Figure 12.

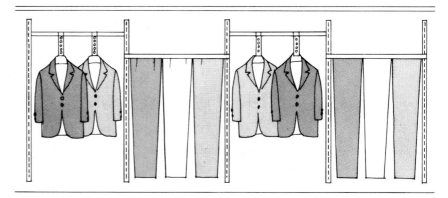

Figure 13.

The use of glass shelving for merchandise presentation is shown in Figure 11. Double hang bars are used for tops and slacks. Key strip waterfalls for coordinates (illustrated in Figures 12 and 13) are an attractive way of enhancing merchandise appeal. Figure 13 depicts the use of bar waterfalls for jackets with coordinating slacks adjacent.

VISUAL PRESENTATION SETS THE STAGE

The store is theater. We have established that a trip to the store is a form of entertainment for many people. Even those who come for a specific purchase enjoy being entertained. Maybe that's one of the reasons they come to a particular store for that specific purchase; they enjoy the atmosphere, there is always something going on. A sense of theater, therefore, is a must for all members of the creative team— display, advertising, and the fashion office. Whether it be store planning, merchandising a fashion floor, display for windows and interiors or special events, visual presentation sets the stage.

The Stage for Special Events

Staging for all special events, whether booked by the sales promotion director or the fashion office, fall directly into the lap of the visual presentation director and staff.

Let us assume that the fashion director has agreed to a magazine tie-in and has requested certain windows and interior displays for support to publicize the event. The visual presentation director, after meeting with the fashion director regarding the details, will undoubtedly turn the project over to the display director. The fashion director knows that the display director needs detailed information (there is usually a packet within the magazine promotion kit designed especially for display's use) on the theme, time and place for events, and what staff will be needed and at what stores.

At the outset of the planning there are certain areas of information about which the display department and the fashion office should consult. These might include:

- Number and location of windows
- Starting and completion dates of displays
- Merchandise to be featured
- Identification needed on signing (magazine logo, etc.)
- Pictures of visiting editors for in-store signing
- Staging requirements

If the magazine sends blowups of magazine covers, enlargements of fashion illustrations or any other material for the event, most of this material should be sent directly to display to be used throughout the store and at the scene of the special event. Most magazines are very good about respecting deadlines and have material shipped in plenty of time for display installations.

If there is a show, demonstration, or seminar in connection with the event, display will erect the stage, plan the lighting, and supply microphones and props. A complete checklist must be submitted to the display director.

Display and Fashion Shows

Behind the scenes of every important fashion show are the talents and efforts of many unsung heros. One of these is the display department, without which the fashion office could not raise the curtain.

Many in-department fashion shows require little more than a small runway, a few chairs for guests, and a microphone. The display department can rig these up a few moments before show time, with little more planning than the notice they have had on the fashion show schedule (a copy of which goes to everyone involved in or affected by the event). Very often, in such cases of shows held "on the floor," little or no decor is required. The only thing that must be planned in advance would be the appropriate sign to go in front of the department or on the runway, announcing the date and time of the show, plus the name of a guest commentator or designer.

When it comes to the big shows—those for which a large audience is expected—the physical setup requires a great deal more attention. Since staging is a major contributor to the effectiveness of a production, the talents of the display department are indispensable. Most stores do not wish to go beyond their own staffs for the majority of their fashion productions, therefore, an imaginative and cooperative display director is a blessing to the fashion office.

If the fashion show coordinator is anxious to give a show a new twist, with something different in staging, lighting, or production, the coordinator needs to enlist the creativity of the display people to come up with good ideas time after time after time. If being creative is dear to the heart of the display director, that person will cherish the assignment.

After the show has been booked, the fashion office must decide where it will be held. The physical setup dictates to some degree what the possibilities of production might be.

Runway. If a stage is available the display director will need to know the theme of the show, how the stage is to be utilized, decorated, and lighted, and if a runway will project from that stage. If so, the display director must know what size runway and what shape.

Most stores have stock runway sections that can be joined together to make a variety of lengths, widths, and shapes. The fashion office needs only to advise display, "we will need a conventional straight runway, projecting three sections from the stage," and the directions are easy to follow. If a T-shape runway is required, a U-shape, a horseshoe, or a zigzag arrangement, the directions should be clearly stated in writing.

If, on the other hand, the standard equipment available is unsuitable for a special treatment, the display department must know the wishes of the fashion office much earlier in the planning stage so that a design may be drawn up and dimensions planned. This design will then be submitted to the carpenter shop for construction. Runway equipment can also be rented.

If the size or shape of the runway requires special covering, that information must also be passed along to display. Perhaps a special color scheme is part of the plan and skirting material for draping around the runway has to be ordered.

If the lighting plan is something other than what the display department has on hand, spots and scoops, or color lenses will need to be obtained to create the desired effect. It is a good idea, therefore, for the fashion office to learn something about the kind of equipment the display department has available. It will make some of the general planning easier for both departments.

The average show cannot require a major production every time, but a few imaginative touches can certainly create the illusion of extensive planning. If the fashion office personnel find they are not "show biz" oriented from a staging point of view, the display director is a good strong shoulder to lean on. Usually a few well-written words regarding the theme of the show, size of audience, and purpose of the event, will inspire display to come up with exactly what is needed.

Props.   In addition to ramps and lighting, props and sets very often must be collected or built to embellish a show. A prop list, if many props are needed, should be drawn up, explaining how each prop will be used. This will clarify the size of each prop and its proportion to other props, how it is to be "set" on stage, and what arrangement will be necessary to "strike" the prop. Will it be carried on and off the stage by a model? Will it be set and removed by a stage hand? The display department must know these details in regard to all props or stage settings ordered by the fashion office.

Display and the Major Production.   Although a fashion office may book and conduct a staggering number of fashion shows per year, perhaps only one or two of these will fall into the category of a major production. The kind of major production referred to requires a major effort on the part of the display department.

For example, the fashion director, presumably the author of the show, has been engaged to produce a fashion extravaganza as a city-wide benefit. It is one in which the audience expects nothing short of a Broadway review, with fashions subtly woven in here and there. It's a big undertaking, and staging is the basic secret of making the whole thing come off as a "first."

The Sets.   The display director and author (fashion director) consult. The author has decided that this year's production should be done in three exciting scenes, each requiring a separate set change. She has designed these sets as she sees them and submitted her three ideas to him for refining. Before the display director can interpret the suggested sets, he must know exactly what she intends to happen in each case.

"I will need motion in scene three," she might explain, "so a turntable at stage right should be rigged to go into motion on cue."

The display director considers that an easy order. The turntable will be electrically operated by a switch backstage that will be turned on by the stage manager at the precise moment necessary. In fact, the display director, most familiar with the workings of the entire production, may very well be called on to serve as stage manager.

Before building begins on the sets, the display director will undoubtedly submit blueprints or sketches of the sets and explain how he feels they would work best. The fashion director will review these plans with the display director, perhaps moving a set of stairs more stage left, taking out an entrance upstage center, or substituting a new idea they both find more intriguing than the original plan. Finally, the plans are passed along to the construction department for execution under the guidance of the display director.

Runways, sets, props, lighting, and sound are usually the responsibility of the display department, unless special outside technicians are hired and outside equipment rented. Many stores, however, prefer to utilize the talents in the family. When something can be done with its own staff, all the better. Actually, this is an advantage for the fashion director. Under this arrangement the director can create with less restrictions. Sets and props, for example, made with loving hands at home are easier on the store's budget; they can be broken down or adjusted for re-use in other shows, display areas, exhibits, and any number of things for which display is called on to contribute material.

Applause, Please. For all this splendid cooperation and creative talent on a major production, when giving credit on a printed program, the display director's name should be very much in evidence along with any other members of the staff he or she may wish to have included. If there is no printed program, then it behooves the fashion director or commentator of the show to acknowledge orally the display director or staff members who have made an outstanding contribution. A little applause is the least the fashion office can do to thank the display department for literally standing on its head to deliver the special effects requested.

AFTERVIEW

A store cannot compete today using techniques of yesterday. New merchandise cannot be housed effectively with old hat surroundings. Department stores cannot always completely renovate or rebuild giant stores, but with fashion-oriented displays (windows, interiors, and shops) they can create the illusion of a "new department," even within those hallowed old walls.

Whatever the focus of display, the important fashion story must be present. That comes first. Too many departments are arranged for the convenience of the clerk, not the customer. The fashion director's role in this entire matter is to keep a watchful eye. While everyone else is busy drawing up floor plans, picking the wallpaper and carpeting, and selecting the fixtures, someone must be sure that the fashion image does not get buried in the rubble.

According to a report in *Women's Wear Daily*, R. J. Pavlik, store designer for Lord & Taylor, said: "basics will be bought by telephone in the near future. Our stores must be geared to theater . . . the merchandise will stimulate excitement and, in a sense, entertain the customer." Most all major stores in our large cities create excitement in their stores with a sense of theater. Marvin Traub, Chairman of Bloomingdale's, said it best: "We are not only in competition with other stores, but with the Guggenheim and the Met."

CHAPTER RE-EXAMINATION

Questions

1. What can a customer learn from a store display?
2. What does a store reveal about itself through display?
3. What is the value of exciting store windows?
4. How does a trend shop differ from a lifestyle shop?
5. Why is the Time and Action Calendar used in conjunction with a Front and Forward Schedule?
6. How do fashion changes affect display mannequins?
7. Where should clearance merchandise be located? Why?
8. Why should the fashion director and buyer be aware of how many garments go on a rack?
9. Why should round racks go to the back of a department and small T-stands or waterfalls be placed at the front?
10. How does a display department help the fashion office with fashion shows?

Workshop

Choose a fashion trend, current or fabricated, and design a display using merchandise illustrating that trend. Sketch or describe:

1. Where the display would be located.
2. Theme of the display.
3. If mannequins used, how they would be dressed, accessorized, and so on.
4. How the display would be signed.

Join u[...]
at the Missio[...]
Valley Store [...]
9:30 Saturday Morning, Feb. 27 [...]
for a special showing [...]
the Spring Dior Collectio[...]
*Available on Feb. 2[...]

FASHION GALLERY

BULLOCK'S CALIFORNIA

What a beautiful way to live.

(Courtesy of Bullock's)

11

FASHION PROJECTION THROUGH ADVERTISING

Everyone loves a good story, and the prime requisite for any good story is that it manages to hold your interest. It is the same with a good fashion story; it must hold your interest. In this case, the customer's interest. Newspaper advertising has long been the source of a retailer's story, complete with words and pictures.

Techniques change, of course, in storytelling as in anything else. People change, and lifestyles change. This is especially true with fashion advertising, because nothing is more closely related or more easily affected by new life styles and trends. Therefore, every year, every season (every item, for that matter) dictates the texture or flavor of telling the fashion story.

Early in the eighties, when Bergdorf Goodman of New York decided that their print advertising needed a new fresh look, they adopted a cleaner, more abstract approach, which they felt was a more personal, more distinctive identity for the store. The new concept provided a dramatic designer's sketchbook feeling with a sense of movement, something modern, yet classic.

To arrive at exactly what the store felt related best to their customer, the store's executives met with Alexander Vethers, the illustrator and discussed the Bergdorf customer, who, according to Dawn Mello, executive vice president of fashion merchandising, is individual, vulnerable, and feminine, with a strong sense of personal style. Using no settings and more succinct copy, the ad technique became, according to Bergdorf's president, Ira Neimark, "a fine reflection of what Bergdorf Goodman stands for."

HOW TO WORK WITH THE ADVERTISING DIRECTOR

The advertising director in a retail organization is a remarkable machine. He or she runs a headful of gears at full speed at all times. The advertising director is programmed for deadlines. With computerized precision routine materials are ground out. The advertising director must also create new advertising ideas for a legion of buyers with a legion of different problems. While resting, this individual is supervising the advertising production department, copy department, and art department and approving, revising, or rewriting reams of layouts, copy, and illustrations.

The fashion director can identify with the advertising director. Neither ever puts on the brakes. There isn't time. However, when creative people meet, both operating in equal pressure chambers, it takes talent, finesse, and patience to accomplish their mutual objectives. An advertising director is a proud professional who would go an extra mile to turn a mediocre ad into a good one. He or she does not enjoy settling for less, and to do so is the greatest frustration. It is in this area that the kinship, or, better still, similarity between the advertising director and the fashion director is so prevalent.

On the basis of all this, it should not be difficult for the fashion director to identify with the feelings, problems, and goals of the advertising director. An excellent way to demonstrate such rapport is to respect the rules of the house—the advertising department's house.

Deadlines

Deadlines must be met; material has to be turned in on time. A whole chain of complications can be created when deadlines are not honored. There are enough "unavoidables" in the lives of advertising directors keeping them well supplied with near-disasters without the plaguing addition of the avoidables. An unqualified respect for deadlines keeps the lines of good communication open. Copy, merchandise for sketching or photographing, and fashion information or direction, must be submitted at the prescribed "not later than. . . ."

Understandable Copy

Copy, the words that accompany the ad's illustration, must be easy to grasp. Speak clearly. Say what you mean. Do it concisely. There are top priority rules for good advertising copy. If a clear, effective fashion point is to be made in a proposed newspaper ad, the copy directions, too, should be succinct, to the point, and thoroughly indicative of the story line. Remember. Assume nothing. The fashion director may know what he or she means, but will the advertising department? Will the customer?

Merchandise for Illustration

After merchandise for sketching is selected and taken to the advertising department, attach to each piece, in writing, what the fashion message is. Usually, a personal appearance is in order, to verbally explain what is intended in the way of a fashion story. Again, assume nothing. The people in the advertising department are very perceptive, alert people, but they cannot be expected to know all the answers in regard to new fashion trends. They may not even know the questions. Even though they have attended the fashion director's educational sessions on new trends, there will still be blank spots in some areas.

A master of the fashion ad campaign is Lord & Taylor. In their "Personal Edit" series, they presented a single fashion idea in each ad with explicit details on how it should be worn, from hair to shoes. *(Courtesy of Lord & Taylor)*

Accessorizing Ads

When submitting merchandise for illustration (assuming it is women's ready-to-wear), the fashion office is also responsible for including what accessories should be used. Hats, shoes, bags, jewelry, scarves, and even hair fashions are part of the story. Accessorizing ready-to-wear illustrations is an excellent opportunity to show new looks from the accessory areas and clarify the new ways they should be used. The more often the customer sees a new fashion trend expressed correctly, the more quickly she is capable of accepting it. The fashion director is involved with fashion ads to be sure that the customer gets the fashion story in the most accurate and effective way.

So strongly did Lord & Taylor New York feel about the importance of the total look that they launched an entire advertising campaign called "Personal Edit," which provided their customers with a complete fashion story. For example, if the ad introduced a new suit look, not only was the photographed or sketched model wearing the right accessories from head to toe, but the copy described the specific accessories shown and identified them by brand name or price. The customer knew at a glance how to put herself together, what the store believed in, and what to ask for when she came into the store.

The key to these thoroughly accessorized ads was to provide carefully edited looks, available in all prices and in departments ranging from designer to juniors.

This comprehensive approach in an ad campaign (it was also used in a Lord & Taylor fall catalog and reinforced with in-store signing and display), not only received customer applause, but garnered much attention from the fashion press and other retailers as well.

In the same way that a customer views a mannequin in a store display, seeing how right the shoe or bag or jewelry is used with the costume illustrated, the reader of an ad may want the exact handbag sketched. If she learns it is not actual merchandise and, in fact, is just a sketch, the disappointed customer feels she has not received dependable fashion direction. On the other hand, if the accessory is sketched from actual merchandise in stock, the customer is properly serviced and the store might enjoy multiple sales.

Ad Preparation

An understanding of the procedure of turning out an ad will aid the fashion office personnel tremendously in working efficiently and harmoniously with advertising personnel. Schedule the ad first, because space must be reserved. Advertising must have, in writing (usually on a form requisition), the size of the ad, the date it is to run, the nature of the ad, and information as to whether it is in black and white or color. If it is to be a fashion impact ad, coming out of the fashion office budget, then the fashion director is responsible for all aspects of the scheduling, preparing, and merchandising. If the ad is part of the advertising budget of the division with which the director is working, all scheduline is done by the DMM. When deadline time rolls around, all copy, instructions, and merchandise for illustrations, must be in the hands of the advertising department.

Followup is important. During the days of preparation (i.e., while the advertising department is planning the layout, sketching, and writing copy for the ad) it is wise for the fashion director to visit the advertising offices and look over the shoulder of the artist to see if the interpretation of the fashion concept is correct. It is far better to correct an error at this stage of preparation than to discover mistakes after plates are made or after seeing a proof sheet. A major change at that point is almost too late. It's also too expensive. Correction of a misspelled word in the copy or a mistake in price on some small thing can be fixed, but a major change, such as the wrong accessories on the wrong model, or the wrong piece of merchandise featured in the major spot, means the whole ad is down the drain. All major changes or adjustments should be made while the artist still has an eraser in hand. It is the same with the copy writer; he or she also has an eraser. Once the layout is finalized, however, and the type is set, beware.

Treatment of Fashion Ads

Timing: the retailer's lifeline. Whatever mistakes a retailer may make regarding a fashion item or trend—buying too much or buying too little—if the retailer has it in the stores at the right time and lets the world know it's there through advertising at the right time, success is more assured.

The fashion director, who advises management of the proper time for exploiting the season's new trends, has a big responsibility to see that fashion ads are scheduled on time for proper exposure. Timing supports the store's goal—to maintain fashion leadership, to have what is new, and to have it *first*.

Fashion ads not only receive different treatment from sale ads but are regarded with different expectations. The sale ad is expected to produce a certain amount of immediate business in proportion to the space devoted to it. For example, if a sale ad costs $15,000, it should produce about $150,000 in sales. This ten percent rule usually does not apply to fashion ads where another guideline is used based on the investment of stock (i.e., the extent in which the item or trend is backed up). If it is a small effort (the introduction of a moderate stock investment), the ad would be small. If the stock investment is major, the ad would reflect it.

To be sure that fashion ads do not in any way resemble sale ads, certain techniques are applied to assure their individuality. The ad should telegraph fashion, the store's image, and the degree of its importance. To strengthen a store's fashion credibility, the following are indispensable advantages for fashion ads:

- Appearance of fashion ads on a regular basis (e.g., every Sunday)
- Appearance of fashion ads in a regular newspaper section or page (i.e., section read by the customer you want to reach)
- Consistent size ad
- Identifiable typesetting
- Continuity in headline or theme (a seasonal "umbrella," or trend that would reinforce its importance and underscore the fashion statement)
- Consistent format in illustration (i.e., sketches or photography)

Even sale ads of fashion leadership stores can contribute an aura of charm or glamour, or even a sense of humor. *(Courtesy of Woodward & Lothrop)*

The presence of all these features guarantees an ambience that cannot be found in any of the store's sale ads. Other special features would be:

- More white space
- A minimum of copy
- Protected placement

Fashion ads are regarded as "clean" because of the existence of more white space and less copy, whereas sale ads are often "dirty" because of lots of black type, much copy, and many illustrations crowded into every available space, with screaming headlines, and so on.

Space for fashion ads is more carefully protected. That is, a full page

It's calypso.
It's captivating.
It's coin dots.
It's crepe.
It's Albert Capraro.
It's black/white.
It's in Designer Collections.
It's On Two at the Plaza.

HARZFELDS

A splendid example of elegance through simplicity. Lots of white space, one graceful figure, a minimum of copy intensified with a single word in bold type. *(Courtesy of Harzfelds, Kansas City, Missouri)*

ad is safe from "dirty" ads. A half page can be protected by "stacking" the ad adjacent to another fashion-type ad (e.g., accessory or cosmetic) that would complement its image.

Photographing Models

When a piece of advertising requires photographing live models with merchandise from actual stock, the fashion director must be on hand to personally supervise the shooting. Usually, a shooting session must be done far in advance of the arrival of stock. It is up to the fashion office, therefore, to obtain the pieces that represent the looks they are trying to sell. The fashion office may also book the models for photography. The fashion director will request the model best suited to the type of garment, look, or theme. During the fitting session, the fashion director will advise the model on the type of hairdo, makeup, and attitude required for the photograph.

Attitude or fashion concept is the prime reason for the fashion director's presence during a shooting. The photographer, receiving instructions from the fashion director, will direct the shooting, but the fashion

For fashion photography, effective lighting is essential in capturing texture and/or mood. *(Courtesy of Tracy Mills)*

director must watch to see that the attitude does not become too sophisticated, too amusing, too elegant, anything, except what it is supposed to be. Attitude is what helps sell the idea. A good model is also a good actress and can interpret the mood of the garment when it is explained to her.

Checking out the model, helping her manipulate the costume correctly (belted right, draped right, tucked in right) is, of course, another important reason for the fashion director to be on hand for the shooting. It is the director's fashion opinion and, ultimately, that of the store, that is reflected in the photograph.

The set, backdrop, or location of the shooting is also part of the attitude. The proper surroundings, either to enhance or dramatize the fashion, must be in keeping with the theme without upstaging the purpose of the photograph.

An example of improper or insufficient instructions from the fashion office to the advertising director, and subsequently to the photographer, was the planned shooting of a new "antique look" for evening dressing. There was no way for the advertising director to know that the fashion office had not been explicit. He is not a mind reader. Whatever instructions of the setting were received were passed on to the photographer. "An evening gown with an antique look." When the fashion director arrived in the studio there was the model, dressed in the delicate antique gown with a Gibson Girl look, standing on the set beneath a huge, baroque chandelier. It was all wrong. It was entirely too massive, too presumptious. The chandelier completely upstaged the soft, delicate attitude of the dress. If the instructions had been more explicit, this would not have happened. At least it would not have gone as far afield. The chandelier had a European grand ball look. The gown was strictly after-the-turn-of-the-century American, a modest, feminine look. Very lovely for evening, but hardly suitable for a grand ball.

The props, the attitude of the model, setting, and lighting must contribute to the fashion look. At no time must they compete. If the costume in question should be a bold print with five or six strong colors, it is important that the background not be too busy. It might be colorful, to help "pull out" one of the important colors, but still not busy. Simplicity of background is often effective in a photograph, in the same way that white space in a newspaper ad enhances the importance of an illustrated subject. It is not necessary for members of the fashion office to design sets for photographing fashion, but it is important to interpret the fashion for those who do build or design sets.

A general knowledge of what is possible and what is needed for fashion advertising is an invaluable asset to the fashion director. Even in stores where the fashion director does not get as completely involved with the fashion projection through advertising or in stores where they do little or no photography, it is still advantageous for the

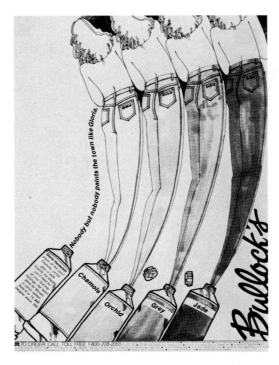

With a minimum of copy, a fashion ad about color, which ran in black and white. *(Courtesy of Bullock's)*

fashion director to have at least an awareness of what makes good ads and what does not. In one way or another, in a future job perhaps, the composite of technical knowledge will put the director in good stead when the challenge presents itself.

HOW TO MERCHANDISE FASHION ADS

The merchandising of the fashion ad starts with the promotion plan. Those "promotables," selected from the fashion director's presentation and then sanctioned by management, are those fashion stories included in the promotion or advertising plan.

On the advertising schedule, where all ads are noted daily, weekly, and monthly, newspaper space is reserved for whatever ads the fashion division has in mind. The leading fashion stories of the season would undoubtedly include new silhouettes, fabrics, colors, patterns, and accessory treatments. Each classification might merit a series or a single ad, but each one is merchandised to relate the message with impact.

The divisional merchandise manager, when consulting with the fashion director, might lay down a series of guidelines. "For this item we are looking for volume, so I would prefer moderately priced examples in the ad." The fashion director will then note that merchandise will be pulled from departments carrying the desired price lines. The director will instruct the staff on what to look for and will advise them about the purpose of the ad. The less they are in the dark, the better.

"This fashion ad, the new look in coats, I think is worthy of a full page. Our coat buyer has selected about four or five pieces she is especially anxious to show. Look them over and see what you think." The fashion director makes a note to visit the coat department. When the fashion director and the buyer agree on which pieces would best do justice to the fashion impact they are after, the fashion director will instruct the staff to pull accessories for the pieces, making sure each one has an individual, effective look. Whenever possible, the fashion office uses actual accessories from stock to be sketched in ads. Very often a customer sees a hat in a coat ad or a piece of jewelry in a dress ad that she wants. If the accessory has merely been sketched from imagination it is frustrating to the customer; she cannot buy it. As mentioned earlier, the real thing gives the ad that much more mileage.

Each ad is merchandised (pieces pulled from stock or flown in ahead of stock arrival) to publicize that which the store has for sale. Each ad must be illustrated with those pieces that best speak for the look, the fabric, and the color, whatever those trends are in which the store believes.

How Fashion Ads Differ

If there was only one fashion story to tell per season, there would seem to be little need to create a ream of exciting, tantalizing, intriguing, and inspired ways to tell the story. "This is it, ladies!" would be enough. Not so. Even if there was only one fashion story or trend, the competitors would be in the same boat—all the more reason to get the fashion message to the consumer in such an irresistible way that you would be assured of her coming to your store instead of the competitor's.

However, there is never just one fashion story; there are many. And it is the differences in the trends and the differences in the customers that dictate the advertising techniques to be applied. The differences influence the frequency, style, size, and kind of space in the magazine section, society page, teen page, business section, and so on. Is it fashion for everyone, or a select few? Is it strictly a here-today-gone-tomorrow fad? Is it fashion with such strong acceptability that it is destined to grow? Is it rehashed fashion, an updated look from last year destined to stick around this year and next year too? The advertising treatment is regulated by the answers to these questions.

Almost all fashion can be pigeonholed into these three areas:

Future or advanced fashion
Now fashion
Basic or bread-and-butter fashion

Each of these, in its own way, is extremely powerful and vital to the total fashion picture. And in the area of advertising, each must be handled in a manner suitable to its characteristics.

Future Fashion

It doesn't take long for word to get around in these days of instant communication in regard to coming fashion trends. Hardly is the idea off the designer's sketch page when fashion forecasts reveal they have it on good authority that the fashion look will be so-and-so. It is not just the retailer who is hearing this prediction, it is the consumer, too. Therefore, to merchandise *ahead* of the consumer and to be a leader of fashion takes some doing. But, having done it (i.e., having succeeded in sampling a coming trend ahead of the crowd) is top priority to tell about in advertising for fashion leadership stores. This is the ad that appeals to the fashion customer interested in being first in her circle, her area, to appear in the new look.

Such a fashion ad, the one capable of giving the store its image as fashion leader, is the one the fashion director gives personal attention to. It is very possible that the sampling or testing of this item or trend was done at the director's urging or recommendation in the first place, and the director is understandably anxious to see customer response to the merchandise and community response to the customer who buys it.

Future fashion is not yet a trend, but future or advanced fashion ads are capable of launching one. If the illustrations, copy, and banner lines or theme are provocative enough, curious, interested customers might drop in to see and try the new idea. Even for those who do not buy this particular piece of future fashion, two advantages are present: (1) the customer has been made aware of the store's leadership and may buy something else during her trip to the store, and (2) she may, through this early exposure of a new look, become one of the more prolific buyers a little later when selections are fuller and the trend is rolling. At any rate, the customer has found her way to the store; she knows where the escalators are and what floor sells her kind of fashion. Exposure is a vital beginning.

Consistency, of course, is one of the greatest boosters for selling future fashion. Ads on advanced fashion trends, appearing often enough, will create the desired dependency of consumers on the store they now feel is on top of everything. Even when a future fashion ad is well done, sometimes the idea is so jolting that it is difficult for the customer to grasp it completely, immediately. She may call the fashion office for clarification.

> "Can a woman my age wear the new look you advertised yester-day?"
> "Would it be all right to wear my last-season's shoes with this new look?"
> "Would you consider this new look too bold to wear to a dinner party at my boss's home?"

A good fashion office is well informed about the newly advertised trend, the appropriate use, accessorizing, and availability in which departments, sizes, and so on. Questions come up most frequently at the introduction of a trend, and a knowledgeable fashion office staff, from beginners on up, can allay a great many fears and doubts of the consumer.

A beginner in a fashion office will soon learn that many a customer feels like a beginner every time the fashion picture has a drastic change. Therefore, even a beginner in a fashion job can feel more confident about individual fashion knowledge, limited as it may seem at the outset, because he or she is closer to the picture than the customer. Observing the kind of questions and reactions stimulated by the newly advertised fashion trends is an excellent teacher. The more perceptive the beginner is of just such small details, the more capable that person will be in watching for details later when he or she has more responsibility.

Now Fashion

The very item or trend that once was projected in an ad as future fashion might very well be that which will eventually emerge as "now fashion." In other words, it is one that caught on. It is the trend that grew important and desirable through acceptance. No matter how great a fashion idea may seem to designers, manufacturers, merchandisers, fashion directors, or magazine editors, consumer acceptance is what puts a trend into motion. Now fashion is a trend in motion.

Unlike future fashion ads, which might be a total of one to announce a coming trend, the now fashion ads might evolve into a full-fledged advertising campaign. Included in the campaign might be ads of the now fashion in the high-fashion area, the moderate priced version, even a knock-off of the look from the budget area. And, in addition to price levels, the campaign might present examples from the women's departments, juniors', children's, and men's. All these ads on a specific fashion subject, if brought together under one umbrella, become an advertising campaign.

Now fashion, that which is currently acceptable and currently in stock, could start out important the first season and grow even more important in the next. On the other side of the coin, now fashion could end up just that, great now, dead tomorrow. Its longevity is not the point; its acceptance "now" is. If it is not obsolete immediately, all the better, but its impact on the now fashion scene is the prime concern of the merchant. The fashion director's great concern is telling the fashion story.

The merchandising of now fashion ads is the most important advertising assignment concerning the fashion director. Here is the big story, the volume story. As a fashion director, everything the fashion division has to sell you must help to herald effectively, here and now, or forever hold your "piece"; the piece, of course, is the advertising copy that must tell what is going on.

Meeting with the members of the merchandising staff, the fashion director would learn exactly how many ads are to be devoted to this effort, what size they are, and when they are scheduled to run. The final advertising schedule would then be drawn up by the DMM and sales-promotion director. The fashion director, now fully aware of which ads are to cover which departments and which ads are to run on which dates, gets out a work schedule for the staff so that they may pull merchandise for the artists in advertising and prepare fashion copy that might be helpful to the copywriter.

Basic/Bread and Butter Fashion

Coming all the way down the pike, future fashion becomes now fashion, and now fashion (if it lives long enough and strong enough) might one day become a classic, a staple, or basic. That is what happens to trends that have endured the test of time.

Advanced fashion, the initial testing, to reach the forward-thinking consumer, is something of the appetizer. The now fashion is the entree, served up in a variety of inviting choices. But the classic old standbys or faithful regulars, no matter what else is on the fashion menu during a given season, are known as the "bread and butter." An advanced fashion might be ignored. A now fashion might bomb. But those classic staples, always dependable, always around, are a store's bread and butter. Whatever other tastes she may have, almost every customer requires some kind of basic or bread-and-butter fashion from time to time.

In music, the new sounds are composed, sung, and flourish for a time. They come and go, but the old standards endure. However, just because a song has become a standard, is no reason to always play it with the same old arrangement. The arrangement, in fact, is the only part that becomes dated, the words and music seldom do. So it is with bread-and-butter fashion; only the arrangement is changed. A newer fabric, sleeve, color, or accent, but still the same song. Still bread and butter. But updated.

Bread-and-butter fashion ads never call attention to their past, nor are they ever called bread and butter in advertising copy. This is strictly an "inside" tag of the retail business. Unlike advanced fashion or now fashion, both of which are perfectly acceptable in advertising copy, bread-and-butter fashion, by any other name, is better. Call it "Updated Classics," "The Classic Look," "The New Standard," or anything that smacks of that which is "new." No woman cares to be associated with the old guard, even though she might recognize the concept as an old favorite. This is not deceiving; it is strictly psychological.

Fundamentally, this is exactly the way bread-and-butter ads are merchandised, with an updated approach, with the new language, new interpretation, new accessory treatment, the whole new thing. Take a sketch of an updated classic placed in an ad with a modern painting drawn in the background and the suggestion makes it new. Take another classic look and include it as part of a season's campaign, say, in an advertising handle such as "The New Spring." All spring fashion ads, upholding the continuity of the theme, would enjoy a fashion spot in "The New Spring"—advanced, now, basic. Together they make up the campaign. Together they tell the entire fashion story for the season. And how well the fashion story is told—with clarity, enthusiasm, and authority—determines the happy ending.

Other Printed Material

In addition to the newpaper ad, there are several other forms of print that come under the jurisdiction of the advertising director. The statement enclosure, booklets, pamphlets, and catalogs are all part of the advertising picture. The fashion director's involvement occurs only when fashion supervision is required. The procedure is much the same as with the newspaper ad. The same things to watch for apply in these cases. Deadlines are always hanging overhead, so timing is essential.

Invitations and Programs

The printed matter that relates immediately to the fashion office is invitations and programs for fashion events. Invitations to fashion shows, for example, are the concern of the fashion office, because it is from the time that the customer is invited that the fashion image or fashion message begins. The color of the stock, the type of print or engraving, the theme and title of the event, are all part of what will be happening at the show, all part of the fashion statement.

A member of the fashion office staff could design and write a sample invitation to stimulate interest in the special fashion event. The format of the invitation might be established. That is, just as the store's newspaper or magazine advertising carries a special look or signature, so invitations might remain a part of the overall concept. Where the established format does not exist, each event presenting a different flavor or need might require or justify an original approach tailored to that event only.

Whatever format or theme the invitation requires, the pertinent information of what is happening where and when is important. The guest receiving the invitation needs to know (in addition to the date, time, and place) whether there is any admission charge, if it is necessary to r.s.v.p., and, if so, the deadline for making reservations. The more understandable and appetizing the invitation, the better the response.

If a printed program is to be provided for guests at the show or fashion event, then this, too, should be drawn up with the theme in mind, perhaps relating to the look of the invitation to establish continuity and greater impact. If the program needs art work for the cover, this must be worked out with the advertising department. The fashion office needs to spell out the kind of art work. An elegant fashion show with a trendy or sporty cover on the program would be obviously a serious contradiction. The fashion office must guide the artist's brush, so to speak, to paint the best picture possible of what the show is all about.

If the content of the program is to include a line-up of those style numbers to be shown, fittings must be made early enough to get copy up to advertising before press time. If names of models are to be included, someone in the fashion office should be assigned to carefully proofread a copy of the program before it is run off. Nothing is more devastating, especially if the guest models are customers, than to have names misspelled. It is the alert, watchful eye that makes for a happy result when it comes to printed material. Once in print, mistakes are recorded for posterity.

MAGAZINE ADS

A fashion ad in a national fashion magazine or special fashion magazine supplement in a newspaper represents more than the specific garment being advertised. If it warrants the price of a full page (and the price is usually substantial), it must accomplish a great deal. The magazine ad, unlike the newspaper ad, is usually a showcase for a single item. One outstanding creation by an outstanding designer. One provocative look dramatizing a special fashion shop within the store. Something special, something that makes a vital fashion statement. The magazine ad, therefore, can be a very important image-maker, for the store as fashion authority, for a department or shop "not to be missed when in town." The selection of the garment to be photo-

Bill Blass as seen through the eyes of Scavullo

The image ad from a Bill Blass campaign that featured the names and styles of a number of the most prominent fashion photographers. *(Courtesy of Peter Rogers Associates)*

graphed or sketched and the theme or mood of the ad must reflect the desired image of the store.

The fashion director's approach to merchandising a national magazine ad, if requested by management to do so, would be to first consider:

1. In which magazine is the ad scheduled?
2. Who is the reader of the magazine?
3. Which fashion look or department would appeal to this reader?
4. What type of fashion would accomplish the greatest impact?
5. In which issue will the ad appear, and what will be the editorial emphasis of that issue?

Answering these questions carefully will be the fashion director's starting place. The fashion director who is consulted about what kind of magazine ad to buy, could guide management into the correct path by stating "we do not belong in this one," or "our customer is the

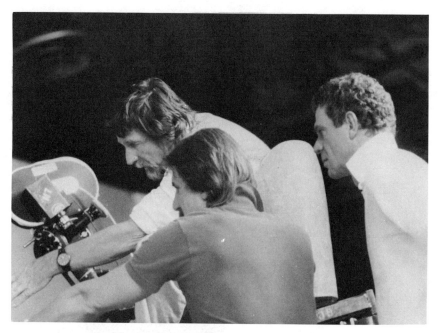

Peter Rogers on a shoot for a client says, "I believe you can do a beautiful ad and still show the merchandise." *(Courtesy of Peter Rogers Associates)*

reader of this one." Also, for certain times of the year one magazine is more suitable than another, such as the back-to-campus issues. It is the fashion director's business to know.

The fashion director might select or recommend which department should be represented in a particular issue of a magazine and which fashion item would be most effective. Since most stores buy space in national magazines for prestige, deciding what will be the greatest image-builder must be the prime factor.

After consulting with the DMM and the buyer of the department from which the item will come, arrangements must be made to obtain a single piece for illustrations or photographs. Also, arrangements must be made to make sure the merchandise will be in the department when the ad runs. This is best accomplished through consultation with the buyer.

Now it is time for the advertising director to get into the act. He or she must be assured that the merchandise will be available in plenty of time for ad preparation. The magazine's deadlines must be met. Also, the advertising director must be filled in with explicit detail on the fashion story the ad is expected to tell.

Magazine Ad Format

If magazine advertising is to be a regular thing, that is, if a series of ads are planned, it is the underlining of the store's image that will make for a more memorable fashion impact. In other words, all the ads with fashion purpose should carry an identification, signature motif, theme, or characteristic that will identify the store and its fashion message. If such a format does not already exist, the fashion director may be of some assistance to the advertising director in arriving at some treatment that would be in keeping with the store's fashion image. It should also be remembered that the longevity of a magazine ad far exceeds the month in which it is issued. Months later that magazine might be reread at home or in a doctor's office or beauty salon. Continuity of format, therefore, helps the ad to stimulate stronger store identification.

All plans for the magazine ad must be submitted to the sales-promotion director for approval. If the ad and its entire conception originates with the sales-promotion director, the person might submit the copy to the fashion director as a double check on proper fashion direction.

Regional Magazine Ads

A department store or specialty shop of national prominence and perhaps in an area attractive to the tourist trade and out-of-town shoppers will be more interested in national advertising in the prestige or currently popular fashion books. A store not likely to benefit from such national exposure but nevertheless anxious to supplement or intensify its fashion leadership on its own home ground, would be more likely to take advantage of ad space in national magazines offered on a regional basis. That is, the ad would run only in those copies distributed in a number of states surrounding the advertiser's location. Thus, even though it does not appear nationally, the ad has the effectiveness of appearing in a highly regarded or much read national magazine. In this way, many stores, who might not otherwise be in a position to take advantage of such an association, can derive the benefit of advertising where the impact would be more immediately rewarding.

Magazine Credits

There is one way that all stores tying in with a national magazine can get national mention, whether they buy advertising space or not. That is the magazine credit, an excellent publicity plus from the fashion books.

In order to advise their readers of what store and in which city the editorially featured fashions can be found, "credits" are awarded by the national fashion magazines to retail stores at no cost. The credits might appear in the back of the magazine or as "on-page" credits. On-page credits are the most desirable. These choice bits of mention are located directly on the ad page or with the editorial feature.

The on-page credit might come about in different ways.

1. Credit may be offered by the magazine to a store involved in a promotional tie-in with a specific issue.
2. Credit may be suggested by the manufacturer whose garment is being featured editorially. The manufacturer advises the magazine what stores are buying the style number involved. The magazine's merchandising department usually checks with the fashion director of each store for verification. "Do you accept this on-page credit?" If the store is buying the style number in question from the resource quoted, the answer is yes and the on-page credit is granted.
3. The last way to obtain on-page credit is store initiated. The buyer or fashion director requests credit mention from the magazine or from the resource being featured.

However it comes about, it is a form of publicity that provides good fashion identification and a share of fashion prestige.

How to Clear Magazine Credits

When the fashion director receives notification from the fashion magazines that credits are available in a forth-coming issue, it is the director's responsiblity to get clearance before accepting. A review of the resource list indicates which buyers might be involved. The director would then send copies of the resource list to those buyers whose merchandise might deserve credit in the book.

The communication might read:

Dear Buyer:
Attached please find the resource list for *Seventeen*'s August issue.
Please check which resources you carry and note if the style numbers to be included in this issue will be in your stock for August selling.
We would greatly appreciate your answer, as we have a deadline to meet, requested by *Seventeen*. They must have immediate clearance to make the issue.

FASHION DIRECTOR

When the replies from all the buyers concerned have been returned, the fashion director sends one copy, with all style numbers and resources to be carried in the store from that issue, back to the magazine. Only those numbers that have been cleared can be included. When a customer reads the magazine and sees the store in her city listed on a page with a dress she wants, she expects to find that dress available.

Some customers far from the city in which a retailer is listed as a *Seventeen* store may write and order the clothes they see illustrated. "Please send me a size 9 of the dress on page 40 of the August issue of *Seventeen*. Please charge to my account."

How Credits Began

Bazaar, Vogue, and Mademoiselle were among the innovators of the magazine credit. At first, only fashion stores in New York were given the nod. Later, in the mid-thirties, major retailers throughout the country were receiving back-of-the-book or on-page credits from the leading national fashion magazines.

In her autobiography, *The World of Carmel Snow*, Mrs. Snow (one of the first great editors of *Harper's Bazaar*) said, "when we were the first to publish out-of-town credits, telling our readers where they might buy the clothes we featured in Chicago and St. Louis and Los Angeles and San Francisco, we were threatened with a boycott from New York stores until Andy Goodman of Bergdorf Goodman brought them back in line."

CATALOGS

In recent years, with the increasingly versatile use of catalogs, and the demand for more sophisticated techniques when they are used for making fashion statements, the fashion director has been awarded a huge responsibility in this connection.

Catalog Types

There are various kinds of catalogs and everyone's mailbox can attest to their skyrocketing number.

Christmas catalogs
Seasonal fashion catalogs (spring, fall, holiday)
Special customer catalogs (working women, large size women, etc.)
Special category catalogs (monogramming, intimate apparel, active-wear)
Home division catalogs
Sale catalogs (white sale)

Of all those listed, the top three (Christmas, seasonal, and special customer books) are of special interest to the fashion director. These require input from the earliest planning stage right through the actual photographing and page layouts. In many stores the special category catalogs would also require the director's help. Coordinators for the home division would be involved with catalogs for that area.

Any of these catalogs might be handled through direct mail (using the store's own mailing list) or as a newspaper insert (or pullout), plus distribution in the store. Some catalogs desired by out-of-towners are purchased either from the stores or through fashion magazines. Some are so famous they have actually become collector's items (i.e., Neiman-Marcus for its unusual Christmas gift suggestions or Sears Roebuck's earliest books).

The Catalog Explosion

In addition to creating catalogs to build traffic in their stores, many retailers with national reputations are recognizing the still untapped potential of catalogs as a means of expanding their trading areas.

Major retailers such as Neiman-Marcus ("N-M by Post"), Marshall Field (Chicago), and Bloomingdale's (New York) go national, so to speak, via fashion catalogs. In the fall of 1981, Marshall Field, for example, issued two fashion books with a combined circulation of one million, for two distinct customer types. One was a slick, high-fashion catalog directed to the fashion customer they hoped to attract to come into the store. The other was a more traditional mail-order piece, which featured classic merchandise.

Some catalogs have taken on another dimension once reserved for other areas of advertising—the "come in to the store and register" contest. A free trip or a special merchandise gift are rewards for the catalog recipient who carefully scrutinizes all the pages.

The so-called catalog explosion, once reserved for mail-order houses, has become a major part of the department store's aggressive advertising plan. And when the catalog moved into the fashion portion of the store's efforts, in addition to the traditional Christmas catalog, the fashion director was awarded another hat to hang on the many-pronged rack in the fashion office.

Catalogs and the Fashion Director

In a speech to AMC fashion directors (May 14, 1981), Paul Nebenzahl, president of Harrison Services, Inc., New York said; "management is finding out that one of the big keys to profit is the fashion director. Suddenly they are discovering that without her or him, no catalog can be successful. I predict that she will be one of the most powerful people in retailing in the next 10 years."

Mr. Nebenzahl went on to offer

THE 10 DEADLY SINS OF CATALOG PREPARATION

1. Planning too late.
2. Unclear marketing direction. Many stores do not know whether they want the catalog to build the store's image, generate store traffic, or increase mail/phone business. The department store catalog should do all three in that order.
3. Heavy dependence on co-op.
4. Retail redundancy: Look-alike catalogs.
5. Uncoordinated spreads—weak statements.
6. Failure to present important looks differently.
7. Unsophisticated standards of taste.
8. Underestimating Santa as a safety net.
9. No one executive in charge.
10. Lack of professionalism.

In summerizing, Mr. Nebenzahl added

10 COMMANDMENTS FOR FASHION DIRECTORS TO FOCUS ON

1. Become involved in catalog from inception.
2. Get management's direction in writing.
3. Spell out direction to divisionals and buyers.
4. Resolve problems with merchandisers in private.
5. Meet with agency Creative Director as soon as marketing direction has been set.
6. Identify the big looks—determine "Are they for us?" "Is it a statement?"
7. Ask: "Is it a coordinated look?"
8. A spread must sell an idea, make a merchandise statement, or support a lifestyle. Watch the subtleties of color coordination and accessorizing.
9. Visualize difference between ordinary and unique statements.
10. Be a differentialist. Be the fashion conscience of your store!

Fashion directors who focus on these forces in their catalogs will have the eyes of their customers focused on their stores.

Catalog Planning

One Christmas over and the New Year rung in and it is almost time again to think of next year's Christmas catalog. The timetable may vary under certain conditions, but, for the most part, the schedule for putting together a Christmas catalog would go something like this:

February/March	Assigned pagination (number of pages for each fashion division)
March/April/May/June	Merchandise selected (during market trips)
July/August	Merchandise samples sent to production company
Late August/Early Sept.	Merchandise photographed
Mid to late September	Final prints and pages approved
October	Book proofed and printed
November	Book mailed

On the early side of this schedule (in February and March) the fashion director would be working with the merchandising team on the fashion statement that should be made and on the theme of the catalog. Will it be an old-fashioned Christmas? Will it be futurist? Would the direction be fantasy? The possibilities are legion, but whatever is decided must reflect the store and its merchandise, the intended image, and the customers to be reached.

Working With the Creative Director

Some retailers have their own in-house agency or production team, but many engage the services of a professional production company that specializes in catalogs. Whatever the situation, the fashion director will work with the creative director to develop the overall look, theme, and fashion statement.

Let us assume that it is agreed that the catalog should have a lifestyle theme. The cover is to have a familiar site in the community (a scenic street, landmark, or building) peopled with the looks to be reinforced inside. Throughout the twenty spreads the theme would continue—a familiar scene, a nostalgic view, with each fashion statement coming forth with proper impact. All the spreads, tied to the cover, would add to the "Home for the Holidays" theme featuring the city and what the people do there.

In addition to the theme plan, there are the specifics for each page, the models in lifestyle situations, exciting but at the same time not upstaging the merchandise. Some will be outdoor shots, some interior. The kind of photographer that will be engaged will depend entirely on the theme and mood of the book. Certain photographers are better at high fashion, others can translate a more folksy flavor to the page. Some have a definite feel for the abstract, some are expert at still photography (gifts, housewares, linens, etc.), while others are specialists in live or animated subjects.

Color Coordinating

Since most catalog pages are in color, the color stories are a top priority. The fashion director is usually solely responsible for color coordination. There are times when an assortment of colors is acceptable on a single page (sweaters, blouses, etc.), but here is the perfect opportunity to illustrate the leading color stories of the season as they relate to the current fashion trends. Even a black and white story in fashion can be enhanced by placing models beside a bright yellow car or red lacquered Oriental screen. Strong color statements can make catalog pages emerge with such irresistable charisma that the competition's look pale.

Plans for what the color stories will be must be shared with the merchandisers and buyers. It is the merchandising team who is responsible for bringing in samples for photographing that will be in keeping with the color plan. Because of the tight deadlines there isn't time for misunderstandings. All plans for all pages must be submitted to each buyer and each division in writing and then discussed for clarification far in advance of target dates.

Catalog Models

The creative director, after working with the store's fashion director, will decide which models to hire. The theme of the book, the mood of the merchandise, and the image of the store will all be considered. Also, the number of pages and pieces of merchandise will determine the number of models needed, plus types—men, women, juniors, children. The schedules for shooting must be very concise and well planned. Good professional models, for a single day's catalog shooting, can cost $1200 to $1500 or more per model, so wasted time is prohibitive.

Shooting Time

Whether the "shoot" is done in a studio or on location, the fashion director is there to supervise. It is the director's responsibility to see that the fashion looks are correctly put together, properly accessorized and accurately interpreted as to fashion trend and the book's theme. Although the photographer will have a stylist on hand who has accumulated special props and accessories, the fashion director represents the store and the translation of its wishes.

Beauty Shots

In addition to the use of live models for the fashion pages, there are areas in the catalog that need animation, even though the merchandise is primarily displayed in stills. For example, the presence of a model's face and hands (closeups) holding and wearing jewelry, in the midst of display shots of jewelry pieces, gives the entire jewelry story a more glamorous aura. On the linens page, instead of seeing just stacks of towels or sheets, a model is cuddled in the bed displaying the bedding story or wrapped in one beach towel while other examples surround her. These are called beauty shots—the inclusion of a model to add beauty to the picture. These are usually made at the same time as the fashion shots (remember those costly daily modeling fees).

A Best Seller

The thrill of seeing the finished photographs is considerable. After so many months of bringing the catalog into reality, it is a very special kind of experience. Fashion catalogs that are very professionally done are always conversation pieces both within the industry and among the store's customers. A successful catalog is as much a "best seller" as any other publication, from the retailer point of view. The pride of publishing a book that is a compliment to the store as well as a producer of sales is a feat made possible by very professional people, including the fashion director.

BILLBOARDS

Another avenue the fashion retailer has chosen to travel toward delivering the fashion message to a broader audience is the outdoor display billboard.

At the outset of the eighties many major retailers adopted this technique as a mass medium to add still another dimension to their advertising program. Often in cooperation with major vendors, the billboards announced with great impact the availability of a vendor's product at a specific store. For a boot ad, the succinct message, along with appropriate artwork, might read: "Best foot forward."

Filene's initial commitment to this format was for six months with a saturation campaign using 250 billboards in the Boston area. In addition to the black and white vendor-shared billboards, Filene's sponsored four-color painted billboards that featured major classifications of fashion merchandise under the store's slogan "Filene's has exactly what you want." It was estimated by the store that the billboards would reach more than 85 percent of the area's adults, at a frequency of 25 times each month.

According to those close to the outdoor scene, the most recognized breakthrough in support of billboard advertising for retailing came from Hastings, a San Francisco-based apparel chain.

Hastings was in need of a new consumer image; it had been losing ground to newer, more progressive competitors. Through a strong saturation billboard campaign, it was able to attract public awareness almost overnight. By using innovative techniques in unconventional advertising (at the time untapped by retailers), Hastings' poster and painted bulletin campaigns caused a local sensation. Newspapers, television stations, and people on the street were talking about this approach. Using the outdoors for retailing was news. Since then, other retailers have discovered the enormous reach of this advertising vehicle, plus the nominal cost, and have used it for sales, fashion, and institutional selling.

VIDEOTAPES

Very often, videotapes are used throughout fashion departments in the store to dramatize or reinforce fashion stories told in advertising. For example, to support the Lord & Taylor catalog and "Personal Edit" campaign (mentioned earlier in this chapter), a 2½-minute videotape presentation ran continuously in the stores to review the fashion stories of the campaign for customers.

In almost any fashion department of a store, vendor-supplied videotape presentations can be viewed by passing customers. They can stop and see how to apply makeup, learn the merits of a specific shoe, observe the easy-care of a washable man's suit, or watch the fashion show of a designer collection. By providing comprehensive product information through the ease of videotape films, the store and vendor can better service customers repeatedly and at the customers' convenience.

AFTERVIEW

"Assume nothing" is a favorite phrase and it has appeared often enough thus far to have made a noticeable point. The point is, wasted time and motion, errors and misstatements, hurt feelings and misunderstandings occur all too often when it has been "assumed" that someone at the other end knows all the answers. Especially in the area of advertising, to assume they know or assume they have been told is suicide. It is far safer, and wiser, to repeat a direction than to omit it. To assume is the mark of an amateur. A pro seldom does.

Advertising is a remarkable area for learning how to project fashion. The beginner who is watchful, even if his or her job is only to run the fashion merchandise from the fashion office to the advertising department, can translate every little bit of information picked up into valuable knowledge. The beginner can almost play a game of skill with meager tasks, such as being a messenger for the fashion office. Why did they select this particular dress to sketch? How will it look with these accessories? What is the point of the ad?

When the person sees the finished product, that dress she carried up for the artist to sketch and those accessories she bagged up and transported, there it is, a huge, beautiful figure in the middle of a full-page fashion ad. The look and the theme begin to have a special meaning and even the department from which it came. "Did it sell? That dress I took up for Sunday's ad?" she might find herself asking the buyer.

"Did it! Over half the pieces we had in that number walked out the next day!"

"Really? That's great!"

Yes, it's great. This beginner shows promise. She is involved and has identified with the whole picture. To empathize with a fashion effort is a mighty strong indication that one could be good fashion office material.

Advertising Terminology

As a reference on advertising terminology, see the Glossary of Advertising Terms at the back of the book.

CHAPTER RE-EXAMINATION

Questions

1. Why is a fashion director involved in fashion ads?
2. Why is accessorizing with actual merchandise important to a fashion ad?
3. What contribution does a fashion director make when models are being photographed?
4. How do fashion ads differ from sale ads?
5. What distinctive techniques should be employed to make fashion ads more effective?
6. What is meant by merchandising fashion ads?
7. How does the magazine ad contribute to a store's prestige?
8. What is a magazine credit?
9. What are three vital contributions a fashion director makes to the production of a catalog?
10. Why is ASSUME NOTHING so important?

Workshop

Draw up a newspaper or magazine ad (an individual ad or campaign). Identify your fashion story, what the illustration will be, select accessories, and write copy. Pinpoint what customer type you are trying to reach.

Ad Stills from TV *(Courtesy of the Television Bureau of Advertising)*

12

FASHION PROJECTION THROUGH BROADCASTING

There once was a time when the retailer and the electronic media (radio and television) seemed destined never to get together. Radio and television were fine for selling soap, refrigerators, automobiles, and cough medicines, but fashion? Not likely. Besides, how?

Advertising to the retailer meant newsprint. Run an ad. See the ad in the newspaper today, and see the people pour in tomorrow. Advertising successes were judged primarily on immediate reaction. Radio and television, seemingly so expensive for the brief moment the commercial was on, appeared too intangible. If a crowd of people was not waiting outside the store when the doors opened on the morning after a commercial, the merchant doubted the effectiveness of the effort. Time sales representatives for broadcasting stations found it difficult to allay the merchants' fears that their messages would be heard and would eventually bring results.

That was the state of affairs of retail advertising on the air several years ago. Even though a great number of products and industries had experienced tremendous success with the broadcasting media almost from its inception, the retailer was the most stubborn, the most skeptical.

HOW THE RETAILER AND BROADCASTING GOT TOGETHER

Before the American listening and viewing public's interests became jaded, radio and television overshadowed most everything else in the area of entertainment. Movies felt the pinch created by television. Rock-music radio stations claimed the teen world. There was reason to doubt that teens did much newspaper reading, and the greater number of cars on the streets and highways, with more car radios, guaranteed a captive audience during regular driving hours.

Retailers began to listen. Broadcasting might have a place in their advertising plan after all. The serious problem facing them now was how to use broadcasting. The car dealer and the hard-sell pitch came off lucky, but how in the world, asked the fashion merchant, can we sell fashion? The networks and advertising service agencies, such as TvB (Television Bureau of Advertising, Inc.), made studies, surveys, and presentations for its members' advertisers or potential advertisers, trying to instill confidence and know-how in the retailers' approach to advertising in the broadcast media.

When the word got around (from the brave, progressive independents and chain stores who recorded successes) that learning the correct techniques and using persistent exposure did the job, things began to happen. Retailers took the plunge, stubbed a few toes on the way, but finally turned out to be one of the largest advertisers in the local broadcasting media. According to a survey of eleven major markets (big cities) by TvB, department stores were in third place in frequency use of local TV as early as 1958. The smaller markets (smaller cities) eventually followed.

Still, retailers were seldom consistent in their use of broadcasting as an advertising vehicle; they could not measure results the way manufacturers of tooth paste, dog food, and detergents could. With all the insistence by the broadcasting executives and their sales agents that retailing was not using the media correctly, the retailer continued to protest that broadcasters did not understand retailing. The tug-of-war never ceased and as late as 1979, when local television stations across the country generated an estimated $1,500,000,000 in sales, retailers accounted for only about 15 percent of that total.

Perhaps what complicated the retailers' approach to broadcasting was their need to sell their wares from more than one angle.

1. Price promotions (sales, clearances, special purchaes, etc.)
2. Fashion (new trends)
3. Image (institutional)

Of these three points, price promotions were the easiest to handle. One could use the hard-sell approach, pound away at the single message—here are bargains, come and get them—and it could be done without costly production. But even here retailers could not list, illustrate, enumerate each and every item the way they were accustomed to doing in the newspaper. As far as they could see, broadcasting was best regarded as a support or reinforcement of what was advertised in the newspaper.

As regards fashion—how could one sell it on radio when you couldn't see it? And how could fashion be sold consistently on television when production costs were so expensive and fashion changed so quickly? After all, a chewing gum commercial could be produced at great cost, but it could run an entire year or more if desired. Gum didn't go out of fashion with the change of season.

It cannot be denied that both radio and television could, and can, do an outstanding job of building image for a department or specialty store, but with limited budgets for advertising (especially in a less than vigorous economy) the retailer has always been hard pressed to let go of dear promotional dollars and use them strictly for institutional selling. This is against everything the retailer has learned about percentage of sales to advertising.

With all this reasoning (called "excuses" by the electronic media), the untapped opportunities haunted both the retailer and the broadcaster and both persisted in looking for workable answers.

NRMA Study

According to a national survey by the Sales Promotion Division of NRMA (National Retail Merchants Association), television advertising received the largest gain in retail media activity during 1980. Percentage increases, according to NRMA, gave television 55.6; newspaper, 52.8; direct mail, 47.2, and radio, 44.4. Their survey further showed that all the stores use newspapers; 95 percent, radio; 80 percent, direct mail, and 65 percent, TV. As of 1980, newspapers received 68.7 percent of stores' advertising budgets; TV, 10.2 percent; and radio, 9.9 percent.

At an NRMA meeting in January, 1982, it was predicted that "retailers will be investing $12 billion in TV by 1990, a figure as large as all of TV advertising in 1981."

Radio Came First

Still regimented by their past experience (the run-an-ad-today-see-immediate-results-tomorrow approach), radio advertising was expected to produce in the same way. It would and it could. However, there was one catch. It was impossible to squeeze the same amount of copy into a minute commercial (later cut down to 30 seconds) as appeared on the page of a newspaper. To tell all the facts about a number of items, or to go into windy detail about one item in a radio commercial with newspaper copy technique, was a disaster. How to use the medium was the big hangup.

There was a time when retail newspaper ads were cluttered with reams of copy and overcrowded with everything, descriptions, illustrations, prices, headlines, floor lines, and store locations. But eventually, even such "dirty" pages were replaced with "clean" makeup. Retailers learned that white space has sales power. This was the lesson that had to be learned in radio and later in television.

How to Use Radio

The retailer was not quick to learn that cramming a volume of words into the alloted time slot was not the way to hold the listener. In the days when almost all commercials were at least a minute long (and sometimes ad-libbed for five minutes, before FCC regulations), the message seemed endless. The announcer rambled on with more facts than the average listener was able to retain. The loaded commercial was not entirely ineffective, but the power of radio, when more of its charms were uncovered, was yet to come.

The merchant learned about hard sell and soft sell. The hard sell, ideal for big sales, close-outs, special purchases, big savings, and hurry, hurry, hurry, was fine in its place, but certainly no way to sell fashion. The soft sell, easy pacing, gentle language, more difficult to write, and more difficult to deliver, was hard for the retailer to utilize.

To begin with, store managements had no one to advise them. The radio stations themselves had much to learn about the problems and needs of retail selling, especially fashion. This was a long time coming.

The designation of advertising dollars into broadcasting met with great resistance even when management sanctioned such a plan. Merchandisers and buyers, responsible for making figures, strongly protested. "Not with my advertising money you don't experiment," was a cry heard regularly from fashion departments. It was understandable. New advertising budget structures helped get the show on the road.

In their use of broadcasting, there was much for the retailer to consider.

1. What merchandise is to be advertised?
2. Who is the customer for this merchandise?
3. Which station has this customer for a listener?
4. At what time during the broadcast day is this customer tuned in?

Buying Radio Time

The careful buying of radio time requires the guidance of the previously mentioned questions. Is it a teen audience to be reached? Then a rock music station is the best choice. Is the merchandise for the working man or woman? Then driving times, to and from work, are ideal slots for reaching employed people. The homemaker? This is more complicated. Ratings must be checked to get some kind of clue as to the share of audience claimed by each station, most desirable listening hours according to programming, and even a survey study of the listening habits of the homemakers of the community.

When the most desirable station or stations have been selected and the best time slots specified, the advertiser has to decide on the kind of schedule to buy. Will it be a regular schedule, day after day, week after week? Will it be just a special purchase of time for special sales, special promotion, or peak periods such as Christmas, back-to-school, Mother's Day, and so on? Will the store run "saturation" campaigns on the air? The saturation campaign (large numbers of spots, continually repeating and hitting hard on a specific item or event) is ideal for sales events but not the most desirable choice for selling fashion. This is not to indicate that large numbers of spots repeated often on a fashion subject are not desirable. The more the better, but fashion commercials are likely to show up on a regular schedule in a compatible time slot so that the correct audience receives the message. By contrast, the sale commercials or those projected in a saturation campaign, might fall anywhere on a schedule, some in prime time and some in less expensive time slots.

This is usually wrapped up in a "package," an assorted time schedule for a specific number of spots.

The fashion director does not buy radio time. Nevertheless, it is important to know what guides the store's purchase of air time and how and where it will be placed. The director is in a better position, therefore, to approach the sales-promotion director and request advertising assistance for fashion promotions or events.

"We will need some help to publicize our big teen show in August. Could you allot a number of spots on the rock stations for this event?" "We will be selling tickets to a fashion show in September and need all the exposure we can get. We need to reach the working woman and young homemaker. How about reserving some of the radio time we own so that we can reach these women?"

The fashion director may even be aware of a particular show or time slot when customers are most likely to be listening. This, too, should be specified. If the director is not aware of which area of advertising would get the best results, he or she may be asking for the wrong kind of help. And, the director must ask. It is not always possible that air time (or any kind of advertising assistance) will be offered unless it is requested. The fashion office soon learns—"them that asks gets."

It is entirely possible that the fashion director will have an advertising budget for everything that comes out of the director's office. Under this plan—and certainly the most efficient one—the fashion director will designate exactly how much of that budget is to be attributed to radio for any fashion event under the director's jurisdiction.

With most major retailers, the broadcast budget is separate from the print media budget. Therefore, the broadcast dollars available in any given month would be allocated to those areas justified in using broadcast advertising. Certainly the junior department would have an excellent chance at capturing August broadcast dollars for back-to-school promotions, the home division would be favored with some of the broadcast money in January for its traditional white sale.

The Advertising Agency and Radio

The actual purchasing of radio time is usually done by the sales-promotion director, in some stores by the advertising director, and sometimes by an outside advertising agency retained by the store. In most cases, the advertising agency is in a better position to survey the market and evaluate the time slots best suited to the store's needs. Also, as a buyer of other air time for other accounts, they are able to take advantage of frequency rates. Through this kind of service, the advertising agency is best equipped to select the most effective time schedule at the best price.

How to Sell Fashion on Radio

The difficult part of selling fashion on radio is deciding what works and what does not. Better still, what works *where*.

The most difficult kind of fashion selling on radio is anything in the prestigious area. The total image of the station must be thoroughly considered, not only the lack of visual illustration, but also the atmosphere in which the message is nestled. If a totally prestigious station is not available (such as an FM or classical station), then at least a more elegant time segment, such as the broadcasting of symphonic music, or some type of lofty-purpose programming would be suitable. Even if the programming were of a lighter nature, and there is no reason why it should not be, it is best if it does not attract the element of hard sell. A personality program (talk show) would be a possibility for selling fashion. In areas where such programming is available, it is important that the program's personality and the store's image are compatible.

In this category, designer fashions, furs, fine jewelry, silver, interior design, or any fashion home furnishings area would be considered possibilities for prestige handling. All of these come under the heading of image-makers. However, many retailers feel that image, per se, is best obtained in other ways. By assigning prestige selling to other facets of advertising they can reserve radio budgets for the places it does the most good.

Regarding the most effective use of radio, more retailers are inclined to include sales and promotions at the top of the list. As regards fashion, the line-up of importance might look something like this:

1. Teen fashions (trendy items)
2. Peak items of new fashion
3. Opening of a new store or shop
4. Announcement of a celebrity or fashion notable's personal appearance
5. Fashion shows and special events

When the minute-long radio commercial became almost extinct (giving way to the thirty-second spot, or less) the selling of fashion by radio improved. Thirty seconds is plenty of time to tell most of the pertinent facts about a specific item or idea.

Teen Fashions on Radio

Naturally, the available listening audience is what draws the advertiser. Young music lovers, with transistors at their ears wherever they go and car radios or bedroom radios turned on at every possible moment, listen constantly to the beat and the sound of their contemporaries. The disk jockeys blurt their language, and report on their interests. They communicate. The advertiser, too, has that very thing in mind—communication.

Copy for the youth market must be written, if not in their language, certainly to their interest. The image of the merchandise and the copy for the commercial must be compatible. The delivery, too, must communicate. Undoubtedly this is why so many personalities on rock stations deliver the commercial within the contents of their music segment. The listening teen customer relates to the total sound. A contemporary station, with contemporary music with commercials from a contemporary store makes it all ring true.

The fashion director, aware of the hottest in fashion for the youth market, makes sure that it gets its share of attention and that the departments have the merchandise. "If we are going to capture the young market, we certainly want them to know, early and repeatedly, that we have the new look in jeans," the director might urge. "This should get top priority in your radio budget."

When the advertising agency begins to write copy on "the new look in jeans," they will need to know what that means. A member of the fashion office pulls out samples, explains the way the garment can be used (with what coordinates, accessories, or new treatments) and what fashion terminology fits the sales pitch.

Peak Items of New Fashion

As indicated earlier, there are limitations to selling fashion on radio. However, with the correct items selected and properly handled, radio can be an important plus in areas outside the youth market.

Advanced fashion, an early projection of a possible fashion trend, has no place in radio. On the other hand, now fashion, with items at their peak, deserves all the attention it can get. In such cases, descriptions are not necessary. Just the mention of the item, letting the world know, "we have them, all sizes, all colors, and all departments," can be the radio approach. The copy will be written and delivered in keeping with the store's fashion image. This time the young disk jockey is not involved nor is the rock station. This time the time slot, station, and delivery is determined by deciding who would be the most likely customer for that item. A new hot trend in sweaters, a new boot, a new look in jewelry, leg fashions, and hundreds of other possibilities. If certain items already enjoy customer acceptance, then additional push on radio, perhaps for specific brands, is a possibility.

With new fashion, the fashion office's services would be enlisted to provide the copywriter with exactly what is meant by that special kind of sweater, that new boot, or new leg fashion. Since the item cannot be seen, the oral facts must be clear, to the point, and tantalizing.

Opening of a New Shop

Radio can be a big plus in this instance. A saturation schedule can be purchased on radio to announce the opening of a new shop in the store. Short, concise commercials presented in the form of an invitation urges listeners to "drop in tomorrow, the opening day of our new shop."

The fashion office needs to be sure that the advertising agency thoroughly understands the fashion image desired for the shop. It is at this time, the beginning and the opening, that the image can be established. So, if it is to have an elegant flavor, a bizarre atmosphere, or a romantic or mystic environment, this message must be carefully carried within the lines of the copy. It is at the outset that the tempo of the shop is established. Careful coordination should be exercised between the fashion department and the advertising agency. A directive, written by the fashion office and submitted to the advertising agency in advance of copy preparation, would be extremely helpful for everyone concerned. Even if it is just a few words describing the intention of the shop or the kind of merchandise carried there, there is less chance for misunderstanding. The fashion office soon learns that to *put it in writing* saves a lot of grief. Better still, in addition to the written directive, a tour through the shop with the agency representative or copywriter would be ideal. A member of the fashion office, acting as guide, can further explain the written description.

Personal Appearances

The immediacy of radio is very often a blessing. Occasionally when something unexpected or unplanned turns up that is too good for the store to pass up, getting out publicity may be a problem. For example, there is an unscheduled celebrity, suddenly available for a personal appearance at the store. A great drawing card, but how to get the word out at such a late date is a problem. It is too late to schedule an ad in the newspaper. Maybe too late for production, or getting enough time on television. However, radio spots, easier to squeeze in and easier productionwise, can get a hurry-up job done. Perhaps a recording of the familiar sound of the celebrity's voice can give the announcement the punch it needs.

Even when the need of exposure is not urgent, the announcement of visiting dignitaries or celebrities is ideal fare for radio. The invitation form of announcement, expressed with the personal touch of the human voice, has a great deal going for it. The fashion office, often responsible for the care and feeding of a visiting personality, primarily in the fashion division, may also be responsible for the celebrity's whereabouts during the visit, and any biographical material necessary for publicity. Where there is a special events director, he or she might take on this responsibility, but if the guest has a fashion identification, the fashion office is also often involved.

Fashion Shows

All channels of advertising can be enlisted to publicize a fashion show, depending how big and important it is. Radio, already saluted as an ideal announcement or invitation media, certainly can lend its usual effectiveness in this way for fashion shows.

Naturally, of all announcement-invitation-type spots destined for radio exposure, the fashion show announcement is the one most strongly associated with the fashion office. In this case, all pertinent information regarding the show must be supplied, in writing, well in advance of the show to permit the advertising agency or advertising department time to reserve air time, schedule appropriate time slots, write the copy, and produce the spot. In thirty seconds, the announcer can tell the listener everything about the show—where it will be, when, what time, admission fee, where to r.s.v.p. (if necessary), who will be there, and what will be shown. If a guest commentator or special attraction is planned, this, too, should be incorporated in the radio spot.

Hard Sell—Soft Sell

All the previous examples of selling fashion on radio are primarily soft sell. If there is any "punching" done at all, it might come under the heading of enthusiasm, excitement, elation. One does not need to strongly bend the listener's ear to sell fashion. What is needed is the true flavor of its intent and purpose. Listeners do not have to be hit over the head, so to speak, with a fashion story; they only need to be informed. The technique used to impart the information would follow, of course, the image of the store.

Hard sell, on the other hand, belongs completely out of the fashion area, into the promotion area. Sale events can stand hard sell. To stir up excitement, to transmit electric urgency about the event (great savings, great buys, great values) is necessary when crowds of shoppers are to be attracted or the sale event is "for a limited time only."

Both approaches have their place. They will appear in one way of another in all areas of the media-mix. Understanding how, when, and where is the way to successful retail selling through broadcasting.

**The Dramatized
Commercial**

Bringing some theater into commercial copy has become a favorite way of injecting personality into what otherwise might be not only dull but sound like all other commercials. Using a two-voice dramatization, for example, with a comedic treatment is a special attention-getter and is more enjoyable to hear when used repeatedly.

TELEVISION AND THE RETAILER

From the early days of television, the paradise for the used-car dealer, the cigarette maker, and the breakfast food giants, retailers saw little or no future in this medium.

They tried, but nothing seemed to work. Television was ineffective, they felt, no matter how cooperative the station seemed to be, offering assistance in production, writing copy, casting, and recommending most suitable air time. The results seemed spotty, sometimes pretty good, most of the time not good. What with all the added headaches of working and planning a TV commercial (a world they found too difficult to understand and for which they could not always draw on their own shop for help or execution), it just wasn't worth the trip. If a store wanted to throw a big sale, an impressive ad in the paper and some hard sell on radio usually did the trick. Why struggle with television when there were other avenues to choose?

Videotape

Before the days of videotape, live commercials were a tremendous chore for retailers. They had to transport stacks of merchandise to the TV studio every time a spot or program was to be aired. In the case of hard goods, truckloads of furniture and appliances had to be transported. If the commercial was to be repeated, the merchandise had to be stored at the TV station and reset every time the advertiser hit the air. For one or two spots this may not sound like too much of a problem, but if any volume of advertising was considered, such as exposing many items from many departments, this became an obviously troublesome chore.

When videotape came into general use (about 1959) the use of television became less complicated. Eventually, one commercial could not only be taped for repeated use on a station, but when equipment on all stations became synchronized, a dub (a copy) of the same commercial could appear on several stations at the same time. Another virtue of videotape was the instant playback. One could tape a commercial and play it back immediately for approval. If approved, it could be edited, dubbed, and used as often as the advertiser desired. If it was not approved, a simple roll of the tape and it could all be cut over. Not only could errors be eliminated, but many a commercial could be improved or changed before being aired to the world. Now there was just one last issue bugging retailers.

Color versus Black and White

Before the mass purchase of color sets, retailers protested strongly that fashion was not getting a fair shake on television because black and white made most clothes look dull. Contrasts were lost. Unless the costume had a definite light/dark contrast, photographing fashion for TV left much to be desired.

The really big interest in fashion selling on television came when local stations acquired color equipment to transmit color, either from the station or remote (perhaps directly from the store or some outside fashion event). Color strengthened the fashion story, made it come alive, and whetted the viewer's appetite for that marvelous red coat . . . that brilliant green dress. Even though many viewers might be seeing the same program on a black and white set, retailers felt encouraged to trust television with their fashion-advertising dollars.

Selecting Television Time

Program selection in television is as important as *station* selection is in radio. A television station is not as susceptible to "image" as is a radio station. An advertiser is more likely to suffer or enjoy audience reaction from TV program association. For example, sponsorship of a regular newscast could reach one kind of audience, sponsorship of a golf tournament another kind, and a cooking show, kiddie show, or horror movie would reach still different audiences. Sponsorship depends on the product being sold, the viewer the retailer is trying to reach, and the image the store is trying to maintain or gain. All these factors guide the purchase of television air time.

The selling of fashion needs special attention. One does not schedule a commercial about formal ball gowns during a tennis tournament. However, what better place to promote the pro shop or active sportswear departments of both men and women? For a more sophisticated approach to television program selections, the retailer considers the viewing habits of various age groups, income groups, and ethnic groups. This is especially important in radio but is also applicable to television.

The Power of Repetition

If merchants were using newspaper to make a sales impact, they might buy a bigger space, a full page, a double truck, or even an entire section to add emphasis to the importance of the event or items on sale. In television, they certainly would not expand the length of their commercial message. They would, instead, use a saturation campaign, repeating the message many times, in many different time segments, or over and over again in the same time slots each day. The advertiser gains two things with this kind of impact: (1) the established audience catches the commercial at the same viewing time each day and gets a repeated exposure to the sales pitch, and (2) the advertiser reaches new viewers that didn't catch the message earlier that day or the day before. In other words, the advertiser gets two cracks at the audience—the regular listener and the newly tuned-in listener.

The power of repetition is most commendable in selling fashion on television. The first time a fashion idea is seen on the screen, the viewer is introduced to the look. The next time the viewer sees the same commercial she considers its merit, identifies with it, and toys with the idea of maybe looking at the garment in the store. The third time she sees it, it reminds her of her former impression and prompts her to action. It is hoped that is what happens to the viewer observing a fashion commercial. If it is well done, related effectively to the type of viewer known to be there, the chances are very good.

This is not to say that the viewer cannot be moved to response or action after one exposure to a commercial, but where apathy or distraction sets in, the power of repetition insures instant recall of the product and the store. Repetition and continuity of scheduling is the secret to the intelligent use of television advertising.

The Success Stories

Observing the national or major market advertisers—perhaps a glamorous cosmetics or fragrance line, an image fashion designer, a mass producer of active sportswear, pantyhose, shoes, or women's under-fashions—the local retailer learned a little about the technique of selling fashion merchandise on television. It showed the retailer how a believable, repeated message could make the product and its maker's name unforgettable. They also saw how such a powerful message could bring the customer into the store looking for that specific item. For example, when designer jeans (or status jeans) became such a desirable form of dress, the television media was credited with a great deal of the success for some jeans manufacturers. Lacking an established name designer, they needed to create another strong desire for their product. Not waiting for retail outlets to sell their product, they went directly to the consumer via television. Their message was so provocative, so effective that merchants, who otherwise would see no reason to stock an unknown brand, were literally forced to carry the line when customers came in asking for what they had seen on TV. When retailers saw the impact on their customers they felt encouraged to take another look at television as a seller of fashion. They were not totally convinced, mind you, but they felt there must be an untapped opportunity in television if it were effectively utilized.

In regard to institutional fashion selling on television, retailers understood this approach better, although they often felt this was a luxury they could not afford. However, when Saks Fifth Avenue launched a three-month million-dollar television advertising campaign in four of its markets to support their new goals for the 1980s, it was watched hopefully by both the networks and potential advertisers. Since the purpose of this campaign was to help Saks change consumers' perception of the store as expensive and not geared toward the youth market, it was felt that television was the best avenue to take. Most television authorities believe that the best way the retailer can use television (aside from sales and promotions) is to sell the store and what it stands for, to promote a store that has been renovated, has adopted a big change in merchandising, or to introduce a retailer in a new market.

The Television Fashion Commercial

The fashion director might be called on to indicate to the sales promotion director which fashion trend in a given season might benefit from television exposure instead of radio or newspaper, or in addition to either or both.

Before the director makes such a recommendation, three things must be considered:

1. The importance of a trend.
2. The strength with which it will be backed up with merchandise.
3. The amount of return on investment expected and growth potential.

If all these points indicate that the trend is not only worthy of the television dollars to be spent but in need of the support, the fashion director submits the request.

Let us assume the trend is expressed with a jungle theme. Safari-type styling with jungle, tropical atmosphere, exotic prints, khaki fabrics and colors. It is available in all departments—for men, women, and children. A big dollar investment has been placed on this trend throughout the company. The fashion director convinces the sales promotion director that all is in readiness in the stores with this trend—the merchandise is in in great supply, displays and shops are up. Advertising support is needed to sell the fashion story.

Here is an opportunity for the creative fashion director. The director recommends a jungle scene—perhaps the zoo will provide a real lion or baby elephant. Samples of the kind of merchandise to be shown are pulled to inspire the plan. The items are selected, the number and types of models needed are determined, and suggested copy is drawn up for the copy writer. Of course, the fashion director will accessorize each outfit to be shown and will be on the set for the filming to protect the proper interpretation of the trend and to be sure that important details are covered.

The Television Spokesperson

It is estimated that ninety-eight percent of all American households have at least one television set, and more than fifty percent have more than one. What's more, the owners of these television sets sit in front of them an average of six and a half hours per day. With that kind of attention, it is very likely that almost everything that hits the air is going to get noticed in some degree.

Never before have there been so many celebrities developed, so many faces recognized by so many. But most encouraging to the television advertiser is the TV commercial celebrity. In countless number of cases, the spokesperson, model, or personality involved consistently in a commercial campaign has become as famous (or even more so) as the star of a television series. The need for recognized spokespersons, to identify the product with image, is so great that "big names" from every walk of life are engaged as television salespeople.

Whether the spokesperson is seen, or simply heard and never seen, the consistency of an identifiable voice is one way to intensify any television or radio sales pitch. When the voice is heard, or the person is seen in connection with a specific product or store, it reinforces in the mind of the viewer where to go for the purchase.

With the fashion commercial, a voice or personality that can be identified as a fashion authority has some obvious advantages. Also, it is felt that the same voice that is heard on hard-sell sales spots should not be heard speaking for fashion. In other words, fashion and image or institutional spots should have an identity of their own. Since the fashion director is the fashion authority for the store, it is a great plus if the director is someone who has the talent to speak for the store in this manner. Of course, it is not often possible, even with talent, because of constant travel time and other distractions, but it must be noted that certain advantages and rewards are worth the special effort.

It must also be noted that the spokesperson for the store on television should be someone who is not heard on competitor's commercials. When using freelance talent this problem could come up.

HOW TO WORK WITH THE ADVERTISING AGENCY

The sales-promotion director and GMM may allot the necessary budget for TV advertising, and buyers and DMMs may decide what fashion items they would like to expose on TV, but someone has to pull it all together from that point on. This is where the specialized know-how of an advertising agency is valuable. Not just any advertising agency, of course, but one expert in television and one with knowledge of servicing the retailer.

What the Ad Agency Can Do

Almost all department stores handle their print advertising with in-house staffs, but when it comes to broadcasting, they rarely maintain a department to service their needs in the broadcasting media. For a 15 percent commission (and sometimes plus a fee) the advertising agency provides the store with creative production and media buys. They also can keep their clients abreast of sophisticated marketing techniques.

In building a store's fashion image, Bloomingdale's of New York is an interesting example. Usually the retailer's in-house advertising people are burdened with the immediate problems of getting customers into the store, making this sale successful, meeting last year's figures for the coming week. Consequently, long-range planning for building the store's image is put on the back burner. The first 75 years of Bloomingdale's existence (they reached 110 in 1982) was seriously devoid of a good fashion image. Around 1970 they engaged the services of an ad agency to help build their fashion image. Today they are one of the great fashion merchants of the world.

The agency, usually working directly with the store's sales-promotion director, is equipped to advise on the best time segments to buy, which stations, and which programs. The agency can report on the availabilities, the ratings, and costs, and can recommend the best way to go.

An important part of an advertising agency's service is its knowledge of television production techniques. An agency is also an idea factory. It is their job to translate the store's fashion or quality image or its promotion message into audio-video effectiveness.

Because television is more than a radio with pictures or a newspaper that moves, the presentation of the store's message has special requirements. Television requires:

Video production

Audio production

Product animation

Within the framework of these requirements, copy must be written, settings planned, action planned, special effects planned, talent selected, and models booked, fitted, and directed. With so much time-consuming detail involved, the agency takes a great deal of the pressure and responsibility off the store's personnel. However, when it comes to fashion projection on TV, the agency works with the fashion office.

Fashion Guidance for the Agency

The store's fashion authority is the fashion director. To guarantee continuity of its fashion philosophy in this advertising medium, as in all the others, the director's guidance is essential.

What is meant by poster-blue? Is it this one or that one?

What accessories go with the new coat look?

What is meant by figurative prints?

How should the new African jewelry be dramatized?

The questions are endless because the change of trends is endless. Only someone who is close to the changes, aware of what they are and what they mean, can direct the honesty of the message.

As noted earlier, the staff members of the advertising agency are also invited to the fashion director's fashion presentations to be sure they are informed of what each season's story will include. But since they are not working with the trends on a day-to-day basis, it is important to specify as each commercial attempt comes up, what is meant and what is needed.

Merchandise Selection

The fashion office figures strongly in the area of merchandise selection. Not only do the fashion coordinators pull fashion merchandise to truly reflect the trend or item in question, but they must also consider the advantages and pitfalls of this intimate medium of communication, television.

The greatest features of fashion, color, texture, and head-to-toe coordination, could only be imagined before color. Tweeds, plaids, and prints, plus the color and contrast of accessories, were difficult to dramatize. Color made it all happen. A tight close-up on a great woven wool tweed, for example, tells the viewer immediately all about the texture, color, and character of the fabric.

Color

However, even with color, some things do not come across effectively. Solid black and dark colors conceal detail, unless the silhouette is all that matters. Stark white, too, although dramatic for a certain type of gown, is usually best replaced with color, even if it is delicate or pastel.

All this the fashion office keeps in mind when the buyer offers pieces for a fashion commercial. "Every piece black, with beige?" If the pieces did not represent a color trend, and they were also available in other colors, the fashion office would be wise to color coordinate the group with more photogenic choices.

Motion

Movement, too, is an exciting advantage that can only be found in television. Wherever possible, this factor should be considered. The fluid, floating feeling of a soft fabric, the swish, flare, and dash of a bold fabric, be it a gentle, understated look or flamboyant avant-garde treatment, if it's the character of the look that carries the message, there is no place it can come more alive than on television.

The Magic of Television

Television is a personal, intimate medium. People come to TV for an emotional experience. They want to be entertained, to be informed, to feel, to relate. Thus, an exciting message, a personable message, an enchanting, glamorous, or amusing message related to fashion can very well jar that viewer out of his or her apathy or resistance to a particular store. For example, many customers who would not look at the store's newspaper ad because, let us say, they do not look to that store for fashion, are exposed and captured (at least in the beginning) by a message on television.

Through this personal medium, a store's fashion image can best come alive. It can talk, move, smile, and entertain. These are not necessarily the virtues that make a strong sales pitch on television successful. If the price is right, and the goods desirable, chances are it will sell. But fashion is different. It depends on image, charm, beauty, and excitement. These and many other emotional ingredients make the fashion message on television sell merchandise, make friends and draw customers to come see.

The selection of fashion merchandise, therefore, carries responsibility to entertain, to inform, and to stimulate desire. All of this and more. A series of well-done fashion commercials by a store could very possibly enhance its fashion image, fashion authority, and fashion leadership, not a small load by any measurement.

How Will It Televise?

When detail is necessary in a newspaper ad, the artist or illustrator can very easily draw every seam, tuck, stitching, pocket, and button. But on television all of this could be lost unless colors of the detail are in strong contrast to their background. A gown of pink taffeta with appliqued pink taffeta petals might be the most divine creation around, but is very likely that most of the precious detail would be completely lost on television. If the petals were in a contrasting color, considerably more detail would come through. Commentary helps, of course, but television is a visual medium. The viewer should be able to see what is shown, not just be told. Television should not be treated as a radio with pictures.

Television is an X-ray machine at times. Every wrinkle, every ill-fitted undergarment, and every crooked line can show and break up the mood. The sensitive television camera, while failing to pick up pale or subtle detail, has an uncanny talent for picking up unexpected flaws. The fashion office must watch carefully for those pieces that will fail to come across or will make the wrong kind of impression.

Guidelines for Choice

A good way to avoid mistakes, especially for the beginner, is to follow a simple checklist on what the merchandise is expected to represent.
  1. What will the merchandise be selling?

A department or shop

A color

A fabric or fiber

An item

A trend

A length

A designer or manufacturer

If the TV commercial is to be on a department or shop, a representation of pieces indicative of that area must be pulled. If it is to be a color, smashing examples from several fashion departments might be included. It is the same with a trend, an item, or a length. When it comes to a fabric or fiber, the garments must be honest representatives of the ingredients advertised. If it is a commercial to herald a designer or manufacturer, the task is much simpler; one must simply select those pieces best suited for television from the named collection; the pieces in stock are the pieces used. It is wise to televise only those pieces that have sufficient backup in the stores. Customers who call or come in for the specific item they see in the TV commercial will be very disappointed if it is not available.

2. How many pieces and how many models have been ordered by the agency? This is important to know before pulling. It is entirely possible that three garments shown will require three models, but is is also possible (through the magic of television editing) for the same model to wear all three pieces. Knowing this in advance, the coordinator responsible will pull the specified merchandise in sizes corresponding to the need.

3. What production facts about the commercial might influence the choice of merchandise? Actually, it should be the other way around—merchandise gets first consideration. Production and format and copy should be drawn up to express the clothes. However, there are occasions when certain special effect or production plans influence a selection.

For example, if a model is going to be "keyed" into a set or prop, the costume cannot be blue. If blue is the key color, her dress would completely disappear. The special effect would not work. Undoubtedly you have seen "keyed" production, a model made to look very tiny, sitting on the brim of a hat, or climbing out of an oversized object.

On the other hand, if the agency advises the fashion office, "We are going to open up on a silhouette shot," it would be understood that the models and the garments will need to be receptive to silhouette lighting. Line and movement are very important in such a shot. If the models are not required to pose in a "freeze" (to stand motionless), the important action of the fabric must be considered, chiffon that floats and can be blown for motion, generously cut crepe or silk can swirl, sleeves can billow . . . tiers of any fabric can show dimension.

The possibilities of production requirements are legion. What's more, they change every season, every year. The important issue is that whoever is responsible for merchandising or selecting fashions for television commercials must be up to date on what's happening.

4. In coordinating a commercial where more than one garment is shown, what is the best way to insure against similarity? It is very possible to select three different garments, a yellow shirt dress, a yellow suit, and a yellow shirt and skirt, and have all three photograph

almost exactly alike. If there is little difference in the line, no difference in trim or detail, and no difference in color, it is very possible for all three to come off enough alike to be alike.

If color is a factor in a commercial, then the example of a dress, a coordinate, a suit, or a coat must be different in almost every detail. Besides watching a more exciting commercial, the viewer can enjoy a thirty-second fashion show and come away with the feeling that the store has a great selection of everything. Accessories, too, help to enhance, dramatize, or punctuate the various looks. Individuality is what each garment should enjoy. Without it, there is no point in its being there, soaking up expensive air time.

Models Make the Clothes

A dress on a hanger is a dress on a hanger. A dress on a bad model would be better left on the hanger. Even an ordinary dress on a good model can stimulate the imagination. Selecting models for television differs in several ways from selecting runway models or showroom models. A fashion show model can be almost any height or size, depending on the clothes being shown and the audience they are facing. Television cameras make a skinny girl look slim and a plump girl look fat. Approximately ten to fifteen pounds can be added by the camera. Height is not as important on television as are body measurements. It is usually difficult to tell how tall someone is unless they are standing next to someone whose height is a known fact. Tall, thin girls, however, usually come off best.

In addition to size and more important than size are a model's photogenic qualities. Sometimes the most sophisticated and colorful runway model will have the wrong kind of personality for TV. Another model, seemingly plain, might photograph like a dream and come across on the screen with everything the viewer likes to see. This is not to say that a ramp or fashion show model cannot also be a good TV model; it does mean, however, that it does not necessarily follow.

A model or personality who is photogenic does not necessarily have to be a beauty. A certain something—a soft look, a pixie look, a dramatic look. Whatever that something is, if it works, it is what it takes.

Movement, too, makes an interesting difference. Many movements and gestures or techniques employed by the model may come off quite well in person, but for some reason, on television where everything seems exaggerated, those same movements are too much, not enough, unattractive, or unappealing. This is not at all unlike some motion picture stars who react to a camera in a way they react to nothing else. The model who has great rapport with the camera can do wonders for a fashion commercial.

**How to Find
TV Models**

A fashion office might be able to pull all it needs for TV right out of its "stable" of fashion models. If the regular crew works out, fine. But if they do not, it is wise to hold auditions specifically for TV modeling. These are best held right in the studio on closed circuit camera. This way it is possible to see the model's photogenic qualities, and scrutinize how she moves, how well she takes direction, and how flexible her effectiveness might be in various moods on camera. Some excellent models, who thrive on a live audience, freeze on camera. Others, not too fond of the live audience, come alive for the intimacy of the camera.

**Personality
Identification**

Just as a store would prefer to have an announcer or commentator whose voice is associated only with them, the models the fashion office engages for television exposure would best serve the store's image or personality identification if they did not appear for the competition. It is obvious that if the same model appeared on the air for two different fashion stores, the viewer might be confused (especially if she is a model who appears often), and memory recall of whose fashions were seen might be difficult.

**Preparation of
TV Copy**

When the merchandise has been pulled and the models fitted, the agency is called in to look over the pieces and write the copy. The fashion office may be called on to provide the copywriter with a fact sheet on what the garment is, what department it is from, who is the designer, what is the fabric, what is its purpose, and so on. Even with a fact sheet, which should also provide the writer with the correct and current fashion terminology, there will be questions.

"What do you call this kind of sleeve?"
"Would such an outfit be restricted to at-home wear, or could it be worn away from home?"
"What will you be calling this new color combination?"

Every new trend and every new commercial will bring new questions. The store's authority is the fashion office. The fashion director should make sure every staff member, even the newcomer, is kept up to date on the new answers.

Theme Continuity

When promoting a fashion trend on television the overall "handle" or "banner" (slogan) theme should be the same as the one used in newspaper ads, in-store signing, or on radio. Referring back to the jungle theme mentioned earlier, if the fashion story is being identified in the store as "Jungle Fever," it should be repeated in ads and broadcast as well.

Taping Time

A representative of the fashion office should be on hand for the taping of fashion television spots or programming. It is good to have an advertising agency that can ride herd on all the details of televising, but fashion interpretation is the job of the fashion office.

As any good fashion magazine will testify, not a single model is photographed or makes the editorial pages of that publication without the presence and approval of the fashion editor in charge. That person is on hand throughout the shooting sessions, making sure the photographer comes up with the accurate interpretation of the fashion and the accurate image or approach of the magazine. It is the same with the fashion director of a store. The director and staff are the editors of the fashion image of the store, the guardians of the fashion stories being photographed.

Every detail of how the costume comes across must be watched—the tilt of a hat, the tie of a scarf, the handling of a bag, the drape of a gown. A mistaken approach can literally change the whole concept. Also, if an economy of shots or takes is involved, the fashion director can give guidance on the most effective way to go. "Don't waste any time panning the waist and skirt; they're not new. But that shoulder and sleeve line is very new. If you are going to hit anything, hit that."

The Television Fashion Show

If a portion of a show, a segment, or complete program is devoted to showing fashion, the pacing and movement must be well rehearsed and "on the button." Unlike a live fashion show, if a model is late, the commentator can ad-lib to fill the spot. On television this is deadly. One model must follow the other with marked precision. Even though most events would be done on tape where there is margin for error, studio taping time is expensive and the more retakes involved, the more changes or revisions, the more expensive the show becomes. A few ways to eliminate problems at the outset include:

1. Be sure there are enough models booked for the show to insure good pacing.

2. Book models who have had previous TV experience so not too much time is spent in explaining which camera is on, where and how to move.
3. Give the models sufficient time to rehearse. Advise them where they "hit their mark" (place where they stand), and what kind of shots will be taken so they can relate their turns or movements to the gown and effect being sought.
4. Time the show during rehearsal so that no one is surprised when it is running short or running long. Rehearsal is the time to fix the pacing.
5. Remember that ten or fifteen seconds is a long time to hold on one model; that is plenty of time for the viewer to get the whole picture. If commentary requires a longer focus on a model, the costume should justify it.

Staging and Lighting

Television is a theatre. A cast of players provided with a good script and good direction must also have a good stage setting and good lighting. Staging on television has unlimited possibilities. One set can become many. A moving camera, another angle, a tight shot, a wide shot, a down shot, all magically transform a static set into a mobile unit.

Thanks to the flexibility of the camera, simple settings can go a long way. Especially when working with fashion, simplicity is most desirable. The intimacy of the camera and the concentrated area of the screen as the viewer sees it should build up an immunity to overdoing. Fashion is most sensitive to competition in backgrounds. Simplicity permits the fashion item to come forth as the main focal point. The less distraction the better.

In addition to sets, the electronic miracles of special effects can create almost any desired atmosphere without the use of props or settings. For contemporary fashions a stylized type of background or lighting, surrounded with special effects in lens patterns, motifs, and movement, can create a contemporary mood that will be more memorable than a fully constructed set. Lighting, a complete art in itself in the television medium, is the best friend fashion can have. Without professional lighting, the most exciting, dramatic, and romantic effects might be missed. Colors and fabrics, too, require special attention. The fashion director, consulting with the television station's engineers, can help them understand what special effect or lighting is most compatible with a specific fashion look. If an advertising agency representative is available, such direction should be relayed through this channel—fashion director to agency to TV director to engineers.

It is sufficient to say that a network of people and responsibilities take place to get a simple commercial on the air. What the viewer sees in a few fleeting seconds has taken many hours, a variety of talents, and no small number of advertising dollars to make it happen.

Filmed Commercials

Not all commercials are taped in the studio. Many are filmed on location. That is, taken to a site more conducive to the merchandise being shown. For a swimwear commercial, cameras and models hit the beach. For nautical-influence in fashion, all hands go on deck of a boat for the filming. For a fashion story of Picasso-inspired prints, one artistic approach might be inside an art gallery or on the steps of the local art museum. For Christmas commercials, it is very common to lease someone's home for a day or two, move Christmas tree, gift-wrapped packages, and other props into the house, light the fireplace, and stage the familiar scenes of opening gifts from the store. Wherever the shooting takes the TV commercial cast and crew, the fashion director is present to oversee his or her specific responsibilities.

Cable TV

The same caution with which retailers approached commercial television manifested itself with the entrance of cable TV. Only this time, instead of waiting to be invited or coaxed into utilizing the medium, retailers launched a systematic investigation of the merits of cable TV as it related to their needs. AMC (Associated Merchandising Corporation) sponsored two seminars on cable television for its member-stores, one for sales-promotion directors and one for special events directors. Since they believed that cable would be a factor in the media mix, they wanted their stores to understand what the potential might be. According to a story reported by *Stores* Magazine (September, 1981), cable television was reaching 25 percent of all U.S. homes through 4,360 cable systems (although ten systems owned 44 percent of the subscribers) at that writing. It was further reported that by 1990, 61 percent of U.S. households will be subscribing to cable television, according to New York advertising agency Ogilvy and Mather. From the research firm of Management Horizons, Inc., came the prediction that 20 percent of all U.S. retail sales will be made by videotex, teletex, or other new electronic media by 1990.

Other opinions indicated that cable television would have advantages to offer the fashion retailer that commercial TV did not.

1. The advertising message beamed to a specific audience. (For example, on a sports network with mostly a male audience, on a music channel aimed at 18–34 year olds, on a news network for a higher-educated audience, etc.)
2. Use of infomercials. Infomercials (information commercials), rang-

ing in length from 30 minutes to four hours, demonstrate and explain the use of a product in an editorial format.

3. The purchase of spots on a regional basis. (A national advertiser could sell one product desirable to specific regions, and another suitable for others—bathing suits to Florida, overcoats to Minnesota.)

The opportunity for shopping at home for cookware, cosmetics, and fashion, to name a few, and seeing how the products work or are applied, is the promise offered by cable television, a catalyst in expanding direct marketing. The new communications technologies—cable TV, video discs, cassettes, and electronic components—add a new dimension to fashion merchandising.

AFTERVIEW

The fashion office can be responsible for many of the pluses that come to a retail store through the medium of television.

Almost all cities have local television shows, which are emceed or hosted by a personality on a regular basis. Such a personality, in need of an extensive wardrobe, is usually an excellent source of fashion exposure for a store who is willing to furnish and dress this person in exchange for a credit line in the roll-ups (credits listed at the end of the show) each day. Sometimes, the personality is willing to mention the outfit, describe it, and tell what department and store it came from in exchange for the generous service of a different ensemble every day.

Fitting and selecting fashions for such an arrangement would normally be the total responsibility of the fashion office. Management is usually delighted to cooperate. The personality is usually invited into the store, and a member of the fashion office escorts the person around from department to department, trying on various looks, deciding what will make the best impression on the air. Eventually, the subject becomes so well known to the fashion office member responsible for handling the situation that an entire week's wardrobe can be selected without any special fittings. Clothes can then be sent to the station a week at a time; clothes from the previous week can be picked up at the same time. Once the routine is established, it is quite painless.

Another television advantage is guest appearances on talk, interview, or variety shows on which store personalities from the fashion area can get free exposure—editorial exposure. Fashion directors or fashion commentators are excellent guests, very often appearing on a regular basis to reveal new aspects of fashion, present live fashion shows, and demonstrate new fashion ideas.

Such arrangements can be made by the publicity director of the store or the advertising agency, but it is more likely to come about through the personal effectiveness of the fashion director. The director's reputation, personality, and authority very often are invited to contribute to shows where personal impact develops viewers' interests. Members of a store's fashion office sometimes become famous as the community's authority on fashion, and television exposure is an ideal area for reaching people on a personal level unattainable to such a degree anywhere else.

If a beginner is preparing for a career in fashion, a general knowledge of the workings of radio and television is certainly helpful. Understanding the language in itself is important in communicating with an advertising agency or the television station personnel. To know what is meant by "on camera" or "a dissolve shot" or "a pan" can make the entire experience more fun, if not more efficient (see Glossary of Broadcast Industry Terms). Television is such an intricate part of our lives, anyway, that it behooves most of us to have enough curiosity to check out some of its mysteries, secrets, and potential.

CHAPTER RE-EXAMINATION

Questions

1. Why were retailers skeptical for so long about using the broadcast media as an advertising vehicle?
2. Where is a good place in broadcasting to reach the teen market? Why?
3. What does the fashion director have to contribute to radio commercials?
4. What are three effective ways a fashion retailer can use radio?
5. What change took place in television that made selling fashion through TV more attractive to the retailer?
6. Why is the choice of a spokesperson so important for a radio and/or television commercial?
7. How does the fashion director work with the advertising agency?
8. What makes one garment more photogenic than another on TV?
9. What responsibility does a fashion director have at a taping or filming session?
10. How does cable TV differ from commercial or broadcast TV regarding advertisers?

Workshop

Create a fashion radio or television commercial. Specify what audience is to be reached, and, therefore, where the commercial should be placed (type of station, program, and time slot).

Bloomingdale's opened its King of Prussia store (Pennsylvania) with a special performance of Broadway's "Sophisticated Ladies." *(Courtesy of Bloomingdale's)*

13

FASHION SHOWS AND SPECIAL EVENTS

In every type of live theatre, a play, a musical, the ballet, and certainly the greatest show on earth, the circus, there is an enchanting ingredient available to the audience, in addition to its obvious purpose of entertainment.

Moved to tears or laughter by the remarkable skill of a fine actor or held spellbound by the daring feats of a circus trapeze flyer, the audience can collectively enjoy the experience, but, more important, people can individually dream a little and identify for a few make-believe moments with the brave and the beautiful, the gifted and the uninhibited. Identification and involvement are part of the thing that is nearest and dearest to the hearts of most everyone—the self.

Where the "self" is involved, the fashion show has much to offer. It has that irresistible ability to draw the audience into a personal relationship. Since what we wear or do not wear enormously represents how we see ourselves or how we wish the world to see us, fashion, ego, and self are highly compatible. In fact, so much so, that it is not uncommon for a woman to walk away from a fashion show with a mood entirely different from the one in which she arrived. She can come away thoroughly delighted and inspired, or she might sulk out feeling totally abused, neglected, and even offended. So close, so fragile, and so intimate is the self involvement that a woman with limited self-confidence or understanding can be slightly shattered by a fashion review if she feels too threatened. To compete, to keep up, and to adjust are all challenges that confront the modern woman. Some meet such challenges with eagerness and excitement; some, whether they admit it or not, fear change, fear their ability to be elastic or versatile.

Fashion Show—
the Educator

A show is not a show without an audience. The better the audience, the better the show. Size is not all-important, but response and communication are. Admittedly, the word communication has become strongly overused. But, let's face it, without good communication, especially in the fashion business, nothing is going to happen. Customers need to relate. They need to understand. They also need to feel welcome and cherished. A good fashion show can, and must, do all of this. Although this is no small task, it is not too difficult if one understands the ground rules.

The customer is the first consideration. A good fashion office must carefully guard against becoming so sophisticated they forget that what is old hat to them may be new and mysterious to the customer. A good fashion show can teach, gently, cleverly, and uniquely, but always with a light touch. To talk down to an audience, or instruct is as deadly as no information at all. The subtle dropping of information is the trick.

Show and Tell

The best fashion guidance in the well-coordinated fashion show is visual. At a glance, the viewer can learn:

How the fabric moves

How the lines of the garment fall and mold

How the ensemble is put together with head-to-toe accessories

How the model's makeup and hair fashion relate to the total look

Most of the fashion story is revealed in the "show," but some audiences require a commentator to "tell" what they have seen. They might like to know the name of the designer, fabric content, fabric performance, purpose of the garment, and perhaps price. Facts that are not obvious are usually welcomed by the audience.

To Comment or Not to Comment

That, indeed, is the question. Some fashion offices would not consider the idea of eliminating a commentator. There are others, a bit more advanced and sophisticated, who avoid commentary wherever possible. Both approaches are right. Both have their place. Again, the audience is the deciding factor or at least the first consideration. In some communities, where the customer is not as well traveled or as involved with fashion, the descriptions and explanations of a pleasant commentator are expected. Even in communities where the customer is very fashionable, well informed, and well traveled, there are times when all women enjoy a professional interpretation or clarification of what they have seen or heard regarding the advanced fashion. Such times might be at the outset of a coming season, the introduction of a revolutionary new trend, or a completely new approach to the use of fashion.

A great number of fashion shows, however, can live very well with a minimum of talk or none at all. For example, let us assume that a collection of knits is to be shown. The entire show is exclusively knits. It would be very simple for the fashion director or fashion show coordinator to greet the guests, make an enthusiastic and succinct introductory speech about the advantages of these knits (their easy-care and versatility, their merits as the perfect packables, perfect travelers, and their general price range). If a printed program is provided, the customer can follow the models in the order of appearance and check those pieces she may like to try on later. In such a case, there is little need to ramble on about each individual piece when the facts are already established. A filler of good background music and a closing statement by the commentator could easily suffice.

Another example of when commentary can be eliminated is when a show is presented as the entertainment feature of a program, a glamorous benefit, or fashion extravaganza, complete with orchestra, choreography, and performers. The important thing in these cases is that the audience knows from which store the merchandise comes. If they have had a good time and go away with a warm feeling, it is very likely they will find their way to the store, even though they may not remember everything they saw in the show. All they need to recall is, "That was a great show . . . some really great looking clothes . . . I think I'll stop by tomorrow and take a look around."

Commentary Know-How

Fashion shows are wonderful for displaying the movement of fabric. (Reproduced with the permission of Ebony Magazine, copyright 1980 by Johnson Publishing Company, Inc. Photo by Maurice Sorrell)

Words can be wonderful things. They can also be a bore. A lovely fire that warms your hearth can also burn your hand. Careful. Handle with care. Words can be equally hazardous; they can draw the listener close or drive her away. Fashion commentary can be a language of charm. It can be exotic, poetic, amusing, trendy, or bizarre. It can be whatever the traffic will bear. The terminology must be the newest, the most fitting. It must enhance the mood and the tempo of the fashion, or it does not belong.

The big taboo of commentary is to point out the obvious. "This red dress is contrasted with a white jacket." If the audience cannot see the dress is red and the jacket is white, no need to pay expensive model fees. Black-and-white photographs would be enough. A commentator is justified in mentioning an obvious color, only when it is a point of fashion. "This new vibrant red is one of the leading brights of the coming season, as a strong ground for the new prints or as a unique combiner with other leading colors." The commentator this time has revealed a color story, one that will give the customer confidence when shopping.

Knowing what to say and how to say it are all extremely important in a fashion show. The more easily and skillfully it is done, the more professional the tone of the show. Women can sense the sound of authority. That's why written commentary is less desirable than just notes. Better still, the ad-lib approach, which is even more authoritative if the commentator is capable. In order to do this, of course, the commentator must thoroughly know her merchandise and her fashion facts. An audience is much more responsive to being talked to than read to.

Commentary Skills

To summarize what the commentator contributes to the show enumerates what that voice at the microphone must do, plus what skills are needed. The commentator must:

1. Represent authority.
2. Hold the audience's attention.
3. Set and maintain the pace of the show.

To accomplish all three of these points (and all three are essential), the commentator will need:

1. For authority—to know the merchandise
2. For audience attention—a pleasant voice, well projected
3. For the show's pace—an energetic, enthusiastic tempo

Nothing is more deadly to a show than a voice that cannot be heard, that drones on at a sleepy pace, speaks in a monotone, and is not in control of moving the models on and off with good timing. Better no commentator at all than an ineffective one, but a charming personality at the mike can make an ordinary show seem extraordinary.

The Ebony Show

A unique way of using a commentator is utilized by *Ebony* Magazine's Fashion Fair show, a production that travels the country as a vehicle to raise money for charities in participating cities.

The commentator, sitting offside on a stool throughout the show, gives brief, poetic, amusing, titilating comments about each garment in a crisp, full-voiced manner that not only identifies the fashion look and its designer, but actually becomes an entertaining part of the show—so much so, in fact, that the absence of the commentator would change the flavor and the excellent pacing of the performance.

Choice of Commentator

The sound of authority, expressed through effective words and delivery technique gives the show the professionalism that helps uphold the store's image as a fashion leader. This would naturally bring up the question of the beginner. A beginner is likely to sound like an amateur, but how does one begin? How does one learn?

It is to a fashion director's advantage to create opportunities for all staff members to exercise their talents, or potential talents, in all phases of assignments in the fashion office. Not the least of these is the job of fashion commentary. For one thing, the fashion director, as indicated in earlier chapters, wears many hats and covers many bases. A director's travel schedule is usually heavy and when absent, it is comforting to know that other staff members can take the microphone and hold the show together smoothly.

For the larger shows, in the fashion director's absence, the fashion show coordinator or assistant can take over. For the smaller shows, area or divisional coordinators can and should step into those shoes. Branch coordinators, often required to handle all aspects of a show, also need to be trained to take on the microphone duties.

But the beginner, the new member of the fashion office, must first serve an apprenticeship in the area of fashion commentary to develop that sound of authority. An excellent place for the young beginner is in the area of children's shows. For starters, a young voice is ideal, and a young woman (even a beginner) can substitute charm for authority. The audience, too, is less sophisticated and the show is less pretentious. The beginner can get the feel of handling the pacing, the models, the words, and the audience, all in an atmosphere of warmth and ease, the general climate surrounding most children's shows. No matter what the children do they are usually loved and mistakes go easily unnoticed.

Shows for All Occasions

A store need never be at a loss for a reason to hold a fashion show. The greatest problem is in holding the number down. The fashion show calendar, maintained by the fashion office, can be bulging at the seams at peak periods and lean at other times, or the steady flow of fashion show action can easily be maintained year round, week after week, day after day. Some stores believe very strongly in the fashion show approach, but some resist it strongly and do only a minimum of "musts."

In an operation that restricts its fashion show involvement to a "must" list, that list alone could be no small undertaking. For example, most stores feel they must do a benefit show or two when asked. They are likely to schedule seasonal shows, such as back-to-school. They might do special showings when a new fashion collection or new shop concept is being introduced. Also, they usually include bridal shows on a must list. That same list could be extended to include special individual showings of wool products, cotton, or man made fibers. And if one added to all the above petite or half-size shows or shows of import collections during special events (such as import fairs) the so-called minimum "must" list can grow quite long.

Whatever direction a store takes on the fashion show idea, it is plain to see that at some time, in some way, every fashion operation will become involved in fashion show business. It's inevitable. It is entirely possible to build a fashion show around almost any new fashion idea or trend that comes along. An alert fashion office, whose store appreciates new and frequent applications of shows, will take special pride in developing a well organized and creative shop, in which all members who are show biz oriented can pitch in when needed.

The Purposes of Fashion Shows

Fashion shows provide many advantages. And right at the top of the list is selling. It is not an easy thing for a woman who is not closely associated with the fashion world to imagine how a new silhouette looks on the human form or how it should be put together. The live fashion show illustrates. A customer can easily overlook a dress seen on a hanger that might inspire her in a show. She needs and welcomes such help.

So it is with every type customer, the teen customer, the male customer, petite-size women, the half-size woman, the debutante, the bride, the mother of the bride, and all customers with special interests. For them, the store has a specialized fashion show. The purpose, of course, is to sell, but in the process a special service is extended: a recognition of individual needs, one of the nicest ways to make friends.

Making friends is a big responsibility of the fashion office. That is why the benefit shows and private shows for women's clubs are so high on the list of some store's public relations projects.

Prestige is another sterling purpose of the fashion show, in the formal presentation of an important name designer's collection or through informal trunk showings of fashions. Other vehicles that carry big prestige insignias are the exclusive or community-wide, annual formal balls, such as St. Louis' Veiled Prophets Ball, Omaha's Aksarben Ball, mardi gras and cotillion balls everywhere.

For all the shows held outside the store to make friends, there are great numbers of shows held inside the store, in the auditorium, in the fashion departments, in the restaurant areas, to build traffic. It all adds up to the same purpose—to sell.

HOW TO PRODUCE A FASHION SHOW

There are so many details to consider when planning a fashion show that the prospect may seem overwhelming. But, in truth, once a good routine is established, the whole project is relatively simple.

The Informal Show

To make the first step an easy one, the informal-type showing is a good place to begin. Under the heading of informal shows go the trunk shows, informal modeling in the store's restaurant areas, fashion departments, and throughout the store.

Trunk shows and informal modeling require no runways, no staging, and no special props or lighting. All that is needed is the merchandise and the live models. Trunk shows (collections brought in for a limited special appearance) usually require a minimum of two or three good models.

The responsibility of the fashion office for the informal show might include:

1. Booking the models. The Fashion Office will need to contact the buyer involved in advance to learn what size samples will be coming in. Since sizes 6, 8, 10, or 12 are the usual requirements, it is wise to have a good file of these size models on hand. The type of model, of course, must be considered; she must be right for the clothes. She should also be personable. She will be in close contact with customers, very often involved in selling a garment if a salesperson or the designer is busy, and it is important that she has a thorough understanding of the fashion concept of the collection involved.

2. Scheduling the models. With informal modeling, models are usually paid by the hour or the day, rather than on the per-show basis. The model will need to be informed as to how many hours she will work, or if she will be working a staggered schedule with other models alternating. For example, a trunk showing schedule might read something like this:

MODEL	DAY	HOURS	PLACE
Diane Schaefer	Monday	11 A.M. to 4:30 P.M.	Crossroads Store Designer Shop
	Tuesday	11 A.M. to 4:30 P.M.	Westroad Store Designer Shop
Jackie Kluza	Monday	11 A.M. to 4:30 P.M.	Crossroads Store Designer Shop
	Tuesday	11 A.M. to 4:30 P.M.	Westroads Store Designer Shop
Gwen Brown	Monday	5 P.M. to 7 P.M.	Crossroads Store Restaurant Area
	Tuesday	5 P.M. to 7 P.M.	Westroads Store Designer Shop
Joanne Cady	Monday	11 A.M. to 2 P.M.	Crossroads Store Restaurant Area
	Tuesday	11 A.M. to 2 P.M.	Crossroads Store Restaurant Area
Darlene Rostetter	Monday	11 A.M. to 2 P.M.	Crossroads Store Restaurant Area
Denise Knapp	Tuesday	11 A.M. to 2 P.M.	Crossroads Store Restaurant Area

All bases are covered. Two girls working the day hours in the Designer Shop, one in the evening, and two during the lunch hours. It is entirely possible for some models to double up on a schedule, such as working the day schedule and evening schedule, but that, of course, would depend on availabilities.

3. Making sure that the trunk collection has been unpacked, pressed and delivered to the appropriate department in time for model fittings and the showings.

4. Accessorizing. Most pieces included in a trunk show (if modeled only in the department) require very little accessorizing, because the garment itself is the focal point, and changes are made repeatedly to allow customers to see several pieces. The important accessories, however, that would be required are the correct leg fashions—hose and shoes. Modeling in the Tea Room, however, might require more attention in the accessory department. A coordinator from the fashion office would fit the models, decide who needs that accessory, and then go chase it down. For the beginner, anxious to learn the ropes, it would be a great idea to tag along, watching, and assisting the coordinator get the informal showing under way. It is a nice, easy-paced place to learn.

How to Pull Fashion Merchandise

Merchandise for trunk shows is brought in from the resource or designer, shipped in (thus the expression "trunk") expressly for the showing (from which orders can be taken), and then shipped back. For most all other shows, except when a designer's collection is flown in to a store for a special runway show, fashion merchandise must be pulled from existing stock. The expression "pull" used in retailing for the removal of merchandise for shows or display, or any other reason it is taken out of a department, is also accompanied with an expression "authorized transfer," which means permission to pull.

Even though the systems used by stores differ, the routine is still a matter of checking out and checking in. To avoid confusion, merchandise checked out by the fashion office for fashion shows, television commercials, or advertising illustration, or merchandise pulled for display, all must be noted on some kind of printed form or record book that clearly states the purpose, where it is going, and who is taking it. Merchandise that has not been checked back into the department or not properly cancelled in the merchandise transfer records will be considered a shortage (missing) and charged to display or the fashion office. The record also serves as a tracer for merchandise that might be needed for some other purpose. If the entry shows that the fashion office has the merchandise, tracing is less of a problem.

Approaching fashion shows with theatrical flare. A chorus line of furs on skaters. *(Courtesy of Chicago Fur Association, Dorothy Fuller Productions, Inc.)*

The Formal Show

Now we get down to the real thing. The types, styles, and possibilities for formal (i.e., runway or stage) fashion shows are astronomical. A good dividing line for instruction and learning how to put the formal show together is the in-store show and the outside show. The in-store show usually represents specialized departmental showings, special fashion promotions, collections, and seasonal approaches. The other (the outside event) can become an entirely different experience. Benefits, entertainment programs for women's organizations, city-wide participations, all of these and more are by their very nature handled with a different approach than the show designed to bring traffic into the store. One is sell, the other public relations.

A Stage for the Show

It is wonderful when a store has its own auditorium. Most retailers prefer to have as many fashion events as possible right on their own premises. Major benefits, however are very often offered in conjunction with a dinner or luncheon or some sort of festivity and require, therefore, the facilities of a ballroom at a hotel or theater or music hall. Every once in a while, however, either through the request of a special

Dancing models in finale showing Halston couture collection. *(Courtesy of Chicago Apparel Center)*

interest group or the special events director, or simply the creative urge of the fashion director, a fashion show will be held around a swimming pool, on the ice of a skating arena, on a private ranch, on a parking lot, in an art gallery, or even on the escalator of the store.

When such unique settings are chosen, the special events director can be of tremendous help. New problems and arrangements must be made to accommodate the show and the special events people are especially qualified for helping in this connection.

The In-Store Shows

A show held in a special department, for a special customer, is the most effective in-store type. A teen show in the junior department, a show for men only in the men's shop, or a bridal show, are good examples. Any show that is designed to attract only those customers who are truly interested is likely to be a show that will sell. The following procedure of show production, with the variance of a few details, would be applicable to almost all in-store shows.

General Procedure

Once the show is booked and cleared on the calendar, the first routine steps include:

A designer collection shown in its own area. *(Courtesy of Neiman-Marcus)*

1. Theme and title
2. Location of show
3. Facilities needed
4. Length of show (number of pieces)
5. Models (what type and how many needed)
6. Commentator (if one is required the person must be committed as to date and time)

Using the above routine as a work procedure, let us plan one of the specialized in-store shows.

The Bridal Show

This show has something in it for every member of the fashion office, and when they get it off the ground they are likely to have learned lessons that will come in mighty handy next time out.

Filling in the answers on the general procedure list will be the framework for action:

1. Theme—Bridal, Title—"I Do"
2. Location of show—Store auditorium
3. Facilities Needed—Stage
   Bridal setting (see display department)

Special rigging for lights (see display department)
Live music
Aisle-wide runway (at least eight feet for bridal gowns)
Microphone (for commentator)
2 dressing rooms (1 for women, 1 for men)
Flowers (see flower shop manager)
Completely set wedding reception table with wedding cake, coffee, etc. (see food service department)
4. Length of show—45 minutes (50–60 pieces)
5. Models
12 young women (brides and bridesmaids)
3 mothers of the bride
2 men (1 groom, 1 father)
2 junior bridesmaids (8–10 years old)
2 flower girls (5–6 years old)
1 ring bearer (5–7 year old boy)
6. Commentator—yes—fashion director

Now the basics are squared away (on paper, that is) and the work begins.

Meeting of the Minds

When a show of such proportion as a bridal show is in the offing, it is wise to have a meeting for all those people involved.

Fashion office
Special Events director
Display department
Advertising department
Bridal shop buyer
Divisional merchandise manager of women's fashion
Divisional merchandise manager of men's fashion
Divisional merchandise manager of home furnishings
Representative of the flower shop
Representative of the food service department
Representative from the bridal registry

All these are usually regarded as vital to the whole picture, but there are even others who might be included: the divisional merchandise manager of accessories and cosmetics, a representative from the photo department, a representative from the stationery department, and the home furnishings fashion coordinator, and the store publicity director.

Home furnishings figures strongly in the bridal show. Bridal services, too, for catering parties or the reception, and for renting everything from the punch bowl for the reception to formal wear for male attendants. This is the one big chance for the whole store to get together to court the bride for all her needs for the wedding and her new home, to reach everyone interested, from what to wear to the wedding to what gift to buy. The bridal show, therefore, deserves everyone's special attention.

At the bridal meeting, where everyone may hear the total plan, exchange ideas, and receive their own specific assignments, the bridal show plan is finalized. The food service needs to know how many people are expected, the flower shop needs to know how many bouquets, what kind, and what colors, the representative of the bridal registry needs to be informed as to when she will be introduced during the show, how long she can talk, and what is to be covered regarding the store's bridal services. One good meeting should do it.

The fashion office is now ready to get on with the show. In every city there is much competition for bridal business, so in order to attract big audiences and customers who will buy, the bridal effort must be an attractive one.

The Setting

The bridal show is scheduled for the store's big auditorium. It may be a very ordinary room at other times, but for this event it must be turned into a breathtaking setting for one of the season's most beautiful shows.

If the setting was traditional last year, it might be contemporary this year, whatever the fashion mood dictates. Never do the show exactly the same way. There is so little that can be changed in a bridal show, every possible change should be welcomed. True, the audiences change every year, but the word gets around. "That store does the most magnificent bridal shows. You are really missing something if you pass it up."

The display department can come up with some ingenious ideas for bridal show settings, but they do need fashion direction regarding the going thing. For example, one season the fashion director felt the usual organ music and traditional vocalist would be best replaced, for the sake of the fashion trend, with a guitarist and folk singer. The wedding setting was a garden. If the display director had not been tipped off by the fashion office as to the "feel" of the show, he could not have given her the compatible background.

A bridal show is a wonderful opportunity to turn an ordinary room into a storybook castle or a beautiful hall. *(Courtesy of J. L. Brandeis, Omaha)*

Pacing

Pacing is another important touch to make the bridal show more exciting. Even when scenes or groups are paraded in ceremonial fashion, and even if wedding marches are slow and precise, a fashion show with maybe a dozen weddings to show, can become a drag if the same here-comes-the-bride pace is maintained throughout. Take a little poetic license and keep the processions moving, smooth and easy, but moving.

Pacing can be improved, not only by the way the models move, but by breaking up the line-up. One can look at just so many bridal or bridesmaids gowns without getting somewhat confused if they are not divided into "theme" categories, color stories, or occasionally sparked with an unconventional bridal approach. One season, when evening pants became big, bridal pants were introduced. When the mini dress was at its height, mini wedding dresses were shown. When cullottes swung into the fashion scene, bridal divided skirts were made available. These novel, breakaways from tradition, are fun and make the show the last word.

Variety

Since an important part of a bridal trousseau includes lingerie, a segment of the show devoted to floating lovelies helps add considerable variety to a bridal show. Some stores have eliminated the travel clothes or going-away fashions in a bridal show, simply because ready-to-wear fashion shows are available throughout the year, and the bridal show is long enough without being overextended. However, a great many stores prefer to take advantage of the large audiences that attend bridal shows and include a sampling of ready-to-wear for the bride's wedding trip and trousseau. This is best done in a separate short scene within the show or just before the final bridal scene. Always open and close a bridal show with the special reasons the brides have come for in the first place—to see clothes for the wedding party.

The Door Prizes

Door prizes are always a delightful addition to such a show, especially if one of the prizes is a honeymoon trip for two, courtesy of some generous airline. If only registered brides are eligible for door prizes, then it is a gleeful experience—lingerie for her honeymoon, a starter set of china, her veil, towel sets, a free wedding portrait, a free trip to the store's beauty salon for the full treatment on her wedding day. Awarding such gifts to the guests and sharing the delight of the surprises gives everyone the feeling of attending a bridal party instead of a fashion show.

Gift for Everyone

A free giveaway always delights an audience. It seems to have a special charm at a bridal show, especially if it is a gift of fragrance or cosmetics, or a gift from the home furnishings department, such as a spoon or some little token that makes everyone attending feel important and part of a "party." Lots of helpful booklets and pamphlets on things of special interest to brides are often available as free pass-outs. All these little additions make the show a special event.

Before the Show

When the guests arrive, while the music is strumming, having young men, perhaps personnel from the store dressed appropriately to serve as ushers and seat guests, gives the store an additional model or two of their men's formal fashions or rental service. It's a nice touch.

The home furnishings fashion coordinator usually arranges to have several beautifully designed table settings available for the guests to stroll past and examine, both before and after the show. These might be part of the lobby decor, part of the auditorium atmosphere, or the commentator might invite the guests to go to the china department to see the special table settings.

Throw the Bouquet

Squeals of delight result from the traditional throwing of the bouquet. Especially if the commentator has just given credit to the store's florist by eloquently describing a crescent bouquet of white orchids. Then to have the bride toss it suddenly into the audience (at the end of the show, of course) provides a fun finish. If fresh flowers are not used throughout the show, it might be wise to at least have one bridal bouquet made of fresh flowers for the "tossing," plus as the center-piece of the reception table.

Even hard-nosed fashion show viewers get caught up in the charm of a bridal show if it is beautifully staged and executed. The audience is moved by the beauty and joy and fun of it all. It's a happy occasion.

That's the Idea

Taking a clue from the bridal show, all in-store fashion events (or anywhere, for that matter) should send the audience away happy and satisfied. That's the whole idea. And that is why specialized shows, tailored to a special audience have a greater chance for success. You are playing to their special interests, talking their language, and communicating with their feelings. It's a winner.

The Box Lunch Show

Another show that has experienced considerable success in many de-partment stores is the box-lunch show. Working women, shopping on their lunch hour, or busy women trying to squeeze lunch and shopping into a short period before dashing home to drive the car pool or prepare dinner, thoroughly appreciate the opportunity to see an exciting show, eat lunch, and dash off to other things. The whole thing can be done beautifully in one-half hour. If the doors open at noon and box lunches are sold at the door, the customer can be seated with lunch on her lap and ready to see the show in only a few minutes. If the show starts promptly at 12:10 P.M. (for this kind of setup promptness is essential) and if only about eighteen to twenty-four outfits are shown, everyone can be out by 12:30 or 12:45. It's a delightful interlude for women of all ages.

THE OUT-OF-THE-STORE FASHION SHOW

Under this category we do not refer to the off-the-premises show the store might itself create by simply holding the festivities at a hotel, music hall, or theatre. We refer here to the show that has resulted from an outside request made to the fashion office for a benefit, a program of entertainment, or a fund-raising project of some kind. For our example, we will use a benefit show. Here the ground rules are a bit different, the procedure very often different with every show of this kind.

Diplomacy

The first rule is diplomacy. Since this is an undertaking more valuable as public relations than as a "sell" vehicle, charm and tact are the watchwords. The women who come to the fashion office to request a fashion show for their project are very grateful for the store's cooperation, though some chairmen or committee members, inexperienced in this area, may not know how to express it. Every member of the fashion office must be trained to bear in mind that they are not dealing with professionals, they are dealing with customers. A woman handling the arrangements of a fashion show for the first time is very unsure of which way to go and what is expected of her, and it is very likely that a charming show of patience and a courteous helping hand will not be forgotten.

General Procedure

The general procedure, used by the fashion office to put a show together in-store or of their own creation cannot apply here. The store may have little to say about the general procedure points listed earlier.

All six points, in fact, the theme and title of the show, location, facilities needed, length of show, models, and commentator may be completely taken out of the hands of the fashion office. It is entirely possible that all that will be required of the store is to furnish the clothes, fit the models, plan the line-up, and work backstage to be sure the models get on and off properly.

Then again, all responsibilities for the show may be completely dumped into the fashion office's lap, leaving everything to the store's discretion. Most fashion directors would vote strongly for this approach. With this routine, the fashion office can move with freedom and in the way they know will bring the happiest results.

Meeting Time

Unlike the meeting for the bridal show, very few in-store people need be invited to this meeting. It is wise, however, for the fashion director, members of the director's fashion office, and the committee members of the organization or group involved to get together to be sure everyone knows what the other is thinking. The only other store member who might be included would be the display director, if the store is involved in handling the staging and settings. There are certain points that should be thoroughly covered at this meeting, and if a plan is worked out, the meeting time can be kept to a minimum.

1. Hear everything the committee has in mind for the show. If what they are requesting is possible, then it's time to go on to step 2, but if it is not, this is the time to clear the air. For example, it is not unheard of for a committee to ask for one hundred models and want a show that will last only forty-five minutes. It is obvious they have no idea about time and the gigantic undertaking of that number of models. A forty-five minute show can easily be handled by as few as six to eight professional models.

2. Get a thorough understanding of how many people are expected to attend, and get as much information as possible regarding the age level, special interests, and lifestyles of the guests. It is also very important to learn, if the fashion office is not familiar with the group, the economic level of the expected audiences. The fashion director can tactfully discover this by asking what type and price range they would like shown. One does not show couture fashions to moderate or budget-priced customers.

Many such events are played to a general audience, from granddaughter to grandmother. That's a tough one. A general audience can be the most difficult to please. There is always one age group or type who feels that not enough things were shown for them. The best way to get around this problem (and every fashion office in the world will testify that it is a problem) is to include as many "ageless" fashions in the show as possible, that is, the classic looks that most everyone can wear, and usually do, at one time or another. If a smaller number of young people are in attendance than the more mature, then perhaps a special category of their new fashion looks would suffice.

3. Discuss the models. This is another delicate area. Some committees insist that their own members or friends be used as models. When it comes to fitting guest models as against professional models there is absolutely no comparison. The professional model wears anything and everything she is told. If she is asked to change her hair, she changes her hair. If she is warned about handling the merchandise, reminded about wearing dress shields, she takes it in stride.

When a show is composed of guest models, the situation changes. Guest models, even though asked by the committee to cooperate when being fitted, are highly sensitive to what fashions are assigned to them. Even the sweetest-natured woman, the best mannered, the most intelligent, can become terribly self-conconscious or upset about fashion when she becomes a model. Many a fashion show coordinator has heard:

"Well, I will wear it if I have to, but I certainly wouldn't buy it."
"This is not *me*."
"Why does she get to wear a ball gown and I have to wear a tweed suit?"
"I'm glad my husband won't be there; he'd die if he saw me in this."
"I love this style, but do you have it in some other color?"

Amusing as it might sound, this is in no way intended to poke fun at the women who react this way in the dressing rooms when fitting for a show. When a woman is invited to serve as a guest model, she feels a strong responsibility. Also, she is being asked to do something for which she has no special training. Those two things make her less than comfortable, even though she is delighted about the whole thing. Down deep, she wants to be at her best, and anything which is shown to her that does not exactly fit her picture of herself at her best is resisted. While the fashion office should not be called to assume the role of doormat, it can be generous and try to alleviate as much pain as possible on both sides.

Not all guest models are painful to fit, not in the least. Some are a delight, some are fun, some are such jewels you want to ask them back again and again, but because of the moments when the guest model-customer is unhappy, some stores make it a firm, blanket rule never to use guest models under any circumstances. Professionals, or no show.

Another strong reason for requiring only professional models for a show is the merchandise itself. It is difficult, because of size and types of guests, to get a balanced show together. Certain peices that would make the show a stand-out might have to be completely eliminated because there were not enough models of that size or look.

Time, energy, and result are three reasons for resisting guest models. On the basis of all the foregoing, most fashion directors of leading stores throughout the country stand pretty pat on the professional show.

4. Be sure and ask if the fashion show is the entire program or just part of it. Every once in a while, a fashion show has arrived to play a benefit or some such event, with a full-scale production, only to learn that they would be surrounded on the bill by a high school band, a church choir, a few dance numbers from a recent dance recital, and a vocalist with an armful of selections. It's a shock, to say the least. Some stores may not mind sharing the program in such a way, but most would prefer not to. After all, a fashion show, while entertaining, is a selling vehicle; too much time and money goes into such an effort to be put in the position of competing for the attention of the audience. Unless the fashion show can be scheduled to go on first, it is best to pass up such a show. To avoid being disappointed or embarrassed, always let your feelings be known regarding such matters. Ask. *Never assume anything!*

5. Be sure and firm up the exact time the show is scheduled to go on. Most models in the average community work very hard for a nominal fee, and usually get paid on a per-show basis rather than an hourly basis. Many models are young mothers who have to pay baby sitters. Therefore, it is only kind to check on the time the model should arrive and leave rather than make her sit and wait a long time unneccessarily. If it is a luncheon show, check the time of the luncheon and at what point they plan to start the show.

Transporting Merchandise

All merchandise that leaves the store for a show must be itemized, checked into a hamper, locked, and sealed, for transporting to the scene of the show. After the show, all merchandise must be checked in again, locked, and sealed, before being returned to the store. The fashion office personnel is responsible for dispersing all show pieces back to the departments from which they came. Shortages is one of the big problems of retail stores, so all departments responsible for transporting merchandise in and out, such as the display department and the fashion department, must keep good records of their transfers and returns.

Keep a Diary

One of the smartest things a busy fashion office can do is keep a fashion show diary. Record on the fashion show calendar or in a special show diary everything pertinent about the show, after it has taken place.

1. Attendance promised—actual attendance.
2. Was the audience the right customer for the store's fashion merchandise?
3. How was it received?
4. Were guest models or pros used?

A year later it would be impossible to remember such bits of information, but a year later, when the same group calls for another show, it is a lifesaver to have the facts at your finger tips. If a group promised an attendance of 500 and only 200 attended, it is entirely possible the fashion director would wish to pass the show up the next time around. Also, next year, there may be a new fashion show coordinator or secretary handling the fashion show calendar; such a diary answers a lot of questions and helps avoid making the same mistake twice.

HOW TO PLAN CATEGORIES

We have reviewed the specifics as they apply to the informal show, the in-store specialized show (bridal), and the outside benefit show, but the one thing that must be developed for all shows, regardless of size (with the exception of informal modeling) is choice of categories or scenes, into which all merchandise to be shown must be assigned.

The Categories

The basis for the line-up is the categories. Just a parade of models in a hodgepodge of fashions does not clearly relate a fashion story. But well-planned groups pulled into clear-cut categories state better than anything a fashion commentator can say that here it is, this is the look, this is the way it goes together, and these are the examples.

The number of categories depends a great deal on these three factors:

1. Length of show
2. Type of show (specialized or general)
3. Current trends (some seasons are much more diversified than others)

For the average-length general show, lasting about thirty to forty-five minutes, five or six categories can be handled. And within those categories five or six examples can be shown, maybe seven or eight, but a category that is short and sweet tells the story well without running it into the ground.

Categories or groups are based on leading fashion trends. If windows and ads are exploiting a certain trend it's smart business to have it represented in the show, at least in one category. A group should not be included unless the merchandise in that group represents the new way to go.

A general show line-up might look like this:

Group One—The Winter Brights
An unusual availability of bright, bright colors for winter in a variety of fashion looks, with all models on stage at once for a bright opening, gets the show off on a high note.

Group Two—The Cardigan Cousins
A new look of the cardigan, showing up in sweaters, jackets, dresses, and coats, all kissin' cousins to other coordinated pieces. A great group to show in diversified modeling. Present some models singly, some in pairs to show companion pieces, and some in trios.

Group Three—New Pickin's in Pants
All the different lengths, combinations, daytime, or nighttime expressions. Avoid the old-hat tendency to show evening fashions only at the end of the show. There should be flourish and fun throughout the show.

Group Four—Applause for Plaids
New plaids showing up in bright and beautiful expressions, not only in lovely wools, but in knits and tweeds, and even printed on velvet and chiffon. It's a pattern story.

Group Five—Dresses: The New Shapes
With so many coordinated looks being shown, so many separates, an elegant category of the new dress silhouettes should be included for the woman who loves to "dress." Show her how to interpret the new lines, how to accessorize, and if individuality is the key here, show an outstanding example of each dress idea separately.

Group Six—The Three Little Bares
A new sophistication for the night side. Bare shoulders. Bare midriffs. Bare backs. The show began big and bright. Give it a little drama and glamor now with everything in black or, perhaps, black and white. A variety of fabrics, of silhouettes, of costumes. Makes a great grand finale.

Number of Pieces

To include six pieces in six categories provides a well-rounded average length show of thirty-six outfits. Naturally, for a smaller show, present fewer pieces in each group; for a larger show, fatten the groups accordingly. For a really big show, each category can be extended and more categories added. However, it is always a good idea to exercise economy in trying to show everything. Pick the top fashion trends, fabrics, colors, and patterns, and develop them in a strong fashion statement. Too much confuses the audience.

Economy should also be prevalent when selecting numbers of garments for an in-department show (sometimes called "on-the-floor" show) because traffic in the department is tied up and other buyers, not involved in the show, are sensitive about customers being kept away from their shopping. Eighteen to twenty-four pieces is enough to show "on the floor."

Props

The use of props by models in a fashion show can add a feeling of staging or even scene changing when there is little or no set decor available. For example, if a category is a color story and models carry artist's pallettes and brushes, perhaps in matching or related colors, the impact is memorable. If oriental influences are played up by having models carry oriental fans, a statement has been made. Anything from helium-filled balloons to a dog on a leash can contribute to the effectiveness of the fashion being shown.

The intelligent use of props in a fashion show can help reinforce the fashion statement. Pictured, a show by Wohl Shoes, announcing big fashion news. The specially printed newspapers are meaningful. (*Courtesy of Footwear News, photo by Thomas Iannaccone*)

Props must be selected and assigned, of course, to those items that would truly benefit from such support. Accessories should not be hampered or upstaged by props. For example, a model carrying a handbag or an umbrella should not be burdened or cluttered with other hand props. The discriminating use of props adds fun and dimension to a show; the indiscriminate use is distracting. As with accessories, careful thought and planning should accompany the use of props in a fashion show.

ACCESSORIZING

Here is an excellent opportunity for members of the fashion office to express their designing talents while providing every outfit in a fashion show with unique interpretation.

Accessorizing is a special skill. This is true certainly in display, but most especially in a show where the model can use the accessory as a prop (umbrella or piece of luggage) or to illustrate its versatility. For example, a model may enter wearing an oblong scarf tied in a bow at the neck. She might then show it tied as an ascot or as a sash at the waist. Accessories not only embellish a costume, they can reinforce its alternatives, change its look, update a silhouette.

Taste

Nowhere does one's taste level surface so powerfully as in the assignment of accessorizing a fashion show. A very ordinary ensemble can be turned into a standout with the tasteful selection and new placement of handsome accessories. Two guidelines will be helpful in making tasteful accessory decisions:

1. Size and boldness of accessories in proportion to the fabric and silhouette
2. Personality of the model (tailored, sophisticated, petite)

Balance

This task is not quite as simple as it sounds. In fact, creating the perfect balance with accessories is not unlike good proportions in any visual art.

It is not unusual to select several variations of a single accessory classification (a half dozen belts, or bags, or earrings, etc.) and hold them up to the clothes one after the other until the right one strikes a positive picture. Not too small, not too large, not too bold, not too conservative.

Balance is also expressed with the frequency or infrequency that accessories appear on a specific outfit. Too many touches of accents (a white collar, white earrings, white belt, white pin, white bag, etc.) are destructive. It is better to choose only two pieces of white accent (perhaps the white earrings and white collar) and let all the other accessory pieces blend with the color of the dress. In most cases accessories are to enhance, not take over. If a belt consists of lots of color and jeweled accents, then it would be wise to deemphasize the neck area, permitting the waistline to be the focal point, or vice versa. Some fashion looks require overstatements; some fashion seasons make this a correct approach. Other fashion trends derive their effectiveness only through severe understatement. Knowing how far to go each way is, indeed, a very valuable talent.

The Paradox

Like so many fashion rules, broken, bent, and even twisted beyond recognition, the theory of taste and balance in accessorizing must still

Accessories that make an otherwise ordinary ensemble hard to forget, even though it is not suggested that the clothes be worn this way. In beachwear by Gottex the "Cleopatra" ensemble is accessorized with heads wrapped with Middle East influence. *(Courtesy of Israel Bond Fashion Show)*

be maintained even though accessories may be overstated for the sake of show business. That is, in a big show, presented in a huge room, unless the accessories are emphatic they might not even be noticed. Costumes are required very often to be "showy" and accessories can play a big part in accomplishing this. A fashion director will very often buy what is known as "runway pieces" because of their show business ability. The bottom line is that even though no one would actually wear an outfit "that way," it is important to make the statement boldly in the show.

Compatible Quality

There is one more accessory rule that is important to observe. Never put a $10 belt on a $1,000 dress. It is equally bad judgment to accessorize a budget-priced outfit with a very expensive designer shoe. Now here comes the contradiction again. If an ensemble is in the moderate to better price range, it is acceptable (and we certainly encourage customers to do this) to accessorize it with an expensive designer bag or scarf or belt. It elevates the image of the wearer and illustrates the power of quality accessories.

A good student of fashion will give special attention to the art of fashion accessorizing. A fashion director soon learns that how well shows are accessorized makes the difference between an ordinary show and an inspiring, highly informative one.

Organizing Accessories

For almost any size show the best way to organize the accessories selected for each ensemble to be modeled is to accumulate them into a plastic bag with a handle and hang it over the neck of the hanger holding the related garment. Additional accessories will be spread out on an accessory table, but when specific choices have been made that relate to a single garment the bagging technique is ideal. Now, when clothes are being arranged on racks in order of appearance for the purpose of planning the line-up, all is in readiness. Also, when the model must take her clothes as she is ready to dress for the show, everything is where it should be, on one hanger.

HOW TO PLAN A LINE-UP

Models need to know the order of the categories or scenes, which of their costumes to wear in which order, whom they follow, if they model alone or in pairs or groups, and if and when there will be a finale. The line-up is the format of the show, the basis of blocking each scene or category; it literally choreographs the action.

Organizing the Line-up

Write it down, everything. For a small or average show, as each model is fitted, tag the outfit with the model's name and category. Then when all fittings are completed, arrange the garments under their specified category. Then when all fittings are completed, arrange the garments under their specified category, in the order of appearance, and transfer the line-up onto a master order-of-appearance sheet.

This system is especially effective in a large fashion office. More than one show might be fitting at the same time, and the person who was responsible for the fitting and tagging the merchandise is off doing something else when the secretary or other fashion office aide comes to transfer the information for the line-up.

With this order-of-appearance sheet clearly filled out, the line-up

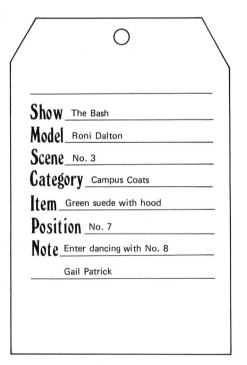

Show _The Bash_

Model _Roni Dalton_

Scene _No. 3_

Category _Campus Coats_

Item _Green suede with hood_

Position _No. 7_

Note _Enter dancing with No. 8_

Gail Patrick

Tag each garment in a fashion show line-up with clear easy-to-read information from which a master line-up can be made.

falls beautifully into place. When the line-up is typed up, it should include approximately the same information as the tag, plus entrance directions for the models, for example, stage right, stage left, or stage center. Also, if models are to appear together, this direction should be shown on the line-up, either by a bracket or note.

Some fashion show coordinators use a file card system when drawing up the line-up, especially for very large shows. A file card typed up at the same time the clothes are tagged provides a complete file on the pieces and their sequence. After the line-up is typed from the cards, they can be punched and bound for the commentator's use.

While getting ready for the show, a model studies the copy of the line-up. Several copies should be posted at all entrances and exits. *(Courtesy of Stores Magazine)*

**How to Use the
Line-up**

Make lots of copies! The line-up must be seen by everyone associated with the show.

1. Post plenty of copies in the dressing rooms and at all entrances and exits. The more models the more copies. Everyone must be able to get close enough to a line-up, on the wall, on the door, near the mirror, and wherever necessary, to check and recheck where they have to be, and when.

2. The starter is a very important person. She stands at the entrance (each entrance must have its own starter), with a line-up in her hand, checking the models about to appear and sometimes literally pushing them out on time.

3. The fashion director or commentator can use a copy of the line-up, instead of cards, if she perfers and if it carries sufficient information about the merchandise being shown.

4. A line-up should be handed to the musicians if there is live music. Very often it can be used as a cue sheet for them on which they can make their notes during rehearal. However, if it is a major production, with an orchestra or group, a more comprehensive cue sheet for music will be necessary. Musicians accustomed to working fashion shows or with a particular store, can draw up their own cue sheet directly from the line-up.

5. The display people involved in the show, working lights, props, or any special effects (such as a media-mix of sound and film and slides), must also have a complete rundown on the line-up. Everyone must know what is expected, and when.

The posted line-up—the one for the models to follow and the starter to check—might look like this:

GROUP ONE—RED, WHITE, AND BLUE SCENE

Model		*Entrance*
1. Diane	Red dress	SR (stage right)
2. Robbie	White dress	SL (stage left)
3. Kerry	Blue dress	USC (up stage center)
4. Stephanie	Red coat/white dress	USC
5. Debi	Blue coat/white dress	USC (with #6)
6. Soralee	White coat/blue dress	USC
7. Donna	Red dress/white jacket	SR
8. Lori	White gown	SL (with #9 & #10)
9. Marla	Red gown	SR
10. Valerie	Blue gown	USC

The change of pace of entrances is as important as any other part of the staging. So also is changing the number of models appearing at a time. Alternating from the single appearance to a duet to a trio, and so on, makes for a choreographed effect, even without a choreographer. It is very important for a well-planned show, especially the long, ambitious type. A single parade of models can quickly become redundant and boring.

Finale

Usually reserved for the end of the show, a finale treatment can also be applied at the end of a scene or category. In the case of the red, white, and blue group in the preceding line-up, the color story would make an exciting impact when all models are accumulated at the end of scene. This same impact might be accomplished by gathering all the models at the beginning of the scene instead; never assemble the group at the top and bottom of the same scene. If there are not enough models to make the changes, of course, a finale treatment would not be possible, unless the show was completely over.

The Rehearsal

Not all shows need rehearsals. The small departmental show, where collections are shown on the fashion floor, are fitted, accessorized, lined up, and put on. The professional models know what is expected of them, the starter is on hand to keep the show moving, and the commentator does the rest. The average club or small benefit show, with professionals, can be handled as well without rehearsal. A short

When an important designer makes a personal appearance at a showing of a collection, the designer usually appears for recognition during the finale. Bill Blass with his collection at Dayton's, Minneapolis. *(Courtesy of Stores Magazine)*

Bob Mackie with costumes he had created for celebrities. *(Courtesy of Stores Magazine © 1981 National Retail Merchants Association)*

Bill Tice, with two of his models. Such illustrious designers usually are available only for major benefits, or major introductions of their collections in a store. *(Courtesy of Chicago Apparel Mart)*

explanation to the models as to where they enter and exit, if the location is not familiar to them, usually covers it.

However, if it is a major production, an important benefit, or a large show with guest models, then by all means schedule one rehearsal or more, depending on how ambitious is the undertaking. Since professional models must be paid for rehearsals, most stores try to keep these extra trips to a minimum. Sometimes, asking the models to show up a little early, to check out some points in the staging, is enough to get the show smoothly on its way.

In the case of a major production with a large cast, it is important for the fashion office to have a check-in list posted at all stage door entrances. If the rehearsal call is 7 P.M., all participants must have checked in and reported to their assigned dressing rooms by that time. The routine is the same on the day or night of the performance. If the stage manager checks the list an hour before show time and names exist that have not yet been checked, it's time to call and find out what's holding up the missing cast members. The curtain cannot go up until all are present and accounted for.

BACKSTAGE ASSISTANTS

There are a lot of unsung heros behind the scenes of every show, especially the major productions. It is very likely that for a small show with five to eight models, showing not more than 30 to 40 pieces, only one or two people may be helping backstage or in the dressing room. But when it comes to the major fashion show, with a cast of professional models numbering anywhere from 12 to 30 or as many as 100 for a so-called volunteer or guest model production, the assistance needed backstage must grow in proportion. When the audience out front sees a smooth, though complicated fashion show, you can be sure there is a very capable crew behind the scene who are doing a beautifully coordinated job.

Backstage Coordinator

A strong overseer is a must. This individual will have planned way ahead of the show, checking on dressing rooms for the models (making sure they are close enough to the stage or runway entrances to allow for quick changes) and will also make sure that the traffic patterns to and from the dressing rooms are unobstructed and safe. During rehearsal the coordinator will take all the models on a tour of the route so everyone understands where they enter and where to exit.

But this is only the beginning. A well-organized backstage coordinator will undoubtedly work from a checklist similar to the following.

- Arrange for adequate clothes racks.
- Place full-length mirrors at stategic places (to avoid having too many models at one mirror), plus one at the door as the models leave for one last check.
- Provide tables for accessories. Jewelry, scarves, handbags, gloves, hats, or any other accessories for the models should be spread out on accessory tables (for those cases where special accessories have not been selected), picked up after the model is dressed and ready to go on, returned as soon as she comes back. Very often accessories are used more than once in a show by more than one model. (i.e., the same scarf tied differently).
- Supply prop tables. this might also be a responsibility of the display crew if props are their assignment. Such a table should be immediately outside the dressing rooms, where models or other cast members can grab the specific prop. Returning of props must follow the same routine as accessories. They may need to be reused or, if not in their proper place, may be impossible to find for the next performance, which is very often the case with major shows.
- Determine what space can be spared for makeup and hair. Be sure tables and chairs and makeup mirrors are set up.
- Be sure check-in lists and line-ups are posted for all to see.
- Be ready for any emergency. The following survival kit will alleviate a great deal of pressure when problems appear (and they do, you can count on it!)
  Cleansing tissue (for makeup, colds, or tears)
  Dress shields (nothing should be modeled without them)
  Hosiery (extra pairs)
  Manicure equipment (for broken nails and touchups)
  Pins (safety pins, straight pins, hair pins)
  Sewing kit (if alteration people are not available)
  Scissors
  Tissue paper (great for stuffing into shoes and hats to make them fit better)

In addition to the survival kit, a first-aid kit is wise to have around. There is often someone who cuts a finger on a pin or develops a headache or trips on a step. Models are always thirsty and hungry, so be sure pitchers of ice water and glasses are available. Some appreciate coffee and candy and nuts to nibble on for quick energy. Alcoholic beverages and smoking in the dressing should be prohibited.

The backstage coordinator (who is usually a member of the fashion office) would be responsible for lining up all backstage helpers.

Dressers

The ideal arrangement is to have one dresser for every model. If this is not possible (and it very often is not), then the line-up should be planned so that the changes are not so frantic. A good dresser can usually handle two or three models as long as the changes are not at exactly the same time. The dresser must review the line-up with the model, understanding exactly what comes first, second, third, and so on. In order to expedite changes without wasted motion, garments should be unzipped and unbuttoned, ready to jump into. When the model is on the runway, the dresser hangs up the outfit just removed and prepares for the next change.

Alterations

Zippers get stuck or break, buttons come off, hems get ripped, straps tear, and a dozen other unforeseen mishaps plague most big fashion shows. Sometimes a model is unable to show up and the clothes originally assigned to her must be fitted into the line-up on other models. Quick alterations may be necessary. It is important, therefore, to have alteration women in the dressing room before and during the show. There is nothing so reassuring as nimble, capable hands that can come to the rescue.

Pressers

Even when clothes are carefully packed and delivered with care to the fashion show site, wrinkles occur. Nothing is more damaging to the store's fashion image than a magnificent gown showing up on the runway in less than showcase perfection. Pressers with steam irons can quickly create miracles. If a professional presser from the store's alteration department is not available, the fashion office usually has a traveling iron as part of its standard equipment. Always bring it.

Hair and Makeup

The best people to receive credit on the program or from the show's commentator are the store's own beauty salon and makeup artists. Very often, when the show is big and prestigious, a cosmetic vendor will send a special makeup artist expressly for the event, simply for a credit line or in connection with an in-store promotion scheduled at the same time.

Know the Merchandise

Even with well-planned line-ups and thoroughly rehearsed shows, in the frenzy of making quick changes some model will put on the wrong costume in the wrong category. The backstage coordinator, or whoever is assigned to do the last minute check of each model as she leaves the dressing room, must know the merchandise well enough to recognize an error in the line-up. She would also check to be sure the hat is at the right angle, the scarf is tied correctly, the correct accessories have been selected. It takes a quick, trained eye to do all this in a couple of seconds and send the model out the door, then quickly turn to the next, and the next. It is important for the starter to know each model by name, otherwise, she might not recognize quickly enough that someone was out of line for the order of appearance. "M'Lee, you're not next. You follow Sarah."

Outside Talent

There are hundreds of details that go into the production of an outstanding fashion show. The fashion director might be the producer-director as well as author, coordinator, and commentator of the show. The director can do a great deal, but usually not everything. For example, if the show requires choreography, it is wise to engage the services of a professional choreographer. If live music is to be used, a musical director to help plan the score should also be a professional or someone who can turn out a professional sound. Audiences have grown very sophisticated and the more polished the show the better image created for the store, if, indeed, that is the aim of the effort.

Staging

The theatre of fashion is never more eloquently served than through the artistry of a well-staged fashion show. To enchant the audience while enhancing the fashion offerings requires theatrical know-how. Especially when playing to sophisticated audiences, professional treatment of fashion shows is important.

If the modeling of clothes is to be supplemented with singers and dancers, a professional choreographer and musical director as mentioned earlier, are necessary. If the production numbers to be offered within the fashion show are ambitious, planning must start far enough in advance to allow for casting and rehearsals. For the major fashion production rehearsals are a must.

Very often, the models themselves are used in a dance situation.

Rehearsals for major fashion productions are a must, especially when an inspired set offers opportunities for exciting staging. *(Courtesy of Joseph Horne & Company)*

Sometimes they might be asked to dance down the runway while modeling. On occasion, if they have the aptitude, they might be taught specific dance routines to reinforce a fashion trend. Dance is used most frequently with models for finale scenes. Whatever the approach, dance has a great deal to offer as an entertainment feature for a fashion show, especially for young presentations, such as back-to-school shows. The type of entertainment should be compatable with the desired image—for the store, the fashion stories presented, and the audience.

Even without dance, models can create marvelous pictures with synchronized movements or through the use of interesting levels. For example, a flat stage does not offer as much opportunity for interesting patterns when several models appear together, or even with one or two. Models moving from steps or platforms, up and down, create a sense of motion and formation not unlike the art of flower-arranging; stems at various heights and clusters of color and texture offer inspired visions of balance. Also, the interesting placement of the stage, such as in the middle of the room, adds to the involvement of the audience. Such staging can provide a fashion show with intriguing pacing, which is, after all, the most important element of a show.

Pacing

Whatever else must be omitted from a show—dancers, singers, multiple stage levels, elaborate scenery or props—good pacing must have top priority. All staging plans must be influenced by the show's pace. Beautiful sets will contibute little to a show that is badly paced, drags in spots, is speeded up when the scene requires a serene treatment, has a choppy line-up rather than one that flows smoothly, and so on. It is good to remember that an audience can be put to sleep with speed as well as with slowness. The important element in good pacing is in alternating speed with easy, relaxed processions of modeling. A well-paced fashion show combined with fascinating staging becomes a memorable event, a selling vehicle for the store and a compliment to the store's image of excellence.

HOW TO WORK WITH THE SPECIAL EVENTS DIRECTOR

If the store has a special events director, he or she is responsible for all events of a special nature such as promotions, fairs, exhibits, and shows that do not necessarily relate to fashion. When a storewide special event does relate to fashion, then the fashion office is involved and works with the special events director.

For example, an import fair may be in the offing for the store, and the special events director is responsible for pulling all the details together. If the fair is from Italy, England, France, Denmark, Spain, Mexico, it is very likely that fashions from that country will have been selected by the buyers during a trip abroad, specifically to embellish the event. The special events director would ask the fashion director to plan on scheduling special shows of the imported couture or ready-to-wear fashions. They will be part of an overall plan of special events with personal appearances and exhibits brought in especially for the fair. It is the special events director's responsibility to balance the program and to have something exciting and attractive going on at special hours every day. The fashion shows will fit into the plan where action is needed. In such a case, the fashion director need not handle any of the details of advising advertising, for example, of what is going on. The director will, instead, submit all information regarding the requested shows to the special events director, who will handle all publicity pertinent to the event.

Another "nonfashion" event that comes under the province of the special events director but calls on a contribution from the fashion director, is the opening of a new store or branch. Such an occasion might be hailed with all the markings of a grand opening, with store officials on hand to greet guests (the fashion director included), with music, cocktail party, and fashion show. The show might be formally staged, or it might be offered as informal modeling throughout the new fashion areas to add to the glamor of the opening event.

The Publicity Director

There are a few stores where the publicity director and fashion director are one and the same. Very often the special events director and publicity director are part of the same office if not the same person. The assignments for these executives vary from store to store. For example, at Bergdorf Goodman New York the publicity department is repsonsible for handling all details of fashion shows.

Whatever the system, fashion shows very often are good news items. When the opportunity is present, the fashion office should provide the publicity department with the necessary information to obtain press attention. Since fashion shows and special events are for the purpose of gaining attention for the store, clueing the publicity department in on what's on the fashion calendar is an opportunity not to be overlooked.

AFTERVIEW

The feeling that "there is no business like show business" is not entirely shared by everyone in the retail fashion business. In the big cities, where the giant retailers prevail, there is a resistance to fashion shows. Big cities, of course, have greater distractions and more sophisiticated audiences, but even more than that, big city retailers have big competition. Their customers are being lured in many directions with quality, price, service, and selection. Merchandising, therefore, is the first consideration for these retailers. The big chains, too, prefer the fashion image of good quality at a price.

In many cosmopolitan cities, large segments of the population have been drowned in fashion shows, hounded to death to buy tickets to fashion show benefits, fund-raising affairs, and club events of their friends. Retailers finding themselves in this climate must excel with every fashion show event. They have to dazzle, enchant, amaze, or shock every time out. Coming up with a new winner time after time can not only be energy and talent consuming, but highly expensive. Smashing shows are not produced on small budgets. This category of retailer resorts to doing fewer shows, but more spectacular ones. They have vowed no more church basements, no more school gyms, no more bridge club programs. Only the occasional star-studded produc-

THE FASHION DIRECTOR

tion, in a grand ballroom of a hotel, in a theatre, in a music hall or art museum, or in the big auditorium of the store, would justify an all-out effort. In the process, these retailers with the big production approach are building very enviable reputations. They are famous in and out of the trade as great show people. Their shows are not to be missed. They make good press. Some even gain national attention and win awards. They are often imitated. When the word gets around, a good promotion idea or show technique sweeps through retail country like brush fire.

In the smaller communities of our nation (and there are more of these) fashion shows are much loved. It is a special event. In fact, women in very small towns, reading about a fashion show coming up in a nearby larger city, will make the trip specifically to see the show. This out of-town customer is very important. She is usually the most appreciative member of the audience.

It all adds up to an obvious truth—when fashion shows are well done, they are still big box office. The fashion show, with its multiple appeals is still the longest running show in the world. Its special merits cannot be lightly passed over. The fashion show is entertainment. It is public relations. It is a service. It not only serves as an educator, but also as a means of expressing the store's community spirit. Many people may not be aware that in the area of benefits and fund-raising projects, the department store gives its personnel, merchandise, and generous assistance free of charge, and that the money raised at the benefit goes directly to the charity involved.

Like all mediums of entertainment, the approach to the fashion show must continue to grow, improve, diversify, and change in order to deserve devoted audiences. That's show business.

CHAPTER RE-EVALUATION

Questions

1. What can customers learn from a fashion show?
2. What are some of the attributes found in a good fashion show commentator?
3. How many pieces are needed for an average size show?
4. What are the first steps in producing a fashion show?
5. How many customer types can be serviced by special fashion shows? (Name the types.)
6. Why do so many areas of the store get involved in a bridal show?
7. What are some of the details the fashion office should check out before committing to a show out of the store?
8. What are three important guidelines to use when accessorizing a fashion show?

9. What is a trunk show?

10. What is a line-up?

Workshop

Plan a fashion show. Specify the type, size, setting, staging, number of models, and so on. List the categories and specify the types of clothes to be shown in each.

From the time of her engagement to Prince Charles, Lady Diana influenced fashion history. The "Lady Di haircut" was immediately imitated all over the world and a little more than eight hours after she became Diana, Princess of Wales, copies of her wedding gown were seen in London shop windows. *(U.P.I.)*

14

HOW PEOPLE, PLACES, AND THINGS AFFECT FASHION

Read the newspaper. Watch the stock market. Watch television. See a movie. See a Broadway or an off-Broadway show. View a new art collection. Walk through a bookstore, or just walk down the street. They are all clues as to why fashion is currently being expressed as it is, and clues as to what might be coming into fashion next. The clues come from people, from their interests, their needs, their behavior, the places they go, the things they do, and the things they create.

The citizens of the fashion community are governed by a multitude of high chiefs who are influenced by a multitude of extenuating circumstances that exist for a multitude of unpredictable reasons. It is a fuzzy thought, but that is the very texture of the fashion business. The fuzziness exists because these high chiefs may function within the fashion community or outside of it. For example, a designer may come forth with one fashion concept, but someone outside the fashion world (a celebrity with great public impact) may appear with a completely different fashion idea. If the public screams, *"We want that!,"* the designer runs back to the drawing board.

To blur the picture even more, fashion is not controlled by any one central governing body—guided perhaps, but not controlled. It may seem to be so because of a Paris that had reigned as the center of the fashion world for over 600 years. And rightfully so. But even Paris, and everyone who goes there for direction, is subject to a higher power: the customer.

CONSUMER POWER

To better understand the indisputable power that the consumer can exert over fashion, examine what transpired in the following time periods.

The Fashion Rebellion of 1970

The fashion year of 1970 is remembered with pain by everyone—designers, manufacturers, retailers, and customers. Paris said it was time for a longer length in skirts. The short look, known as the mini and accepted with favor for nine years, was over. It had been introduced in England, intensified by English designer Mary Quant's interpretations, and carried to new expressions by French designer, Andre Courreges. The sixties had bowed to the directions of the young, whose mini look was adopted by all who wanted to look like the young. However, after almost a decade of sameness, there seemed little more that designers could do to make the short skirt look fresh. The alternative, the longer length, reaching midcalf or above the ankle and called the midi or longuette by the press, was accepted by Parisian women but rejected violently by American women. "Absolutely no," they screamed. And their "no" was heard around the world. Their resistance to the longer lengths was a bloody battle. Designers failed to exert their influence, manufacturers by the dozens closed their doors, customers stopped buying, and retail fashion figures took a big dip downward. During the ensuing witch hunt, *Women's Wear Daily* was blamed for starting or perpetuating the whole midi mess.

New Tale of Two Cities

During that fashion revolution, two fashion capitals—Paris and New York—experienced their own version of the worst of times and the best of times. The worst was the fashion industry's inability to please the fashion customer. But, on the other hand, it proved, indeed, to be the best of times for the consumer. For the first time the customer's power was felt and a new respect for her wishes emerged. Haute couture, already showing signs of losing its power to dictate, bowed its head to the omnipotent command of the American customer. The following year, after the severe thumbs down on the longer length, the very designers who had proposed the fashion idea came back with a complete reverse: short shorts for day or evening wear (hot pants), skating skirts (hot skirts) shorter than the mini had been. They also made a compromise on length, in the neighborhood of the knee, and many women were willing to agree that where daytime dresses and suits were concerned, it was not a bad neighborhood.

The Fashion Reaction of 1980

The time had arrived for another major change. Being careful not to get burned again, the fashion designing community put out feelers by including some above-the-knee and thigh-high looks in their collections. The reaction was unique, to say the least. The women who had protested so fiercely in 1970 were now of an age where the short skirt did not appeal. Even great numbers of younger women hesitated (except for social and activewear) because they had become career-oriented.

The result was a new approach to instigating a major change. The designers offered both for fall 1982—very long skirts, very short ones. They knew it would be only a matter of time until women would tire of the long versions and the eye would get trained to accepting the shorter proportion by spring 1983. Maybe.

The fashion world, in its modern state, is not a true dictatorship; it is strongly democratic. There is even a two-party system existing in the ranks of the consumer—those who want to be individuals and those who want to emulate others. In some fashion years, as in the sixties, there is a radical fringe group who may wish to overthrow the entire system by creating anti-fashion. In the late seventies it took the form of "punk" fashion. The eighties will record its own version.

Because fashion influence can come from any direction, almost without notice, it is very tough for the high moguls of fashion, wise and talented as they may be, to predict in any given season which way the customer will vote.

The Importance of Awareness

There are signs, however, that all citizens of the fashion community must watch. For example, which fashion is likely to get the customer's vote depends on how she lives, what she does, and where she goes. The perceptive fashion director soon learns that *researching the market tells what is available for sale and researching people tells who will buy it.*

Although it is impossible to avoid mistakes, through constant awareness it is entirely possible to avoid major disasters. One of the fashion director's most valuable assets is *awareness.*

This book has hammered away pretty hard in previous chapters, urging thoroughness and checking and rechecking of facts before suggesting that the store put its money on the line for any new trend, color, fabric, or classification. Those earlier chapters deal with the available information and guidance *within* the fashion industry and its relative services. The awareness we speak of here deals with the available information and guidance *outside* the industry in the world at large, from people, places, and things.

THE PEOPLE

To say that a man "looks like a Greek god" is to pay him the ultimate compliment. To say that a well-dressed woman "looks like a page out of *Vogue* " is a salute to her fashion excellence. Whatever the comparison, to "look like" something or someone highly admired, is a very desirable form of recognition. As far back as fashion records show, it has been as important to successfully "look like" someone as to be totally original. This inherent desire to imitate the celebrated, the rich, the powerful, the beautiful, and the revered, has been a basis for fashion trends and change throughout history.

Royalty

Fashion history has never been more magnificently embellished than in the days when fashion was led by royalty. Pre-Renaissance was a period of Spanish elegance. Many fashion firsts came out of that time—the corset, the hoop, silk stockings, and the ruff that encircled the neck holding it high and proud ("dressed to the teeth"). During the Renaissance, when the cultural center of Europe switched to Rome, fashion, too, began taking direction from Italy. Opulent fabrics such as brocades, satins, and velvets encrusted with jewels, were the status of those of high rank. Law prohibited persons outside of royalty or high society from wearing such elegant fabrics. From this period, great new techniques for embroidery developed and the fashion for lace was introduced. In fact, the lace industry was founded in Italy during the sixteenth century.

When fashion supremacy was taken over by the royalty of France, it was the beginning of a reign of dominance from then on. During the sixteenth century, Catherine de Medici of Florence became the queen of France and brought with her the grandiose influence of Italian Renaissance. France became the new cultural center for Spain and Italy.

Throughout the long reign of Louis XIV and then Louis XV, the importance of fashion was elevated to a new height. Both of these brilliant courts were the criterion for all European society. During the Louis XV period, names like Madame Du Barry and Madame de Pompadour took the fashion lead for the French court. Madame de Pompadour spread the taste for Chinese motifs. In 1780, the court of Marie Antoinette was influenced by Spanish fashions. During the eleven years that Napoleon was emperor of France, the Napoleonic influence on fashion and art was remarkably extensive. From his empire came the fashion word and look that remains today: empire, the high-rise bodice, the silhouette that is synonomous with Empress Josephine.

Hair fashions, too, were carefully copied from the royal courts of France. Wigs, for example, were out of fashion during the reign of Louis XIV, until he started to get bald. When he adopted the wig, his court followed.

The court of Napolean III and Empress Eugenie provided the last of the royal innovations. The crinoline was created as a new kind of reinforcement for ball gowns, overlayed with several bouffant skirts. Through the patronage of Empress Eugenie, the House of Worth, the first couturier, gained recognition all over Europe. Other royal clients followed, and society women everywhere were clamoring to identify with the couturier who dressed the royal ladies.

With Napoleon III, the French court, that glamorous, romantic, plush, extravagant fashion showcase came to an end. Around 1871, when the Republic of France was established, royalty's influence on fashion ended.

The Theatre

New queens of fashion were destined to be born, not of royal blood, but equally as glamorous. The actress, that unique lady of the theatre, took the fashion lead. Celebrated, adored, and applauded, she was indeed a woman to copy. France had the divine Sarah Bernhardt, Italy had the inspiration of Eleonora Duse, and across the sea, America had the hour-glass fashion image of Lillian Russell, who dazzled the world with her magnificent costumes and hats.

Society and Early Couture

Perhaps not everyone wanted to be an actress, but everyone wanted to be rich. To associate with the rich and powerful through imitation was perhaps the next best thing.

Before the turn of the century, many notable couture houses had opened in Paris, and their clientele, the socially prominent, were in a position to have gowns made exclusively for them. The designer received little publicity, but his client was observed in her original creation wherever she went. She was photographed for the new fashion magazines that were appearing about this time, and her fashion choice, admired and envied, was copied.

Designers Gain Stardom

Even though we are dealing here with influence on fashion from *outside* the industry, in the case of the name designer, an exception must be made. It is difficult to separate the celebrated designer from other celebrities influencing fashion. It was the same star quality, the same stimuli, that brought worshipers to their thrones. In other words, just as the masses of the consumer community chose an illustrious personality to imitate, the citizens of the fashion community chose to copy the celebrated designer.

Poiret, the First Trend Setter

After the turn of the century, a change took place with the couture, initiated by Paul Poiret. Instead of being guided by his clients, Poiret, an original thinker, preferred himself in the role of guide. From the time he opened his own Paris shop in 1904, he became a bold, if not brash, advocator of freedom and individuality in women's dress, imposing his direction with a tyrant-like command. As the first great trend setter, and perhaps the first fashion dictator, he spoke out often about his strong convictions.

In an article he wrote for *Harper's Bazaar* in the early 1900s Poiret said, "I dined the other day in a fashionable restaurant. At the tables around me I noticed at least half a dozen women whose hair was dressed in exactly the same number of puffs and switches. All were dressed in equally expensive gowns, although I was not able to judge of the colors because they were all equally overloaded with beading, embroideries, gold, silver, or steel ornaments, with laces and fringes. . . . Instead of hiding their individuality, why did not each woman try to bring out her own personal type of beauty?"

The unconventional Poiret, who was determined to free women of rigidity in dress, denounced the corset. At the same time, however, he provided them with a new restriction—the hobble skirt. Nevertheless, he provoked a new fashion awareness among women, awakened their taste buds, and gave them a sense of theater in their clothes.

Perhaps as a carryover from the days when he designed costumes for actresses, such as Sarah Bernhardt, his creations were an embodiment of garish colors, lavish Oriental and Russian influences (from the ballet and visual arts), startling jewelry and makeup. He even introduced a perfume called "Roseine." The perfume, the jewelry, and the simplifying of cut in women's fashions seemed to pave the way for a parade of celebrated fashion designers that followed, many of whom literally shaped the fashion destiny of women the world over.

Chanel

Next came the incomparable Chanel, a provactive, enchanting rebel. Her longevity of fame in the fashion world was unprecedented. Her contributions are unforgettable. With Chanel's understated lines and simplified construction, the wholesale fashion business was born. The elaborate, complicated creations that preceded her prohibited mass production.

Chanel immortalized the fabric of jersey. She started the vogue of costume jewerly. She gave fashion the indestructible Chanel suit, the most copied idea of its kind. She was the first dressmaker to popularize a perfume under her name, the famous Chanel No. 5. Why No. 5 when it was the first? It was her lucky number.

Chanel, the designer who dominated Paris fashion in the nineteen-twenties, was preparing a new collection at the time of her death in 1970, at the age of eighty-seven. Her last collection, shown a couple of weeks after her passing, was hailed as "good Chanel," a splendid classic look, welcomed in a period that was returning to "civilized" fashion.

Mlle. Gabrielle Chanel, the great French couturiere, photographed in her salon in the late 1930s, the embodiment of her fashion credo of understated elegance and luxury. *(Courtesy of Chanel, Inc.)*

More Great Fashion Designers

The great talents of Haute Couture became illustrious stars. Above, Yves Saint Laurent, long reigning king of trendsetting, and possessor of the world's most famous initials.

Each great designer in the French couture was famous for special innovations. Each was imitated and copied with pride. Patou raised the waistline that Chanel had lowered. Recognizing the value of publicity, he was the first to offer a preview showing of his collection for the press. Vionnet contributed the bias cut. Schiaparelli ended the slouch look by bringing up the shoulder. Christian Dior made fashion front page news with his shocking new look in 1947. It was a turbulent change to return to small waistlines, full skirts, and longer lengths. Dior's look lived its nine lives until the crown was passed on to Yves Saint Laurent after Dior's sudden death. St. Laurent released the waistline and eased clothes into a relaxed simplicity. Another new trend began.

The sixties brought a star-studded era of European couture. St. Laurent, Courreges, Cardin, Givenchy, Pucci, Valentino, and others became so illustrious that they were paid the kind of homage once enjoyed only by stars of the stage and screen. Instead of an autograph, their signature on a scarf of their design became a new status symbol. American designers, too, such as Norell, Beene, Blass, and de la Renta were "signing" their accessories, or adding a fragrance line bearing their name. Adolfo signed his hats with bold script. Wearing the label on the "outside," so to speak, appealed to the affluent society that now could afford the "names" of high fashion, a privilege once confined to the fortunate few.

In the late sixties, the name designers branched out even more, to design and endorse in areas outside their original efforts. Their names appeared as the creators of everything from shoes, jewerly, children's clothes, and men's fashions, to towels, sheets, and bedspreads. A store might have St. Laurent or Cardin in the linen department, in accessories, in the cosmetic and fragrance department, in men's fashions, and in women's fashions as well. A woman might receive a silk-print-on-Florentine-leather checkbook cover designed by Emilio Pucci, for opening her accounts at a New York bank. She might buy lipstick or nail polish and find colors named after American designers Bill Blass and Norman Norell—Bill Blass Red or Norell Red. The merchandising of the big names was an undisputable testimony to their star quality. They were good box office; their names sold.

The Beauty Stars

The stars of fashion reached beyond the couture and ready-to-wear, toward the woman herself. Her hair and face, regarded as part of the total look, had to change with the fashion trends, relate to the trends. To every potential Helen of Troy, the bottles of hope provided by the cosmetic industry held a promise of youth and beauty few women could resist.

Just as women loved to follow a fashion authority when selecting a wardrobe, she preferred "authority" for her hair and face, too. Because of this star system, the sixties developed authorities like Sassoon with his unique short haircut for women, Alexandre, Kenneth, and many others whose hair fashions were designed to relate to the whole fashion picture. The wig makers followed the hair designers and provided replicas of the newest trend.

Even the most original designers of fashions for the hair were influenced by the people whose celebrity overshadowed anything they might propose. In the seventies a Farrah Fawcett (TV and films) might be their direction, with hair full, long, and undisciplined. At the ouset of the eighties, film star Bo Derek's braided and beaded hair produced imitators everywhere.

The Face

As a way of relating to lifestyle dressing, Ralph Lauren presented his cosmetic line with separate color stories for active, day, and night.

Face fashions had their own moments of glory. The sound of the name of the beauty leaders of the cosmetic industry was indeed the sound of authority. Helena Rubinstein ruled in her time like a queen. Elizabeth Arden considered the total woman so completely that she even had exclusive fashion collections designed to carry in her salons the world over. Max Factor's name was synonymous with the glamour of Hollywood. Charles Revson (Revlon) personified the magnitude of color for nails and makeup. Many famous beauties, film stars, and socialites either started their own cosmetic companies or lent their name and image to hype a cosmetic line's clout. Such efforts, like all fashion trends, come and go, but their power to sway is why it all happened.

Estee Lauder, who would personally cover the Paris couture every season to be sure her beauty creations were fashionably compatible, demonstrated tremendous staying power by relating to the lifestyles of women.

The change in a fashion silhouette is motivation for a cosmetic change. A trend in color, fabric, texture, along with the lifestyle use of these features in clothes, inspires the direction for cosmetic color and even treatment.

Just as a point of focus on a woman's body shifts with the transposing of line in fashion, so does the focal point on the face.

In the forties (and revived in 1971), the bright red mouth was the important feature. In the sixties, the eyes had it. A rainbow of eye shadows and eyeliners, from romantic to sultry, was created to glorify the eyes. False eyelashes became the big accessory on every woman's dressing table. For the seventies false eyelashes disappeared and the natural look prevailed. The eighties ushered in a multitude of mood changes—specific faces to relate to lifestyle dressing—for the office, for the tennis court, for a candlelight dinner.

Bill Blass

Halston

Giant American designers whose leadership in fashion propelled their respected and authoritative names onto fragrances and other products with major success.

The Creative Director

Fashion designers create clothes. Creative directors fashion faces. The creative director of a cosmetic house researches the fashion market to learn what the new colors, fabrics, silhouettes, and trends will be. If a new color is proposed as important, a congenial color in lipstick, for example, must be available to relate to the clothes. Makeup techniques must also be redesigned. If clothes have a classic, country feeling (i.e., tweeds and checks), the face should belong, with color and application in harmony. A delicate, romantic costume would be prettier with a gentle approach to makeup than a dramatic look intended for a slinky, sophisticated gown. Creative directors whose makeup artistry appear on magazine covers and in cosmetic ads inspire women to adopt their ideas.

To help the average woman choose the correct products and to teach her the new techniques of application, many leading cosmetic companies conduct makeup clinics in department stores or send trained consultants to demonstrate. The adult customer may have to forget old

Calvin Klein

Oscar de la Renta

tricks and learn new ones, and the young customer,perhaps using makeup for the first time, needs instruction in the approach best for her. Whoever she is, whatever age, the cosmetic customer looks for authority for her makeup as strongly as she does for her clothes.

Fragrances

From fashion to fragrance has been a predictable track for a great many giants in the fashion world. Their famous names that provided prestige on a garment, through excellence and originality, carried a magic worth millions into the fragrance business. Going back as far as Chanel's first fragrance, even as far back as Poiret's Roseine, the enchantment with a star-designer's product has continued to flourish.

Stardom for the Fashion Model

At the outset, the fashion model was comparatively unknown as a personality. In the 1860s, Charles Frederick Worth, of the House of Worth, used his beautiful wife as a model. Poiret, also, used his wife as his model in the mid-1900s. The early fashion magazines used sketches

Diane Von Furstenberg

of fashions, or photographed the celebrated in their own creations. It was much more chic to follow the prominent.

Through the innovation of previewing couture collections for the press, and the growth of the fashion magazines, the fashion models position grew in importance. She was selected as carefully by the designer as his fabric, and by the magazine as carefully as the photographer. *Harper's Bazaar* called Suzy Parker the model of the fifties. The sixties brought unprecedented fame to a very young English girl who came to be known the world over as Twiggy. A product of the Mary Quant generation (a time of skinny minis), Twiggy's very thin, long body personfied the young look of the day. Equally famous were the Twiggy eyes, eyelashes drawn on the face, a new approach to eye makeup.

In the late seventies and early eighties, many a young model hopeful longed to be another Cheryl Tiegs or Beverly Johnson. Photographic models, perhaps because of the exposure, became much more famous than runway models—especially if they were actresses like Brooke Shields or had the potential of appearing in the role of actress, such as in television commercials.

Fashions in models, of course, change with fashion. Measurements, types, looks, and personalities flow in and out with the tide of public acceptability, the reigning fashion ideal, and the dominating concept of designers.

Movies

Of all the influences of fashion, perhaps the movie star enjoyed the longest and most powerful influence on the greatest number of people. In the twenties, from America's sweetheart, Mary Pickford, and the profound Helen Hayes, to the screen "vamps," every American woman could find a favorite to emulate. Theda Bera was the screen's sex symbol, and among the first to be toasted for their stirring pulchritude were Greta Garbo, Gloria Swanson, and Mae Murray. Even though much of what they wore was more suitable for reel people than real people, their "look" was enough to inspire adaptation.

The thirties brought another crop of celluloid queens, and their fashion impact is a matter of history. Shirley Temple was a merchandising dream, and the Shirley Temple doll became a household item. Mae West became an institution. Jean Harlow made blond hair a national craze, and the indisputable fashion powers of the screen, whose wardrobes were worth the price of admission alone to movie goers, included Katharine Hepburn, Bette Davis, Joan Crawford, Loretta Young, and Carol Lombard. Adrian, fashion designer for the screen, created such unforgettable looks as the padded "Joan Crawford shoulders." The Jean Harlow–Carol Lombard slinky look of the bias-cut and plunge backs and the Garbo slouch hat, all lived to be revived in the seventies. All these bright stars, plus Norma Shearer, Ginger Rogers, Hedy Lamarr, Claudette Colbert, Rita Hayworth, and Irene Dunne, created an age of adoration from movie fans, the like of which was never quite known before and seldom achieved again.

From then on, an occasional great fashion force developed from the screen (Marlene Dietrich and Merle Oberon in the forties, or Audrey Hepburn and Grace Kelly in the fifties), but the heyday of movie influence was giving way to other outside powers.

Television

The impact on fashion via television did not occur in the same star-studded manner as it did through the motion picture. From the outset, television had its stars, but they were not innovators so much as models. Their names were household words, but their fashion image was forgotten almost as quickly as one series replaced another.

What really happened with fashion through the medium of television was unique. By the very nature of its continuity, television promoted fashion in four separate ways.

1. **Exposure.** A current fashion trend gained great momentum by the repeated exposure. Personalities in contemporary situations (a drama, an interview, a variety show) dressed in the current fashion. Over and over again, the viewer saw the new trend, saw its various interpreta-

tions by people of all types and sizes. Consciously or subconsciously, the viewer might pick up a fashion idea here or there suitable for his or her own use.

The so-called "talk" shows were ideal showcases for fashion. The famous men and women who appeared as guests provided a constant fashion show. From time to time, formal fashion shows were included as part of the format. These usually were parades of the way-out looks coming in, many of which became not-so-way-out after general acceptability.

Fashion's role in television specials is one of the big attractions. Throughout the award shows—the Oscar, the Emmy, the Grammy—the fashions that the celebrated wear to present or accept awards is as intriguing as who the winners are. The reviews of such shows almost always mention who the fashion stand-outs were. Days after the excitement of who the winners were has died down, women might still be talking about what the stars wore at the Academy Awards.

The women in the viewing audience may not wish to copy the fashion look of the stars (more often criticized than applauded for their choices), but it cannot be denied that such a parade of fashion dramatizes its ability to be provocative, stirring, glaring, and bold. Stars do not select their gowns for such occasions to win fashion awards; they select fashion to get talked about and make the press. At the same time, the viewing audience discovers that fashion can be exciting enough to steal the scene. And there are times when it should.

As regards news broadcasts, not only does fashion make the news when a new season ushers in newsworthy innovations, but how the anchorperson is dressed also is part of the show. When a Barbara Walters does an interview news special, what she wears contributes to the program's image.

When certain programs have great impact on viewers, a fashion influence could emerge. For example, television provided a strong influence for Oriental fashion ideas following a highly successful televised version of the novel *Shogun*. Giorgio Armani of Italy offered an outstanding Japanese-inspired collection at the time, while Gianfranco Ferre produced a collection in the Chinese mood. Touches of Oriental feelings appeared in collections everywhere.

The world came to know Kermit, a lovable frog, and Miss Piggy, a sexy blond pig, through a puppet show on television called "The Muppet Show." Merchandised in every area of the store imaginable, the beloved characters appeared on towels, sheets, pillows, and quilts created by Martex. Same with "Big Bird" from Sesame Street, a television show for children. This eight-foot yellow bird, along with other Sesame Street characters, showed up on bedding designed for Burlington in a pattern called "Sesame Street TV Time."

Whole trends have been intensified by television's impact—the western look and the ten-gallon hat ("Dallas"), the juniors' interest in hospital scrub greens as casualwear ("General Hospital"), plus T-shirts bearing the names and pictures of favorite TV characters or show titles.

The power of the tube is indisputable. Every year new images appear on that small screen and new fashion ideas are born as a result of its exposure.

2. **Merchandising.** Because television personalities, plus the famous from all other areas of entertainment, are such excellent models of fashion, and because they have such personal rapport with the consumer, opportunities for merchandising fashion as a tie-in with such celebrities is a natural. That's why we see a Brooke Shields modeling Calvin Klein jeans, why a fragrance is named for Sophia Loren or another is identified with Candice Bergen or Jaclyn Smith. It is because of the power of television that there was great interest in Johnny Carson suits.

Johnny Carson, star of the "Tonight Show," having demonstrated his excellence in taste and effectiveness with fashion, not to mention his unqualified acceptance with his viewing audience, was a top choice for merchandising. At a time when men showed a growing interest in fashion, when they were ready to take lessons in color and fashion coordination from the men they respected and admired on the air,

Johnny Carson's well-dressed look on television made him an excellent personality for merchandise endorsement. (*Courtesy of Johnny Carson Apparel Co.*)

Jacqueline Kennedy, as First Lady, was the undisputed fashion leader of the 1960s. *(Portrait by Richard Avedon, courtesy of Harper's Bazaar)*

merchandise endorsements held promise. For several years, Carson and his musical director, Doc Severinsen, bantered around the merits of what they were wearing (Johnny illustrating the contemporary, Doc the avant-garde). Later, when fashion changed, Johnny continued as the perfect model for the traditional look, Doc opted for the relaxed contemporary.

3. **Credits.** Many of the men and women on television are supplied with clothes by manufacturers, sometimes for cost, sometimes for credit. Since the fashions we choose are very indicative of our personalities, the actor in an episode or the cast of a drama must be clothed in a manner in keeping with the tone of the character involved. It would be impossible for performers to have a different change for every show, week after week, if they had to use clothes from their personal wardrobes.

Contemporary wardrobes might be furnished by a manufacturer in exchange for a credit noted in the roll-up at the end of the show. If the viewer admires the fashion look of the star on a particular show, he or she can learn from the credit line, "Miss Star's Wardrobe furnished by _____," where such fashions are available. Also, when a customer sees the manufacturer's label on a garment in the store, she is reminded that this is the label her favorite TV actress wears.

4. **Commercials.** Commercials can relate to fashion in two ways: (1) as wardrobe for the actor playing a role in the commercial or (2) as a direct fashion sell. The latter might be a commercial by a fiber company, fabric mill, manufacturer, or retailer.

The commercial selling a product unrelated to fashion is very often a fashion vehicle all the same, though usually subliminally. Whether the woman is baking a cake, or waxing a table, or illustrating makeup or hair shampoo, she is wearing fashion. If an automobile commercial includes people, their fashion look will relate to the style and image of the car.

The combined stimuli absorbed by the viewer through televison exposure, provides fashion with considerable influence.

Public Figures

Public figures who become fashion influences, do so because they are intriguing and colorful in a way that is uniquely theirs.

Jackie. Of all the personalities to influence fashion trends in the latter half of the twentieth century, none was so effective as Jacqueline Bouvier Kennedy Onassis. As the wife of President John F. Kennedy, she was the most photographed, most talked about woman of the decade. The sixties were aglow with the fashion leadership of Jacqueline Kennedy and designers such as Yves Saint Laurent were elevated to greater recognition by her approval. The interest in the "Jackie Kennedy look" was enormous and, therefore, big business.

Nancy Reagan, on her way to Buckingham Palace, for the wedding reception of Lady Diana and Prince Charles, wearing a look that not only continued desirable fashion but provided the designer with an elevated public image. (*Courtesy of Women's Wear Daily*)

Nancy. In 1981, when Nancy Reagan became America's first lady, a new flutter of fashion influence was notable. She was described by Adolfo, whose designs Nancy Reagan had chosen since 1967, as "chic upper-class American." This understated, perfectly groomed style of Nancy Reagan was called "American Thoroughbred" by *Women's Wear Daily*.

Because of her love of red, the color prevailed as good fashion. Her gown for the inauguration ball (a Galanos creation, said to be valued at $10,000, loaned to Mrs. Reagan for the occasion and later donated to the Smithsonian Institution) was a one-shoulder silhouette. The one-shoulder look for gowns was adoped widely. American women, who were relating to classic, functional fashion, were comfortable adopting the soft chanel jackets, suitings, and soft dresses Mrs. Reagan chose.

Unlike the "Jackie look," Nancy Reagan's did not revolutionize fashion; it just reinforced women's feelings about dressing chic. What did happen is that sales of the designers whose clothes Nancy chose were elevated considerably. For example, Saks Fifth Avenue reported sales of Adolfo suits and eveningwear increased 200 percent the month of the inauguration of President Ronald Reagan.

Gloria. Gloria Vanderbilt is a case of a celebrity outside fashion becoming a celebrity within the industry. Combining her distinguished American family name with a remarkable designing talent, Gloria came on the status jean scene with a power that equalled or surpassed the leading fashion names already established in this area.

Other socially prominent personalities entered the fashion business, some actually participating, some just lending their names as endorsements. In any case, they provided prestigious labels to fashion merchandise that appealed to the status-conscious buying public.

Weddings

A new kind of star in the fashion business. Combining her remarkable talent with an already-celebrated name, Gloria Vanderbilt gained extraordinary acclaim for her creations.

Weddings involving public figures have always influenced fashion trends. When Wallis Simpson married the Duke of Windsor, the English king who abdicated his throne for "the woman I love," the romantic public appointed the new Duchess of Windsor a fashion leader. What she selected for her trousseau, her wedding, and everything she chose in fashion for some time thereafter was news.

The wedding day is an important day, and who would be better to copy than someone very important? Even without a wedding in the offing, the general public is interested in the fashion story for the sake of fashion itself. When the younger daughter of President Nixon, Julie, was married, her fashion choices were reported by the press in detail. For Tricia Nixon's wedding to Edward Cox in 1971, her attendants wore long silk organdy gowns of mint green and lilac, with off-shoulder necklines and handkerchiefing surrounding the hemlines. It was expected by the industry that the public interest in this creation by Priscilla of Boston would be stimulated; copies of the fashion idea and the color scheme were inevitable.

Undoubtedly, the most heralded, and certainly the most watched wedding of many decades, perhaps of the century, was the royal wedding of England's Prince Charles and Lady Diana Spencer. At a time when the news was heavy with conflicts between nations, within nations, strikes, unemployment, and concerns about the economy and inflation, the world took a one-day respite from all these concerns and entered a fairyland of beauty and romance. The two-million-dollar wedding extravaganza held the attention of millions of viewers around the world, but nothing was more anticipated than Lady Diana's wedding gown, held secret until her appearance.

Being aware of the likelihood of a rush to make copies, details of Lady Di's wedding gown were released in a sealed envelope on the morning of her wedding, to be opened when the 20-year-old bride stepped into the glass coach at Clarence House on her way to St. Paul's Cathedral. The designers of her gown, David and Elizabeth Emanuel, made three gowns, so that a switch could be made in case details of Diana's choice leaked out before the wedding.

As soon as a detailed description of the magnificent ivory silk taffeta and old lace gown became available, copies were started. While the royal couple was still on their honeymoon, copies in England were offered for $500. Designers elsewhere in the world agreed that some version of this spectacular wedding gown (perhaps not its 25-foot train) would be requested and imitated. Even the color of the new bride's going-away dress (a pale salmon), as well as the dress worn to the wedding by America's representative, Nancy Reagan (also a pale salmon), was an immediate clue that the following season would see a similar color incorporated into fashion collections everywhere.

Also, according to gem dealers and retail jewelers, after Prince Charles gave Lady Diana a sapphire and diamond engagement ring, the demand for sapphires went up.

These, of course, are not all the people who influence fashion. The numbers are legion. They are, however, highly indicative of how people can promote a trend or create a new one. An awareness of who these people might be, what they are wearing, and to what degree they are admired, is an important guide to which way fashion will take its inspiration and general fashion acceptability might be going. This is the way, or at least one of the ways, a fashion director takes the public pulse.

THE PLACES

Even people who are not famous are capable of influencing fashion. Great fashion trends have come into being, for example, from fashion innovators at vacation resorts. Something contagious in fashion might sweep through the Riviera one season, another fashion idea might begin in the discotheques of Paris another season, in St. Tropez, at St. Moritz, or at Swiss Klosters. Other trends might be brought home from Corfu, the Greek island playground, or Greece's Mykonos, from Acapulco, Hawaii, or Palm Beach. Everywhere. At home or abroad, fashion-conscious travelers bring, exchange, and borrow fashion ideas from the natives or fellow travelers.

The Big Attractions

Special events the world over bring fashion into the spotlight. During the Grand Prix de Monaco in Monte Carlo, race car fans from Europe and America can be observed day and night in an international fashion exhibit. From the Cannes Film Festival to renowned horse racing tracks such as the Royal Ascot in England where the sport of kings attracts the fashionably prominent, the new way to dress is extensively demonstrated. Every year the calendar is filled with special events that stimulate fashion awareness in those who come to participate or in the press who come to report on who was there and what was being worn.

Fashions Where the Socially Conscious Gather

The presence of the press at an inaugural ball, the dedication of a famous-name library or art center, or any occasion that merits the attendance of the rich and famous, will invariably provide fashion representation on a level of special interest to the reading public. Benefits and charities, too, of the $1,000 or more per person vintage, bring photographers and reporters to translate the festivities of the event for their readers. What the guests wore to such important and exclusive events reveals the highest utilization of current fashion.

Fashions Where the Masses Gather

There was a time when fashion filtered down only from the top, from the choices of the rich and powerful. Everything thus far indicated in this chapter testifies to this system. However, beginning in the sixties, fashion made a complete reverse; it moved from the bottom all the way up to the couture. The street influence might have started in Greenwich Village of New York, Carnaby Street, Kings Road of London, or any street in any city in the world where young rebels of fashion explored new horizons of dress. They were their own designers, their own coordinators. What might have started out as a put-on was picked up and developed as new fashion by fashion authorities in the industry.

Young designers, especially receptive to this new system of freedom in dress, glorified the out-of-the-attic, surplus store, granny's old clothes kind of looks. The followers became the leaders. For example, some resourceful, fashion-free thinkers in the Village tied knots in their white jeans, tossed them into some colored dye, and when they dried the patterns created by the knots were fascinating. The fad not only caught on with the young, but was picked up by designers and fabric mills and reinterpreted on luxury fabrics from velvet to chiffon. Tie-dyeing is an old art, discovered long ago in Indonesia, popularized in the twenties, and revived in the sixties along with many other old crafts.

Any college campus is an excellent source of fashion direction. An alert fashion director, anxious to get an accurate reading on what the student might want for back to school, for classroom or social occasion dressing, would benefit by visiting college campuses.

Totally different from the grubbies of the sixties and the jean scene of the seventies, the outset of the eighties found the student body cleaned up with a strong interest in the preppy look (a throw-back to an earlier prep school or ivy league look), which included plaid skirts, tweed jackets, shetland sweaters, and button-down shirts. The preppy man was also evident with similar type shirts and sweaters, some with varsity stripes. Every incoming class, of course, will interpret its own version of what is best for campus, so there is nothing like a firsthand look at what's happening to spot a trend or discover an emerging change or unique idea.

Wherever the masses gather, a college campus, a fashionable vacation resort, a world premiere of a motion picture, the opening night of a Broadway show, a visit to a fashionable restaurant, or a walk down any prominent street in a fashion-aware community, from Southhampton to San Francisco, from Minneapolis to Dallas, anywhere, everywhere, fashion is happening.

THE THINGS

Fashion is reflected from and onto the things that surround us. Because change affects fashion and fashion is created for change, all the things that coexist with us—the shape of a chair, the color of drapery, the texture of the carpet, a trend in art, decor, collections—fall in and out of favor depending on the fashion.

Fashion and Art

As far as archaeological discoveries and the preservation of art forms can testify, fashion and art are inseparable. Mode of dress is revealed on pottery, vases, plates, reliefs, statues, frescoes, mosaics, stained glass windows, tapestries, drawings, and paintings. The artists of the world have recorded fashion for posterity, and from all these art forms, fashion artists have repeatedly revived and reinterpreted ideas to their own art form. From ancient Greek culture, for example, comes the Grecian drape, revisited again and again, indestructible in its grace and versatility.

There is unquestionably enough influence to be traced from the paintings of the old masters alone to fill another volume. When expressionistic or surrealist styles of art became popular, fashion picked up more inspiration. For example, Schiaparelli's "lobster dress" and a hat in the shape of a shoe with a shocking pink velvet heel, was inspired by surrealist Salvador Dali. Makeup created by Estee Lauder with a delicate Renoir touch was inspired by the paintings of Auguste Renoir. Every area of fashion calls on art at one time or another to validate its motives.

Fashion design is electric with art inspiration. A color, a balance, a pattern, a rhythm, or a mood, originally captured on canvas by the artist, can reappear with an undeniable resemblance or feel on the designer's sketch pad. Artists themselves have had a kinship with fashion. Many have designed fabrics, jewelry, clothes, accessories, and even hairdos. Watteau (1684–1721), for example, designed a fashion look recorded in many of his paintings. The Watteau train, which falls from the back of the shoulders to the floor, is a look often seen in wedding gowns.

When a retrospective exhibit of Pablo Picasso art was brought to New York's Museum of Modern Art, not only were fashion designers inspired to pick up on the current interest, but retailers incorporated Picasso colors and Picasso art and impressions as part of a fashion promotion or display decor.

For his 1981 collections, Yves Saint Laurent announced that he was "in a Shakespearean mood." The influence, which seemed destined to carry over into other seasons, brought words like "Lady Macbeth velvet," "Shakespearean sleeves," "Elizabethan mantilla," and "Renaissance motifs." Yves Saint Laurent also saluted the greats of the art world, such as Matisse, Ingres, and Van Dyke, with his fashion artistry.

A magnificent collection of Hapsburg costumes was displayed in New York at the Costume Institute of the Metropolitan Museum and once again designers found inspiration. Oscar de la Renta, plus many other designers, translated the ornate, luxurious Hapsburg looks into current fashion. With inspired passementerie-embroidered accents, luscious velvet, satin, fur, silk and braid, the splendor of Marie Antoinette was brought into the twentieth century.

Still another art form served as a inspiration for fashion in bed linens. For their "L'Opera Collection," Burlington offered La Boheme, Madame Butterfly, and Carmen pattern interpretations.

The first major United States showing of textiles and gowns created by the Spanish master Mariano Fortuny opened first in New York and then traveled to Chicago. The exhibit, which included 22 priceless fabrics and a display of 75 gowns loaned by museums and private collectors, reinforced the influence that was appearing in contemporary ready-to-wear. Dresses, blouses, sleeves, and scarves appeared with Fortuny pleats.

Fashion and Cartoons

A fashion director's awareness will not stop with the art forms mentioned above. The director will notice that even a poster craze for old movie stars, for example, indicated a nostalgic interest in fashions of the thirties, forties, and fifties. Such fascinations with the past stimulate revivals.

An art form that is as American as apple pie—cartoon and comic strip characters—has been merchandised time and again, in one way or another. A revival of Walt Disney characters or a movie about Popeye or Superman will bring their specific charm to the fashion floor. For spring 1982, the renewed interest in the nautical influence brought Popeye and his world into favor again.

Stage and Screen

In addition to the stars of stage and screen who influence fashion, the vehicles themselves (the play or the movie) become merchandising material. The production might be showcasing a costume or fashionably acceptable trend that is susceptible to fashion exploitation. A manufacturer might tie in with the picture promoter to market a collection influenced by the costumes or story line of the show.

All areas of fashion—cosmetics, hairstylists, and ready-to-wear designers—are possibilities for tie-ins that would ultimately be offered to the fashion retailer. What happens is that the store that stocks the fashions related to the show usually helps promote the production when it hits town. Windows, displays, ads, and fashion shows, all using the theme of the production, plus maybe even giving away free tickets, help stimulate interest in the fashion items.

Fashion and the Front Page

Reference was made earlier to Tobe's belief that "front page news makes front page fashion." This truth has been confirmed with every fashion change resulting from a war, a drastic stock market change, a new breakthrough in science, or a new comic strip character.

When the moon shot put men on the moon, outer-space fashions were improvised for that last word for the modern fashionables. When country music became such a national hit, country-and-western looks were included with a new impact every season. What started out as fashion soon became a fashion department's mainstream.

News has always affected fashion, even way back when Columbus set off to explore the New World. The Spanish were awarded fashion leadership after the discovery of America. The prestige of their involvement in this great moment of history was enough to bring fashion followers to their door.

AFTERVIEW

All the people, places, and things that influence fashion are offshoots of lifestyles, what people earn, where they live, and what they do. But in addition to their external environment is their internal environment, their emotional needs, their dreams, their goals. All this is reflected in the heros they choose, the standards they accept, the roles they play, and, ultimately, the fashions they select.

In the first edition of this book I stated that fashion directors, along with manufacturers and retailers, take calculated risks because not they nor any magic power known to humans can predict fashion when it is impossible to predict woman. I also stated that first woman wants something nobody else has. When she can get it, she will not have it until she is sure everybody else wants it. When everybody else is wearing it, she doesn't want it. The only reliable thing one can predict about woman is that she is unpredictable.

Today, the above statement is only partly true. It *is* possible to predict in some degree what, for example, the working woman might want, if we relate to the kind of job she holds and its dress requirements. We can also predict that she is health oriented and, therefore, will want and need a certain amount of casual and functional clothes for active sports or just plain relaxing on weekends. With casual and working clothes having their own special look it is very likely that the glamour side of woman will need to be expressed differently after five. Three wardrobes with their own special character are predictable for most active women at this writing. However, what will influence the design, color, fabric, the blend, mix, contrast, balance, and proportions within those three wardrobe types depends in large part on those areas discussed in this chapter. In any given season a new personality, a newly applauded visual art, a front-page story, or lifestyle change will be the guideline to watch for fashion's next direction.

CHAPTER RE-EXAMINATION

Questions

1. How was the fashion change offered in 1980 handled differently by the fashion industry than that attempted in 1970?
2. Why is "awareness" one of the fashion director's most valuable assests?
3. Throughout history what kind of people have influenced fashion?
4. How did Poiret open the way for Chanel's wholesale approach to fashion?
5. What conditions brought fame to the fashion model?
6. What are three ways television can influence fashion?
7. How does the fashion influence of TV differ from that of motion pictures?
8. Name three types of places where fashion influences can be traced.
9. What modern art forms affect fashion?
10. What affects fashion changes in cosmetics?

Workshop

Examine the current news. Pick a story, a famous personality, movie, TV show, Broadway play, dance trend, and so on that is or has the potential of influencing fashion. Write a report on how and why it has had an influence.

The people likely to enjoy the greatest success in any fashion career are those who are the best prepared. Pictured, a student at the Fashion Institute of Technology. *(Ken Karp)*

15

FASHION COORDINATION CAREERS OUTSIDE RETAILING

Fashion is everywhere. And as the old observation says about smoke and fire—where there's fashion there's fashion coordination.

Before fashion gets into the stores, there is an army of agencies and institutions working in many different ways to make fashion happen. Fashion directors, coordinators, stylists, and consultants guide the fashion expressions coming out of all those areas outside retailing.

A fashion firm or fashion authority can be found making a contribution in dozens of areas, from manufacturing of fashion ready-to-wear and accessories to home furnishings, to fiber producers and fabric mills and converters, consultant firms, and buying offices. All these areas and more depend on fashion direction. However, many of these areas might be overlooked because those seeking fashion careers could be unaware of their existence.

A decision to seek a career in the field of fashion direction or coordination should also include a consideration of all the available possibilities, before deciding which job in which place seems more attractive and more suited to one's individual talents. A general inspection, therefore, of each prominent area outside of retailing is a good way to begin.

FIBER INDUSTRY— FABRIC INDUSTRY

The fiber industry can create miracle fibers and yarns for mills and converters to turn into yards of cloth for apparel and home furnishings, but it takes a fashion director to help turn a piece of fabric into fashion. Yarns, blends, textures, weights, and performance are all very impressive and important terms, but without a fashion message the consumer would turn a deaf ear. In a season when fashion looks are expressed with soft lines, soft fabrics make it happen. In fabrics, therefore, fashion comes first.

The day is gone when people buy fabric or clothes that will wear forever. Nobody wants clothes that will wear forever. If they did, they would buy bulky, stiff, rugged clothes and the fashion be damned. Not so. They may insist that the fabric holds its shape and be wrinkle-resistant, but chances are they will by-pass a durable fabric if durability is all it has to offer. A beautiful fabric, one acceptable to the current fashion picture, is more likely to get the nod. After fashion, there would be more interest in easy care. Is it washable? That question would come up long before how does it wear? The translation of fibers and fabrics into fashion is one of fashion directors' giant contributions to the apparel industry.

The Textile Fashion People

At the place where fashion begins (with the fabric), fashion research is as intense, or more so, as it is on the designer or retail level. At this place, working much further ahead than any other phase of the fashion industry (with the exception of the leather people), the fabrics that garments for men, women, and children are made of, must be available (and available in desirable textures, weights, colors, and patterns) early enough to be utilized by those who would turn them into finished products. Since designers and manufacturers are guided strongly by the fabrics available, the fabric designers are something of a power behind the throne of fashion.

The Fashion Director in the Fiber Industry

Before the garment comes the fabric, and before the fabric comes the fiber. Therefore, working far ahead of the garment and fabric makers, would be the fiber company's fashion director. If the director learns through research that a forthcoming season will be expressed with filmy, draped, or constructed silhouettes, the director will work with the mills, to develop that type of fabric with a company's fibers.

An Example

The program that the fashion director of Celanese Fibers Marketing Company, instigated to assure maximum use of Celanese fibers, is a good example of the contribution of fiber company needs from its fashion director. Her three-step plan included:

1. Working with fabric mills a year or more in advance to develop fabrics (using Celanese fibers) that will be desirable for the type of clothes that cutters will be making for a particular season.
2. Providing sketches, illustrating how the fabrics can be styled. These then become the subject of a slide and film presentation shown by appointment at the Celanese offices in a specially-designed little theater to designers looking for fabrics.
3. Revamping the slide and film presentation (after the designers have made their fabric selections and incorporated them into their designs) to show visiting retailers what specific styles they can buy that are made of the specific fabrics.

Color Coordination

The fiber fashion director must research the color story for each season. If a company sells colored yarns for fabrics, like woven plaids or space-dyed knits, (as against fibers that are made into fabric and then printed and dyed), a director must advise the company on the exact tint as well as the right color to dye the fibers. For example, if the director decides red is important but recommends an orange red instead of the preferred blue red, all is lost. Yarn dyed the wrong color or wrong shade won't sell.

The Fabric Library

Most fiber houses maintain a fabric library or fabric room, as a visual file of everything that is new and important in fashion fabrics containing their fibers. It is an available reference for the company's merchandising staff, a display of the range of fabrics available to designers and manufacturers. It is a fashion information center on fabrics for buying offices, the press, and retail fashion directors and buyers. Completely changed each season, the library is visited (by appointment) by many people in different areas of the fashion industry who take away fabric swatches as samples and information on which mill made the fabric in question and the price of that fabric.

Fashion Presentations

From this up-to-date fabric library, the fiber fashion director creates fabric presentations on men's and women's wear to be sent to designers, manufacturers, buying offices, fashion magazines, chains, and other retailers. Communication with retailers is another aspect of the job. For the retailer this director performs a most comprehensive service (see Chapter 8), supplying color and fabric forecasts, fashion forecasts, and reports on European fabric and apparel collections.

Fashion Shows in the Fiber Industry

Very often, fashion shows of a manufacturer's line or a designer's special collection will be shown at the facilities of the fiber company for members of the press, buying office representatives, and retailers. These collections, of course, would be made of fabrics using the company's own fibers.

Also, fiber companies often schedule special events to launch a new fiber or show new uses of an existing one. The fashion director might work with a name designer to create garments illustrating what can be done with the fabrics incorporating a company's fibers. These are usually one-of-a-kind collections (such as a Qiana Paris designer collection created by Du Pont) launched at a show for the press, designers, and manufacturers, and then they are sometimes made available for special showings or benefits sponsored by retailers throughout the country.

Sometimes, through such efforts, new and exciting fashion ideas are inaugurated and fashion history is made.

The Fiber Fashion Director and Imports

Through her travels in Europe, the Orient, and anywhere and everywhere in the world where new things are happening and new inspiration is available, the fiber fashion director might seek out and bring back collections for a special gala fashion show for the trade or for display to special segments of the fabric and apparel trades. Knitting mills, for example, might be invited to view some European knits, to examine their construction and technique, and to discuss how they might be interpreted in the American market, using the fiber company's products.

The Fashion Director in the Fabric Industry

Most major mills and converters have coordinators, usually called fashion directors, to research the trends and advise the technicians if working with a mill, then the colorists and print stylists on all fashion decisions relating to their fabric production. This is a tremendous responsibility because of the huge investment in setting up a warp for a new weave. A fifty-thousand yard warp costs thousands of dollars. A dye-lot of a color or a strike-off of a print also involves several hundreds of thousands of yards. Naturally, the converter must be sure that the colors dyed and the prints created are fashionably accurate and salable.

Color Coordination

The colorists and print stylists rely on the fashion director to help them translate the company's color choices into the exact shadings and the right print looks for a forthcoming season. In this connection, the fashion director works with the dyer and finisher on the colors. There is usually someone at the converter's who handles all matters with the dye plant. She works through him. Hand dips are made first with a few yards to perfect a color, and to see how it looks in a certain weave. "No, that's too light . . . too dark . . . has too much yellow in it . . . " she might say, until it comes out right. Color accuracy is established before big dye lots are put in.

The colors that have been incorporated for a coming season or a coming year are organized into a fashion presentation and color card. The fashion director usually designs the color presentation, names the colors, and writes the copy. A sample line of the fabrics and color cards is available for customers in the showrooms of the mills or converters. Also, a capsule version is designed as forecast fashion information, complete with fabric and color swatches, for buying offices, manufacturers, chains, and department stores (see chapter 8).

More Bases Covered by the Fabric Fashion Director

The fabric fashion director sees designers, manufacturers, and buying offices for a mutual exchange of ideas and to learn "what is in the air."

The director will review the lines of manufacturers, who have sampled their fabrics to see which fabrics were actually used (not all fabrics sampled are used) and to get the style numbers made with a company's fabrics. Ultimately, the fabric fashion director will use this information in various forms of publicity, to advise retailers, for example, what resources and what numbers are available in their fabrics.

The fabric fashion director works ahead of the fashion magazines (as does the fiber fashion director). When her new fabrications are ready, she shows the fabric samples, colors, and prints to magazine editors. She will also provide the editors with the names of cutters who have sampled the fabrics since an editor may be interested in certain numbers created by the manufacturers named.

In addition to providing fashion information for consumers, the press, and retailers, the fabric fashion director must also assume the role of educator within the company as well. In a manner similar to the retail fashion director, the fabric fashion director is responsible for the fashion training of the company's personnel. In her case, the sales staff is of prime importance.

Trend Shows

To make the sales representative's job easier and more efficient and to help establish the mill's fashion image to the consumer, the fashion director presents trend shows, perhaps in a multi-media form, of film, slides, sound, and music. After the sales representative and internal personnel have seen the production, it is available for showings to designers, manufacturers, buying offices, and retail executives. Also, school groups studying textiles and fashion, benefit from such a presentation, because it teaches how fashion happens.

Import Shows

Textile fashion directors research the foreign fashion markets, just as their retail counterparts, but their function goes a step forward. The textile fashion director not only writes and distributes a report on her findings on fabrics and fashions abroad, but she also buys samples of merchandise (men's, women's and children's) for import shows at home. Such a show helps American designers to think more about what is being done fashionwise around the world and it helps them translate what they see into suitable adaptations for mass production here.

General Shows

The textile industry, through its fashion departments, is a source of all types of exciting fashion presentations. Their live fashion shows might be held at a hotel for a benefit luncheon, at the offices of the company for buying office representatives or retail buyers, or on the deck of a ship for the press. Such shows are excellent for exhibiting fashions created by important designers using the fabrics of a particular mill. For these shows, the fashion office staff coordinates, accessorizes, and lines up the models in much the same way as the staff in a retail fashion office (see Chapter 13).

The In-Store Fabric Show

In a previous chapter we examined the in-store fashion show provided by an outside source, from the vantage point of the retail fashion director. Now we will take a look at it from the other side.

Most of the big pattern companies engage fashion coordinators who handle all details of fashion shows held in retail stores. Most mills and converters tie in with a pattern company and are available for fabric shows. Sometimes it is the stylist of the pattern company who puts the show together and travels with it, or, the pattern company and the fabric company will divide the cities, presenting the show separately in different areas.

Tied to the fashion fabric department, the show is offered to the store or requested by the fabric buyer. The visiting coordinator does all the advanced work on the show before making a personal appearance. The coordinator has put together a collection of sew-at-home fashions. These show pieces usually arrive ahead of the coordinator (from the last city in which the coordinator appeared) and are directed to the store's alteration department or fashion office for pressing.

When the coordinator arrives at the store, he or she must fit, accessorize, and line up the models. Sometimes the coordinator brings accessories that are special for the wardrobe shown in city after city, or may use accessories out of stock from the store, mentioning in the commentary what departments they are from. The models and backstage dressers are supplied by the store's fashion office. To represent the fabric company to the consumer, the traveling coordinator usually serves as commentator for the show. The coordinator also supplies a printed program for audience distribution. This program is especially essential for fabric and pattern shows; customers can check the pattern numbers and note their fabric choices as models appear.

A great number of fashion department stores as well as chains have completely eliminated fabric departments, but where they still exist, (and certainly for the specialty fashion fabric stores) the fabric-pattern show is very likely to be a part of each major season.

Advertising

Fiber firms and fabric companies are among the biggest national advertisers in the fashion business. In telling their fashion story, certainly a yard of cloth or a cone of polyester fiber would do absolutely nothing for the company's fashion image. But a show-stopping garment from a designer's collection made with the company's fiber or fabric product, certainly could do the job.

The fashion directors, therefore, of both fiber and fabric companies, are called on to select exciting fashions from collections or even to have something special made up for advertising purposes.

Naturally, all fashion directors, as so often indicated throughout this book, work differently. This holds true in many ways in the area of fibers and fabrics. The essence, however, is that they all must do research to arrive at the decisions on which they base their highly influential recommendations. They must interpret the fashion picture for their company and their company's customers. All of this they must do far enough in advance to keep one step ahead of the speeding treadmill of changing fashion.

NATURAL FIBERS

In addition to the fiber and fabric companies developing man-made fibers discussed thus far, there are the fashion arms of the producers of natural fibers, such as Cotton Incorporated and The Wool Bureau, Inc. The purpose of such agencies is to assist mills, manufacturers, and retailers in promoting their products. A major service that reinforces the validity of using natural fibers is the constant flow of up-to-the-minute fashion news and direction.

The Wool Bureau

The Wool Bureau/ IWS (International Wool Secretariat) are supported by the countries that produce nearly 80 percent of the wool in international trade: Australia, New Zealand, South Africa, and Uruguay. The IWS, although a nontrading organization, is strongly commercial-oriented. It has fully staffed branches in 29 countries, which include:

- For women:
  IWS Fashion Office in Paris, France
  The Wool Bureau Fashion Office in New York
- For men:
  IWS Fashion Office in London, England
  Wool Bureau Fashion Office in New York

**Wool Bureau
Fashion Services**

All phases of fashion development—from conception to consumption—are covered by the Wool Bureau to serve every area of the fashion industry. These services include:

- Forecasting the newest textures and dyes in yarns and fabrics.
- Offering fashion direction in the development of new products.
- Commissioning designers to create exclusive pacesetting fabrics, and making them available exclusively to wool licensee mills/ manufacturers.
- Reporting world-wide style trends, color news, and latest designer collections to the fashion industry.
- Offering fashion direction in new product development to spinners, weavers, knitters, and manufacturers.
- Publishing reports on Interstoff, the annual Fabrics Fair held in Frankfurt, Germany.
- Working with mills to create new fabrics and color styling and showing finished swatches in The Wool Bureau Fashion Studio in New York.
- Sending out "Wool Flash" reports on color/fabric/silhouette trends as production guidelines for manufacturers.

The Wool Bureau provides further specific services to manufacturers and retailers by:

- Displaying new Woolmark and Woolblend Mark approved fabrics to the trade in the Fashion Studio so manufacturers can plan their new lines.
- Producing catalogs for retailers featuring fashions chosen from individual coat, suit, dress, and sportswear manufacturers. Such catalogs might include over 150 manufacturers and be sent to 5,000 key retailers as a designing, buying, and selling guide.
- Creating slide presentations, showing pret-a-porter collections from Paris.
- Coordinating wool fashion displays and in-store events.

The responsibilities of the wool bureau's fashion people, as listed here, are indicative of the kind of service provided by many fiber and fabric fashion departments. Cotton Incorporated operates in much the same way.

PATTERN COMPANIES

A great deal of fashion happens in this industry. Women who sew want their fashion to be up to date, just as women who buy ready-to-wear, so the pattern companies must create patterns that are indeed the last word in fashion. These might include designs from their own design department or from name designers who create especially for the pattern catalogs.

Fashion Research

Fashion inspiration for what goes into the pattern line and catalog is not unlike every other fashion area that must look ahead and anticipate what will be happening in fashion next season, next year. Fashion trips abroad, are made perhaps four to eight times a year, to visit couture showrooms, inspect the boutiques in Italy, Spain, England, France, or wherever important fashion is happening. Such research also includes a survey of the best of American fashion, and the composite of all the findings is what influences the design department to create patterns that will go into the catalog. A hot trend can be crash programmed and inserted in the catalog in a few weeks. The fashion people of pattern companies, like the retail fashion office, carefully scrutinize fashion information as it comes into focus. To be sure that the sketches or photographs in the pattern catalogs are properly accessorized and that the hair fashions and makeup of the models are the correct ones for the clothes, members of the fashion staff shop the accessory market, gathering the last-word information on shoes, gloves, bags, belts, jewelry, and scarves, plus trends in hair and makeup fashions.

The Celebrity Pattern Designer

To add authority to its fashion offerings, most major pattern companies include collections by major name designers created especially for their catalogs. A leading designer from Paris, Milan, or New York might be included. Even designs by celebrated personalities grace the pages of the pattern catalogs. All these efforts tell the people who sew that the same up-to-the-minute fashion that exists in ready-to-wear is available in patterns.

Pattern companies reinforce their fashion authority and glamour with name personalities. Pictured is Peggy Fleming, Olympic Gold Medalist wearing a dance or exercise design she created for McCall Patterns. *(Courtesy of McCall Patterns)*

The Fabric Library

The silhouette is only part of the fashion for home sewers. The fabric is the other part. Pattern companies, therefore, maintain remarkable fabric libraries, complete with every new and important fabric, the newest colors, textures, and patterns, to inspire the designers further and to help with the illustrations for the catalog. The library is also available to editors and to retail store executives who wish to come and look.

In conjunction with the fabric library, which might include over-the-counter fabrics from 200 resources or more, the fashion staff of the pattern company supplies a comprehensive report for spring and fall with swatches of fabric trends for subscribers to their pattern catalogs.

The Pattern Fashion Show

As mentioned earlier, almost everything that happens in conjunction with the fabric in-store fashion show also takes place with the pattern show. For example, J. P. Stevens fabrics might cooperate in a show with Vogue Patterns. The pattern company's fashion representative brings individual show pieces (about 20 garments from patterns in the current catalog), and usually handles all details of the show, fittings, accessorizing, and commentary. Of special interest in stores that still provide this kind of service is the show for special sizes, such as the "14 Plus" show by McCall Patterns.

In addition to consumer shows held in department, chain, or independent stores, pattern companies sometimes unite their efforts into one large show for the trade in both Los Angeles and New York during the AHSA (American Home Sewing Association) markets.

The pattern companies' fashion consultants or representatives not only travel throughout the country with their shows, but also report back to their management on any fashion trends they spot, such as fabrics and patterns that are selling, what people are wearing, requesting, and the type of merchandise the stores are carrying.

FASHION MANUFACTURING

Another area and a completely different use of fashion personnel is in the world of manufacturing. As in retailing, it is certain that no two firms use their fashion specialists in exactly the same way. Markets are different. Juniors, coats, sportswear, dresses, and intimate apparel all have different needs, different approaches to fashion projection. But in spite of these differences, their objectives are similar enough for a fashion specialist, consultant, director, stylist, representative, sales manager, or whatever the title, to train with one manufacturer and be qualified to serve another.

Internal Fashion Training

From the manufacturer's point of view, perhaps the most important service their fashion authority can make is in fashion presentations for the sales force. Four or five times a year (spring, summer, fall, winter, holiday), or whenever a new line has been produced, the company's fashion specialist organizes shows for all personnel involved in selling fashion. In the designer and better houses, the name designer is strongly involved. In cases of the mass producers, a fashion consultant and/or stylist might be engaged to assist. The stylist might book the models, supervise the fittings, accessorize and coordinate the pieces.

Bearing in mind that the sales representatives are being presented with a whole set of new ideas, the stylist or fashion director might write descriptions of the fashions, specifying all the new terminology, new combinations, new purposes. In the commentary, the fashion presenter would point out the various possibilities of mixing pieces in a group with parts of another group. This is very important if the manufacturer has a sales force on the road. The sales representative, in turn, can instruct the retailers on whom they call.

Also, in the area of training, the manufacturer's fashion expert might be called on to produce or coordinate films and slides for staff use in the national office, or for those in the field throughout the country.

For retailing, the manufacturer's fashion authority is someone who might arrange for fashion shows or trunk showings in the store. If it is a full-fledged fashion show, that person might make a personal appearance, provide the commentary if needed, but in most cases would work directly with the store's fashion office.

Other Hats

The manufacturer's fashion expert usually wears another hat—or two. She may work in the showroom, reviewing the line piece by piece for retail buyers. He may have the assignment of working as liaison with the fashion magazines, putting editors in touch with designers, sending over fashion pieces the editor may have selected for editorial exposure, or even have something designed especially for the magazine.

She may shop the stores to check out what is being displayed and sold. He may find design ideas worth the company's attention and buy a fashion garment and take it back to the firm's designer (more likely in the mass market or knock-off house) to examine for cut and construction.

Such fashion expertise might result in help with creating mailing pieces to be sent to customers or distributed by the company's sales representatives.

ACCESSORIES AND INTIMATE APPAREL

Fashion directors make a strong contribution to the internal workings of accessory and intimate apparel firms, as well as to their customers. They research the ready-to-wear markets, keep in close touch with what colors and fabrics are developing, and maintain good contacts with the fashion offices of leading retailers and buying offices. Through these dependable channels they obtain a reliable flow of what's happening in fashion and how it affects their company's product.

Direction for the Designer

By sharing findings with the company's designers, realistic products can be created. For example, if full, swinging skirts are predicted for a coming season, the fashion director of an intimate apparel company can recommend that flared, flounced, and tiered petticoats are needed. If slim, sleek knits are going to be a strong trend, the director would certainly encourage the appropriate dress liners. If necklines or backlines will be pluging, bra lines will need to be accommodating. If fabrics in ready-to-wear are projected as sheer, underfashions will require fabric, color, and design to support the look.

Since all accessories need to support and reinforce the ready-to-wear trends, good fashion direction must be present. The belt industry becomes strong, not only because belts might be in, but because creative fashion expressions of belts make them irresistible. A trend for wide belts, jeweled belts, soft wrap belts, bold constructed belts, whatever the look, becomes important when belts contribute to the total fashion picture.

In the hosiery industry, the fashion director not only works with the ready-to-wear industry but the shoe people as well. For a season of delicate pastels in dress fabrics and pale leathers in shoes, the leg should complement the picture with sheer, delicate shades of hosiery. English tweeds might be important fashion for a fall/winter season, but unless the hosiery industry is informed, there would be a lack of exciting textured or opaque leg fashions.

In addition to providing their companies with good fashion direction, the fashion directors of intimate apparel or hosiery or shoe houses might compile a catalog or booklet of how they see the season's trends relating to their merchandise. These are often very handsomely done for use by the retailer, who, in turn, can share the information with the consumer.

Another way the accessory or intimate apparel fashion director gets involved with the rest of the fashion industry is when new collections are shown during New York market openings. For example, all hosiery for an Anne Klein or Carol Horn collection might be specially dyed to match the garments. All such plans are arranged and executed through the hosiery firm's fashion director.

When new products are being developed and consumer education and exposure are vital, the fashion director of an intimate apparel firm might take to the road and visit retailers coast to coast, supplying a number of services for those who stock their merchandise.

For example, when Formfit Rogers established their "Cut Above" concept (daywear, sleepwear, and loungewear for the large-size woman), their fashion director, together with a New York model, toured stores across the country to carry their message. The fashion director conducted training seminars for the stores' fashion sellers, advised store people on display possibilities, participated in fashion shows, appeared on local television, and was interviewed by the local press.

COSMETICS AND FRAGRANCE INDUSTRY

Few of the titles of the fashion people found in other areas are evident in the cosmetics and fragrance industry. Titles like creative director or publicity director identify the fashion executives here. Fashion direction is administered in one or both of these offices. The creative director researches the fashion world to find guidance for fashion decisions in cosmetics. The season's new colors and trends will need to show up in "face fashions." Face designers, therefore, will create new trends in cosmetics as readily as fashion designers do in the couture and ready-

How a major cosmetic fashion ad is created: shown here is a campaign to support Estee Lauder's Venetian Court Colors. The wardrobe stylist, working from instructions by the senior vice president of Creative Marketing (whom she is using as a model) has gathered clothes from the best designers. She also brings in enough accessories to stock a boutique; it is important to review lots of choices before the final ones are made. *(Courtesy of Estee Lauder Public Relations Dept.)*

On the set, a hairdresser arranges Karen's hair for the first photograph. *(Courtesy of Estee Lauder Public Relations Dept.)*

to-wear field. Not unlike the accessory market, cosmetics must be compatible with what's happening in the fashion world as a whole. (See Chapter 14.)

Cosmetic Fashion Forecasts

The cosmetic buyer, the merchandise manager, and the store's fashion director are kept well informed about what the cosmetic world is planning for a coming season through releases issued by the publicity director (see Chapter 8). These might include interpretations of the apparel market, especially as it relates to makeup trends. Fashion authority is very important in cosmetics. The endorsement of a famous beauty, fashion designer, or celebrated star provides the product with the impact it needs to be recognized as a bearer of miracle gifts of beauty and fashion excellence. After all, it is dreams that are being sold, requiring the stuff that dreams are made of.

Fragrance and Fashion

Fragrance is always in fashion. What makes it appeal to the consumer, however, is the level of her fashion and emotional needs. Inspired copy in advertising, plus stirring fashion environment in ads, sell fragrance. Image sells fragrance. To accomplish all this and relate it to the fashion world, fragrance companies often name, package, and promote their products with an ambience that is in keeping with the fashion image of their designer, or the current fashion/lifestyle trend. Fragrance companies often tie in with fashion shows in stores where the fashion image is compatible with their own. Gifts of fragrance to the audience in exchange for a few words from the commentator or credit on the program help keep the name and the product before the fashion consumer.

Beauty Advertising

The creative director or publicity director for cosmetics and fragrances are also involved with selecting or approving costumes for models in their image ads. Sensational forward fashion is as important as the face, therefore, good fashion direction is paramount.

LINENS AND DOMESTICS INDUSTRY

From the moment white sheets and white towels fell from favor and were gloriously upstaged by color and then by a windfall of never-before-heard-of patterns for bed and bath, the linen and domestic industry became a fashion market.

At the outset of this major change, a fashion director came into being in some cases as an offshoot of the office of the publicity director. White sheets needed no fashion direction nor did unimaginative blankets, bedspreads, and rugs, but when fashion colors, stripes, florals, and unlimited patterns and trimmings were employed to bring interior-design type of high fashion into this area, fashion direction was definitely in order for the home.

The Early Fashion Director for Linens and Domestics

In almost all businesses where a fashion director is required, the fashion information for personnel, as well as for the customer, is a top priority assignment of the fashion office.

The early linens and domestics fashion director worked with the company's designers, sharing with them all he or she had learned about relative fashion trends. The director made fashion presentations at their company's sales meetings and interpreted the new collections in current fashion terms. On the retail level, the director would travel to the major accounts and present the new fashion story to store management and the selling staff. Salespeople were more likely to push a product they understood, one they were excited about, and one with whose representatives they had a warm rapport (this is still true). The personal touch of an effective fashion director did wonders to convey the new fashion stories at the store level.

But as fashion became synonymous with linens and domestics, there was less need to travel to the stores, where their own fashion directors and coordinators were providing the necessary fashion direction. Of greater importance were the internal fashion decisions—what the company should be offering a season or two or more down the road. That is, fashion concepts that would be compatible with what was happening in fashion elsewhere. For example, if Oriental feelings were prevalent in the news or in art or in apparel, Oriental themes would undoubtedly be in order for the home, including bed and bath.

Director of Design

Geoffrey Beene (*Courtesy of Fieldcrest*)

The director of design is very likely to be the title of the fashion person influencing what fashion will be translated onto sheets, pillows, bed spreads, and towels.

By market research, by being totally aware of social change, lifestyles, economic trends, as well as traveling extensively, subscribing to fashion forecasting services, and being in touch with the fiber and fabric industries, the director of design can bring back "pieces of reference" as inspiration for the company's team of designers. Also, when a firm licenses a name designer, such as a Mary McFadden, Pierre Cardin, Oscar de la Renta, or Geoffrey Beene, considerable direction is available for pattern design excellence. Whether a piece of reference comes from a work of art, a fabric, wallpaper, or a picture in a magazine, it must inspire an idea that has integrity.

But, in the final analysis, how does the director of design back up the recommendations for what fashion looks should be going forward? According to the vice president, director of design for Fieldcrest, "In addition to thorough research of potential trends, a lot has to do with what you are feeling. Take all marketing research and if it doesn't have to do with feelings and emotions (the intimate rooms of homes such as bedrooms and baths have emotional ties), it won't work. The important thing is to channel those feelings into product."

Perhaps a good example of how feelings and research work together was the season when there were very strong indications that people were leaning toward romantic nostalgia. They were buying books that featured romantic heroines and were looking for lifestyles and special interests that made their world more tranquil, gentle, pleasant. It was time, it appeared, for ruffles, ribbons, and lace. Fieldcrest offered lace for bedroom decor. Ready-to-wear supported the romantic look with total poetic, feminine expressions for several seasons. The "feeling" was that women not only wanted and needed a respite from strict

Fashion translates into linen and domestic markets through famous designers of apparel. Geofrrey Beene's Trousseau Flower design for Fieldcrest. *(Courtesy of Fieldcrest)*

business attire in their clothes, but that they cherished the escape of being surrounded by such delicate charm in their bedrooms.

This case is a definite testimonial to how fashion or design directors, in all areas of the fashion world, must be strong on awareness, as well as skilled in the technicalities of their fields.

ADVERTISING AGENCIES

Although most advertising agencies no longer have fashion departments, per se, they are constantly in need of fashion direction, especially if they handle fashion, cosmetics, or fragrance accounts.

Fashion-oriented staff members of such advertising agencies usually wear other hats. For example, the fashion consultant for the creative team of J. Walter Thompson might also be an account executive. For product development, launching a new fashion firm, or creating a new image, much of the direction would come from the office of the creative director. On the other hand, if a special fashion event is to be produced and executed by the agency, such as a press fashion show for a foreign fashion industry interested in attracting American buyers

(Japan, Israel, Brazil, Germany, etc.), it is very likely that an outside consultant and/or stylist will be engaged to handle the project.

The Freelance Stylist

If you would ask a fashion stylist how he or she got into the business, the answer very likely would be "by default." The stylist might have majored in fashion merchandising in college, been an English major, been a fashion model, worked in a retail fashion office, for a fashion manufacturer, for a fashion magazine, advertising agency, pattern company, or could be a student fresh out of design or art school. Whatever the background, this person soon learned that a good stylist had to have a great deal of fashion savvy, be highly perceptive of the client's needs, and, most important, be absolutely accurate; a stylist must get an assignment right the first time because there seldom is a second chance. It's not the easiest fashion job around, as any stylist will testify, but it's very rewarding insofar as it is not confining and every day is different.

Also, a multitalented stylist can get a variety of assignments not unlike the retail fashion director. A stylist might serve as a spokesperson for a product, traveling the country, appearing on television, producing fashion shows, or even designing or hosting press parties (perhaps as an assistant to a publicist).

While we may refer to the stylist on these pages as an agency stylist or studio stylist (primarily to identify the assignment they have at the time) it is very likely that this stylist is one and the same person. That is, freelance stylists work for advertising agencies, photographers, magazines, publicists, whoever has need for this particular kind of fashion service. Rarely do any of the these areas employ full-time stylists, although it is possible that a stylist will be repeated for a specific client and continue in an association with an agency or photographer because of a satisfactory and smooth relationship.

What the Agency Stylist Does

Whether the product of an agency's client is advertised primarily through print (magazines, newspapers, billboards) or through television, fashion coordination is needed. The actors, the settings, the mood, theme, graphics—everything must be fashionably in tune with the product's message and purpose.

Having learned a client's needs and special likes and dislikes, most agencies feel it is more efficient to assign the same stylist to the same client for all fashion work done for that account. For a small agency, or one that has few fashion accounts, one stylist might be used to handle all fashion details. In any case, a stylist or fashion consultant working with an advertising agency, selects, fits, coordinates, and supervises the use of fashion by actors or models in print ads or television commercials. However, in making decisions about what clothes to select, several points are automatically taken into consideration.

1. What is the client's message?
   Elegance or economy?
   Glamour or confort?
   Luxury or necessity?
2. Who is the client's customer?
   Young, mature or ageless?
   Affluent or mass market?
3. Will the ad be in black and white or color?
4. What is the location for the shooting?
5. What are the details of the set, motif, patterns, colors?
6. Is the ad a one-time shot or part of a series in a campaign with an established theme?
7. What is the budget?

The answers to these and other questions are obtained by the stylist and/or fashion consultant through consultation with other staff members working on the account.

Staff Consultation

The account executive relates the client's message to the agency. He or she spells out exactly what should be told through print or television, or both. The budget is established. The creative staff of the agency takes it from there. The writer, art director, and producer (the art director for print, the producer for television) create all aspects of exactly what will happen on the printed page or the television screen.

The Writer

The fashion consultant or stylist talk over specifics with the writer and art director to learn how the ad will be "dressed." The writer may say, "the message is for real people doing real things. Keep all sophistication out of it." Or, the case may be to "tempt with glamour." Or, the message might have a lighthearted, young approach, "the look must be the last word in young fashion." The fashion consultant knowing the facts, knows what to select.

The Art Director

Perhaps next will come a separate conference with the art director or set designer. How is this individual expressing the writer's language into the physical atmosphere? Will it be an outdoor location? Will it be a specially designed set? Will it be shot in someone's fascinating apartment?

What happens in the background is highly pertinent to what clothes the actors or models will wear. If the wall is going to be red, a red costume would be lost. If the background is extremely "busy" in pattern or decor, a strong pattern in the fabric of the costume might be deadly. Coordination, all the way, gets it all together.

The Producer

Where TV commercials are involved, the producer pulls the whole production together. How will the message be interpreted? Lots of movement? Will the story come across quiet and soothing? Will it be jump-up-and-cheer stuff? A storyboard is drawn up as a guide, from which the producer will instruct which way to go with the fashions. Covering the ground thoroughly at the outset will help avoid gross errors in costume choices.

The Casting Director

A casting director will be responsible for bringing in the appropriate models or auditioning actors for the television commercial. Based on the type, mood, character, personality of the message, the casting director brings in cast members to be approved by the producer and/or client. If they relate accurately to the texture of the client's message, the stylist gets the go-ahead to start work on wardrobe.

When casting a print ad, the fashion consultant may book the models, or sometimes the art director or the photographer books the models. When the model is highly identifying with the product's image, the choice may be reviewed by the client on a "go-see" (see Glossary of Fashion Industry Terms), photograph, or "name" basis. The mere mention of the name of a well-known model may be sufficient.

When the personalities or models have been booked for a TV commercial, the fashion people find it more efficient to check out sizes, heights, measurements, and so on, directly with the talent, instead of through the casting director. For print ads the procedure may differ. When models have been booked by the photographer, for example, the studio would send to the agency composite photographs (comps), which all professional models have, with their sizes for dress, shoes, pants, and so on, plus height, figure measurements, and other necessary information. With all these details established, the fashion consultant or stylist is ready to shop.

Shopping Time

If the agency is in New York or California, it is very likely the agency stylist will shop the wholesale apparel market as well as the manufacturers of fashion accessories. Sometimes sources will loan fashions in exchange for a credit (mention), and sometimes they charge for lending. It is also very likely that the stylist will shop The Broadway, I. Magnin, or Bullock's of California, or Bloomingdale's, Macy's, Bonwits, Bergdorf's, B. Altman, or Saks, New York, and pick something right out of stock. And, maybe, something right out of stock from the Salvation Army.

The fashion requirement might be such, however, that something more exclusive is in order. In such a case, the stylist might contact a name designer, such as Oscar de la Renta, to have something special made. Another occasion might prompt the stylist to approach a theatrical costume designer to create something original. Or, the stylist might make a trip to a costume house to rent the clothes. This would be especially true when period fashions are in order.

There are still other sources for costume selection. It is very possible that the agency might maintain a wardrobe, accumulated from other ads or commercials, still current and suitable for reuse as is, or adaptable to a new look with the help of a seamstress. A wardrobe of shoes, for example, can be reused while still in fashion by dyeing or covering with fabric to relate to the costume.

Occasionally, the agency is responsible for having fashions made from scratch. For example, all pattern companies have garments made up especially for ads from their patterns.

When budgets are a contention, the actors are sometimes asked to wear something of their own, especially when the roles they will play are to depict a realistic flavor of real people in everyday situations.

If something out of the ordinary is needed and is difficult to find (and it is amazing with all the resources available that "that certain something" can be difficult to find) the stylist might take the initiative to rig something with loving hands at home. One might even ask an assistant in the office who is extremely talented in knitting, for example, to go to work on something that provides that certain look, maybe in the colors or motif of the client's packaging which is not for sale anywhere.

In other words, the fashion people use every ounce of ingenuity at their disposal to accumulate the best possible wardrobe for the required theme of the ad, even if they have to cut up some drapes or a bedspread (makes a great evening coat) to do it.

Fitting Time

As soon as the wardrobes are accumulated, fitting times are set up for the models or actors. A national print ad or national television com-

When working on fashion ads, the agency of Peter Rogers Associaties uses freelance stylists. From one of his famous advertising campaigns, Carol Burnett for Blackglama. "Don't focus on the mink," said Jan Trahey, who conceived the campaign, "but what's in it." *(Courtesy of Peter Rogers Associates. Photograph by Bill King)*

mercial consumes a great deal of the client's advertising budget, so all fashion details are carefully executed.

For a display print ad, the stylist handles all aspects of the fittings, maybe calling the art director in if there are any serious questions. To consult on a TV fitting, it is possible that the producer or art director will be present. Here is the place to take a final check and reacquaint everyone with the possibilities before the actual shooting. Since there are deadlines to meet and everyone is more or less working against time to meet shooting schedules, fittings should be thoroughly prepared. If any changes or adjustments are to be made, the fitting session is the end of the line.

It should be noted, however, that models' clothes are sometimes deliberately fitted too loosely for easier movement as instructed by the photographer, art director, or producer. The clothes are then pinned to fit properly, according to the required action or pose, right on set.

As to accessories, the agency stylist often borrows from manufacturers, and, therefore, they are not available much before the day of shooting. The agency stylist usually brings several possible choices for each costume change. The stylist may review the selection with the photographer and art director, giving them a choice, or may try a variety of ideas with each outfit and personally decide on the best way to go.

Hair and Makeup

The head must fit the body. A good stylist, well versed on the newest trends, will carefully instruct the models on the required hair fashion for the specific shooting, as well as type of makeup. If the fashion is bizarre or extremely high fashion, a hair fashion expert or makeup artist may be called into design something special.

What Fashion Can Do

How often we have picked up a magazine and seen a beautiful model in an ad, draped on a magnificent couch, dressed in an opulent gown, so uniquely elegant and so ultrafeminine that it completely dazzled the imagination with a pampered life of luxury. The ad was not selling couches or gowns, but perfume. The stirring association of the beautiful woman with the product did the job—a fragrance that could make you feel like this. That is, in part, what good fashion selection can contribute to the ad and to the client's product.

In a television commercial, another wonderful thing can happen with fashion. Movement of flowing chiffon, swirling wool or crepe, or crisp lines of linen can help underscore the mood of an automobile, a diet food, a laundry product, or the fabric itself. Whatever the case, the presence of effective fashion unmistakably enhances the story.

The Unforgettable Focus

To help identify an ad, or create a memorable focal point, a single accessory or fashion item might be called into play. For the close-up of a hair-color or shampoo ad, a devastating earring. A hand lotion or nail enamel ad might be glorified with a totally unique ring (maybe borrowed from Tiffany's). A bath product may be dramatized with a bath towel bearing the same special design and colors of the packaging. If it caught on, the makers of the bath product could tie in with a towel manufacturer to market the item in a new collection. Stranger things have happened, and all through the inspiration of an effective fashion presentation.

Shooting Time

All is in readiness. Whether the shooting is on location (anywhere in the world), in the photographer's studio, or in the television studio, along with the agency production crew comes the stylist engaged by the agency. If the commercial or ad is a simple one, with only one or two people involved and only one change, the agency stylist may not be required to remain on the set for the shooting. The stylist may just see that the wardrobe is pressed and delivered to the shooting site and be sure that it is returned when the job is finished. However, for more complicated productions—sometimes there are twenty-five to thirty changes of wardrobe—the stylist's presence and supervision are a must.

The stylist makes sure every ensemble and every change is checked out as planned. It is a stylist's responsibility to see that everything is laced up correctly, fitted properly, draped effectively, according to plan. The preferred tilt of a hat, drape of a scarf, closing of a jacket, handling of an accessory, all these are in the stylist's province. The agency's stylist works closely with the photographer and photographer's stylist, if there is one, to help transmit lighting, movement, and mood in regards to fashion.

PHOTOGRAPHERS' STYLISTS

While some photographers' stylists move along to work with the advertising agency, some stylists from the agencies transfer to the photographer as studio stylists. The studio stylist (an absolute must for the commercial photographer) is finding more opportunities in this area than ever before. Even when an advertising agency stylist is on hand for the shooting, the photographer's stylist also needs to be present. Small agencies, having only an occasional need for a stylist, depend entirely on the photographer and the photographer's stylist to interpret the client's message.

Requirements of the Studio Stylist

Most photographers will testify that taste is a prime requirement— good taste and an alert awareness of what is happening in fashion. Next, the photographer must have a stylist who can accurately interpret directions. Naturally, a rapport with any employer is important, but in the case of the photographer with a stylist, it is the incomparable combination that produces the best results.

The studio stylist keeps close tabs on fashion trends by checking the wholesale market, the stores, and the fashion magazines. The stylist must anticipate what is coming in strong, what is going out. As stated earlier, ads become quickly outdated if the fashion image is not plucked from advanced trends.

Responsibilities of the Studio Stylist

Like the agency stylist, the studio stylist sometimes buys fashions for models or actors and sometimes borrows them. Personal contacts are helpful. Also, there are places that specialize in renting clothes and props of various types to photographers' studios. Knowing who these people are and what they have saves the stylist a great deal of time and shoe leather.

The studio stylist is not only responsible for the production's wardrobe but the props as well. The stylist works with the photographer and client on what kind of setting and props will be used before going out to look for them. Very often, all the details that contribute to a setting, the props, furnishings, accessories, and sometimes even the set, are chased down and assembled under the supervision of the stylist.

At the shooting session, the watchful eye and assistance of the stylist is imperative. He or she helps interpret, organize, and arrange the props and the fashions selected for a job. It is also the stylist's responsibility, with the aid of messengers, to be sure that everything borrowed is returned when the job is finished.

When an agency stylist has done the fashion coordinating, that person has all the outfits and accessories sent over to the set, where the photographer's stylist takes over. The agency stylist may be on hand, as noted earlier, but the photographer's stylist knows how to slip onto the set to make adjustments exactly when it should be done and when it will not interrupt the photographer.

The stylists with some photography studios also book models. They keep in touch with the agencies, reviewing their needs and supplying them with composites for model selection or for the agency's information regarding types, fittings, and so on.

Smaller photographers' studios prefer freelance stylists because their shooting schedules do not always require the help of such fashion guidance. Or, the load of a photographer with one or two stylists already on staff becomes so heavy that it is necessary to call in an additional freelance stylist to help, perhaps one to collect props and wardrobe and one to work on shootings. Most stylists work completely on a freelance basis, establishing contacts with photographers and serving them as their work load permits.

**OTHER
IMPORTANT
AREAS FOR
COORDINATORS**

Grouping the following possibilities together under this heading does not mean that they are less important than those areas highlighted separately in this chapter. In fact, some of the following are bigger and present even greater opportunities for the coordinator. However, to cover in detail the functions of the buying offices, for example, would be unnecessary repetition because they have already been covered earlier in the text (see Chapters 7 and 8). Also, the consultant firms, their service and the duties of their coordinators, were included earlier. The buying offices and consultant firms, both very close to the fashion scene and both keeping their members or subscribers informed on what is happening and what it means to their store specifically, have places for retail-trained fashion people.

The Shoe Industry

The fashion director or director of design of a shoe company works far ahead with the tanners to make leather selections for coming seasons. The colors and textures selected are to be expressed in designs of footwear suitable for the forthcoming fashion apparel season. The fashion director of a shoe company researches those areas that influence fashion decisions, the apparel market (usually abroad, because they work far ahead of the domestic market), the fabric market, and the magazines.

The classics or staples come up with a fresh look, and the very new or high-fashion models are carefully designed to win friends as quickly as possible. It is expected that some looks will be slow getting off the ground, but a trend that is expected to be around for a while requires patience. The fashion director helps relate the fashion story in this area in much the same way as it is done in other fashion areas, by training the selling staff of the company.

Publicists

The publicist is concerned with selling the client and/or the client's products through good publicity. With fashion accounts, this means dealing with the fashion press. It follows, therefore, that the publicist handling fashion accounts must be totally conversant with current and incoming fashion trends.

The publicist's fashion research is not too unlike that of the retail fashion director. A publicist might work with fabric editors of fashion magazines, be a member of Fashion Group (get direction from their fashion shows and presentations), read *Women's Wear Daily* and other trade publications, be a people-watcher, evaluate the news, subscribe to a color service, or follow any current avenue that is influencing fashion.

In order to get editorial space from discriminating fashion editors, the publicist must provide press pictures that are beautifully done. Since getting as much good press space as possible for fashion clients is a prime responsiblity of the publicist, this area is very important. For example, publicist Charlotte Lipson may hire a stylist to do the leg work (make the contacts in the fashion market) to obtain the requested clothes and accessories, but she would personally supervise the shoot. Coming from a fashion magazine background, and working very closely with fashion and beauty editors of all the leading fashion books, Ms. Lipson would know not only what would make her client's image most effective, but what each fashion or beauty editor would find acceptable. In other words, fashion know-how is paramount to the publicist.

The Fashion Magazines

Not all fashion magazines have fashion directors. The fashion arbiter for fashion and service magazines is usually called fashion editor. However, some magazines have a fashion director (i.e., *Gentleman's Quarterly, Esquire, Ladies' Home Journal, Town & Country, Seventeen*) who may be over a fashion editor and staff. The editorial pages are created by the fashion editors and the merchandise is selected, coordinated, and photographed under their watchful eye and direction. In researching the fashion market, one editor may cover the coat and suit market, one the dress market, another the accessory market, and so on down the line. Each brings back individual findings, and they are utilized as they relate to the concept of the magazine. The merchandising department of the magazine develops all the promotions and fashion tie-ins with retailers, working closely with the store's fashion director and merchandisers (see Chapter 8). Because of their close association with retailers, many of the national fashion magazines have on their payrolls (especially in the merchandising division) people whose background includes fashion experience in retailing.

THE SIMILARITIES OF FASHION COORDINATION JOBS

Touching on a diversified list of industries where careers in fashion coordination are available, one very prevalent fact shows up: the requirements and responsibilities are similar enough to permit a crossing of boundaries from one area to another. In other words, training in one fashion job is good preparation for another, even though the industry and the product may be different. Advertising agencies, photographic studios, and public relations companies can easily interchange fashion personnel, and any of these can move back and forth from fabric or fiber companies or magazines. A staff member of *Women's Wear Daily* or of a pattern company might invade the world of the advertising agency; a member of a department store fashion office might migrate into the area of freelance stylist, become a publicist or be a magazine fashion editor. Even students fresh out of college or graduates from professional schools specializing in fashion education are likely to find good experience with on-the-job training in any of the areas mentioned in this chapter because of their fashion preparation.

For every area mentioned in this chapter (those fashion careers outside of retailing but closely related) retailing is the great training ground. Consider the similarities:

1. All are involved in researching the fashion market for future trends.
2. Most are responsible for fashion presentations and/or training of personnel.
3. Most are involved in fashion shows, promotions, and public relations activities related to the consumer.
4. All are concerned with ultimately selling a product.

These points alone more than substantiate the relationship of the entire profession of fashion directors, embracing all areas of the fashion business.

MISCELLANEOUS CONTRIBUTIONS FROM THE FASHION INDUSTRY

The public relations or promotional efforts of fashion departments in any or all the fields included in this chapter have made unique and valuable contributions to the fashion industry and to the nation as a whole. Through the ingenuity of a fashion department with vision, seeing a need and filling it, careers for young beginners have been launched, consumers have been aided, and retailers have been benefited. Some efforts contributed to public morale and well-being. Some benefited the underprivileged. Scholarships, contests, competitions, sponsored by all phases of the fashion industry to discover and encourage new talent, have started many a promising career on its way. The worthy efforts are legion, and new ones are being instituted every day. The following example is highly indicative of the meritorious work being done.

Until 1968, the United States parade uniforms at the Olympic games were hit-and-miss selections, sometimes just some left-over fashions off the pipes of the manufacturer's back room. It took some time before it was generally noticed that the U.S. Olympic teams were the worst dressed among the nations represented. Something had to be done. The executive director and members of the Olympic Committee came to Burlington Mills for help. From this meeting came the idea to have the young design for the young. Several hundred entries were submitted by colleges and professional schools participating in the United States Olympic Apparel Committee's national competition. At last, for the 1968 winter and summer games, United States Olympic athletes paraded in fashions that demonstrated American apparel know-how and presented the team as a shining example of well-dressed young Americans. The 1972 Olympic parade uniforms were executed under the direction of Sears Roebuck and Company. The fashion director of Sears had several groups of fashion ideas specially designed and submitted to the United States Olympic Apparel Committee for final selections.

Uniforms for national and international sports events come as a contribution from the American fashion industry. Pictured, uniforms supplied by Levi Strauss & Co., outfitter of the U.S. Teams to the 1983 Pan Am and 1984 Olympic Games. *(Courtesy of Levi Strauss & Co.)*

A four-year association between Levi Strauss & Co. and the U.S. Olympic Committee started the summer of 1981 with the National Sports Festival III through the 1984 Olympic Winter Games (Sarajevo, Yugoslavia) and the Summer Games (Los Angeles, California). In addition to parade, award, and travel apparel for all participating American athletes, an estimated 14,000 event workers and officials (to give America a coordinated fashion look)—from ticket takers and parking lot attendants to judges and officials—all were outfitted by Levi Strauss at the Los Angeles Olympic Games. Levi Strauss also committed to a cash payment toward the cost of staging the 1984 Olympic Games.

Actually, the Levi Strauss association with the Olympics began with the dressing of America's athletes for the Pan Am Games in San Juan, Puerto Rico, in 1979. The company then outfitted the 1980 U.S. Olympic Winter Games team at Lake Placid, New York. The American team did not go to Moscow for the 1980 Summer Games.

The fashion influence, resulting from those games, was most prominent at the Lake Placid Winter Games. The western trend was escalated when, at the opening ceremonies, the American athletes wore white cowboy hats, as was the interest in fashion activewear when the American hockey players were awarded their gold medals dressed in royal blue Levi's warm-up suits.

Legions of Benefits

It is well known that the fashion industry—designers, manufacturers, fashion retailers—have contributed enormously with money, talent, and time to the raising of millions of dollars annually to support benefits of all kinds. Health agencies, churches, schools, benevolent institutions, museums, symphony orchestras, ballet, opera, and theatres in cities coast to coast have looked to the industry or the local department store to help them raise money. The fashion show benefit, one of the major forms of entertainment and fund-raising throughout the world, can be found on the calendars of cities, small or large, every year.

Fashion's purpose is to make life more pleasant. Certainly it would follow that the fashion industry in all areas would feel a responsibility and, by its very nature, be sensitive to the needs for beautification.

AFTERVIEW

With all the choices available in the field of fashion coordination, finding the right place presents an interesting challenge. A good starting point would be to relate to the area or kind of product that interests you most. The shoe industry? Ready-to-wear fashion houses? The advertising agency or public relations world? The photographer's studio? The fiber or fabric business? The retail field?

Of course, a great deal depends on where you live, what is available, and where you are willing to go. New York or Chicago may be a good place for a top advertising agency, but Boston or St. Louis may be better for the shoe industry. New York or California may be the wisest choices for good fashion houses, but department stores all over the country provide the kind of training ground that will equip the beginner with the necessary experience.

The records are filled with case histories of fashion coordinators who have left retailing to go to fashion magazines, to fiber companies, to fashion consultant firms, or to advertising agencies, and then back to the retail business for high level responsibilities. As indicated earlier, whether it is used as a springboard to other fashion associations or as a permanent career, retailing has much to offer.

CHAPTER RE-EVALUATION

Questions

1. Why is color consistency important throughout the fashion industry? What is the fashion director's role in developing color trends?
2. What is the difference between fibers and fabrics?
3. What are natural fibers? Through what type of organization is their fashion message related?
4. How does a pattern company keep its pattern catalogs currently fashion-right?
5. What purpose does a fabric library serve?
6. How does a pattern fashion show differ from a traditional fashion show?
7. What are three things a fashion specialist of a manufacturing firm teaches the sales staff about a new fashion line?
8. What kind of business gets its fashion direction from the director of design? Which from a creative director?
9. How does a stylist find clothes needed for a fashion shoot?
10. Why is it important for the U. S. Olympic Team to be well dressed?

Workshop

Assume you are a stylist who has been assigned by an advertising agency to dress a glamorous model for a fragrance magazine ad. The fragrance is called Flame. The copy accompanying the picture will read: "Flame . . . to fire his imagination—to add a glow to your image." Sketch or describe the ad as you see it. Show in outline form what guidelines you use to learn all about the ad and what leads you to your final choice of clothes, hairstyle, and so on.

Dressed with polished informality for her journey into the world of fashion.
(Courtesy of The Wool Bureau, Inc.)

16

ONE MORE
THING . . .

The moment has come. It is time to place all the facts face up, end to end, for a final review. It is time to ask for a realistic total of the rewards and the demands, the advantages and disadvantages, the blessings and privations of a career in the field of fashion.

On the basis of aptitude and interest, one could conceivably give the area of fashion coordination a try, take a flyer, and see what develops, but no one can or should give the full measure of devotion required by the fashion business without having a pretty good idea of how well or to what degree it pays off. Economy is important, of course, but the kind of money one can make in this field is only one of the many reasons for pursuing such a career. Money or no money, if the pros do not outweigh the cons, the joys of satisfaction might be sadly lacking.

THE ADVANTAGES

Every career has its share of advantages, but the character of those found in the fashion business makes a very attractive list.

Action

There is lots of it. Every scratch on the calendar represents a whirl of activity; up and down escalators to see fashion departments, display, advertising, publicity, special events; to talk with store executives, merchandisers, buyers, training directors, store managers, and sales associates; in and out of meetings, dressing rooms, ballrooms; in and out of airports, hotel rooms, conference rooms, fabric rooms, showrooms; in and out of cars to visit branches that might be strung from one end of the state to the other, plus surrounding areas.

Action, always running in high gear in the fashion business, can be classified as an advantage only by those who thrive on such an atmosphere. If one is fortified with boundless energy, the constant flow of action will be met head on and, in most cases, thoroughly enjoyed. Without a good flow of top-level energy, the surge of activity could be too overwhelming.

The versatility of the action, however, is in itself a stimulant. Heavy action of one kind might be harder to handle, but a busy schedule, bursting at the seams with all kinds of different activity, different assignments, different challenges, and different people, provides renewed stimuli. This is the kind of action that is considered by those involved in fashion coordination as a true advantage.

Personality Asset: ENERGY

Creativity

Creative people need to create. If one does not possess enough excellence to pursue a career in the world of visual or living arts, but is possessed, all the same, with the temperament of a creative person, a home can be found in fashion coordination. Here is a chance to create with ideas, with showmanship, and with innovations for the merchandising of fashion.

Paralleling the physical action of the job is the mental action. With all the guidelines provided in this book, there is still latitude for bringing to the job what the individual, and only the individual, can provide. Because the product with which we work, fashion, is never static and always changing, so must be the relative occupations dealing with it, especially fashion coordination. The changes are felt more readily in this area than perhaps others. They do, however, make possible the elastic creative opportunities.

To make things happen, to properly use those creative instincts, the person most likely to succeed in fashion coordination creates unselfishly, not only to please oneself, but especially to please the customer and the store. That is a big order. It can only be filled by a big person.

Also, creativity in this field cannot be hemmed in by tradition. There will be those who will say "We have never done it this way before." It will take strength to reply, "it is time that we did." Live dangerously now and then.

Personality Asset: COURAGE

People

People can be the biggest advantage or the biggest disadvantage; it all depends on viewpoint. In an accounting firm, for example, many of the people would be of a typical nature, similar in temperament, similar in educational preparation. This is not so in fashion. Personalities are extremely different—running the gamut from the very gentle to the very tough, from the quiet and easy-going to the very vocal and up-tight types. Prima donnas in fashion can easily tie with those found among opera stars or the acting profession. Giants of strength, pillars of accomplishment, stand tall and firm at the heads of fashion institutions, and those on top, plus those on the way up, come from all walks of life, all kinds of backgrounds, bringing to the industry the wealth of their combined experiences.

Whether the person at the top inherited the throne or slaved for it, the style of dedication and contributions to the industry have often been pace setters of imitation by those following. Their message has been a very clear one. Halfway measures in fashion don't work—not for the president, not for the fashion director.

Surrounded by people, therefore, who demand such a great deal of themselves, it can well be expected that they will demand a great deal of everyone else as well. If kept in proportion, such demands can urge the best performance to come forth, and can carry one to heights that otherwise might not have been attained. Whatever brings out the best in us is undeniably an advantage.

The melting pot of personalities found in the fashion industry contributes largely to its special charm. The composite of influences, and the blending of ambitions and goals, ignite a bombardment of happenings that make the industry an explosive powder keg most of the time. Even though the fireworks are not going off all the time, one is aware of their presence, especially in the area of retailing. If every day is not the Fourth of July, some inventive merchant will find a way to make it so. The feeling arises that in the world of fashion, even though some days could be very ordinary, no one in the fashion community would want it to stay that way for very long.

The citizens of the fashion community are colorful, hard working, aggressive, unique, spoiled, ambitious, temperamental, hungry. Such qualifications might be death in other professions, but in fashion they are splendid. They make things happen—remarkable things. To work with such people can be totally enchanting or completely unnerving. The effect is entirely dependent on one's viewpoint, love them for what they are, or at least accept them for what they are. It must be remembered that they, too, will need to love you for what you are or just accept you for the same reason. An interplay of respect and sympathy for others' efforts (very important) will help make a fashion director the people-person the job demands.

Personality Asset: PATIENCE

Travel

This can be, if one is endowed with a sense of adventure, one of the best advantages on the list. Fashion directors travel considerably. Their travels not only take them to the market places, from New York to California, but to many stops in between. They are often on a plane to new cities to check out other fashion stores, to examine branches of the company if it is a chain operation or conglomerate, or to attend special meetings in cities near and far.

In addition to the above, a director might be taking off on a junket as a guest of a fiber company to examine their mill operation. Not the least of all this packing and unpacking are the fashion trips to Europe, to the Orient, to the Middle East, to all the fashion capitals of the world, those known and some trying to be known.

The beginner in the fashion office might eagerly await word as to when he or she might get in on some of this travel-is-broadening education. It is entirely possible that a fashion director will take an assistant along on some market trips, area or divisional coordinators, or anyone else on the staff if the trip is relative to their function. These instances usually are for meetings or showings in the United States. To go abroad, get promoted.

The art of getting the most out of travel is very important to fashion coordination. To look and not see is something of a tragedy for one seeking fashion knowledge. From the time one boards the plane, one watches what fellow passengers wear, checks into the hotel, and notices travelers in the lobby, out to dinner, at the theater, at the meetings, everywhere.

Combining people-watching with what is learned from the industry, one comes home inspired, refreshed, and informed. A meeting inside a room in any city can provide only what goes on inside that room. But what one sees outside that room, on the street, in the restaurants, in the stores, in the homes, is what makes a visit from one city to another, one country to another valuable.

Personality Asset: CURIOSITY

Research

At first glance you may consider it strange that "research" could be considered on advantage. However, many a fashion director, with the soul of a sleuth, has found the role of fashion detective to be the most exciting and satisfying part of the job. Following hot on the heels of a new fashion idea, tracking down clues on colors, uncovering hidden facts about fabrics, scrutinizing every trend with Sherlock Holmes perfection, a director soon can put a finger on the fashion looks that promise to be heroes and eliminate the villians.

The fashion director is a trained observer. Being able to evaluate what he or she sees and hears, having the judgment to piece together all the clues and recognize what they mean to the whole, is being a good fashion detective. For example:

> *Clue No.1*
> The strong emergence of details—middy collars, sailor ties, brass buttons, marine motifs and lacings.
>
> *Clue No. 2*
> Biggest color story—red, white, royal, and navy.
>
> *Clue No. 3*
> Most dominant pattern—stripes.
>
> *Conclusion:*
> The *nautical trend* will be major.

If you enjoy research and are intrigued with arranging the puzzle until the picture comes into focus, then this aspect of the fashion director's responsibilities is definitely an advantage. Furthermore, a good researcher, one who is also capable of translating that research into profitable fashion decisions, can utilize that talent in every area of merchandising not only as a fashion director but as a divisional or general merchandise manager.

Personality Asset: **PERCEPTION**

Economy

In exactly the same proportion that one gets out of a job what one puts into it (there are some who testify this does not always follow), so are the economic rewards in proportion to the service. The world is certainly not without injustice, but most injustices suffered on the pay scale are vulnerable to change. Good fashion jobs in the fashion office might range anywhere from $16,000 to $75,000; in some cases, the pay is even higher. In addition to the paycheck itself, fashion people enjoy the privilege of house discounts on all merchandise, and sometimes special arrangements are made for contributions to their wardrobes. These side benefits usually apply only to those in retailing areas.

Perhaps in very few fields are there more opportunities for good paying jobs, faster promotion, better chance for growth than in the fashion world. Even if one is merely using the fashion office as a stepping stone to other things, it is a splendid training ground for related careers with bigger paychecks. It all depends on one's individual needs, one's drive and scope of ambition, what the traffic will bear, what heights may be reached.

Personality Asset: **HUNGER**

Fringe Benefits

There are many fringe benefits that pop up for those in the fashion office. They are sometimes small and intriguing, sometimes large and enviable. For example, free samples of a new product. Sometimes these come under the heading of small and intriguing, not significant but fun—a new lipstick, a new lotion, a new fragrance. One should never expect these things because their appearance is spasmodic and sometimes nonexistent, but when they do appear it is delightful.

Freedom of movement, too, is a decided advantage, the kind of fringe benefit that some might consider of top importance. For the temperament that resists being tied close to a desk on regular nine to five schedules, the freedom of the fashion office has much to offer. There are days when some members of the staff do not even set foot into the office; they are off on location for an ad or catalog shoot, executing a fashion production, visiting the branches. The versatility of the activity permits this freedom of movement.

For the fashion director who has become individually distinguished in the industry and has been highly visible as a fashion authority, there is the occasional reward of celebrity. If you recall what was said about the aura of glamour surrounding this business in the first chapter, you can recognize the possibility of such an image being earned (and it must be earned) by an outstanding fashion director.

Contacts are not the least of the fringe benefits. The freedom of movement places fashion office personnel in contact with every level of professional in the fashion business, from the stock clerk to the top executive. Outside one's own organization, one will meet sales representatives, promotion people, designers, manufacturers, magazine editors and publishers, members of the press, celebrities, company presidents, civic leaders, and political officials, to name a few. Where these contacts lead can have very interesting results, a way to make friends for the store, to make personal friends, to make points for another career. The constant flow of personalities in itself guarantees sparkle to the life of the fashion director.

The unique exposure to a wide variety of people, the experiences of travel and the education one can reap from it, the experiments with creativity, the constant need to explore and dig and uncover, to discover, invent and direct, to set one's pace as fast or as easy as the job will allow, to taste the joys of being a self-starter, self-explorer, to gamble and lose, and gamble and win (expecting both, enduring both), to take a stand, stick the proverbial neck out, live dangerously, all add up to remarkable advantages. It is all there. Few careers offer so wide a sweep of involvement. And for the beginner, hidden between the folds of all this experience comes the most rewarding part of all, the chance for personal growth.

THE DISADVANTAGES

So that we do not overglorify the merits of a career as a fashion director, an honest appraisal of the disadvantages must go on the record. There is no doubt that some of the points listed as advantages could also be noted under disadvantages. Take travel, for example, for the person who hates to leave home, hates to pack, is afraid to fly, dislikes strange places, this would certainly be a big problem.

Pressures

Now here is a point that would immediately seem only acceptable for listing under disadvantages. Not necessarily. There are those who thrive under pressure, and everybody needs some. But we deal here with the excessive pressure that can realistically appear in the life of the fashion director. For example, a fashion director serves so many lieutenants it is entirely conceivable that they might start pulling from different directions, all at the same time, and often they do.

Even the most organized fashion office will find that projects will pop up unexpectedly, situations beyond the fashion department's control will demand immediate and special attention. Shows will be back to back; business trips; merchandising decisions, and fashion presentations requiring lots of preparation will run neck and neck; meetings, interviews, fittings, shooting schedules, and personal appearances will take place alomost simultaneously. All busy offices are busy, naturally, so why the big fuss about pressure? For one thing, the expected and the planned can usually be handled without too much pressure, no matter how busy. It is the unexpected and the unplanned lunging out of nowhere that puts the pressure on high. It is part of the nature of the retail business, however, it is also a basic truth in fashion.

Another thing—the different types of hats the fashion director wears, requiring a different set of personality traits or approaches, add considerably to the kind of personal demands on energies and feelings that regulate the pressure gauge. A pressure even more basic where the fashion office is concerned is the pleasing of a multitude of personalities: please the customer, please the boss, please the press, please the buyer, please the audience. This routine can provide an undercurrent of pressure, ever present and unrelenting.

Whatever the pressures, they are not pointed up here as unendurable. Thousands of fashion office people endure them very well, indeed, even enjoy them. But the so-called fools who rush in where angels fear to tread should be tipped off to all the ramifications. In other words, if pressures are expected, they can be challenging, not devastating.

"We never know what might be coming up when we unlock the fashion office door in the morning or pick up the phone," one fashion director said, "but that is what makes us go."

Personality Asset: SENSE OF ADVENTURE

Hours

Oh, the hours. There are plenty of them. Tabulating all the fashion directors queried in the country, this is very likely to appear at the top of the list of disadvantages. The hours—often long, often irregular—disqualify many people who have other strong demands on their time, home, marriage, family, recreation. All these will feel the pinch of the demanding hours. Sometimes only during peak periods, sometimes only during a special promotion, but it is wise to have a realistic awareness that consuming hours come on strong very often. The bigger the responsibility, the bigger the clock.

Even though a fashion director and staff arrive at 8 A.M., it is not unusual to work straight through until 8, 9, 10, or even midnight, with a dinner break consisting of candy bars from a vending machine. As a hectic day wears on, the fashion office staff, preparing for a big fashion event, might be wading knee-deep in plastic clothes bags, tissue paper, hangers, boxes, and clothes racks, after unpacking carton after carton, or trunk after trunk of just-arrived clothes. Soon tired feet required kicking off shoes, no time to retouch fading makeup, hair goes limp, and the so-called glamorous fashion staff is anything but glamorous.

It is also very likely, on location for a catalog or magazine shoot, that the wakeup call would be 5 A.M. in order to capture the precious morning light. And if going on location means packing and unpacking and repacking and checking two dozen suitcases through customs, after a week of rising at daybreak, the fog of weariness becomes very heavy, even for the most energetic.

Clock-watching, per se, is a no-no. Not that anyone is keeping tabs or clocking in or out, but just as the pace may be slowing down to a healthy jog, along comes another one of those "unexpecteds." Clock-watching is just not practical, even though the freedom of movement permits an ease of coming and going. Flexibility helps considerably. The calendar, not the clock, dictates the time for coming and the time for going. Overtime pay? Not for executives.

Personality Asset: **ENDURANCE**

Dedication

Whether or not this factor can be considered a disadvantage depends, of course, on the extent of dedication or the reason for it. The fashion business is a very jealous lord demanding total devotion, no other false gods, total commitment. For some, this may be asking too much. Some cannot give it. Others may pledge total devotion but do so with resentment. Unthinkable. Unworkable.

Dedication given because of one's eagerness to get the most out of what they are giving makes a plus out of a minus. Dedication because the challenge itself becomes totally consuming pays off better. For those who dream of a spot at the top in the field of fashion coordination, dedication will become unavoidable.

Personality Asset: **SURRENDER**

Frustrations

Vying for first place among the disadvantages, right up there with the pressures and long hours, is another often unavoidable ingredient in the fashion business—frustrations.

Perhaps reasonable portions of any one of these—long hours, pressures, and frustrations—would not be all that devastating, but it seldom works that way, especially in retailing. Usually they appear as a hyphenated team, a tough combination that might cause the faint-hearted to fall away.

Imagine putting forth a major effort, let us say a storewide promotion for the purpose of opening a new store. After weeks of planning and preparation, invitations are out, expensive ads have been run, grueling hours have been spent right up to the last minute. Everything is in readiness and a snow storm of blizzard proportions hits. Almost no one shows up or the whole thing is cancelled. Many might consider this a minor frustration compared to the others that are so often available.

The best defense against any frustration, or the pressures, or the long hours, is excellent health. With good physical health and a healthy outlook one can handle all the challenges with style.

Personality Asset: RESILIENCE

SPECIAL PREPARATION

Even though some past fashion office personnel came from many directions (from the ranks of models, teen boards, buyers, merchandisers, publicity and advertising areas, to name a few), a good educational background will help you arrive better prepared and in a position to command a better salary.

A college degree need not be restricted only to the areas of fashion and merchandising, although this is, naturally, most desirable. A couple of the biggest fashion coordination jobs around were held by people who majored in political science. However, it must be noted that a career in fashion was not yet their goal while in school, nor was specialized fashion training available.

For the young person who knows what he or she wants, who looks to fashion as a goal, the sooner this individual gets into specialized education, the better. Competition has become keener and requirements set higher. The retail fashion business has become more specialized, and specialized people are more in demand.

Management Training Program

Almost all leading retailers build their internal source of future executives through very comprehensive executive training programs. Applicants who are accepted for such training and successfully complete the program are usually the first recipients of appointments in the merchandising division when openings occur.

For students entering the fashion business in the area of retail merchandising, it is recommended that applications on such executive training programs be a first priority when seeking employment.

To give you some idea of what such a management training program has to offer, the following outline, used by Brandeis, Omaha, Nebraska, is typical of what to expect.

BRANDEIS RETAIL MANAGEMENT DEVELOPMENT COURSE

Objectives:

To familiarize management trainees with the function and responsibilities of all vital divisions of retailing.

To provide realistic on-the-job training in Operations, Stores, Advertising, and merchandising divisions.

Resources:

Brandeis Management Development Manual
NRMA *The Buyer's Manual*
Articles of Leadership from the *Harvard Business Review*

Course Content:

1. ORIENTATION
   History of the company
   Goals of the company
   Structure of the company (organization chart)

2. STORES
   Job Descriptions:
   General Store Manager
   Assistant Store Manager—Operations/Personnel
   Assistant Store Manager—Merchandising
   Divisional Sales Manager
   Sales Associate I
   Sales Associate II
   Visual Merchandising procedure
   Sign Shop policy
   Schedule of store hours
   NRMA Store Visit Checklist

3. OPERATIONS
   Distribution Center: Checking and Marking
                          Traffic
                          Purchasing
                          Invoice Office
   Security and Safety

4. PERSONNEL
   Sales Associates Performance Evaluations
   Leadership and Supervision
      Understanding Leadership
      Skills of an Effective Administrator
      Taking Charge
      Supervising by Example
      Guidelines for Handling Conflict
      How to Stay on Top of Your Job
   How to Prepare a Job Description
   How to Conduct Performance Evaluations and Salary Reviews

5. FINANCE
   Control Division:
      Sales audit

Payroll
Shortage
Statistical
P.O.S. (Point of Sale)
Credit

6. MERCHANDISING
Basic Retail Math Concepts
Merchandise Information Systems:
FLAIR (Fashion Line Automatic Information Retrieval)
Basic Stock
Classification/Changes
CRT (Cathode-Ray Tub—computer input device)
Seasonal Merchandise Planning:
Open-to-Buy Policy/Forms
Purchase Order Policy/Forms
Seasonal Merchandise Planning/Forms
Sales Promotion/Advertising Forms
Fashion Director:
Function of the Fashion Director
How to Work with the Fashion Director

7. MANAGEMENT-SUPERVISION SKILLS
How to Ask Questions/Listening
Assertiveness versus Aggressiveness
No-Fault Confrontation
Time Management
Management by Objectives
Goal Setting
Professional Salesmanship
9 to 5 Dressing

Fashion Design

Fashion design is excellent background for fashion coordination. There is no better place to learn respect for the intricacies of fashion creation. A solid knowledge of construction, detail, balance, and manipulation of fabric is a good background for the professional fashion director.

The workmanship, the special finishes, the trims of a garment, all contribute to its cost, all in proportion to the degree of excellence and skill. Without an exposure to such details, the novice will be a longer time catching up on facts that will prove highly valuable. Such a tiny detail, for example, as understanding that color-coordinated pearl or bone buttons, perfectly matched to the fabric, or the addition of a belt or pocket, increase the cost of the garment. Such understanding helps the fashion director appreciate the manufacturer's efforts and the buyer's choices. Yes, and even the customer's preferences.

441 *ONE MORE THING . . .*

Home Economics

The fashion business is alive with home economics graduates, especially in the textile area of fashion. Many of the relative fashion courses offered in some universities and most junior colleges who are anxious to update their programs come under the department of home economics. These are good places to start the program of fashion, together with on-the-job training in a retail store that cooperates with the school.

Merchandising Schools

In addition to merchandising divisions of universities, there are excellent professional schools that specialize in merchandising and fashion training. They offer highly comprehensive programs for careers in fashion, taught by staff members who have been formerly active or are currently active in the field of fashion.

These institutions are famous for their alert approach to the current methods of merchandising fashion, with a continuous updating to meet the personnel demands of retailers, manufacturers, agencies, and mills who are likely prospects to draw from their student body for new talent. In other words, they keep a constant finger on the pulse of the industry to develop accurately trained fashion people to fulfill realistic needs.

The Professional Fashion Director and Schools

Specialists in the fashion industry are often invited to serve as instructors or as guest speakers. The retail fashion director, or the fashion director of a fabric company, fiber producer, fashion design house is often invited to universities, professional schools or local colleges to speak on their industry and fashion experience. Also, teaching aids for home economics teachers or instructors of specialized fashion schools are often provided for classroom use by the industry. And, very often, it is the fashion director who compiles the material.

FOR WOMEN ONLY?

Is the field of fashion coordination, the career of the fashion director, strictly a woman's world? Not really. This book has been directed to the female student or reader, because over ninety percent of the fashion directors are women. However, in the places where men have assumed the duties of fashion director, their records have been impressive and indicate that there is a place for creative men, depending on the responsibility structure and types of assignments in a given store or company.

In the realm of retailing, male fashion coordinators or directors have been more in demand in home furnishings divisions and in the men's and boys' ready-to-wear divisions. There have been a few men (enough to prove it can be done) who have distinguished themselves as corporate or divisional fashion directors for women's ready-to-wear. For example, Rich's in Atlanta, Wanamaker's in Philadephia, and Sanger-Harris, Dallas, Macy's, New York, and May Co. Los Angeles, have employed men fashion directors. In the fiber industry, Monsanto enlisted the services of a male fashion director.

AFTERVIEW

The very existence of so many ways to go in fashion coordination, inside and outside retailing, is an immediate testimonial to the importance and scope of the area. The fashion industry continues to grow. The field of fashion coordination, spanning a wide range of possibilities and choices, also continues to grow in proportion. The surface has barely been scratched.

With fashion growing more complicated, bigger changes, faster changes, and fashion institutions expanding and spreading, one great cushion against future shock is the well-equipped fashion director who can pull the entire fashion picture together for management.

The ever-present needs to meet competition, to make a profit, exploit a new product, create a new market, uphold an image, and keep in personal touch with the consumer require dependable fashion know-how. The well-trained fashion director, coordinator, stylist, consultant, or director of fashion merchandising, whatever the title, intellectually and emotionally equipped to direct fashion with a here-I-come-world initiative, can be the most exciting and most profitable thing that can happen to her firm.

When dealing with the advantages and disadvantages noted here, there are two more extremely important Personality Assets that will make every effort easier and more pleasant. In fact, the sincere and consistent application of these usually guarantee greater success in every area of the fashion business.

Enthusiasm. This is a must. It is the charmed ingredient that will propel you to attack each assignment with the kind of strength and excitement that filters into the work itself.

A Sense of Urgency.   The desire to do it now, follow through immediately, is the quality that will bring novices to the attention of superiors, and help push the prepared up the ladder to higher places.

One more Personality Asset: **A SENSE OF HUMOR**

Bring it along. One who has it is blessed, and the fashion industry will applaud it.

GLOSSARY
Fashion Industry Terms

Accessories All articles, ranging from intimate apparel to hosiery, shoes, belts, bags, gloves, scarves, jewelry, hats, etc., worn to enhance or complete an outfit of apparel.

Accessorizing The process of adding accessory items to relate to apparel for purposes of display, advertising, modeling in fashion shows, or for customer's clothes on request.

Alta mode Italian couture.

Apparel The all-embracing term applied to men's, women's, and children's clothing. Wearing apparel.

As ready Expression used by vendors regarding estimated delivery time of merchandise purchased by retailers. The promise of orders being filled when merchandise is ready precludes the commitment of an exact shipping date.

Assortment plan A report usually compiled by the buyer to indicate within each classification an item's style number, color, size, and store or branch to receive this item. With assortment plans, store managers can see what merchandise has been alloted to their individual store. Larger assortments are usually sent to the larger branches, pared down versions are sent to the smaller branches. The assortment plan is also a tool for the DMM and the GMM to see how assortments of merchandise have been allocated throughout the company.

Atelier French word for studio or workshop. Designer workshop for dressmaking and tailoring.

Bad press Term meaning unfavorable, in regard to reviews, notices, or general coverage by the press. (See **Good press**.)

Basic stock Merchandise that is constantly in demand and is stocked on an ongoing basis.

Body In manufacturing of fashion, body refers to the concept of a garment, its silhouette. (A designer or manufacturer might use the term when indicating that "all the bodies in our line this season are slimmed down.")

Boutique   A shop or area within a retail store, devoted to specialized merchandise for a special-interest customer. Usually includes new and unique apparel and/or accessories, a special classification, a special segmentation for a designer, or items not found elsewhere in the store. (See **Specialty shop.**)

Branch   In retailing, a suburban or other extension of the downtown, flagship, or original store, operated under the same ownership and often carrying the same merchandise, or merchandised to accommodate a certain customer type. Larger branches carry larger assortments of merchandise, small branches stock pared down versions.

Brand name   A trade name used to identify the product and/or the maker.

Branded goods   Products that are identified with a brand name, a device that often helps reinforce the product's image and at the same time establishes responsibility for quality.

Bridal registry   A registration service provided for the bride-to-be in selecting preferred gifts. When a bride registers at a store's bridal registry, she indicates her choice of patterns in china, glassware, silver, etc., and the registry keeps a record of gifts purchased to avoid duplications.

Brown goods   Merchandise such as radios, television sets, electronics.

Buyer   In retailing, an executive who views, selects, and writes orders for merchandise for a specific department or classification. In many retail organizations, the buyer is also involved in policing shipments of merchandise purchased and working on advertising and merchandise presentation on the floor of their department or departments.

Buying plan   System used to guide what a buyer will buy during a specific period or season. The buying or market plan is based on the buyer's current stock condition and sales expected. (See **Open-to-buy.**)

Chain   Retail store group, centrally owned and operated with policies regulated and most merchandise selected and bought by a regional or national office.

Classic   Fashion trend or style that has enjoyed longevity of acceptance.

Classification   Merchandise divided into classes or groups, according to types (coats, dresses, blouses, sweaters, etc.). In fabric departments, classifications would be according to fabric content. In the linens departments, blankets would be one classification, bedspreads another.

Collection   A manufacturer's or designer's group of fashion creations for a specific season. The season's total number of fashion pieces, accumulated for presentation to buyers, constitute a collection. More often used in referring to a designer or couture group.

Completion date   The date designated on a purchase order by the retailer. Any merchandise that has not left the factory of the vendor by the completion date is subject to cancellation.

Confined   When a line or label is sold to one retailer in a city on an exclusive basis. Also, when a fabric is used exclusively by a designer or manufacturer, such fabric is considered confined.

Consumer   Customer or user. Often used as a collective term when referring to the buying public (the young consumer, the affluent consumer, etc.).

Consumerism   Consumer rights to protect against unfair or dishonest marketing practices.

Contemporary   Term used in fashion to identify updated styling. Fashion designed for the young adult who wants sophisticated, individualistic looking clothes.

Converter (textile term)   A concern handling gray (greige) goods (unfinished goods) as they come from the loom. The converter gives the goods their finish—print, color, and any other treatment. The process of converting textiles into fashion fabrics.

Cost price   Price at which goods are sold to a store. Wholesale price.

Costume jewelry   Often trendy creations, less expensive, less valuable than jewelry made of gold, silver, and precious stones.

Cotton   A vegetable fiber obtained from the boll of cotton plant.

Couture   French word used to describe the ultimate of fine sewing. It is used throughout the fashion industry when referring to high fashion houses.

Couturier   French term for (male) proprietor or designer of a couture house. Couturiere (female).

Cut-and-sewn goods   Garments that are cut and sewn (as against knitted).

Cutter   Apparel manufacturer. One who cuts and sews the fabric into a garment.

Daywear   That portion of intimate apparel that includes slips, camisoles, teddies, warmwear, panties. (See **Intimate apparel.**)

Delivery date   A date by which a resource commits to ship an order. If a delivery date has not been met, an extension must be requested or cancellation of the order will be automatic. (See **Completion date.**)

Department Manager   The person who oversees the stock, personnel, and sales in an assigned area. The department manager usually reports to the store manager.

Department store   A sizeable retail operation, selling men's, women's, children's apparel and accessories, other soft goods and merchandise for the home (hard lines), plus other accommodations. Not all department stores will carry everything, but all major operations provide large assortments of those classifications they do carry.

Design   An original or individual manipulation of fabric, color, and line to create a style concept.

Designer   One who creates in his or her own manner an interpretation or concept of a style in apparel, fabrics, accessories, etc.

Display   The visual presentation of merchandise in interiors, windows, cases, etc.

Distressed merchandise Damaged merchandise or any goods that must be sold at a sacrifice.

Distribution center Centralized depot that receives all merchandise for a retail organization, and processes, marks, tickets, and distributes the merchandise to the various branches.

Division In retailing, a segment of the business, divided according to customer or merchandise types (men's division, home division, etc.)

Divisional Merchandise Manager (DMM) Retail executive who heads up a division of the store's business (DMM of women's RTW, DMM of men's, etc.)

Domestics The original name for yard goods from which sheets, towels, etc., were cut. The all-encompassing name applied to the finished products of this type merchandise.

Dominant sell Item or items dominating a big share of a department's sales. Also known as volume sellers.

Dominant store In retail, the store that dominates in a given area. A store enjoying the largest market share in the area.

Editorial credit Publicity extended by consumer magazines at no charge to retailers (on-page credits or back-of-the-book credits) in order to advise the reader where items featured editorially are available in which city, and at which store.

Employee discount Special privilege discount given to employees for the purchase of merchandise from their employer for their own use.

Engineered pattern A pattern in a garment that is woven into the fabric as distinguished from being printed on.

Executive trainee One who receives on-the-job training for an executive position in a store; usually candidates are college graduates or those with backgrounds in retailing and fashion merchandising.

Explosive Term used in retailing to describe the success of an item, trend, or merchandising concept. A best seller.

Fabrics

Filling—Any yarn interlaced with a warp yarn at right angles in the weaving; sometimes referred to as pick.

Thread count—Number of warp yarns and filling yarns per fabric inch.

Wales—Ridge or rib fabric, such as corduroy or pique.

Warp—Any yarn running lengthwise in fabric made on a loom.

Weave—Process of forming a fabric on a loom by interlacing the warp and filling threads with each other. Plain, twill, and satin are the basic weaves. One of these three types is used in all weaves.

   Plain weave—One warp yarn over and warp yarn under the filling throughout the fabric.

Satin weave—Smooth shiny surface created by floating (skipping) of warp yarns over the filling yarns, or vice versa.

Twill weave—Diagonal lines on the face of the fabric.

Weft—The yarn that runs crosswise in a woven fabric, or at right angles to the warp threads. Also called filling.

Fabric dyeing

Piece-dyeing—Dyeing of fabrics in the piece after weaving or knitting.

Space-dyeing—A yarn dyeing process in which one strand receives more than one color at irregular intervals. Space-dyed yarn produces an effect of abstract design when woven or knitted into fabric.

Stock-dyeing—Dyeing of fiber prior to yarn spinning.

Vat dyeing—Dyeing of fabric with a chemical-oxidizing process for producing highly colorfast fabrics.

Yarn-dyeing (skein-dyeing)—Dyeing yarn in skeins before knitting or weaving, usually in a solid shade.

Face-out   In retailing, a display term describing a display fixture that faces out to better reveal merchandise on which it hangs (See illustration in Chapter 10.)

Fad   A fashion trend that comes in and goes out quickly. Short-lived fashion.

Fashion   Term awarded to styles or trends during a reigning period of strong consumer acceptability. That which is no longer widely accepted is no longer fashion.

Fashion look   Design, style, or silhouette of wearing apparel.

Fashion press   Periodicals and/or reporters who specialize in covering fashion news; consumer magazines, newspapers, broadcast media, trade journals.

Fiber   An individual strand, either natural or manmade. *Natural fiber*—obtained from animal (wool), from vegetable (cotton), mineral (asbestos). *Man-made fiber*—derived from cellulose (rayon, acetate) or from petrochemicals (nylon, polyester, acrylic).

First Cost(FC)   Wholesale price quoted by vendor abroad to export. Wholesale cost before shipped. (See **Landed Cost.**)

Four-way   A type of fixture, a unit with four extended arms used for hanging merchandise. A display term. (See illustration in Chapter 10.)

F.T.C. (Federal Trade Commission)   Rules and regulations set by the F.T.C. govern the granting of promotional and advertising allowances by a vendor to retailers.

General Merchandise Manager (GMM)   Retail executive to whom all divisional merchandise managers report, and through whom the GMM supervises the merchandising activities of the divisionals' buyers. In most stores, the immediate supervisor of the fashion director.

Go-see   Term used in the modeling agency business when a model goes to see a prospective client with his or her composite for consideration.

Good press   Term meaning favorable, in regard to reviews, notices, or general coverage by the press. (See **Bad press.**)

Gross margin   The difference between net sales and the cost of merchandise sold. Gross margin is the result of several elements: initial markon, markdowns, and discounts.

Gross Margin Return on Investment (GMROI)   Combines gross margin, sales, and inventory factors. GMROI represents the number of gross profit dollars returned for each dollar investment at cost. GMROI can be calculated as follows:

$$\frac{\text{Gross Margin Dollars}}{\text{Net Sales}} \times \frac{\text{Net Sales}}{\text{Cost of Average Inventory}}$$

Half size   The sizing of a garment for a woman who is usually short-waisted, short in stature and full-figured.

Hard goods   Term referring to refrigerators, freezers, washers, dryers, ranges, heaters, air conditioners. Major appliances.

Hard lines   Term describing certain classifications in the home division of a retail establishment. (i.e., furniture, appliances, etc.)

Haute couture   The leading dressmaking houses of Paris, and important designers of custom-made clothes anywhere.

High fashion   Fashion that has limited acceptability. Fashion that is more unique, advanced, and individual versus mainstream fashion.

Highly promotional   A classification of store and/or merchandise that concentrates on volume. Promotes price instead of just fashion. Many highly promotional stores offer fashion at a price.

Home division   Area in a retail establishment devoted to merchandise for the home. Fashion departments of the home division would include furniture, draperies, linens, carpets, pictures and lamps, china and silver. (For other classifications in the home division, see **Hard lines.**)

House organ   Publication intended for employees only. Form of communication for a store's associates often spread apart by many branches. Usually supervised by the store's personnel department.

Ideacomo   Trade fair of Italian fabric producers held in Como, Italy, every November and May.

ILGWU   International Ladies' Garment Workers' Union.

Image   Impression or understanding the consumer has of a retail store's position on fashion leadership, quality, service, selection, price level, and general personality.

Institutional advertising   Advertising designed to reinforce a store's image, prestige, or community responsibility. Such advertising usually excludes specific merchandise.

Inter-Color   A meeting held twice a year in Paris, attended by representatives of the fashion world to establish future color directions.

Interselling   Salespeople's assignment or permission to sell in more than one department, as against being confined to one department or a single classification or line.

Interstoff International fabric trade show held in Frankfurt, Germany, each November and May.

Intimate apparel Retail name for merchandise that includes feminine undergarments (innerwear or daywear), foundations, sleepwear, loungewear. Lingerie. (See **Daywear**.)

Irregulars Merchandise with some kind of defect or imperfection that is visibly not perfect but still very useful or wearable. Usually available to the consumer for less than the regular price.

Juniors Identified with a size scale of odd numbers: size 3 to 15. Even numbers are assigned to sizing for misses apparel.

Keystone Term used to describe technique of markup of merchandise to be sold at retail. Keystone markup is to double cost price.

Knits A general term describing fabrics composed of an interlocking series of one or more yarn loops. Can be a jersey (circular knit) or tricot (warp knit) produced in a variety of plain, stockinette, rib, and novelty-stitch patterns. Knits are highly resilient in many weights and designs for men's, women's and children's clothing.

> *Raschel knit*—A versatile type of warp knit with intricate overlays and open-worked design. Coarser than other warp-knitted fabrics and available in a great variety of patterns.

Knock-off A copy of a higher priced garment. An imitation.

Landed Cost Retailer's actual cost on imported merchandise. First Cost, duty, transportation, insurance, handling, and commissions must be added to establish Landed Cost. Where applicable, inland freight must be added, plus a discount load, depending on the store's policy.

Leased department A department within a store that is ostensibly run by the store, but is operated by an outside specialist or organization who leases the space and pays the store a percentage of sales.

Leaving paper The process of writing an order and leaving the order (the paper) with the vendor for the merchandise seen.

Lifestyle merchandising Selecting merchandise that is geared to lifestyles of customers (i.e., active sportswear for sports enthusiasts).

Line In apparel, the contour of a silhouette, design, or style.

Line (collection) The all-embracing term for a manufacturer's collection of styles in a given season (i.e., spring line, fall line, etc.).

Linen A vegetable fiber obtained from the stalk of the flax plant. Pure linen in a garment has the character of wrinkling easily, an appealing feature for many fashionable customers.

Lineup   Fashion show term, referring to procedure, order of appearance of models, groups, or categories of clothes to be shown. Lined up as to who follows who, what follows what.

Low end   Lowest price point available in a given department, or classification.

Mainstream   Another word for merchandise classified as traditional in look. A description of merchandise other than updated or advanced.

Making plan   Successfully attaining goals of projected sales. Retailers go against last year's figures on a day-to-day basis; if a planned percentage of increase this year is achieved against last year's figures, the making of plan is realized.

Man-made fibers   Synthetic fibers. Made from chemicals (petroleum, coal, and gas), or from cellulose.

Markdown   The process of reducing the original retail price of merchandise to a lower retail price. A markdown results in a lower profit.

Markon   The amount added to the cost price to make the retail price.

Markup   Another term for markon, perhaps of longer standing, and used by many retailers.

Mass merchandise   In retailing, merchandise that has greater acceptability to large numbers of people. Merchandise that is capable of contributing to a store's volume, because it is sold in large quantities. Usually this is merchandise in moderate to budget price ranges.

Merchandise transfer   The transfer record of moving merchandise from one accounting area to another. Merchandise might be transferred from one department to another, one store to another.

Merchandising   The business of buying and selling merchandise, in direct response to consumer need and demand. Managing inventories, meeting competition, presenting merchandise in an attractive and understandable manner (visual merchandising).

Misses (missy)   System of sizing feminine apparel. Misses apparel is always found with even numbers (4 to 16). Odd size numbers identify junior sizes. (See **Split ticket**)

Moda pronta   Italian ready-to-wear.

Natural fibers   Fibers from sources of nature; materials created from natural fibers include cotton, silk, and wool.

NRMA   National Retail Merchants Association. Trade association of leading American retailers.

On order   Merchandise that has been purchased but not yet received.

Openings   The time for showings of new collections by fashion producers and designers at the beginning of a season. Term used most frequently in connection with designer collections. (See **Showings**.)

Volume producers do not have openings, per se; they announce the beginning of a season when "the line is ready."

Open-to-buy (OTB) The amount of money a buyer has to spend monthly for merchandise. At the beginning of a period, usually a month, it would be the amount of planned purchases for that period based on where the stock level should be at the beginning of the next period in relation to sales and current on hand.

Point-of-sale Where all retail sales transactions are made. The point at which the merchandise for sale is sold to the customer.

Pret-a-porter French term describing ready-to-wear apparel.

Preticketed Merchandise that comes into the store with price tickets already attached from the vendor.

Private label A special brand name created for and owned by a specific store or store group for its exclusive use in its area. The merchandise bearing the private label or brand name may have been developed especially for the store or purchased from a vendor's line and relabeled.

Proportion In apparel, the balance of design. The size or length in direct relationship to other aspects of the design.

Proven body Silhouette or style in a garment that has sold well. A fashion design with a history of success.

PSM Indicating sizes petite, small, or medium. Sometimes used as PSML, which also includes size large.

Pull An expression used by the retail fashion office or display department in connection with selection (pulling) merchandise from stock for temporary use in a fashion show or store display. In advertising, to "pull" an ad is to eliminate or cancel it from running.

Rag business An old, inside term used to refer to the apparel business. Used mostly at the manufacturing level.

Ready-to-wear (RTW) Wearing apparel manufactured in a variety of styles and sizes, available for selection and ready to wear for the consumer. Apparel distinguished from that which is custom-made.

Receipts Term used by retailers when referring to ordered merchandise that has been received.

Reorder number An item that has received strong consumer acceptance and, therefore, is a style number to reorder, to replenish the stock for continued demand.

Rep An individual or wholesale company representing a manufacturer in a particular sales territory. One who solicits and takes orders for merchandise for the company he or she represents. Salesperson.

Resource The retailer's term for supplier of wholesale merchandise (manufacturer). (See **Vendor**.)

Retail price   Price at which goods are sold to the consumer by the retailer.

Rounder   Name of display fixture, used to hold large numbers of garments. (See illustration in Chapter 10.)

Runway   Area or aisle (on the floor or elevated for visibility) for fashion show modeling. Audience space is usually provided on either side or surrounding runway area. Also called a ramp in some parts of the country.

Sales plan   A merchandise budget based on anticipated sales during a given period.

Sales promotion   The combined efforts of advertising, publicity, public relations, and special events are coordinated to promote sales for a retail establishment. In some organizations display would also be included. The executives heading these areas, lead by a sales promotion director, are sometimes referred to as the creative team.

Sell-through   The amount of sales on any merchandise at retail (i.e., if an item sells out, it has a 100 percent sell-through; if half of the supply of this item sells out, it has a 50 percent sell-through). Also called sell-off.

Seventh Avenue   The street in New York where most of America's leading designers have their showrooms. Also the term used to identify the garment district's authoritative fashion area.

Showings   The presentation of new lines or collections at the beginning of a season by manufacturers and designers. (See **Openings.**)

Signing   Retail display term for identifying merchandise in interiors and windows with signs. This department is usually under the supervision of the display or visual presentation director.

Silhouette   Term for fashion look or style. (See **Body.**)

Silk   A natural fiber obtained from cocoons spun by silkworms.

Sleeper   An item or trend that received a small amount of attention from the retailer, but became important because of consumer demand. Also, an item with strong potential if supported with aggressive promotion.

SML   Meaning small, medium, and large. A manner of indicating sizing on certain types of merchandise. Abbreviated initials used by manufacturers.

Soft goods   In retail circles, the term used to classify all ready-to-wear merchandise. Also term applied to towels, linens, blankets, bedspreads, etc. sold in the home division of a store (distinguished from hard goods, i.e., housewares, small electrics, etc.).

Special event   A retail effort to attract traffic (customers) to the store. Usually presented as an exhibit, show, demonstration, or fair. A special attraction or unique merchandising presentation offering entertainment or special information.

Special Events Director   The executive whose responsibility is to create and supervise all special events for the retailer.

Specialty shop   A retail outlet, usually a free-standing establishment or separate shop within a shopping center, that carries classifications of merchandise for a special customer block (i.e., children's only, men's furnishings only, gift shop, etc.). Sometimes called a boutique.

Specialty store   Usually a fashion store, devoted to wearing apparel and accessories, excluding budget areas and home furnishings departments, such as furniture, large appliances, or hard lines found in the complete department store.

Split rounder   A display fixture. A split round rack for hanging garments. Split level—half of the rounder is elevated at a higher level than the other half for better visibility of the merchandise. Usually used to distinguish two colors of a garment, two different concepts of a item, etc. (See illustration in Chapter 10.)

Split ticket   A dual manner of indicating size of a garment (i.e., 7/8 or 9/10). A garment that is split ticketed is not a true misses size nor a true junior size; a size presumed to be suitable for either customer type.

Staples   In retailing, merchandise that is always in demand and is always kept in stock.

Stock condition   Of special interest to all buyers and merchandisers when planning open-to-buy or any buying plan. Heavy stocks can mean an overbought condition. Depleted stocks can mean assortments are skimpy, in need of replenishment.

Stock-to-Sales Ratio   The formula used for planning inventories based on sales. While expressing a relationship between sales and stock, Stock-Sales Ratio differs from turnover in that the stock is divided by sales, instead of sales by the stock. The ratio is generally for a month, and is found by dividing the inventory at the beginning of the month by the net sales of that month. It shows the length of time it would take to dispose of the first-of-the-month inventory at the rate of sales for that current month.

Stock turn   See **Turn.**

Style   In clothes, the special concept or distinguishing feature. A style is not necessarily fashion. Style is the term used to categorize a garment's individual look. (i.e., a pleated trouser is a pant style.)

Swing shop   A term used to describe a department store shop concept. Usually an area designated as a special shop, changed periodically with different trends or items. A process of swinging the look of the shop from one idea to another, depending on leading fashion trends during the height of special interest in them. A retailer's way of maximizing attention for such trends.

Tanning   The technique of turning animal skins into leather.

Target market   Consumer block to whom manufacturers and retailers aim their advertising.

Taste   The ability to recognize and understand what is appropriate as well as beautiful. One who has a high taste level is usually regarded as one who has good taste.

Textile fabrics   Cloth made from textile fibers, by weaving, knitting, etc.

Textile fibers   Slim strands of raw material from which textile fabrics are made.

Texture   The look and feel of all fabrics.

Toile   French word for muslin used in creating a sample garment.

Tonnage   Expression used by retailers regarding an item or items bought in large quantities. The kind of merchandise that is capable of generating volume sales, usually associated with budget or low-end merchandise.

Toppers   A term used for signing in a store.

To write   To order. The writing or placement of orders for merchandise by the retail buyer.

Traffic (Customers)   The retail term for collective customer presence in a store. Heavy customer traffic indicates a good possibility of stronger purchasing. Hence, special events and advertising are created to build "traffic."

Trend   Fashion trend. A fashion concept or idea that is enjoying acceptability. The direction in which fashion is moving.

T-stand   Display fixture, shaped in a T, for hanging a small amount of merchandise. Usually placed at the front of a department or near mannequins to highlight newly arrived merchandise or a special look, group, or item. (See illustration in Chapter 10.)

Trunk show   A designer's collection of samples, brought into a store for a limited time to show customers the selection from which customers can order style numbers in their size or color for later delivery.

Turn   A retail term denoting the number of times during a specific period that merchandise is sold and replaced. By dividing the net sales for a specific period by the retail value of the inventory during that period, the turn figure can be established.

Twig   A retail operation offering merchandise in limited portions of certain classifications (i.e., cosmetics and ready-to-wear accessories and/or some ready-to-wear). Usually a small shop, away from the parent store.

Unit control   System used to record the number of units of merchandise on order, in stock and sold.

Update   In the physical plant of a store or a department within the store, update means to remodel, refurbish, bring the ambience up to date. In the merchandising concept of a store, update may mean to bring the store into a more favorable position to service the customers' current needs.

Updated In fashion, a style that is made current by updating lines, details, fabrics, or colors. Updated fashion incorporates newness without being advanced or too forward in concept (i.e., updated classic.)

Upgrade In fashion merchandising, to upgrade usually refers to upgrading the quality of merchandise, elevating to higher price points, or upgrading the total fashion concept of a store. In manufacturing, upgrading may mean improved quality, and/or improved fashion direction. In all cases, upgrading is for the purpose of servicing and attracting a more discriminating customer.

Vendor One who sells to the retailer, vendor is another term for resource or supplier of wholesale goods.

Vendor returns In retailing, often referred to as RTV (Return to Vendor): the process of returning merchandise to the vendor for credit or replacement.

Vignette In a retail store, a special display area devoted to the presentation of merchandise in a dramatized manner.

Volume Amount of gross sales annually done by a retail store.

Volume seller A merchandise classification or item that is capable of generating big sales, thus contributing in large measure to the store's volume.

Warp (textile term) Yarns that run lengthwise in woven goods. (See **Fabric.**)

Waterfall Display term. A display fixture for hanging garments on a retail floor. The arms on this fixture are slanted forward so that a cascade effect is created when merchandise is displayed here. (See illustration in Chapter 10.)

Wool

All-wool—Fabric of any description in which yarns are 100 percent wool from the sheep.

Heathers—Wool yarn of multi-colored fibers, combined to produce a blended-color appearance. Used in tweeds, homespuns, cheviots and Shetlands.

Lamb's wool—Wool shorn from lambs up to seven months old. Very soft wool possessing superior spinning properties.

Merino—A very fine soft wool from the Merino sheep. Worsted yarn spun from Merino wool is excellent for dress fabrics and knitted goods.

Naked wool—A general term describing any very lightweight sheer wool fabric. Usually a crepe but may be other lightweight fabrics either solid, patterned or printed. Used year round for women's dresses, blouses and sportswear.

Shearling—The soft, natural, short-wool pile backed with sheepskin. Used in making powder puffs, slippers, rugs, and coats.

Sheepskin—A general term for hide with the wool still intact on the pelt or leather.

Virgin wool—Defined by the Wool Products Labeling Act of 1939 as "wool that has never been used or reclaimed from any spun, woven, knitted, felted, manufactured or used product."

Wool fancies—A general term describing numerous novelty wool fabrics in various yarns, colors, weights, and designs. Used for high-fashion coats, suits and dresses and sportswear.

Woolens—A general term describing various fabrics woven from woolen yarn, spun from the shorter wool fibers, which are not combed to lie flat as in worsted yarn. Soft surface textures and finishes are produced and the weave of individual yarns does not show as clearly as in worsted fabrics. Woolen fabrics include tweeds, fleeces, and meltons.

Worsteds—A general term describing various fabrics woven from worsted yarns containing the longer fibers spun from combed wool. Usually refers to tightly woven, smooth, clear-finished goods in a variety of twill or fancy weaves. Worsted fabrics include gabardines, crepes and serges.

Yarn   A thread produced by twisting fibers together. A continuous thread that can be used in weaving, knitting, etc.

Carding—A mechanical process in yarn development by which fibers are brushed up, made more manageable with foreign matter removed in the process (i.e., carded cotton).

Combing—A mechanical process after carding that removes undesirable cotton fibers and foreign matter. Produces longer, better quality fibers for the manufacture of fine yarns (i.e., combed cotton).

Denier—Describes the thickness of a yarn, generally used when referring to silk and man-made filament yarns. The higher the number, the thicker the yarn.

Filament—An individual strand of man-made fibers or silk.

Mercerizing—A finishing technique, used on cotton yarn to increase its strength, affinity for dyes, and luster.

Monofilament yarn—A single filament yarn.

Pima—Higher quality, smooth, strong cotton yarns, made of long fibers.

Spun yarn—Either natural or man-made fibers incorporated into a single yarn by twisting in the spinning process.

Yarn ply—Two or more single yarns twisted together.

Yarn size—Yarn number. The thickness of yarn, generally used when speaking of cottons, cotton blends, spun silk, and wool. The lower the number, the thicker the yarn.

Youth market Merchandise for babies, children, subteens, teens, young juniors, and young men or women, in contrast to older generations. Merchandise geared to young thinking, tastes and interests, in opposition to mature concepts.

GLOSSARY
Advertising Terms

Black plate Anything that is printed in black in an ad—type, borders, rules (boxes), etc.

Blowup An illustration or other material that has been enlarged, perhaps several times, from the original size.

Blue line A blue-colored copy, made on a diazo machine, from a tracing layout. Used for those concerned to see in advance what the finished ad will look like.

Broadside Another name for section. An advertising section that is made up of any number of pages, all the full size of the traditional newspaper page.

Buzz word Fad in terminology. Popularity and adoption of a word for a new or special meaning. Important in advertising copy; using the latest buzz word keeps the communication fresh and current.

Camera-ready Art work and type pasted up and ready to be photographed.

Campaign In advertising, a series of ads, a special format used for emphasis.

Color separation A process used in the preparation of a color ad. Accetate flaps (clear plastic-like material through which you can see) are laid over the black plate, one color at a time (i.e., a red flap, a blue flap, etc.). The printer photographs one color flap at a time, according to the percentage of color, then assembles the composite for the final color ad.

Column inch Term describing a measurement of printed space. A column-inch ad would be as wide as a single standard-size newspaper column.

Co-op A term used in retailing to indicate the cooperation of a vendor to share in the cost of advertising. A 50–50 co-op would indicate that the vendor would pay half and the retailer would pay half.

Copy All lettering, numbers, etc., that appear in type for an ad. The legend, story, general information about what is advertised.

Crop   To cut down, trim, or in some way exclude part or parts of a picture, illustration, etc., not to be included in the printing.

Direct mail   Advertising that is mailed to the customer (i.e., catalogs, statement enclosures, etc.).

Double truck   Two full pages of advertising, placed facing each other. Used to make a strong statement for either fashion or sales merchandise.

Finished art   Taken from the layout and executed by the artist with India ink, a wash, paint or pencil, for photographing.

Flap   A clear plastic-like material, transparent, used in processing color separation for ads. (See **Color separation.**)

Format   The plan, theme or otherwise outline of an ad, ad campaign or ad series.

Impact ad   Usually an ad of considerable size, designed to make a strong statement. A fashion impact ad would feature with emphasis in illustration, copy, and ad size the importance of the fashion story.

In-house   Referring to an operation or service handled within the store with its own personnel (i.e., a house organ, written and published internally; a catalog photographed and produced within the company, in lieu of hiring the services of a catalog production company; in-house production).

Insert   A special section that is inserted into a newspaper in free form to be pulled out independent of the rest of the newspaper. A broadside or tab may be an insert.

Kill   To kill an ad is to stop its publication. Eliminate it before it goes to press.

Layout   The arrangement of art and copy, based on material or directions given to the layout artist who designs the ad.

Line drawing   Sketch or hand-drawn illustration.

Logo   Abbreviation for logotype. Term describing the format or character of an insignia, trademark, or name. A retail store's logo (type or style of name identification), used in all its ads, helps identify the store and its image.

Merchandising ads   (for fashion ads) The process of selecting those fashion pieces that are to be sketched or photographed for an ad. To merchandise is to provide the choices that best represent the fashion story to be told.

Paste-up   Copy and art for an ad, pasted into position, in preparation for camera reproduction. (See Camera-Ready.)

Proof   Copy of an ad or advertising piece, with art and copy assembled exactly as it will appear when printed, offered for correction before publication.

Pull   In advertising, to "pull" an ad is to eliminate or cancel it from running. (See **Kill.**)

Sizzle   A term denoting the hype or stimuli for whatever merchandise or event being touted. (i.e., often used in broadcasting, to add sizzle to what may be cold, hard facts (colors, sizes, prices, etc.) in a newspaper ad. Copy that is colorful, exciting embellishment.

Slick   A glossy print of an ad.

Space   That area needed for placement of an ad. To reserve space is to commit it for a particular ad or group of ads.

Stack   The process of placing one ad next to another for purposes of effectiveness or defense against competitive or undesirable ad adjacencies. Several small ads might be stacked together to fill up a page, rather than have several small ads scattered throughout the paper.

Tab   A type of section. Smaller than a broadside (i.e., 8½ × 11). Also used as an insert in a newspaper edition.

Tear sheet   Duplicate copy of a published ad, often supplied to vendors involved in co-op advertising as proof or documentation of advertising as it appeared.

White space   Unused, clean area of an ad. Space without art or type, left blank to dramatize what appears in the ad. Often used for fashion ads. An economy of art and copy on a large space.

GLOSSARY

Broadcast Industry Terms

Ad-lib Action or speech that is impromptu, not written into a script.
Audio The sound portion of a telecast.

Boom Television equipment. A cranelike device for suspending a microphone or camera in the air.
Bridge Music or sound, film or slide, used to link one scene or sequence of a show with another.

Closed circuit Telecast that does not go over the air, but is shown from camera to monitor only (i.e., closed circuit television usually used for private viewing, not broadcast for public viewing).
Close-up (CU) Camera shot of an object or person seen close-up.
Cue A signal (by sight or sound) to indicate start of action.
Cue sheet A list indicating cues for a show or production.
Cut In television, an order (usually given by the director) to stop action.
Cuts Portions of a script or program to be eliminated.

Dead mike Microphone that is not connected or not working.
Dissolve A television technique for overlapping (fade-out) of one picture and the bringing up (fade-in) of another picture.
Dolly A movable platform or truck carrying a camera, to be wheeled around for advantageous shooting positions during a production.
Down-and-under Instruction given to sound effects or music to bring volume down to a soft level so that the voice of announcer, actor, or singer can be heard.
Dry run Rehearsals prior to actual performance.
Dub Recording of a sound track on a film. Also, a copy of a sound recording.

Edit   Electronic technique for adding one portion of taped TV program to another portion.

Feedback   Squeal or howl from improper mike hookup.
F.C.C. (Federal Communications Commission)   Guardians of broadcast practices and station licensing.
Fluff   A mistake in speech or action.

Instant replay   Video tape repeated, played back. Used extensively for taking another look at action in telecasts (i.e., sporting events).

Key   To key in a camera shot. Superimpose one image over another. A process through which an object or person can be made to look miniature or giant in contrast to surroundings.
Key lighting   Strong light directly on the object or person, eliminating background.

Live   Telecast that is not pre-recorded, but is transmitted and seen on the air at the moment of happening.

Minicam   Television term for a small, sealed electronic television camera that uses video tape instead of film. This self-contained video unit can be carried easily by the camera operator for any remote telecast.
Mock-up   Facsimile of products.

On camera   Talent or announcer seen on the air. As opposed to off camera, when the announcer is heard but not seen.
Open cold   To start a show without theme or musical introduction, usually without titles.
Open end   A show or film with the commercial parts blank, to be filled in at the time of broadcast.

Pan   Moving the camera from one object to another or across a set to view other parts of the scene or items.
Participating program   A television program sponsored by more than one advertiser.

Remote   A broadcast made away from the radio or television studio (i.e., on-the-scene news reports).

Scoop   Large light, used for lighting sets in a television studio.
Script   The complete written material for a television show or commercial.

Simulcast   The broadcasting of a show or program on television and radio at the same time.

Slow-mo disc   A slow-motion record (disc), used instead of tape to record action in slow motion or stop action.

Special effects   Electronic technique for audio and/or video treatment, to create special animation, lighting, movement, or any other effect not created by the camera or microphone alone.

Stand by   A cue or alert that a television program is about to go on the air.

Station break   Intervals during broadcast time designated for station identification.

Story board   A set of illustrations showing the sequence of action or pictures (video) as related to sound (audio). A planning board for the television production of a commercial.

Telecast   The broadcast of a television program.

Teleprompter   Electronic device used for on-the-air people to read their scripts while looking into the camera. Used instead of cue cards.

Video   The picture or visual portion of a telecast.

Videotape   The process of transferring video and audio into electronic waves. These are recorded magnetically onto the videotape for viewing over the television system.

Voice over   The commentary or narration of a film or show, usually filmed or taped without sound, with sound or "voice" added later.

BIBLIOGRAPHY

Brady, James. *Superchic*. Boston: Little, Brown, 1974.

Calasibetta, Charlotte. *Dictionary of Fashion*. New York: Fairchild Publications, 1976.

Cassiday, Doris and Bruce. *Fashion Industry Careers*. New York, Walts, Inc., 1977.

Charles-Roux, Edmonde. *Chanel*. New York: Alfred A. Knopf, 1975.

Editors of Menswear Magazine. *75 Years of Men's Wear Fashion 1890–1965*. New York: Fairchild Publications, 1965.

Fraser, Kennedy. *The Fashionable Mind*. New York: Alfred A. Knopf, 1981.

Frings, Virginia S. Fashion: from Concept to Consumer. Prentice Hall, 1982.

Gold, Annalee. *75 Years of Fashion*. New York: Fairchild Publications, 1975.

Greenwood, Kathryn Moore, and Mary Fox Murphy. *Fashion Innovation and Marketing*. New York: Macmillan, 1978.

Hamburger, Estelle. *Fashion Business: It's All Yours*. San Francisco: Canfield Press, 1976.

Hartley, Robert F. *Retailing: Challenge and Opportunity*. 2nd ed. Boston: Houghton Mifflin Co., 1980.

Horchow, Roger. *Elephants in Your Mailbox*. New York: Times Books, 1980.

Horn, Marilyn J. *The Second Skin: An Interdisciplinary Study of Clothing*. Boston: Houghton Mifflin, 1968.

Jarnow, Jeanette A., Beatrice Judelle, and Miriam Guerreiro. *Inside the Fashion Business*. 3rd ed. New York: John Wiley & Sons, 1981.

Le Vathes, Christine, ed. *Your Future in the New World of American Fashion*. New York: Richard Rosen Press, 1980.

Marcus, Stanley. *Minding the Store*. Boston: Little Brown, 1974.

Marcus, Stanley. *Quest for the Best*. New York: The Viking Press, 1979.

Pistalese, Rosana and Ruth Horsting. *History of Fashions*. New York: John Wiley & Sons, 1970.

Stegemeyer, Anne. *Who's Who in Fashion*. New York: Fairchild Publications, 1980.

Stevens, Mark. *Like No Other Store in the World: The Inside Story of Bloomingdale's*. New York: Thomas Y. Crowell, 1979.

Troxell, Mary D. and Beatrice Judelle. *Fashion Merchandising*. New York: McGraw-Hill, 1981.

Walz, Barbra and Bernadine Morris. *The Fashion Makers: An Inside Look at American Leading Designers*. New York: Random House, 1978.

Wingate, Isabel B. *Fairchild's Dictionary of Textiles*. 6th ed. New York: Fairchild Publications, 1979.

Winters, Arthur and Stanley Goodman. *Fashion Advertising and Sales Promotion*. 5th ed. New York: Fairchild Publications, 1975.

INDEX

Pages in *italics* refer to illustrations.